Ronald Bradfield
Understanding the Future

Ronald Bradfield

Understanding the Future

An Introduction to Scenario Planning

DE GRUYTER

ISBN 978-3-11-161719-0
e-ISBN (PDF) 978-3-11-161744-2
e-ISBN (EPUB) 978-3-11-161798-5

Library of Congress Control Number: 2024949458

Bibliographic information published by the Deutsche Nationalbibliothek
The Deutsche Nationalbibliothek lists this publication in the Deutsche Nationalbibliografie;
detailed bibliographic data are available on the internet at http://dnb.dnb.de.

© 2025 Walter de Gruyter GmbH, Berlin/Boston
Cover image: lechatnoir/iStock/Getty Images Plus
Typesetting: Integra Software Services Pvt. Ltd.

www.degruyter.com
Questions about General Product Safety Regulation:
productsafety@degruyterbrill.com

Contents

Preface

Dr Ronald Michael Bradfield
The focus of this book is to develop the capability of individuals and organisations through scenario planning, to perceive what is happening in the business environment and to act on this new knowledge. The contextual environment facing organisations has always been complex and dynamic; however, the economic, technological, scientific, social, cultural, and political forces are becoming increasingly complex, along with factors such as mass migration, caliphates, terrorism, rogue states, biodiversity loss and climate change. The consequence is the need to understand the future unknowns is especially high. One of the benefits of scenario planning is that it can provide structure and understanding through exploration and discussions of what is going on in the contextual environment, to think through what this means, and then act on this new knowledge. The benefit of scenarios is they change mindsets and reframe perceptions in organisations, improving strategic decision-making.

While there are several books on scenario planning which cover a range of scenario techniques, the value of this book is that it presents a detailed step-by-step guide to the "Intuitive Logics" method of scenario planning.

This book has three possible audiences.

– The first group which is very large, comprises students working on MBA and other university programs focused on business planning, who need to analyze and understand the contextual environment in which organisations operate, and how and why it may change in unanticipated directions.
– The second group comprises practitioner-scholars involved in scenario work who already know much about scenario work, and this book provides a practical foundation for the Intuitive Logics scenario development process.
– The third group are managers, leaders, professionals, and policy-makers across a broad spectrum of private and public sector organisations, who may be familiar with the topic of scenario planning but want a much deeper understanding of the topic, its conceptual framework and process, and its value in addressing specific business challenges. This book will enable them to be more aware of and prepare for, alternative futures and provide the means to challenge conventional thought.

https://doi.org/10.1515/9783111617442-203

My scenario journey

After completing a full-time MBA program at Strathclyde University Business School in 1992, I joined the Business School as a lecturer. During the MBA I undertook a scenario planning module (EIBE-Exploring the International Business Environment) developed and taught by Professor Kees van der Heijden who joined the Business School following his retirement from Shell. I spent hours talking to Kees about his experience with scenario planning, and he suggested that I join the Business School and undertake a PhD in scenario planning with him as my supervisor. I was fortunate to be offered a position as a lecturer at the Business School, and I spent the next 4 years as Kees's scenario apprentice, working with him on scenario projects in the UK, Singapore, and Barbados, teaching the MBA EIBE course and working on my PhD. Kees retired from Strathclyde and in 1996 I took over the role of EIBE 'Subject Coordinator' and was posted to Asia as Director of Strathclyde postgraduate programmes. I spent the next 25 years managing postgraduate programs in Asia (India, Malaysia, and Singapore), the Middle East (Bahrain, The UAE, Muscat) and Europe (Greece and Switzerland).

Alongside my Business School activities, I led and managed numerous scenario and strategy development projects with a wide array of public sector bodies, MNCs, SMEs and NGOs in numerous countries (Barbados, China, Finland, Hong Kong, India, Indonesia, Malaysia, Singapore, South Africa, Thailand, UAE, UK) in diverse sectors ranging from Airlines to Pharmaceuticals. I also worked with the World Bank in India and the World Economic Forum in Sharm El Sheikh, Egypt. Alongside scenario projects, I have run numerous 5-day scenario training workshops, including 45+ for Indian Railways.

In 2022 I retired from Strathclyde and following encouragement from individuals I had worked with on scenario projects and students I had taught the Strathclyde scenario course, in 2023 I decided to write this book.

Acknowledgements

Over the years I have had many interactions, exchanges, conversations, debates, and emails with a wide variety of individuals, all of whom I owe a great deal of thanks. This includes Pierre Wack, Kees van der Heijden, Peter Schwartz, Napier Collyns, Paul Shoemaker, Art Kleiner, Ted Newland, Charles Quah, and George Tan; my colleagues at Strathclyde including George Wright, George Cairns, Robert van der Meer, Fran Ackerman, Colin Eden, and Peter McKiernan; and the many scenario clients and students I have worked with and taught. Finally, my thanks and appreciation to Matthew Smith, the Senior Acquisitions Editor, Business and Economics, De Gruyter, for all his hard work and to my wife (Laetitia), my two daughters (Kerry and Sarah) and my son (Michael) for all their love and support.

Chapter 1
Introduction

Uncertainty about the Future

Throughout history, society and its foundations have periodically undergone pro-found transformations. These transformations include the rise and fall of empires, the French, American, Spanish, Algerian and European Revolutions, the Agrarian, and Industrial Revolutions, and the two World Wars. According to Gidley, (2017), we are currently in the midst of another transformation that she describes as the 'Post-Industrial Revolution'. This era is characterized as an age of uncertainty and paradox, in which our world is being transformed at an exponential rate as many of our socio-cultural and ecological systems unravel. The causes of this Post-Industrial Revolution are numerous, complex, multifaceted, and planetary, including the:

– impact of climate change.
– mass migration of refugees.
– extinction of species.
– increasing amplitude of economic cycles.
– unprecedented speed of technological innovations.
– ideological, cultural, and societal value shifts.
– changing demographics.
– unparalleled explosion of knowledge, and
– the advent of globalisation.

Furthermore, Kees van der Heijden (2004) notes that we learn from network science that everything in life is not solitary, but part of a wider, non-linear, self-organizing, and interconnected milieu. The intractable nature of these systems arises not from the inherent complexity of the individual components or their number, but rather from the patterns of combinations and interactions between these systems.

Meanwhile, Slaughter (2012, p 119) looking at planet Earth, asserts that:

> *Humans have wrought such vast and unprecedented changes to our world that we might be usher-ing in a new geological time interval and altering the planet for millions of years. Recent human activity, including stunning population growth, sprawling megacities, and increased use of fossil fuels has changed the planet to such an extent that we are entering what can be called the Anthro-pocene Epoch . . . represent[ing] a new phase in the history of humankind and of the Earth when natural forces and human forces became intertwined so that the fate of one determines the fate of the other, the outcome of which will be unprecedented and extreme*

Take our increased use of fossil fuels as one example. The Economist magazine (November 5th–11th, 2022 p 13) claims that "our failure to curb CO_2 emissions as a di-rect result of burning coal, oil and gas, will be catastrophic". Gidley (2017, p 1) builds on this, suggesting that:

https://doi.org/10.1515/9783111617442-001

The future we face today is one that threatens our very existence as a species. It threatens the comfortable urban lifestyle that many of us hold dear and the habitability of the earth itself. The times we are in are critical, and the challenges we face as global citizens are complex, intractable, and planetary. The impact of the climate crisis alone is pointing to frightening futures of rising seas and drowning cities, mass migration of climate refugees, drastic food shortages due to loss of arable land due to floods, drought and salination, and the mass extinction of species. Several Pacific Islands have already disappeared, and, in the USA, the first climate refugees are being resettled from low-lying islands to higher ground.

And this Gidley suggests, is just the beginning.

The consequence of the above is that governments, institutions, companies, and individuals must today deal with larger, systematically interwoven, and confusing problems than at any time in the past. The result is that public policies are becoming increasingly complex, and their development requires one to understand the future and the deep trends and their interplay influencing its evolution. Gowing and Langdon (2016, p 4) argue that while the rate and scale of change are much faster than most are prepared to concede or respond to:

a proliferation of 'unthinkable' events over the past two years has revealed a new fragility at its highest levels of corporate and public service leaderships. Their ability to spot, identify and handle unexpected, non-normative events is shown not just to be wanting, but perilously inadequate at critical moments. The overall picture is deeply disturbing.

A persistent aspect of human history is the occurrence of major incidences and events which have taken governments and organisations by surprise, even though in most cases clear signals were forewarning of these happenings. Taleb (2007, p 12) notes that once major incidents have happened, we have no trouble concocting post hoc explanations for why they should have been obvious. In complex situations, we only know right and wrong after the fact. The problem with this retrospective coherence, as Snowden (2002) warns, is that connecting the dots backwards does not unfortunately direct us on how to connect the dots forward.

Three decades ago, Handy (1989) suggested that we are living in confusing times, a world of uncertainty and discontinuities in which major unprecedented changes are taking place, the result of which is that invocations of profound uncertainty about the future have become something of a mantra. Fitzsimmons (2019, p 42) meanwhile suggests that "many seem to believe that this old-fashioned problem is today, worse than usual – or maybe worse than ever". The question is, are these mantras of intense uncertainty about the future a new 21st-century phenomenon? The answer is no. For example, a quote in the Atlantic Journal Editorial on June 16th, 1833, declared:

The world is too big for us. Too much going on, too many crimes, too much violence, and excitement. Try as you will, you will get behind in the race, despite yourself. It is an incessant strain to keep pace and still you lose ground. Science empties its discoveries on you so fast that you stagger beneath them in hopeless bewilderment. The political world is news seen so rapidly you're out of breath trying to keep pace with who's in and who's out. Everything is high pressure. Human nature cannot endure much more.

Although the complex global systems in which we live may have resulted in an accelerated rate of change, Godet (2001, p 9) states that: "Every generation has the impression that it is living in an era of unprecedented transition. Nothing could be more normal!" A more recent example of the idea that we are living in a dangerous era of transition is the book, *The Population Bomb* (authored by Paul Ehrlich, published in 1968). The book predicted a worldwide famine due to overpopulation along with other societal upheavals and called for immediate action to limit population growth. However, while none of these and many other pessimistic predictions have not (yet) come to pass, change today is regarded as accelerating, resulting in a state of flux which has become the norm in certain areas of the business world and is described by the term VUCA.

VUCA

VUCA, a term developed by the US army and first used in 1987 to describe the state of the world after the end of the Cold War, is an acronym that stands for Volatility, Uncertainty, Complexity, and Ambiguity. It has become a trendy managerial acronym that describes the situation of constant, unpredictable change that is now the norm in the world and according to Wikipedia, has taken root in emerging ideas that apply in a wide range of organizations (https://en.wikipedia.org/wiki/Volatility,_uncertainty, _complexity_and_ambiguity).

Bennet and Lemoine (2014) state that the characteristics of these four distinct types of challenges are:

- **Volatility:** relates to the speed, volume, nature, and magnitude of phenomena in an industry, market, or the world in general, resulting in change which is usually associated with fluctuations in demand driven by new technologies, regulations, and cultural trends. Although unexpected and usually of unknown duration, it may not be difficult to understand as knowledge about it is often available. An example of this is price fluctuations in the stock market following a natural disaster.
- **Uncertainty**: relates to the rapidly decreasing predictability of the future, increasingly shorter product life cycles, and projections for the surprise of an event. This is because there are no concrete trends or patterns, making it difficult to establish what will happen next. Although there may not be much information about the event, its cause and effects are known, and change is possible. An example is the COVID-19 pandemic and the difficulty of governments to determine what measures to implement which would be effective, and what the subsequent impact would be on society and the economy.
- **Complexity:** relates to the different states a system can get into because of the interconnectivity and interdependence of multiple components that create systems leading to non-linear and emergent behaviours. The more numerous the fac-

tors and the greater their diversity and their interconnections, the more complex the environment. Although information may be available or predictable, the sheer volume of it is overwhelming and can lead to wrong decisions. An example of this is doing business in a wide range of countries, each with unique regulations, tariffs, and values.

-   **Ambiguity:** this refers to a case of 'unknown unknowns' (Rumsfeld, 2002) as causal relationships are vague, incomplete, or even contradictory. There are no precedents and multiple interpretations are possible, potentially leading to misreads and cause-and-effect confusion. An example is a decision to enter new and untested emerging markets, or to launch new products outside of the organisation's core competencies.

These four interrelated elements present the context in which organisations view their current and future state, and include the boundaries for planning, their capacity to understand the consequences of issues and actions, and to appreciate the interdependence of variables.

As highlighted earlier, change is not new, so what is different now? The answer is that the pace of change, the immediacy, the extent of the impact and the number of factors to be considered, have all dramatically increased. The omnipresence and growing intensity of VUCA in the business world increasingly change how companies view the world, interact with each other, and respond to their environments. Numerous suggestions and processes are offered in the literature aimed at surviving in a VUCA world by learning to master the paradox and become more flexible, agile, and resilient. The problem as Zakharov (2021, p 53) notes, is that ". . . as greater complexity and ambiguity lead to greater uncertainty, we devise even more complex system to try to reduce the uncertainty, which itself adds another layer of complexity to the whole system." Bennett and Lemoine (2014) suggest that three significant problems exist in how leaders have employed the term VUCA. The first is that it has become a trendy way of saying 'unpredictable change' and offers a mixture of things that are dangerous in their consequences, as useful differences between the terms are glossed over and their value lost. The second is that even when experts and leaders are sensitive to the differences in meaning, there is a lack of information regarding just what it is that leaders should do to confront one or more of these conditions. The third problem is that because there is a dearth of actionable advice, many leaders are confronting this VUCA world by throwing up their hands, the response being how can you plan anything in a VUCA world?

The many moving and evolving parts in the VUCA environment call for risk management methodologies to incorporate a robust risk foresight that answers the question, is the organisation's risk management system appropriate for the VUCA context faced by the organisation? The problem according to Sunter and Illbury (2021), is that risk management is usually viewed as an internal affair and seldom covers the external risks that come from a VUCA world. However, there is a radical difference between calculable risk and essentially unknowable uncertainty which was independently stressed by Frank Knight in his book *Risk, Uncertainty, and Profit* (published in 1921), and John Maynard Keynes's *A Treatise on Probability*, also published in 1921 (Dimand, 2021). According to Knight (2018), 'risk' stems from repeated events and therefore refers to a situation in which the probability of an outcome can be determined through repeated observations, enabling the estimation of the frequencies with which different outcomes will arise. 'Uncertainty' by contrast, refers to a situation where both what is going to happen next, and the probabilities of their occurrence are unknown, so one cannot know what the possible statistical distribution looks like. Therefore, the essential difference between risk and uncertainty according to Knight, is that risk is measurable while uncertainty is not measurable or predictable.

Keynes meanwhile believed that while the financial and business environment was characterised by radical uncertainty, probability was about believability not frequency (Packard et al, 2021). Although the views of Knight and Keynes are quite different, the two are often cited because of their agreement regarding the fact that most business decisions are made in the absence of any numerically definite probabilities of the factors that might influence their consequences to go on. This establishes the distinction between situations in which decisions are informed by objective numerical probabilities of contingent outcomes (decision-making under risk) and situations in which there are no such probabilities to go on (decision-making under uncertainty). In the 1920s Keynes became engaged in an intellectual battle with Ramsey, Savage, and Friedman, who insisted that all uncertainty could be described probabilistically by a wide-ranging list of outcomes with well-defined numerical probabilities attached to them. The reason for this was the rise of the Bayesian interpretation of probability, pioneered by Ramsey, de Finetti, and Savage, under which probability is interpreted as a measure of an actor's strength of reasonable belief in a contingent outcome, instead of the frequency or propensity of a phenomenon. Thus, so long as they are rational, it is possible to argue that rational decision-makers always act as if they have sharp numerical probabilities at the back of their minds even in situations in which there are no objective probabilities to go on (Syll, 2015). The consequence is that Keynes and Knight lost that debate and the probabilistic approach to uncertainty has maintained academic primacy ever since. More recently, Kay and King (2020) contend that probabilistic thinking gives us a false understanding of our predictive power. They emphasize the difference between the wide range of possibilities that lie between the world of unlikely but imaginable and well-defined events to which probabilities can be attached (i.e., uncertainty), and the world of unimaginable events and unpredictable consequences (i.e., radical uncertainty), which cannot be described in probabilistic terms. Ormerod (2015, p 16) suggests that "uncertainty is increasingly a feature of the real world, considerably more so than it was when the economic theory was first formulated in the late 19th century". Thus, the model of economic rationality "is applicable in a declining number of situations, resulting in the limits on computational capacity applying more in seemingly everyday situations."

Uncertainty is measurable in both magnitude and duration and there are according to Courtney et al. (1997), four levels of uncertainty:

- **Level 1:** Low uncertainty where there is a single and clear view of the future and dependable outcomes.
- **Level 2:** A limited set of possible future outcomes and sufficient historical precedents to estimate outcomes with reasonable certainty.
- **Level 3:** Outcomes are indeterminate, and events are unique but bounded within a range; and
- **Level 4:** The uncertainty is a limitless range of possible outcomes with many unknowns.

While levels 1 and 2 represent the world of 'problem-solving', levels 3 and 4 are regarded as the world of 'dilemma exploration'. In this case, a dilemma is a situation where there is no clear easy choice or answer, a choice must therefore be made between two or more alternatives that may seem equally undesirable.

When making decisions, economists have found that although people tend to dislike risk, humans are particularly averse to ambiguity when the risk is unknown. According to Ralston and Wilson (2006), traditionally, there have been three different answers to the need to reduce uncertainty by anticipating changes. The first is to throw more resources into the process of forecasting, expanding data gathering and analysis, improving forecasting techniques, and using better tools. The second answer is to acknowledge that change cannot be anticipated; the idea is that owing to the ever-growing complexity of the environment, speculating about the future is a waste of time and resources. The third answer is to accept uncertainty as a fact and to deal with it, not just with one simple anticipation on which to gamble everything, but with a range of feasible alternative futures that might arise from the forces of change. This accords with Wack's (1985) view that:

> We abhor uncertainty even when it is an irreducible part of the problem we are trying to solve, but . . . uncertainty today is not just an occasional, temporary deviation from reasonable predictability, it is a basic structural feature of the business environment. This being the case, you cannot ignore uncertainty and hope it will go away. The only solution is to accept it, try to understand it, and make it part of your reasoning.

Having established that we live in very confusing times in an interconnected world, a world of uncertainty, of constant discontinuities in which major unprecedented changes are taking place and where "experience is rapidly devalued and familiar landmarks no longer serve as guideposts to the future" (Hamel and Pralahad, 1994), the following sections look at techniques commonly used to try and identify unexpected, non-normative events and the boundaries between what may happen or what may not, beginning with prediction.

Prediction

We live in a world that is obsessed with prediction. It is a routine human preoccupation inherent in all social behaviour and it is essential to survival. An example of this in social psychology is stereotyping which is a generalized belief about a particular group or category of people, and is an expectation that people might have about every person in that particular group. The type of expectation can vary widely, ranging from expectations about the group's race, religion, personality, preferences, beliefs, or ability. While the stereotypes can on occasion be accurate and useful, they are also often overgeneralized and inaccurate.

Box 1.1: The Prophets

Every era in the history of humankind seems to have its prophets who are reported to have foretold future events, some that occurred a long time after their deaths, or in some cases, are yet to happen. One of the legendary, and most powerful women of the classical Greek Empire, was the high priestess Pythia who served the god Apollo at the sanctuary of Delphi in ancient Greece after he had slain Python, the dragon who protected the navel of the Earth (Cartwright, 2013). The Delphi sanctuary was situated northwest of Athens located on the slopes of Mount Parnassus, and its oracle was so well-known that droves of people visited the Pythia, not just Greeks, but also foreign dignitaries and leaders who came to Delphi for a chance to put their questions about their plans to the Delphic oracle, and then waited to receive a response about what the gods thought of them. However, "the real work lay with the priests, who behind the scenes, used a wide network of contacts to gather information that would provide useable answers, thus maintaining customer satisfaction" (Strathern, p 13).

One of the most famous prophecies uttered by the Oracle was that of the defeat of Croesus by the Persians. According to Herodotus, Croesus the King of the Lydians, wanted to know if he should wage war on the fledging Persian Empire. The Oracle replied that if he attacked Persia, Croesus would destroy a great empire. To question the oracle was unthinkable as this was tantamount to questioning the gods, and so satisfied with this answer, Croesus prepared to invade Persia unaware that the 'great empire' referred to by the Oracle was not that of Persia, but actually, his empire (Barnes-Brown, 2018).

Delphi was not the only site of oracular consultation in ancient Greece. In the northwest of Greece was the oracular site of Dodona, where consultants wrote their questions on small lead tablets, which still survive today. Additionally at the oasis of Siwah in Egypt, lay the oracle of Ammon, which Alexander the Great visited during his conquests. Although the sanctuary in Delphi lasted for almost 1,000 years, between 391 and 392 Emperor Theodosius I banned pagan practices and closed Greek temples, including those at Delphi; with its religious function stripped away, the site fell into decay as did other sites.

A more recent renowned French prophet was Michel de Nostredame, better known as Nostradamus, who reportedly predicted many of the world's biggest events. In his book *Les Prophéties*, written in 1555, Nostradamus wrote about events that he believed would happen in the next two thousand years, ranging from the French Revolution of 1789, the outbreak of World War II, the assassination of John F. Kennedy, and even the terrorist attacks of September 11, 2001. However, the most crucial predictions of Nostradamus are the ones that have not yet materialised, which include the emergence of a third Antichrist, a third world war, and the exact year the world would end (History.com).

Along with stereotyping, human beings are remarkably prone to supernatural beliefs and beliefs in invisible agents in seeking to foresee and understand the future. We have for millennia sought answers from clairvoyants, mystical oracles, palm readers, prophets, psychics, sibyls, witch doctors, and others, all with alleged special powers of healing, divination, and the ability to gain information through extrasensory perception, making wildly inaccurate predictions with metrics that turn out to be nonsense. In his book, *The Evolutionary Psychology of Religion,* Pinker (2004, p 28), notes that "in all human cultures people believe that illness and calamity are caused and alleviated by a variety of invisible person-like entities: spirits, ghosts, saints, evils, demons, cherubim or Jesus, devils and gods". History is replete with stories in many cultures about people who could supposedly see into the future. These include foretelling the future from forecasters in ancient Babylon using a vast range of techniques of divination based on beliefs in the supernatural and magic, ranging from the distribution of maggots in a rotten sheep's liver, observing the patterns a fire makes as it burns, reading bones, and watching cheese coagulate, to the interpretations of dream (Hyndman and Athanasopoulos, 2012).

Bishop and Hines (2012, p 3) contend that people believe that to predict the future all they need to do is to understand the laws that govern human behaviour. However, prediction is exceptionally difficult in the world of human affairs, and most predictions about human behaviour are usually wrong. They suggest that the reason for this is that although there is an abundance of theories in the areas of psychology, anthropology, and sociology, there is as yet "no good, scientific theory of human behaviour. The consequence is that there is much more uncertainty in predictions involving humans than in predictions involving the hard sciences." This, however, has not stopped a plethora of books predicting the future of humans such as *Future Shock* (1970) by Toffler, along with numerous press articles and websites devoted to the subject. The question is, why is there such an interest in foreseeing the future? The simplest answer is that by having an idea of how future events may unfold, one should be able to better plan, prepare for, and manage events as they occur.

In conclusion, Martelli (2014, p 13) states that VUCA makes "exact predictions so prone to error as to make them futile or useless" and that this conclusion stretches back to the writings of Cicero and Seneca. However, Bell (2003, p 6) states that divination may have one major advantage over modern future research in that "in many nonliterate societies, people had great faith in their diviners, more, no doubt, than many more people in industrial societies have in their futurists." On a more humorous note, Arthur C. Clarke formulated three 'laws' of prediction (Gidley, 2017): The 1st Law: When a distinguished but elderly scientist states that something is possible, he is almost certainly right; when he states something is impossible, he is very probably wrong. The 2nd Law: The only way of discovering the limits of the possible is to venture a little way past them into the impossible. Finally, the 3rd Law: Any sufficiently advanced technology is indistinguishable from magic. However, the final word on prediction comes from Nils Bohr, a Nobel laureate in Physics, who said: "Prediction is very difficult, especially if it's about the future" (https://www.brainyquote.com/quotes/niels_bohr_130288).

Forecasting

Prediction and forecasting may appear to be the same and are often used interchangeably as it is assumed that they both relate to the same concept, i.e. the future, and risk and uncertainty are central to both. They are not, however, the same thing; the distinction between the two is that forecasting is an estimation of a future event that one can make by incorporating and casting forward past data in a systematic manner. Thus, forecasting relies on the scientific analysis of past data and linear models and regression techniques are the fundamental models used. Martelli (2014, p 4) defines forecasts as "statements referring to the explicit or implicit probability of the occurrence of a certain variable assuming a certain (usually) single, value". Prediction on the other hand is an estimate of future events made by subjective considerations; it is a statement that attempts to explain a possible outcome or future event with or without any prior evidence and requires no specific skills.

Forecasting is necessary, we cannot live without it and use it every day, albeit we are usually unconsciously aware of it. For example, before crossing a street we usually look left and right and forecast the movements of the approaching vehicles, deciding if there is enough time to safely get to the other side. We do this instinctively and forecasts of this type involve relatively closed systems, the number of variables is well-defined and the relationship between them is understood. Forecasting is also an indispensable management tool used in almost every field, and the Institute for Business Forecasting and Planning (2018) states that virtually all business decisions are based on assumptions of happening in the future which, by definition, are forecasts. Sunter and Ilbury (2021, p 23) state that forecasts are only as good as the models used which "represent a set of pre-defined rules that govern the forces or variables driving the system into the future underlying which is a set of assumptions . . . based on past trends and probabilities revealed by statistical analysis"; and they are only useful in the short term where things are reasonably predictable, and uncertainty is relatively small compared to the ability to predict. As Pierre Wack (1985) notes, "although forecasts can be reasonably accurate on many occasions, this paradoxically is their greatest danger, because sooner or later they fail to predict some major shift . . . and this occurs at precisely the moment when organisations most need to know, or sense, what the future may hold, and more particularly, what elements of it may make their strategies obsolete."

One of the best-known forecasters is Nathaniel Silver, an American statistician who first gained public recognition for developing a system for forecasting the performance and career development of Major League Baseball players. In 2009 he was named one of 'The World's 100 Most Influential People' by Time magazine after he developed an election forecasting system that correctly predicted the outcomes in 49 of the 50 states in the 2008 US presidential election and the winner of all 50 states in the 2012 presidential election. His book *The Signal and the Noise: Why So Many Predictions Fail – But Some Don't* (2015) was one of the Wall Street Journal's Best Ten Works of Nonfiction in 2012. However, the system he developed failed to predict Trump's victory in the 2016 election. In defence, Silver (p 68) contends that:

> The explosive, accelerating growth of knowledge in a rapidly changing and increasingly interdependent world gives us so much to know about so many things that it seems impossible to keep up – we are flooded with so much trivial news that attention to serious issues gets little interest; the result is that too much time is wasted going through useless information and noise obscures signals even when there is no doubt that the signal does exist.

In the long term, little is in reality, predictable, and the fundamental problem with forecasting is not just the unpredictability of events, but also the fact that most models we use are predominantly bad; they tend to extrapolate from the past assuming that the situation we are familiar with will continue indefinitely, even though history shows us that there is inevitably a point in time where variables will break with the past resulting in trend breaks. van der Heijden (2004, page p 96) provides the metaphor suggested by Albert Olensak of Sun Oil, to illustrate the situation.

> Forecasting can be thought of as analogous to the illumination by the headlights of a car driving through a snowstorm at night. A bit of what lies ahead is revealed, but not very clearly. The driver merely tries to avoid danger and pick out enough detail to arrive at his destination intact. He needs to be prepared for sudden major obstacles, be aware of his limited view and try to adjust his speed accordingly. Obstacles will appear suddenly, and then it may be too late to adjust. The obstacles the driver must be prepared for are outside the limited view that he has. The reaction required is an adjustment of speed in response to limits in perception.

The point of this metaphor is that we cannot live without forecasting, but it is important to understand our limitations, as making forecasts beyond our capability will inevitably cause a crisis of perception; the further we look into the future, the higher the degree of uncertainty, the lower the degree of predictability, and the more dangerous it is to forecast.

J. Scott Armstrong, an eminent authority on forecasting (founder of the Journal of Forecasting and the International Journal of Forecasting, editor of *Principles of Forecasting*, and the co-founder of forecastingprinciples.com), suggests that one of the major problems of forecasters is overconfidence, i.e. people's tendency to process information by looking for, or interpreting, information that is consistent with their existing beliefs while ignoring information that is inconsistent with their beliefs, a characteristic known as confidence bias. There are several causes of this. The first is that the confidence of forecasters enables them to generate supporting data that makes almost any outcome seem probable, and it is, therefore, unlikely that they will potentially seek disconfirming information. The second cause of overconfidence is that forecasters often fail to obtain the data needed to diminish their confidence and even when there is feedback, forecasters are prone to discount disconfirming information. Thus, Armstrong indicates in the seminal book *Principles of Forecasting*, that forecasting processes should be systematically judged against 139 forecasting principles, organized into sixteen cate-

gories, ranging from formulating problems to evaluating methods and using forecasts. He provides the following six methods for selecting forecasting methods:
- Convenience: It is often not worth spending time choosing a forecasting method when minor change is anticipated.
- Market popularity: Determining what methods are commonly used by others.
- Structured judgment: It is useful to select a method when several criteria and methods are possible, by developing explicit criteria and using these to select the best methods.
- Statistical criteria. Confined primarily to quantitative methods.
- Relative track records: Comparative performance of methods assessed by systematic, unbiased, and reliable procedures.
- Principles from published research: Guidelines on methods that have worked well based on prior research.

Additionally, Armstrong provides a detailed set of recommendations listed below, on how to use and structure appropriate forecasting systems to substantially reduce forecast errors and improve the accuracy for typical types of forecasting problems:
- Match the forecasting method to the situation, as no one forecasting method works for every situation.
- Use domain knowledge when developing forecasts which can be important for forecasts, but is often ignored.
- Structure the problem by breaking the problem into manageable pieces, solve each piece then reassemble them, which can substantially improve the accuracy of the forecast.
- Model experts' forecasts can be expensive, and the alternative is to rely on 'judgemental bootstrapping' which unfortunately is seldom used by practitioners.
- Represent the model realistically by starting with the situation, and then developing a realistic representation, rather than the other way around.
- Use causal models when there is sufficient information to understand the factors affecting the forecast variable and data, to develop a causal model.
- Use simple rather than complex quantitative methods when there is a lot of uncertainty about a situation, as they are easier to understand, are less prone to mistakes, and are more accurate.
- When historical data shows a long steady trend, extrapolation of the trends is appropriate but faced with uncertainty, discontinuities, and reversals, make conservative forecasts.
- Combine forecasts employing several experts through methods such as Delphi, as this reduces biases, and several experts usually possess more knowledge than an individual expert, producing more accurate forecasts.

Given the above discussions, it is understandable why predicting the future of the weather using temporal information is known as 'forecasting' rather than weather 'prediction.' Turn on the television or radio and following the news will be the weather report with forecasts of the weather for the next 2 to 10 days. An infamous weather forecast gaffe by the BBC Weatherman Michael Fish on 15th October 1987, illustrates this point; a woman called the BBC and said that she had heard there was a hurricane on the way. Fish's response was: "Well if you're watching, don't worry. There isn't." That night Storm Ophelia, a major storm with hurricane-force winds, struck southern England resulting in the death of 18 people and substantial devastation across the country. Around fifteen million trees were uprooted and fell onto roads and railways causing major transport delays and taking down electricity lines leaving thousands of homes without power for more than 24 hours. However, according to Finlay Greig (2017, p 3), a repetition of this kind of error is unlikely to happen again because "technology, computer modelling, and forecasting techniques have advanced meteorically in the intervening years."

The UK Meteorological (Met) Office is a large organisation with around 2,000 staff and weather data coming from many sources including the meteorological organisations of other countries through the World Meteorological Organisation (WMO). As a result of the above, billions of pieces of data pour into the Met Office every day. The rhetoric from the US National Oceanic and Atmospheric Administration is that given all this data, a 4-day weather forecast today is as accurate as a one-day forecast was 30 years ago and a 7-day forecast can accurately predict the weather 80% of the time. However, a 10-day forecast is only right 50% of the time (https://scijinks.gov/forecast-reliability/). This raises the question, why with all the data and computing power at our disposal, can we not forecast weather more than a few days out, why is there still so little predictability when storm systems are involved? The answer is that we do not have perfect knowledge of the earth's atmosphere; it is too complex and chaotic to accurately model because the smallest, almost imperceptible changes can compound as a dynamic system develops and triggers massive changes in the development of the system, a phenomenon known as the 'Butterfly Effect.' The concept of the Butterfly Effect is credited to Edward Norton Lorenz, a meteorologist and mathematician who searched for an alternative to linear models as a means of predicting the weather. He discovered that a trivial change in the initial specified weather conditions could result in huge changes in the weather at some later point i.e., variables that may seem insignificant over a short period, may be extremely impactful over a longer period. This meant that it was not practical to engage in long-range weather forecasts, because firstly, it would not be possible to make all the necessary observations in sufficient detail; secondly, what seemed trivial non-meteorological events could cause big problems (Cornish, 2004). At a meeting of the American Association for the Advancement of Science in 1972, Lorenz posed a question: "Does the flap of a butterfly's wings in Brazil set off a tornado in Texas?" The phrase refers to the idea that the flap of a butterfly's wings might create tiny changes in the atmosphere that could ultimately alter the path of a tornado, or delay, accelerate or even prevent the occurrence of a tornado in another location. The purpose of his provocative question was to illustrate the idea that some complex dynamical systems exhibit unpredictable behaviours, such that small variances in the initial conditions could have profound, widely divergent effects on the system's outcomes. Because of the sensitivity of these systems, outcomes are unpredictable and because there is no way to know exactly what will tip a system, Lorenz concluded that attempting to predict the weather over a longer period was impossible. The idea that minuscule changes in a system compound as the system progress and there is no way of discerning exactly what tipped a system, became a branch of mathematics known as chaos theory, which applies to forecasting in general (Gleick, 1987). The concept of chaos theory is well summarised in the novel *Good Omens*, by Pratchett and Gaiman, who state that while it used to be thought that it was big things that changed the world, it is according to chaos theory, the little things.

While our ability to predict the weather and continues to improve, Pearson of the Organisation for Economic Co-operation and Development (OECD) states that we are getting worse at making forecasts. This is because the world is getting more complicated; the forecasting record was not great to begin with, as evidenced by the fact that an analysis by Prakash Loungani from the International Monetary Fund found that "economists have failed to predict one hundred and forty-eight of the past one hundred fifty recessions" (Shaw, 2017). Even well-known futurists/scenario planners such as Peter Schwartz have been prone to significant forecast errors; in his book *Inevitable Surprises* published in 2003, he referred to the saving and loan crisis in the USA and said that nothing like this would happen again. However, only 5 years later a larger global banking crisis occurred.

Types of Forecasts

Forecasting serves many needs in our lives and there are many types of forecasting models classified by criteria such as their complexity, the amount and sources of data they use, and how they generate the forecasts. There are essentially two forms of forecasting techniques, qualitative and quantitative, with an ongoing debate concerning the relative advantages of each approach (Mathews and Diamantopoulos, 1986).

Qualitative Techniques

Qualitative techniques often labelled as judgemental methods, are used when past data is not available or is unreliable, are subjective, and are based on intuition, experience, expert judgment, and the opinion of consumers and experts. Techniques vary widely in terms of cost, complexity, and value and can be used separately, in combination with each other, or in conjunction with quantitative methods. It is more difficult to measure the usefulness of qualitative forecasts and although doubts are often expressed about its value, qualitative forecasts frequently provide useful information for managers.

These forecasts are essentially used to supplement quantitative forecasts, rather than to provide specific numerical forecasts; they are most useful in situations where it is suspected that future results will depart markedly from previous period results, and which therefore cannot be predicted by quantitative means. An example this is changes in government policies, or changes in consumption patterns. Qualitative forecasting can also be useful to discern trends in situations where there is an abundance of narrowly focused local data that a more quantitative analysis might not find, and in situations of newer or smaller companies that lack sufficient historical data to produce accurate quantitative results (Makridakis et al., 1998).

Quantitative Techniques

Quantitative forecasting techniques, meanwhile, are supposedly objective, data-based processes used to forecast future data based on applicable empirical past data. This is made possible when numerical information about the past is readily available and there is an assumption of continuity. An underlying premise of all quantitative models is that it is realistic to assume that aspects of past patterns will continue into the future and there are a wide range of quantitative forecasting methods developed within specific disciplines for specific purposes. These methods use data collected over regular time intervals (time series) or at a single point in time (cross-sectional) and there are several well-known models of time series data collection methods:

- Naïve: this uses the last period's data as a forecast and does not account for seasonal trends or other patterns which might arise in the data.
- Simple Mean Average: all past data is used to generate a forecast.
- Simple Moving Average: this uses an average of a specified number of the most recent observations, with each accorded the same weight.
- Weighted Moving Average: as above, this uses an average of a specified number of recent observations, but with each accorded a different weight.
- Exponential Smoothing: this is a weighted average procedure, with the weights declining exponentially as the data become older.
- Trend Projection: this technique uses the least squares method to fit a straight line to the data; and
- Seasonal Indexes: this technique adjusts the forecast to accommodate any seasonal patterns evident in the data.

In terms of human attempts to predict economic futures, John Kenneth Galbraith purportedly stated that "The only function of economic forecasting is to make astrology look respectable" (The Economist, 2016). Drucker (1973, p 124) meanwhile suggested that ". . . forecasting is not a respectable human activity and not worthwhile beyond the shortest of periods." The benefit of forecasting is that it gets one into the habit of looking at past and real-time data to try predicting future demand. The disadvantage, of course, is the fact that forecasts will never be 100% accurate and undertaking them can be time-consuming and costly. However, as forecasting knowledge and forecasting techniques have improved over time, forecasting has become acceptable and widespread, and there are, as Armstrong (2001) suggests, some features common to all forecasting models, namely:

- Forecasts are about the future and involve uncertainty, and therefore it is impossible to develop perfect predictions; the goal of forecasting, therefore, is to minimise errors.
- Forecasts are easier to make and appear more credible when using more data, including strong patterns which have been around for some time.
- The shorter the time horizon of the forecast, the lower the degree of uncertainty and therefore the more likely a more accurate forecast; and
- Forecasts are generally more accurate when developed by groups rather than by single individuals, as when grouped the individual high and low values tend to cancel each other out. Evidence to support this comes from a 2003 study by researchers at the Federal Reserve Bank of Atlanta which found that the monthly 'Blue Chip Consensus Forecast' by fifty economists was consistently better than that of any individual economist forecast (Kiviat, 2009).

This last point, initially known as 'crowd forecasting' originated from Sir Francis Galton, a British scientist, and statistician, who in 1907 asked 787 villagers to guess the weight of an ox. None of them got the right answer, but when Galton averaged their guesses, he discovered that the average arrived at a near-perfect estimate of the weight of the ox. This demonstrates a phenomenon that has become known as the 'wisdom of the crowds' whereby collective intelligence by the aggregation of information in groups, results in better decisions than could have been made by the individuals in a group, and big groups consistently outperform little groups. The concept was popularised in the book *The Wisdom of Crowds: Why the Many Are Smarter Than the Few and How Collective Wisdom Shapes Business, Economies, Societies and Nations*, by James Surowiecki, published in 2004. Numerous research articles on the subject of the wisdom of crowds have been published; for example, Simoiu et al (2019) found that crowds do indeed consistently outperform individuals in the crowd, often by a large margin, and that crowd performance is generally more consistent than that of individuals. However, there was evidence that social influence can, in some instances, lead to herding resulting in decreased crowd performance. According to Surowiecki (2004), the crowd is far from infallible and wise crowds have several key characteristics; the first is that the crowd should be diverse and have a diversity of opinions. The second characteristic arises in situations in which individuals in a group are more likely to be wrong than right because few of the individuals comprising the group have access to accurate information. In such a case, the likelihood that the group's majority will decide correctly falls toward zero as the size of the group increases. This is supported by Lu Hong and Page (2004), who propose three criteria based on a theoretical model of group decision-making: first, a diverse group of problem-solvers make a better collective guess than that produced by a group of best-performing individual solvers. i.e., diverse minds do better than expert minds when their decisions are averaged. Second, individuals should remain independent of those around them; the crowd should arrive at their opinion based on their individual knowledge, without being influenced by the opinion of others. Third, crowds should ideally be able to aggregate individual opinions into one collective decision.

Makridakis et al. (1998, p 3) state that there are two important comments to be made about forecasting. The first is that despite the improvements to forecasting made over the centuries "successful forecasting is not always directly useful to managers and others." Two examples support this contention: firstly, predictions made over a hundred years ago by Jules Verne regarding the development of submarines, nuclear energy, and travel to the moon; secondly, the predicted need for and the proposed design of a computer in the mid-1800s by Charles Babbage. Although both sets of predictions were accurate, they were of little value in helping organisations to realise those possibilities or achieve greater success. The second point is the distinction between "uncontrollable external events . . . and controllable internal events." Makridakis et al. state that while the success of a company depends on both types of events, forecasting applies directly to the former (external events) whereas decision making applies directly to the latter (internal events), and planning is essentially the link that integrates them.

Forecast Failures

While effort usually correlates with outcome in most fields, and the more effort put into a forecast should increase the confidence in its accuracy. History has shown repeatedly that this is not true. Ralston and Wilson (2006) state that the problem of predicting the future has become more, not less, intractable despite the increased sophistication of our forecasting tools. An example of this is the 2007–2008 monetary crisis during which an unprecedented number of financial institutions collapsed resulting in a freeze of global credit markets and requiring government interventions worldwide. Cornish (2004, p 162) suggests that the forecasters of the last century fell victim to two fundamental problems; the first is that while "important developments occur constantly all around the world, they may not appear significant, and most people would remain unaware of them". The second problem was that recent events, "especially those we experience personally, tend to dominate our thinking about the future." These problems apply equally to modern-day forecasters; as Tversky and Kahneman (1986) have demonstrated in their works, heuristics, and cognitive biases such as 'availability' and 'representativeness' skew human judgment and have pernicious effects on forecasting, which is discussed in more detail in Chapter 6.

Cornish (2004) states that one of the most significant failures of the century by the forecasting community was to anticipate the collapse of the Soviet system and the end of the Cold War, which was inevitable in hindsight. One small group of people, however, correctly anticipated the collapse. Faced with a multi-billion-dollar decision about building a natural gas platform in the North Sea, Shell asked Peter Schwartz, the head of scenario planning in Shell and his team, to develop scenarios in which the price of natural gas might fall. At the time, most natural gas came from the Soviet Union and as part of longstanding Soviet policy, the vast gas reserves had never been fully opened to the free market. Schwartz stated that on digging deep into the Soviet economy, they discovered a mismatch between the official energy demand and the economic numbers i.e., the Soviet Union was using less energy than the CIA's official economic numbers indicated. There were two possible interpretations of this, either the Soviets were far more energy efficient, which was unlikely, or the CIA numbers were wrong. After much detailed research and rigorous analysis, they recalibrated the numbers using Shell's energy data and discovered that the Soviet economy was, in fact, facing an imminent economic collapse; the world, however, had not yet recognised this. At the same time, Schwartz's team identified a few obscure politicians, any one of who's rise to power would likely signal a new era of economic cooperation with the West. One of those identified was a largely unknown individual to West democracies, Mikhail Gorbachev; if Gorbachev came to power, one of the two scenarios developed by the scenario team ('Incrementalism' and the 'Greening of Russia') postulated there would be massive economic and political restructuring; an opening to the West and declining tensions, resulting in a free and open natural gas marketplace.

In 1973, the scenario team presented the scenarios to the senior management, and although there was some scepticism, what the scenarios depicted was what actually transpired. When Gorbachev began his ascent, Shell took it as a sign of changes to come and saved themselves from disastrous investment decisions (Schwartz, 1997).

Although clairvoyants, oracles, palm readers, prophets, and psychics still exist, today pollsters, statisticians, and scientists have largely taken over the function of prediction and have built complicated computer-based models to predict almost everything from the economy to epidemics, to earthquakes. However, Orrell (2018) contends that the majority of these traditional models cannot predict with any degree of accuracy, because they do not work in the case of organic systems dominated by emergent properties which cannot be modelled or predicted. An example of this was the poll of forecasters by Bloomberg at the start of 2008; the expected gain for the S and P 500 index was 11%, with no one predicting a decline. However, by year-end, the market had actually fallen by 38%, which Orrell suggests is confirmation that the science of prediction has a considerable amount of baggage attached to it; as the economist Paul Samuelson humorously put it: "The stock market has called nine of the last five recessions" (https://www.azquotes.com/).

Economists, Sommer (2011) suggests, have an even worse record, particularly when it comes to predicting downturns; for example, in 1929 the Harvard Economic

Society declared that a depression was outside the range of probability, when in fact the country was already at the beginning of a depression. While economies are very complex, forecasters usually predict short-term trajectories with reasonable accuracy but fail miserably when it comes to the long term. For the past 20 years *The Economist* magazine has kept a database of projections by banks and consultancies for annual domestic product (GDP) growth which contains 100,000 forecasts across 15 rich countries. The projections were reasonable when covering short time periods but unsurprisingly, got progressively worse the further out into the future they projected.

Evidence of the extreme difficulty in accurate future prediction is the fact that there are many predictions over the years by experts or individuals who should have known better, and which in retrospect, turned out to be preposterous. Some examples of this are:

– In 1876 the President of Western Union, William Orton, dismissed telephones as a toy when Alexander Graham Bell offered to sell him the patent. Orton wrote an internal memo stating: "The idea is idiotic on the face of it. Furthermore, why would any person use this ungainly and impractical device when he can send a messenger to the telegraph office and have a clear written message sent to any large city in the United States?"

– The statement in 1899 by Charles Duell, Commissioner of the US Office of Patents that: "Everything that can be invented has been invented".

– In 1946, 20th Century Fox CEO Darryl Zanuck predicted: "Television won't be able to hold on to any market it captures after the first six months. People will soon get tired of staring at a plywood box every night."

– In 1950, Associated Press writer Dorothy Roe allegedly used scientific evidence to predict that by the year 2000: "All women would be six feet tall with perfect proportions because science will have perfected a balance of vitamins, proteins, and minerals that will produce the maximum bodily efficiency with a minimum of fat."

– In 1977, Ken Olson, founder of Digital Equipment Corporation (DEC) in a talk given to a World Future Society meeting in Boston, stated: "There is no reason for any individual to have a computer in his home."

– More recently comments in 2007 by Ben Bernanke, the former Federal Reserve Chairman that the housing market was stable even while it was falling apart; that Fannie Mae and Freddie Mac were in no danger of failing just before they failed; and the audacious statement on 10th February 2008, that "the Federal Reserve is not currently forecasting a recession" when in fact a recession had already started (Bernanke, B. 2007).

The above examples along with numerous other predictions by well-known individuals that turned out to be humorously ludicrous are available in the book, *The Experts Speak: The Definitive Compendium of Authoritative Misinformation* (1998), written by Victor Navasky and Christopher Cerf.

The fact that history is littered with failed predictions raises the question, why do we persist in producing predictions? Daniel Gardner, author of the book *Future Babble: Why expert predictions fail – and why we believe them anyway? (2011)* suggests it is simply because it is indispensable to our lives, it is part of human nature, and it serves many needs. We have an innate desire to want to know the future and when our predictions prove to be wrong, we make up kinds of excuses to justify it. Prediction and the commitment to forecasting in organisations has grown over the years because of several factors. The first is the increased complexity of organisations because of interrelated elements such as multiple organisational structures, the increasing activism of investors, stakeholders, regulators, and the changing the value of brands and customers, media coverage, and competitors. Secondly, the complex and rapidly changing VUCA environments facing organisations. Third is the changing expectations of an organisation's employees in most countries. The 2013 PricewaterhouseCoopers global generational study (https://www.pwc.com/gx/en/hr-management-services/pdf/pwc-nextgen-study-2013.pdf). suggests that the Millennial generation who make up the bulk of the global workforce, value a work-life balance and seek more flexibility as keys to greater job satisfaction, including the option to shift their work hours when required, and the freedom to work outside of the office periodically while remaining connected through technology. In the UK one of the consequences of COVID 19 and enforced working from home, is changing how people in general want to work in the future. A report by Chung et al (2022) has shown that the experience of homeworking has influenced the preference for continued flexible working to reduce commuting times, to spend more time with family, to increase productivity, and to improve general wellbeing. The fourth point as to why the commitment to forecasting in organisations has grown, is as Makridakis et al (1998, p 7) suggests, because of the development of "forecasting methods and knowledge concerning their application that enable their application by practitioners rather than solely by expert technicians".

'Superforcasters'

Philip Tetlock, a Canadian political scientist, is one of the leading academic authorities on forecasting. He has spent 40 years collating predictions from hundreds of academics, analysts, and pundits and has established a precise measurement system to track political forecasts made by experts, the objective being to understand just how good humans are at foreseeing the future, and what habits of thought improve their forecasts. In general terms, his findings were that the average expert's ability to make accurate predictions was only slightly better than that of a layperson using random guesswork, and was no more accurate than that of the proverbial dart-throwing chimpanzee. However, the more famous the expert, the more credibility and confidence in their predictions there is, and they are particularly good at defending their views, albeit their thinking is often trapped by their expertise. When wrong, experts are seldom held accountable and rarely admit their mistakes; instead, they insist they were just off on timing, blind-sided by an improbable event, or were almost right, or wrong, for the right reasons. Tetlock concluded that the best forecasters are analytical and numerate but intellectu-ally humble, they gather as much information from as many sources as they can, and they talk about possibilities and probabilities, not certainties. They are self-critical, aware of their cognitive biases, readily admit when they are wrong, are not wedded to any one idea, are quick to change their minds in light of new data, and are open to different, even contrary perspectives (Tetlock and Gardiner, 2016).

Tetlock also found 'superforecasters,' individuals who significantly outperformed others despite a lack of subject-specific knowledge, and who comfortably beat the av-erage of professional intelligence analysts using classified data. He also established that training programmes could yield big improvements. The book *Superforecasting: The Art and Science of Prediction* (2016) written by Tetlock and Gardner, explores the nature of these unusual individuals and shows that it is possible to make better fore-casts of certain phenomena. However, better forecasters must have the right mix of traits, limiting themselves to forecasting things that are forecastable and showing im-provement when trained in probabilities and bias awareness. Furthermore, continu-ous feedback and keeping score on good and bad forecasts is essential to the learning process of forecasters. Some 63 years earlier, the Oxford philosopher Isaiah Berlin di-vided thinkers into two categories, hedgehogs, and foxes (Gopnik, 2014). Hedgehogs view the world through the lens of a single defining idea while foxes draw on a wide variety of ideas and for whom the world cannot be boiled down to a single idea. Hedgehogs know a few important things and have a single grand idea that they apply to everything; foxes meanwhile know a lot of things and produce a new idea for every situation. Foxes, therefore, make better forecasters than hedgehogs, because hedgehogs are singular thinkers who tend to make predictions based on their un-shakeable belief in what they see as a few fundamental truths. Foxes on the other hand, entertain multiple perspectives and are guided in their forecasts by drawing on diverse strands of evidence and ideas. When new information becomes known, a fox is likely to adjust its forecast, whereas a hedgehog will likely discount the new data. For a fox, being wrong is an opportunity to learn new things. Given these qualities it may be said that foxes essentially share the traits of superforecasters.

'Cosmic Bazaar' the largest forecasting tournament in Europe combining super forecasting with crowd-based forecasting and representing the gamification of intelli-gence, is run by the UK's Professional Head of Intelligence Assessment. A recent article in The Economist (April 17th, 2021, p 71) titled 'Welcome to the Cosmic Bazaar' states that since April 2020, more than 10,000 forecasts have been made on the Cosmic Bazaar website. These forecasts have been made by 1,300 forecasters from 41 government de-partments and several allied countries to offer their best guesses on questions ranging from "whether China will invade Taiwan by a particular date, or whether Artic Sea ice will retrench by a certain amount". Users are ranked by a single, simple measure i.e., the accuracy of their predictions. The purpose of Cosmic Bazaar is to identify a group of persistently successful forecasters who would be able to improve the British government intelligence analysis and provide answers to tough questions in a crisis. The objectives of Cosmic Bazaar include encouraging cognitive diversity by ensuring that British Intelligence does not rely solely on its small pool of analysts; stimulating debate and discussion regardless of status and/or rank of the users as the system is anonymous and unclassified; and identifying blind spots in analysis. While The Economist suggests that Cosmic Bazaar's insights are reportedly 'trickling into policy teams' that work on issues such as COVID-19 and counterterrorism, there are two downsides to such a forecasting platform. The first is that the forecasts could outperform the work of traditional analysts thereby up-ending existing hierarchies; the second is that a forecast number alone is not useful even if it is good, a detailed description is required that explains to the reader how and why the number developed.

Utopias and Dystopias

The future state of the world Samuel (2018) suggests, has historically been portrayed by futurists as a polarized one, with the world of tomorrow often imagined in hypothetical fiction imagery as either utopian or dystopian. A utopia is an ideal world, the depiction of a flawless society representing perfection of an egalitarian society in which there are no problems such as war, disease, poverty, or oppression. From the biblical *Garden of Eden* in Genesis, writers have written about utopias for centuries, some of the well-known ones being Plato's *Republic* (360 BC); *Utopia* (1516) by Sir Thomas More; *News from Nowhere* (1892) by William Morris; *A Modern Utopia* (1905) by H. G. Wells; and *3001: The Final Odyssey* (1997) by Arthur C. Clarke. A dystopia on the other hand is a world in which nothing is perfect, and the world is plagued by extreme and oppressive societal control. Dystopian fiction emerged as a response to utopian fiction and well-known dystopias include *Brave New World* (1932) by Aldous Huxley; *Fahrenheit 451* (1953) by Ray Bradbury; *Animal Farm* (1944) and *Nineteen Eighty-Four* (1949) by George Orwell; and more recently, *The Handmaid's Tale* (1985) by Margaret Atwood. There have also been a number of dystopian films such as *Minority Report, Blade Runner, The Matrix* and *The Hunger Game*, all which proved to be popular.

A common feature of both utopian and dystopian societies is technology; however, those writing about the future have significantly underestimated the quantum leaps in technology. For example, while H.G. Wells correctly identified several emerging technologies such as the advent of space travel, nuclear weapons, satellite television, radio and air-conditioning, he underestimated by more than one hundred years when they would appear. Alongside the criticism that futurists have missed the rapid evolution of technology, a more important criticism has been their failure to anticipate major social change, in particular the women's rights and civil rights movements of the 20th century. Arnold Toynbee, a British historian and author, published a 12-

volume *A Study of History* between 1936 and 1961, to trace the development and decay of world civilizations and detail the five stages through which they all pass (genesis, growth, time of troubles, universal state, and disintegration). He developed a theory which stated that the biggest changes in history and methods for meeting challenges for society come not from technology, but a creative minority and their ideas. Support for this comes from Samuel (2018, p 24) who suggests that the bias towards predicting technological versus social progress has "been and continues to be the Achilles heel of futurism, with the next wave of gadgets and gizmos easier to see coming than a cultural tsunami".

While the use of prophets and seers is far less common today, the need to know what the future holds has not diminished, rather it has increased because of the growing uncertainty and complexity of the world. As a result, we are constantly bombarded with predictions ranging from the economy to politics and everything in between. Though we may be reasonably good at making short-term predictions, it is general developments, changes in a situation or in the way that people behave which precipitate further change. The general direction in which the change is happening, either upwards or downward during a specified period of time, is known as a trend.

Trends and Trend Cycles

Trends are part of everyday life, and trendspotting, popularised by books such as *Megatrends* by Naisbitt and *Microtrends* by Penn, has become an important intelligence tool for identifying and tracking consumer interests and behaviour in terms of fashion, food, music, and films, to name a few. Trendspotting can be performed either qualitatively by trend hunters who comb through life searching for signs indicating major shifts in consumer values, beliefs and needs, or quantitatively by analysts who monitor individual indicators such as the frequency of keywords searched, blogged, or tweeted.

A 'trend' can be defined in several different ways, but trends are essentially sequences of events concerning the same phenomenon over a particular period with a relatively predictable character. They vary in their breadth of application as a function of time, increasing, decreasing, or fluctuating as they move from history, through the present, and onto the future. While trends are usually determined through the extrapolation of historical data using statistical models, this does make using them straightforward, nor that the projection will always be correct. There are a number of reasons for this:

- There are often unexpected events that can (and often do) influence a trend with unforeseen consequences.
- The further into the future the projection, the more uncertain is likely to be the result with opinions invariably differing on historical developments.

- The future may not be a smooth continuation of past trends, some trends do not take the form of straight lines, some may be reversed, or emerging trends which are barely visible, may become critically important as the future unfolds.
- In the world of human activity, every trend creates its opposite, or countertrend (Weiner and Brown, 2006), and
- "Technology has made it difficult to distinguish between a trend and something that is simply trendy, and that is because much of it is complicated and confusing. Or it is invisible" (Webb, 2016, p 47).

Webb (2016, p 55) states that all trends intersect with other aspects of daily life, and "they share a set of conspicuous, universal features" i.e., they are driven by a basic human need, they do not emerge overnight, they evolve as they emerge, and they can materialise initially as a series of unconnectable on the fringes. Because there's still so much uncertainty, trends don't tell us the future, they simply give us some way points to help navigate the future. Webb suggests that as trends develop over time, progress increases exponentially partly because of Moore's Law, but also because the acceleration of change causes the rate of technological change to accelerate. She makes two further points: the first is that game-changing trends can enter society without initially attracting media attention or arousing interest, an example being the global adoption of the mobile phone. The second is the issue of confusing short-lived fads with major trends; fads are common worldwide and spread fast but usually last a brief time and can disappear before many people are even aware of them. Examples include *Gangnam Style, Heelies, Yo-yos and Planking.* The methodological issue in trend research is always how to measure them – their impact, relevance and importance.

Dobbs et. al (2015) state that four global disruptive forces are breaking all trends and producing monumental change, albeit most seem to be unaware of this. These four disruptive forces are:

- The shifting locus of economic activity to emerging markets such as China and cities within those markets, with nearly up to half of the global GDP growth to 2025 projected to be coming from 440 cities in emerging markets. Although there is no direct evidence to support this claim, the Conference Board Global Economic Outlook published in March 2023 (https://www.conference-board.org/topics/global-economic-outlook) suggests that Asian economies are expected to drive most of the global growth in 2023, with emerging economies remaining the key engine for global growth and by 2035, their share of global GDP will have risen to 61%.
- The exponential change of technology beyond the power of human intuition to anticipate, along with the data revolution provides consumers with unprecedented amounts of information. The total amount of data created, captured, consumed globally reached 64.2 zettabytes in 2020, up from 2.0 zettabytes in 2010, and is projected to grow to more than 180 zettabytes in 2025 due to more people working from home and the proliferation of technology-enabled businesses (https://www.statista.com/statistics/871513/worldwide-data-created/).

- Dramatic demographic shifts resulting from ageing populations and falling fertility rates will for the first time in history, result in the global population plateauing in most countries. The resulting smaller workforce will increase the need for increased productivity and the need to care for large numbers of ageing people, which will put severe pressure on government finances.
- The fourth force is how the world becomes progressively interconnected through trade, and the increasing speed of movements in capital, people, and information, leading to a dynamic new phase of globalisation.

There is a fifth force not mentioned by Dobbs et al. which has been slowly accelerating for the last 70+ years, but now growing at a precipitous rate, i.e. the issue of refugees. The global refugee population has more than doubled in the past decade and according to the UNHCR, at the end of 2021, the total number of people who were forced to flee their homes due to conflicts, violence, fear and human rights violations was 89.3 million which excludes those escaping the current Ukrainian-Russia and Israel-Hamas wars (United Nations Digital Library 2022). Conflict has traditionally been the major contribution to mass migration with the Middle East and North Africa being the most affected regions with 45 plus armed conflicts. (https://geneva-academy.ch/galleries/today-s-armed-conflicts). However, the UN estimates that 20 million people are displaced in their countries each year due to famine conditions (https://www.unhcr.org/climate-change-and disasters-.html).

As these forces grow and gather pace simultaneously, they disrupt long-established patterns in every sector of the global economy, causing a break in trends. This plays havoc with traditional forecasts based on intuition and extrapolation of experiences as assumptions that have long proved dependable.

Megatrends, a confluence of smaller trends that are often intertwined with each other, are the biggest trends, and their direction usually remains constant for a long time. Megatrends are global, long-term change developments and represent disruptive forces that take place over extended periods. They affect everyone and everything, with well-known examples including globalisation, climate change, urbanisation, and digitalisation. Tse and Esposito (2017, p 24) have developed a DRIVE framework representing five major megatrends:

- **D**: Demographics and social changes.
- **R**: Resource scarcity.
- **I**: Inequalities in terms of how resources and outputs are allocated and distributed.
- **V**: Volatility, scale, and complexity of the external environment; and
- **E**: Enterprising dynamics related to technologies and emerging business models.

The DRIVE framework, similar to the four global disruptive forces of Dobbs et. al (2015), is not intended as a prescriptive formula for analysing the contextual environment. It is however a tool that allows an understanding of what is happening in the contextual environment and the interconnectedness of forces, by focusing on the five key interrelated perspectives that impact our lives.

Trends can have a long-term and strong impact, but also a shorter-term character with a lower impact which may be a part of the cause of an issue in all sorts of ways. They tend to follow a predictable cycle: a trend usually emerges on the fringes of society and is initially of interest to a small band of individuals; over time the media begins to take an interest in the trend, and it is then taken up by early adopters. Finally, the trend becomes mainstream. Trends, however, can also reverse direction, and when they oscillate between positive and negative phases, they become known as cycles.

One of the best-known but controversial cycles in economics is the Kondratieff Wave, a concept introduced by Russian economist Nikolai Kondratieff in his 1925 book *The Major Economic Cycles* (see Box 1.2). While the theory of Kondratieff Waves does not conform to orthodox economic theories, the poor economic conditions of the 1970s and 1980s has revived interest in the Konratieff cycle.

Box 1.2: The Kondratieff Wave Theory
Kondratieff observed that agricultural products and copper prices underwent long-term economic cycles that he believed to be a result of three phases:
- The first cycle (1780-1830) was fuelled by the invention of the steam engine and the growth of textile manufacturing, which produced a period of prosperity, alternating with stagnation and economic decline. Underlying the central concept is that major capitalist economies tend to grow, boom, bust and grow again in long waves or 'supercycles'.
- The second cycle (1830-1880) was triggered by the birth of the steel industry which facilitated the inexpensive process for mass production of steel from pig iron leading to the spread of rail transport of people and cargo, resulting in rapid economic growth.
- The third cycle resulting from the electrification and innovation in the chemical industry which allowed the mass production of commodities, ran from 1880 through to 1930.

There have since been two further cycles. The fourth (1930-1970) powered by the growth of the petrochemical industry which supported the advance of the automobile market. The fifth cycle started in the 1970s, initiated by the advent of computer-based information technology which began transitioning the industrial society to an information society (Marr, 2018).

Another reasonably well-known cycle used to analyse and forecast financial market cycles is the 'Elliott Wave Principle' (see Box 1.3) developed by Ralph Elliott and published in his book *The Wave Principle* in 1938. Elliot, an accountant, developed an analytical model for the underlying social principles of financial markets by studying their price movements, and developed a set of analytical tools in the 1930s. He believed that stock markets which were generally thought to behave in a somewhat random and chaotic manner, in fact traded in repetitive patterns by identifying extremes in investor psychology and price levels, such as highs and lows, and by looking for patterns in prices. The theory identifies impulse waves that establish a pattern and corrective waves that oppose the larger trend. More commonly known today are economic cycles, also known as business cycles, which are the circular movement of an economy as it moves from expansion to contraction and back again. The economic cycle is characterized by four stages:

- Expansion: During an expansion stage the economy experiences rapid growth, interest rates tend to be low, production increases, and inflationary pressures build.
- Peak: The peak of a cycle is reached when growth hits its maximum rate, and the growth typically creates some imbalances in the economy that need to be corrected.
- Contraction: A correction occurs through a period of tightening when growth slows, employment falls, and prices stagnate.
- Trough: The trough of the cycle is reached when the economy hits a low point and growth begins to recover.

Box 1.3: The Elliot Wave Principle

Using stock market data as his research tool, Elliott discovered that crowd behaviour trends and reverses in recognizable patterns. From this discovery, he developed a rational system of market analysis. He isolated, defined, and named several 'waves' and hypothesized that public sentiment and mass psychology move in five waves within a primary trend, and three waves in a countertrend. Once a five-wave move in public sentiment is completed, then it is time for the subconscious sentiment of the public to shift in the opposite direction in a natural cause of events. This arises as a consequence of a deeply embedded set of behavioural patterns in the human psyche in what is known as the 'herding principle', defined as "a form of convergent social behaviour that can be broadly defined as the alignment of the thoughts or behaviours of individuals in a group through local interaction and without centralized coordination" (Raafat et al., 2009, p 420), or as Banerjee (1992) puts it - a case of "everyone doing what everyone else is doing, even when their private information suggests doing something quite different." Herding has a broad application and is a biological response shared with animals because as with animals, humans are hardwired for herding within their basal ganglia and limbic system within their brain.

The primary purpose of Elliott's wave principle is that it provides a context for market analysis, albeit critics of the wave principle state that it is too vague to be useful, it is impossible to consistently determine when a wave begins or when it ends, and therefore forecasts are prone to frequent subjective revisions.

Trend Forecasting and Trend Reports

There is a difference between 'trend spotting' and 'trend forecasting and analysis.' 'Spotting' allows brands to copy what is happening now and requires an immediate response; 'Trend forecasting and analysis' on the other hand, is a deceptively simple technique that looks ahead, collects, and assesses information, considers the broader cultural shifts driving change and attempts to spot a pattern (Trend Bible, 2016). Aside from the fashion and consumer industries, it is widely used in business and management to predict developments such as sales and profits, stock market prices, and time series data of economic, financial, and geopolitical importance. Neither trend spotting nor forecasting are however, new, they have long been a component of media and marketing in the fashion industries as fashion designers have used these tools to predict what individuals will wear in the seasons ahead. What is new however, is the widespread adoption of these tools by organisations in almost every industry today, including the likes of Wal-Mart, Campbell's Soup, Marks and Spencer, and Virgin. These were industries that traditionally did not use trend analysis, but who now reportedly use these tools as part of their processes to anticipate what their customers will want in the future.

Trend forecasting systems are essentially analytical processes using consumer insights, designed to spot patterns and identify upcoming trends across a variety of different areas such as fashion, technology, economics, politics, and culture that shape the social mood and can become catalysts for change. It is all about identifying underlying consumer trends that have the potential to impact consumers' everyday lives and ultimately their choices. One tool for doing this is 'Google Trends' which explores how particular words and phrases are trending in internet searches across parts of the world (Wikipedia). The management challenge is to align the firm's innovation initiatives with the consumer needs, to improve the probability that consumers will adopt the innovations, which will then increase the probability of the commercial success of the innovation.

Traditional market research methods used by practitioners incorporate interviews, focus groups, and questionnaire surveys, all of which focus predominantly on the current markets, identifying problems with products, and assessing current consumer needs, motivations, and values. What they do not do, is help customers articulate their future needs and identify directions for radical innovation – there is a misfit in that corporations increasingly rely on innovation as a major source of corporate progress, while consumers on the other hand want new products and services; however, neither party seem to be on the same page. Given that future consumer needs and related innovation, opportunities are not discernible in advance, traditional market research has proved to be insufficient and trend forecasting, and spotting emerged as a tool for marketers to monitor changes in the technology and market environment and to adapt their actions accordingly. The goal of trend analysis is to uncover hidden insights i.e., trends, by combining data from a wide range of sources including the internet, social media, texts, and documents. Matching innovation efforts with consumer trends constitutes a valuable approach for surviving the challenges of a rapidly changing consumer market as it will not only improve the odds of innovating something new and of value to consumers, but should also aid innovators in detecting new opportunities.

One of the best-known trend forecasters who works with businesses to identify future trends which will impact their business, is Faith Popcorn (born as Faith Plotkin and legally changed her name to Popcorn). She initially worked in the advertising industry for several years, then in 1974 founded a futurist marketing consultancy firm called 'BrainReserve' which helps clients reposition existing brands, develop new strategies, and innovate new products and services; according to Restauri (2016), the company has a 95% accuracy track record for predicting cultural trends. Exceptionally well-known, The New York Times has labelled Popcorn 'The Trend Oracle,' while

Fortune magazine named her 'The Nostradamus of Marketing.' She is recognized as America's foremost trend expert and trusted advisor to the CEOs of a range of Fortune 500 companies including American Express, Avon, Citigroup, Coca-Cola, Johnson and Johnson, Kellogg's, and KFC (Cummer, 2014). Following the success of BrainReserve, Popcorn created 'TalentBank' a company comprising 10,000 experts who by analysing newspapers, magazines, and the media, and conducting thousands of interviews annually, provide trend forecasts to organisations covering many topics.

Popcorn is probably best known for coining the term 'Cocooning.' In the early 1980s, she detected a shift in the way people were living their lives as more people desired psychological shelter to protect themselves from the unpredictable realities of the outside world by spending time at home and enjoying quiet leisure activities or entertainment, rather than going out to socialize. The word cocooning became so well-known and used, that it is now included in the dictionary. Alongside this, Popcorn has predicted a range of societal movements and was purportedly the first to predict the demand for four-wheel drive vehicles, food coaches, home delivery, and working and shopping from home. She has also authored and co-authored books, including: *"The Popcorn Report: Faith Popcorn on the Future of Your Company, Your World, Your Life"* (1991); and *"The Dictionary of the Future: The Words, Terms and Trends That Define the Way We'll Live, Work and Talk"* (2001) co-authored with Adam Hanft.

Trend reports are not only a common outcome of foresight and forecast initiatives, but there are organisations such as *Trend Hunter, Trend Hunting,* and The *Future Laboratory* who comb through billions of consumer conversations, news, and search data, to detect emerging trends, use frameworks to predict the potential of a trend, map the audiences and communities behind each trend, and produce reports and podcasts. Some such as The *Future Laboratory* provide online modules to train individuals on how to explore trends and create accurate forecasts, develop scenarios, and sharpen strategic foresight skills. Although there are numerous trends that individuals and organisation monitor and analyse, it is often difficult to quantify development tendencies with reliable, historical data and to determine which developments are important, and which are only short-lived fads. It is often therefore, the case that is it only when many things are put together and analysed, that the questions raised by each can provide a basis for speculating and providing a rich picture of how a particular sector might develop in the future. Although there is some value in analysing, understanding, and extrapolating from the current state of trends, Zaidi (2020) suggests that this can be problematic as they:

– Simplify and compartmentalise data, the analysis, and interpretation of which are subject to human error.
– Are simple and linear and do not consider wildcards, unpredictable events, or unintended consequences.
– Often emphasize noise rather than knowledge and can be wrong or misleading when based on short-lived fads.
– Are not all equal and given the number of trend predictions, it can be difficult to determine what is critical and warrants attention.

In summary, whether talking about predictions, forecasts, or trend spotting, reliable predictors of the future and the pace of change can be difficult to anticipate, albeit over the years there have been predictions that nobody expected to come true such as Wi-Fi, digital colour photography, mobile phones, pre-prepared meals, debit cards, the slowing of population growth and so on. Meanwhile, Ogilvy (2011, p 165), working at SRI (formerly Stanford Research Institute), interpreting the results of a VALS (values and lifestyles) programme in 1985, came to the realisation that while the programme had been successful in correlating purchasing patterns with lifestyles, the system was losing its predictive powers and "would no longer be predictable. "And indeed, customers around the world have been unpredictable ever since. No general system of market segmentation or analysis has managed to capture their patterns of behaviour in any reliable way."

Conclusions

Although this introductory chapter discusses prediction and forecasting, this book is not about these subjects but provides an overview of techniques used to try and identify what may happen or what may not, in the future. Scenario planning is about understanding how, and why, the future will evolve in diverse ways from that imagined, based on a grouping of important environmental influences and drivers of change, about which there is an elevated level of uncertainty. No effort is made to predict or forecast the future business environment or to attach probabilities to a set of events. "It is a process to prepare the organization to see discontinuities, to accept and understand change and to do so earlier, or at least better than anyone else, and so be able to seize new opportunities as well as avoiding the undesirable effects of misconceived actions" (Mintzberg, 1994: p 233) while van der Heijden suggests that the greatest power of scenarios is that they provoke and encourage, rather than suppressing strategic conversations in organizations.

Book Structure

Chapter 2 which follows, traces the origins and evolution of scenario planning and associated techniques. Chapters 3 through to 6 then proceed to detail the Intuitive Logics scenario development process, from Stage 1 through to Stage 5.

References

Armstrong, J.S. (2001). Principles of Forecasting: A Handbook for Researchers and Practitioners. ISOR Volume 30.

Banerjee, A.V. (1992). A Simple Model of Herd Behaviour. The Quarterly Journal of Economics, 107, 3, pp. 797–817

Barnes-Brown, A. (2018). The Oracle of Delphi: How the Ancient Greeks Relied on One Woman's Divine Visions. History Answers Ancient Civilisations, 28th June.

Bell, W. (2003). Foundations of Futures Studies: Volume 1: History, Purposes, and Knowledge. Human Science for a New Era, Volume 1. Taylor and Francis.

Bennet, N. and Lemoine, J. (2014). What VUCA really means for you. Harvard Business Review, January-February 2014.

Bernanke, B. (2007). No Recession On The Horizon. Moneywatch, CBS News, March 28th, 1:31 pm.

Bishop, P. and Hines, A. (2012). Teaching about the Future. Palgrave McMillan.

Bohr, N. (https://www.brainyquote.com/quotes/niels_bohr_130288).

Cartwright, M. (2013). Ancient History Encyclopaedia. 22nd February

Chung, H., Seo, H., Forbes, S. and Birket, H. (2022). Working from home during the covid-19 lockdown: Changing preferences and the future of work. https://www.birmingham.ac.uk/Documents/college-social-sciences/business/research/wirc/epp-working-from-home-COVID-19-lockdown.pdf

Cornish, E. (2004). Futuring: The Exploration of the Future. World Future Society.

Courtney, H., Kirkland, J. and Viguerie, P. (1997). Strategy under Uncertainty. Harvard Business Review. November-December, 75, 6, pp 66–79.

Dimand, R.W. (2021). Keynes, Knight and Fundamental Uncertainty: A Double Century 1921–2021. Review of Political Economy, 33, 4.

Dobbs, R., Manyika, J. and Woetzel, J. (2015). No Ordinary Disruption: The Four Global Forces Breaking All the Trends. Public Affairs, New York.

Drucker, P. (1973). Management: Tasks, Responsibilities, Practices. Harper and Row, New York.

Fitzsimmons, M. (2019). Scenario Planning and Strategy in the Pentagon. US Army War College Press. https://press.armywarcollege.edu/monographs/385.

Gidley, J.M. (2017). The Future: A Very Short Introduction. Oxford University Press, U.S.A.

Gleick, J. (1987). Chaos: Making a New Science. Viking Penguin.

Godet, M. (2001). Creating Futures: Scenario Planning as a Strategic Management Tool. Economica, London.

Gopnik, A. (2014). In Life, Who Wins, the Fox or the Hedgehog? Wall Street Journal, August 15th. https://www.wsj.com/articles/the-reality-behind-isaiah-berlins-fox-and-hedgehog-essay-1408144444.

Gowing, N. and Langdon, C. (2016). Thinking the Unthinkable. A New Imperative for Leadership in the Digital Age. An interim report by Nik Gowing and Chris Langdon. Chartered Institute of Management Accountants.

Grieg, F. (October 16, 2017). The worst weather gaffe in TV history – 30 years on. https://inews.co.uk/news/environment/weather-great-storm-michael-fish-97570.

Hamel, G., and Prahalad, C. K. (1994). Competing for the future. Harvard, MA: Harvard Business School Press.

Handy, C. (1989). The Age of Unreason. John Wiley and Sons, London, U.K.

Hong, L. and Page, S.E (2004). Groups of diverse problem solvers can outperform groups of high-ability problem solvers. PNAS November 16, 101, 46 pp 16385–16389.

Hyndman, R.J. and Athanasopoulos, G. (2012). Forecasting: Principles and Practice. Monash University, Australia. 2012.

Kay, J. and King, M. (2020). Radical Uncertainty. The Bridge Street Press.

Kiviat, B. (July 17, 2009). Why are Economists so bad at Forecasting? Time. content.time.com/time/business/article/0,8599,1911011,00.html

Knight, F.H. (2018). Risk, Uncertainty, and Profit: The Economic Theory of Uncertainty in Business Enterprise, and its Connection to Profit and Prosperity in Society. Adansonia Press.

Makridakis, S., Wheelwright, S.C. and Hyndma, R.J. (1998). A review of Forecasting: Methods and Applications. John Wiley and Sons, third edition.

Marr, B. (2018). The 4th Industrial Revolution Is Here – Are You Ready? Enterprise Tech, Forbes. https://www.forbes.com/sites/bernardmarr/2018/08/13/the-4th-industrial-revolution-is-here-are-you-ready/?sh=53058ea1628b

Martelli, A. (2014). Models of Scenario Building and Planning: Facing Uncertainty and Complexity. Bocconi on Management, Palgrave Macmillan.

Mathews, B. P. and Diamantopoulos, A. (1986). Managerial Intervention in Forecasting. An empirical investigation of forecast manipulation. International Journal of Research in Marketing, 3, 1, pp 3–10

Mintzberg, H. (1994). The Fall and Rise of Strategic Planning. Forbes, January-February.

Navasky, V. and Cerf, C. (1998). The Experts Speak: The Definitive Compendium of Authoritative Misinformation. Pantheon.

Ormerod, P. (2015). The economics of radical uncertainty. Economics Discussion Papers, No. 2015–40, Kiel Institute for the World Economy, Kiel.

Orrell, D. (2018). The future of everything: the science of prediction. From wealth and weather to chaos and complexity. Avalon Publishing Group.

Packard, M.D., Bylund, P.L., Clark. B.B. (2021). Keynes and Knight on uncertainty: peas in a pod or chalk and cheese? Cambridge Journal of Economics, 45, 5, September 2021.

Pinker, S. (2004). The Evolutionary Psychology of Religion. Freedom From Religion Foundation, Inc.

Popcorn, F. (1991). The Popcorn Report: Faith Popcorn on the Future of Your Company, Your World, Your Life. Doubleday.

Popcorn,F. and Hanft, A. (2001). The Dictionary of the Future: The Words, Terms and Trends That Define the Way We'll Live, Work and Talk. Hyperion

Raafat, R.M., Chater, N. and Frith, C. (2009). Herding in humans, Trends in Cognitive Sciences, 13, 10. pp 420–428.

Ralston, W. and Wilson, I. (2006). The Scenario-planning Handbook: A Practitioner's Guide to Developing and Using Scenarios to Direct Strategy in Today's Uncertain Times. Thomson South-Western.

Restauri, D. (2016). Forbes. When This Woman Changed Her Name, Her Career took off. March 8th

Rumsfelt, D (2002). A phrase from a response US Secretary of Defense gave to a question at a U.S. Department of Defense news briefing on February 12, 2002.

Samuel. L. R. (2018). Why Do We Think So Much of the Future? It is impossible to predict, but that doesn't stop us from trying. Psychology Today Aug 09.

Schwartz, P. (1997). The Art of The Long View: Planning for the Future in an Uncertain World. New York, Currency Doubleday.

Shaw, A. (2017). Why economic forecasting has always been a flawed science. The Guardian, September 2nd.

Simoiu, C., Sumanth, C., Mysore, A., and Goel, S. (2019). Studying the Wisdom of Crowds at Scale, Vol. 7 No. 1: Proceedings of the Seventh AAAI Conference on Human Computation and Crowdsourcing, pp 171–179.

Slaughter, R.A. (2012). Welcome to the Anthropocene. Futures, 44, 2, pp 119–126.

Snowden, D.J. (2002). Complex Acts of Knowing: Paradox and Descriptive Self-Awareness. Journal of Knowledge. Management. 6, pp 100–111.

Sommer, J. (October 8, 2011). An ugly forecast that's been right before. The New York Times https://www.nytimes.com/2011/10/09/your-money/a-recession-forecast-that-has-been-reliable-before.html

Strathern, O. (2007). A Brief History of The Future. How visionary thinkers changed the world and tomorrow's trends and are 'made' and marketed. Robinson, London.

Sunter, C. and Ilbury, M. (2021). Thinking the Future: New perspectives from the shoulders of giants. Random House, ZA.

Surowiecki, J, (2004). The Wisdom of Crowds. Anchor Books.

Syll, L. (2015). The Keynes-Ramsey-Savage Debate on Probability. https://larspsyll.wordpress.com/2015/07/22/the-keynes-ramsey-savage-debate-on-probability/

Taleb, N.N. (2007). The Black Swan: The Impact of the Highly Improbable. Allen Lane, U.K.

Tetlock, P.E. and Gardner, D. (2016). Superforecasting: The Art and Science of Prediction. Crown Publishers/Random House.

The Economist, November 5th 2022. Page 13. Special Report: Challenge of the age

The Economist, April 17th, 2021. Page 17. Science and Technology. Predicting and Uncertain World: How spooks are turning to superforecasting in the Cosmic Bazaar.

The Economist, January 9th, 2016. Finance and Economics. A mean feat: Despite forecasters' best efforts, growth is devilishly hard to predict.

Trend Bible https://www.trendbible.com/contact-trendbible/

Tse, T.C.M. and Esposito, M. (2017). Understanding How the Future Unfolds. Using DRIVE to Harness the Power of Today's Megatrends. Lioncrest Publishing.

Tversky, A. and Kahneman, D. (1986). Rational Choice and the Framing of Decisions. The Journal of Business, 59, 4, Part 2: The Behavioral Foundations of Economic Theory.

United Nations Digital Library 2022. UNHCR global trends, forced displacement in 2021.

van der Heijden, K. (2004). Scenarios: The Art of Strategic Conversation. John Wiley and Sons, Chichester.

Wack, P. (1985). Scenarios. Unchartered Waters Ahead. Harvard Business Review. September.

Webb, A. (2016). The signals are talking: Why today's fringe is tomorrow's mainstream. Public Affairs, New York.

Weiner, E. and Brown, A. (2006). Future Think. How to Think Clearly in a Time of Change. Pearson Prentice Hall, New Jersey.

Zakharov, D. (2021). Future Fluent. How Organisations use Foresight to Thrive in Turbulent Times. New Degree Press.

Zadi, L. (2020). The Only Three Trends That Matter: A Minimum Specification for Future-Proofing. Journal of Future studies, 4, 24.

Chapter 2
Scenario Planning Origins & Evolution

Introduction

In a VUCA world, competitive advantages erode rapidly and the formulation and application of appropriate strategies, are becoming increasingly complex and dependent upon the ability of policymakers to absorb a multitude of facts. Furthermore, an understanding of the deep trends influencing the evolution of the future is required, in addition to the interplay between these trends, structural elements, and their outcomes. However, Hamel and Prahalad (1994, p 123) contend that:

> *About 40% of a senior executive's time is devoted to looking outward and, of this time, about 30% is spent peering three, four, five, or more years into the future. Of that time spent looking forward, no more than 20% is devoted to building a collective view of the future . . . thus, on average, senior managers devote less than 3% (40% x 30% x 20%) of their time to building a corporate perspective on the future. In some companies, the figure is less than 1%,*

The authors suggest the consequences of this are:
- difficult management questions go unanswered because they challenge the assumption that top management is in control;
- the urgent drives out the important, firefighting becomes the mode of management and the future is left unexplored;
- the capacity to act rather than think and imagine, becomes the measure of leadership;
- when problems arise, the scalpel (cost-cutting) becomes the answer to everything.

Although Hamel and Prahalad wrote this in 1994, Gowing and Langdon (2016) claim that 22 years later there has been no improvement. The primary focus of senior executives' consideration of the future continues to be based on forecasting and identifying one future, rather than developing a deep understanding of discontinuities. Gidley (2017, p 3) supports this argument, arguing that "as the rate of change accelerates and the world becomes more complex and confusing, the term 'future' is becoming omnipresent in media, business literature, and education." She claims that consultants everywhere call themselves futurists, with the use of the term 'future' leading to a "global proliferation of government departments, corporate agencies, consultancies, and trend spotters, all claiming to be future-focused." Despite this proliferation of 'future-focusing' entities, governments, businesses, and the education industry continue to operate on short-term thinking "with little evidence of engagement with the future studies literature established over several decades" (p 3).

What is required today is a new way of thinking, one focused on understanding the forces and their combinations that are driving change in the future. This thinking

https://doi.org/10.1515/9783111617442-002

can provide an understanding of, and insights into how and why the future may develop in unanticipated ways, leading to the development of a deep understanding of
discontinuities. This is the essence of future studies, an interdisciplinary and systems
thinking approach about the future, with several organisations specializing in this
field. Illustrating the future by means of scenarios is one way to study the future; scenario planning is a fundamental part of the framework of this future, and it is perhaps the most emblematic foresight method.

The Origins of Scenarios

The use of scenarios as a strategic planning tool is rooted in the military, having been
employed by military strategists throughout history in the form of war game simulations. The first documented evidence of what today would be regarded as 'scenarios'
appears in the writings of von Clausewitz and von Moltke, two 19th century Prussian
military strategists credited with having formulated the principles of strategic planning
(von Reibnitz, 1988). Following the First World War, a focus on the future became a subject of national interest to a wide range of professions, and national predictive forecast-
based planning became the established norm in governments. In the United States of
America (USA) President Herbert Hoover established the Research Committee on Social
Trends in 1929. This committee used historical statistics to chart trends and extrapolate
the future, with the objective of finding better ways to understand and predict the future; following the Second World War, the future became the focus of increased US
state planning. This provided the platform in 1946 for the founding of the RAND Corporation (an acronym for Research and Development), a leading think-tank that evolved
out of a joint project between the United States Airforce and the Douglas Aircraft Company in 1945. The objective of the RAND Corporation was "to assist with US war efforts,
focused on developing prediction and forecasting methods for military and industrial
goals" (Gidley, 2017 p 43) using mathematical models supported by newly acquired computing power. Andersson (2018, p 23) describes it as "RAND built an epistemic Cold War
arsenal: these techniques were used to know an enemy whose future behaviour was to
be revealed through forms of virtual experimentation and synthetic fact in the absence
of conventional knowledge." From this emerged contemporary scenario planning, with
the 1960s witnessing the development of two geographical centres in the advancement
of scenario techniques, the USA and France.

Foundations of The USA Scenario Centre

After World War II, one of the tasks facing the US Department of Defence was deciding what projects should be funded for the development of new weapons systems.
Given the increasing complexity of weapons systems arising from advances made

during the war years, this was a difficult undertaking. Compounding this difficulty was the significant uncertainty faced by the decision-makers on three fronts. Firstly, the development of new weapons systems generally required long lead times. Secondly, with the lowering of the 'iron curtain,' there was a high degree of uncertainty as to the future political environment in which the systems being developed might be deployed. Finally, the uncertainty about the effectiveness of the systems developed would be largely dependent upon what weapons systems other nations were developing (Raubitschek, 1988). Decision-making in this situation gave rise to two specific needs: a methodology to capture the reliable consensus of a large and diverse group of experts, and simulation models of future environments to facilitate investigation by policymakers of their consequences.

The necessity to elicit and synthesize expert opinion inspired the development of the Delphi technique (discussed in detail later in this chapter), while the need for simulation models led to the development of an approach known as 'systems analysis' (Raubitschek, 1988), both of which were developed in the 1950s by the Rand Corporation. This, in combination with the progress of computers which provided the data processing capability required for simulating solutions for obstinate problems, a game theory which provided the theoretical structure for the investigation of social interaction, and the US military's need for war game simulation models, provided the platform for the emergence of scenario techniques as depicted in Figure 2.1 at the Rand Corporation (Schoemaker, 1993).

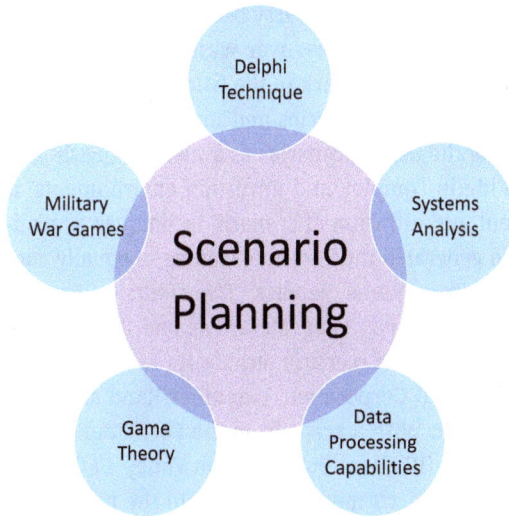

Figure 2.1: Components providing the Platform for Scenario Planning.

Using this platform, Herman Kahn, the ranking authority on Civil Defence and strategic planning at the Rand Corporation in the 1950s, began developing scenarios for the

Air Défense System Missile Command, a large-scale early warning system. Kahn variously described as a 'super genius' and a 'policy intellectual of unquestioned genius' developed a disturbing critique of US military strategy in the thermonuclear age (Bruce-Briggs, 2001). Credited with having coined the phrase 'thinking about the unthinkable,' Kahn demonstrated through a combination of facts and logic, that military planning tended to be based on wishful thinking rather than realistic expectations. The existing doctrine he contended, was disastrous, and he demonstrated this by developing scenarios of a 'nuclear war by miscalculation' (Millet, 2003). The objective of using scenarios as a vehicle to think about the unthinkable was to search for serious alternatives to annihilation and surrender, and his work had a major impact on the US Pentagon's thinking in the 1950s. However, due to the classified nature of this work, the content and methodology of this pioneering scenario work were not widely publicised until 1960 when Kahn published a book entitled *On Thermonuclear War*.

In 1961, Kahn left the Rand Corporation and, together with Max Singer and Oscar Ruebhausen, established the Hudson Institute at Croton-on-Hudson where they refocused scenarios from the theatre to government, and then to corporate planning (Millett, 2003). The Institute used hypothetical scenarios as well as game theory and systems analysis, to conduct a wide variety of projects for both government and corporate clients. Kahn subsequently authored and coauthored numerous magazine and journal articles and published books incorporating futuristic scenarios, the most controversial of which was *The Year 2000: A Framework for Speculation on the Next Thirty-Three Years*, co-written with Anthony Wiener and published in 1967 (Shoemaker, 1993; Godet, 1987). Although Kahn's work gained notoriety, provoking controversy because of scenarios describing conflict situations leading to a potential nuclear war with the Soviet Union, Raubitschek (1988) maintains that the book is a landmark in the field of scenario planning, providing one of the earliest definitions of scenarios and introducing the term into the planning literature. In validating the use of scenarios as a methodological tool for policy planning and decision-making in complex and uncertain environments, it influenced the subsequent development and diffusion of scenario techniques as planning tools in the USA. Kahn's book also generated much debate leading to equally controversial studies, for example, the Club of Rome Reports, *The Limits to Growth* (Meadows et al, 1972), and *Mankind at the Turning Point* (Mesarovic and Pestel, 1974), heightening the focus of attention on scenarios and scenario techniques.

Soon after Kahn departed from the Rand Corporation, two other Rand alumnae, Olaf Helmer and Theodore Gordon also left. With a grant from the Ford Foundation, they co-founded the Institute for the Future (IFTF) in 1968 in Silicon Valley, California. IFTF's mission was to take leading-edge research methodologies into the public and business sectors, with the commitment to building the future by deeply understanding it. Encouraged by the publicity and controversy caused by Kahn's books, Helmer and Gordon, along with several individuals at the Stanford Research Institute (SRI) Futures Group and the California Institute of Technology, began to experiment with scenarios as a planning tool, becoming pioneers in the field of future studies in the

USA. Although concerned primarily with scenarios as a tool for public policy planning, it was not long before their work migrated to the business community. The first widely documented use of scenarios in the context of business was the experience of the Royal Dutch Shell (Shell) company which adopted scenario planning as a corporate strategy in 1973 (Lorenz, 1990). This, along with the work of SRI, gave rise to what Godet (2000) describes as the Anglo-American School of scenario planning, better known in the literature as the 'Intuitive Logics' (IL) school, or methodology, of scenario planning (Huss and Honton, 1987).

The Intuitive Logics School

In 1965, Shell introduced a complex, computerized, six-year time horizon, model-based, financial forecasting system called the Unified Planning Machinery (UPM). However, it was not long before the realization that many of the company's commitments extended beyond UPM's six-year time horizon, and even within the six-year time horizon UPM tended to get a lot wrong. As a result, UPM was shut down and Jimmy Davidson, the head of Economics and Planning for Shell's Exploration and Production Division, worked with Ted Newland, a company veteran, to start an activity at Shell's London headquarters called Long-Term Studies. In 1967, together with Henk Alkema, Newland began to develop scenarios around the long-term outlooks for oil, with the scenarios presented to senior executives in 1971. While this first generation of scenarios was not considered successful providing little in the way of new insights beyond that which was already known, there was recognition that scenario planning was a potentially useful tool and that the technique had promise. This prompted the decision to experiment with scenario planning as a better framework for thinking about the future rather than continuing to rely on conventional forecasts, which were typically wrong in the face of discontinuity (Wack, 1985; Kleiner, 1996).

Davidson then brought in Pierre Wack who was the head of planning for Shell Française, to work with the scenarios in London, to try to secure the attention and interest of Shell's senior executives. Wack had already met Herman Kahn and was familiar with the scenario approach, and he decided to experiment with the technique using his native France as the testing ground. The set of scenarios developed in 1971 by Newland and Alkema was revised, and two new scenarios were presented to the senior management in 1972. These new scenarios suggested that a change in the Middle East was about to destroy the stability of the existing oil regime which oil companies had dominated, resulting in an impending oil crisis. Wack and Newland examined a range of potentially possible angles of the situation, focusing in particular on pressures faced by the governments of Iran and Saudi Arabia. They concluded that it would take a miracle to avoid an energy crisis; the oil price could soar from $2 per barrel to an unimaginable price of $10 per barrel (by 1975 it hit $13) and they warned the Shell management to prepare for it. Consequently, Shell "began to put in place many of common sense, mundane frugality that had been lost amid the frenetic growth of the 1950s and 1960s" (Kleiner, 2003). In 1973, a year after Wack's team presented their new scenarios, came the so-called 'Energy Crisis' which the scenarios had proposed and which put Shell in an enviable position. OPEC countries placed an embargo on their oil exports, resulting in an increase of 400% in the global price of a barrel of crude, causing turmoil in the oil industry (Millett, 2003). As a consequence, shortly thereafter scenario planning was extended throughout Shell, replacing UPM, and it has since forewarned Shell's managing directors about some of the most bewildering events of their times including the price shock of 1979, the collapse of the oil market in 1986, the fall of the Soviet Union, the rise of Muslim radicalism, and the increasing pressure on companies to address environmental and social problems (Kleiner, 2003).

The Shell approach to scenario development has now been in use in Shell for more than 50 years and has spread to other corporations globally. However, despite its successes, there have been periods during which Shell's senior management has struggled to see the value of scenario planning. In fact, "it has come close to being shut down at least three times" but it has continued "to evolve and help shape the company's global thinking . . . and, at times, its strategy" (Wilkinson and Kupers, 2013, p 1) This is quite remarkable given the difficulty in determining the contribution scenario planning makes to the organisation's bottom line, and that rather than producing predictions, scenario planning instead emphasizes the uncertainty of the future. At the same time, Shell has used scenarios to create new value by developing scenarios with key stakeholders in prospective joint projects, building networks, and sharing their expertise. While there is no clear evidence that scenarios have helped Shell anticipate future developments ahead of anyone else, they have helped make the executives comfortable in navigating a VUCA world, and in preparing for futures which could happen.

At about the same time that Shell started using scenarios, General Electric (GE) began to experiment with the technique and in 1971 produced four alternative scenarios of global and US economic and socio-political conditions in 1980. Ian Wilson, a corporate planner from GE's corporate offices, befriended Kahn and met with him and Wack to discuss the application of scenarios to the business world. Although both Wilson and Wack decided to initiate scenario projects as an innovative approach to traditional corporate and financial forecasting, there were two substantial differences in their approaches to scenario development. The first was that GE scenarios comprised four alternative futures, whereas Shell generated only two, representing extreme ends of a spectrum of possible futures. The second difference was that Wilson assigned expert judgment probabilities to the GE scenarios; Wack, however, resisted this urge, not wanting scenarios to be seen as akin to traditional forecasts (Millett, 2003).

The question is which approach works best, Shell or GE? While there is little in the public domain regarding GE and scenario planning, Shell has become the celebrated corporate exponent of scenarios and Shell's definition of scenarios and process methods for scenario generation has become the gold standard of corporate scenario planning. This is why the IL methodology is sometimes referred to as the 'Shell approach' to scenario planning (Millet, 2003). Indeed, the name 'Pierre Wack' and 'scenarios' are used almost synonymously, with Wack widely considered 'the founding father of modern-day scenario planning' and the 'undisputed intellectual leader in the domain of scenario-based strategic thinking' (Ringland, 1998: p 19). Wack, who passed away in 1997, wrote no books and only published three articles; however, two of the articles, *Scenarios: Unchartered Waters Ahead* and *Scenarios: Shooting the Rapids*, published in Harvard Business Review in 1985, are among the most frequently cited articles in the scenario planning literature.

Over the years variations of the IL model have been published, each identifying a set of discrete steps varying from 13 steps (Orru and Relan 2013) to 10 (Schoemaker, 1993), to 6 (Gugan, 2008), and down to 4 steps (Kahane, 2012), depending on what features of scenarios are either highlighted or ignored. Practitioners have in some cases branded proprietary scenario developmental models, examples of which include:

- *Future Mapping*®, an approach used by Northeast Consulting Resources Inc. based in Massachusetts;
- *TAIDA*™ (an acronym for 'Tracking, Analysing, Imaging, Deciding, and Acting'), an approach developed at Kairos Future in Sweden (Lindgren and Bandhold, 2003);
- *Idon Scenario Thinking*, an approach using visual tools developed by the Idon Group in Scotland (Galt et al, 1997); and
- Futureworlds™ a foresight development methodology to create customised scenarios, by PA Consulting (https://www.paconsulting.com/insights/2020/futureworlds/).

Efforts have also been made to develop simpler and less resource-intensive models, and when it comes to the IL model, there are now almost as many ways of developing scenarios as there are practitioners in the field. While the IL methodology has received most of the attention in the literature, following a review of the literature Bishop et al (2007) identified more than two dozen variations, with some difficult to classify because they include processes from various categories. The more commonly known categories of these techniques include Trend-Impact Analysis (TIA), Cross-Impact Analysis (CIA) Backcasting, Field Anomaly Relaxation (FAR), and Morphological Analysis (MA), each of which will be briefly discussed in the following sections.

The Probabilistic Modified Trends School

TIA and CIA, developed by Theodore Gordon and Olaf Helmer, have been used in many different contexts and share a common foundation of a mathematical amelioration of extrapolated time series data. They can therefore be justifiably viewed as a coherent group of techniques that for convenience, can be labelled the 'Probabilistic

Modified Trends' (PMT) school. They are, however, different standalone quantitative and probabilistic forecasting tools that generate a range of alternative futures rather than a naïve single point extrapolation of historical data, and when combined with narratives about these futures, constitute scenarios.

Trend-Impact Analysis (TIA)

The TIA model developed in the early 1970s is most often associated with the Futures Group based in Connecticut and was first introduced by Theodore Gordon and John Stover. According to Gordon (1994), TIA evolved out of the fact that traditional forecasting methods relied on the extrapolation of historical data without considering the effects of unprecedented and unexpected future events. As Gordon (2003, p 3) puts it, "TIA is a simple approach to forecasting in which a time series is modified to take into account perceptions about how future events may change extrapolations that would otherwise be surprise-free; it permits an analyst, interested in tracking a particular trend, to include and systematically examine the effects of possible future events that are believed to be important".

The concept of TIA is reasonably simple, being designed to modify simple extrapolations involving four sequential steps:
1. The collection of historical data relating to the issue being examined.
2. An algorithm is used to select specific curve-fitting historical data and extrapolate this to generate 'surprise-free' future trends.
3. A list of unprecedented future events which could cause deviations from the extrapolated trend is developed; and
4. Expert judgments which are then used to identify the probability of occurrence of these unprecedented events as a function of time and their expected impact to produce adjusted extrapolations. Three different impact points are identified and estimated, the first being the point of the first noticeable impact when the trend deviates from its original course; the second is the time to the maximum impact when the trend deviates furthest from its original trajectory, and the third is when the deviation impact reaches a steady state and is fully integrated into the trend. A new trend line is then developed and compared to the original baseline trajectory (Bishop et al, 2007).

The TIA method is particularly suited to policy evaluations. It is relatively simple and easy to use and has been employed by numerous US agencies including the Federal Aviation Administration, Federal Bureau of Investigation, Joint Chief of Staff, National Science Foundation, the Departments of Energy and Transportation, and the State of California. Compared with other forecasting methods, the main advantage of the TIA method is that it links events with trends and allows forecasters to specify factors that may alter a trend, and then assess the probabilities of this happening. Criticisms of TIA include the fact that the list of future events developed is unavoidably incomplete and historical data may not give a true picture of underlying trends. Additionally, the accuracy of the probability of occurrence and the impact judgments can be questionable.

A major problem in forecasting trends regardless of what process is used, is in identifying the turning points. In hindsight, turning points are usually clearly visible, but it can be difficult to tell when working on a forecast whether they are mere anomalies or the beginning of new trends. At the same time, the further out the forecast, the greater the possibility for error, because it is inevitable that as time progresses, new and unknown variables will appear. While accepting these criticisms, the benefit of TIA is that it raises assumptions about the future which might not otherwise have been raised. At the same time, it can enhance the accuracy and usefulness of approaches to trend extrapolation, by allowing users to focus on tracking a small but important set of events.

Cross-Impact Analysis (CIA)

CIA was based on a simple card game called *Future* developed in 1996 for Kaiser-Aluminium by Theodore Gordon from the Futures Group, and Olaf Helmer. This was in response to a shortcoming of Delphi surveys in that they did not consider mutual influences existing between events i.e., that events can be interrelated and not be independent of each other (Wiemer-Jehle, 2006). The objective of CIA was to gain additional insights into the future development of selected issues by evaluating interactions between a set of events, and changes in the probability of the occurrence of the set of events, following the actual occurrence of one of the events. As with TIA, the CIA methodology essentially attempts to evaluate changes in the probability of occurrence of events, which may cause deviations in the naïve extrapolations of historical data. This is based on the premise that events do not happen in a vacuum and that other events in the surrounding environment can significantly influence the probability of certain events occurring. The processes underlying TIA and CIA methodologies are similar; however, CIA incorporates an additional layer of complexity. Rather than accepting the a priori probabilities attached to future events by experts, CIA attempts to determine the conditional probabilities of pairs of future events, given that various events have or have not occurred, through cross-impact calculations. The premise of CIA is that it is essential to be conscious of the interdependencies of events to move from a system of initial unprocessed probabilities to a set of corrected probabilities (Godet, 1987).

Although different variants of CIA have been developed and extensively applied across a wide range of disciplines, there still exist several shortcomings with the technique. Firstly, while it focuses on interactions between pairs of events, real-world interactions often occur in more than just pairs. Interactions between three or more events would add significantly to the issue of causality and conditional probability judgments, and the collection of these judgments. Secondly, it requires judgments of the conditional or joint probabilities of pairs of events or marginal probabilities of events These judgements require knowing what interrelationships exist in a system and understanding the impact this will produce, which requires both mental integration and the possession of insights. It also assumes that conditional probabilities are more accurate than estimates of a priori estimates, which is unproven (Gordon, 1994). Finally, the underlying mathematical structures are difficult to understand in many generic cross-impact models, and their computational routines are difficult to explain (Weimer-Jehle, 2006).

Researchers have since developed several proprietary causal and cross-impact methodologies, including:

- KSIM a simulation technique developed by Julius Kane based on the expected interactions among time-series variables rather than events;
- IFS (Interactive Future Simulations) previously known as BASICS using software developed by the Battelle Memorial Institute (Millet 2003);
- EXPLOR-SIM also developed at the Battelle Institute by Duval, Fontela, and Gabus; and
- INTERAX (Interactive Cross-Impact Simulation) developed by Selwyn Enzer at the University of California; and SMIC, a French acronym for Cross Impact Systems (Avella, 2016).

New Techniques

Alongside CIA, several new techniques discussed below, have developed over the years and are used in particular scenario planning instances.

Backcasting

While most scenario development techniques extend from the present to the future, the Backcasting technique which is essentially a normative scenario development technique, works backwards. It begins by envisioning a desirable future state at a specified horizon year; having created the desirable end state, one then works backwards step-by-step to the present to determine what policy measures, implementation, and follow-up programs would be required to reach that desirable future (Quist, 2016). The fundamentals of the method were first outlined in 1980 by John Robinson from the University of Waterloo. Robinson proposed 'Backcasting' as an alternative planning methodology for electricity supply and demand, suggesting the term 'energy backcasting' to capture that future energy demand is mainly a function of current policy decisions. Today the approach is increasingly applied in urban planning and resource management, and has become the most commonly used approach in futures studies dealing with urban sustainability, smart cities, and other sustainability-related challenges. This is because it is viewed as a natural step in operationalizing sustainable developments (Bibri, 2020).

Unlike most scenario techniques, Backcasting is not concerned with developing plausible futures but rather determining how desirable futures can be achieved. This is especially useful in developing normative scenarios where there is a normative objective and fundamentally uncertain future events that influence the objectives. There are numerous examples of normative scenarios, one of the first being 'Wawasan 2020' (translated as Vision 2020), a Malaysian ideal introduced by the Prime Minister of Malaysia in 1991. This scenario calls for "the nation to achieve a self-sufficient industrialised nation by the year 2020, encompassing all aspects of life, from economic prosperity, social well-being, educational world-class, political stability, as well as psychological balance" (Wikipedia). There have since been many examples in the literature of countries developing and publishing normative scenarios, such as the Sultanate of Oman where the stated objective is that of "Oman joining the World's Developed Countries" (Oman Vision 2040.)

The main characteristic of the Backcasting approach is that it is a participatory process involving stakeholders at an early stage in the foresight process in developing a long-term normative scenario. Thereafter the participants can translate this into necessary actions and define their required roles to achieve the scenario. The rationale for a Backcasting approach is essentially twofold. First, the ability to predict the likelihood of alternative outcomes for complex human systems in the longer-term future is severely limited and compromised. These restrictions are due to fundamental uncertainties about future events, stemming from the lack of knowledge about systems, their conditions, dynamics, and the prospects for innovation. Second, even if the future were predictable, for long-term societal problems such as sustainability, the most likely future may not be the most desirable. In such a situation it is important to explore the feasibility of alternative normative futures, which also introduces the examination of policy choice into the analysis. Thus, the major distinguishing characteristic of Backcasting is that it involves working backwards from a particular desired future end-state to the present, to determine the practical and relative feasibility of that future, and the policy measures required to reach that point.

To permit time for futures significantly different from the present to come about, endpoints are usually chosen for a time of 25–50 years into the future. Unlike predictive forecasts, Backcasts are not intended to reveal what the future will likely be, but to indicate the relative feasibility and implications of different policy goals (Robinson, 2003). It is particularly useful when "the problem to be studied is complex and there is a need for major change; dominant trends are part of the problem; the problem to a great extent is a matter of externalities, and the scope is wide enough and the time horizon long enough to leave considerable room for deliberate choice" (Dreborg 1996, p 820). van der Duin (2016) documents five distinct steps involved in a conventional step-by-step Backcasting process:

Step 1: Strategic Problem Orientation.

The initial steps are:

– Establish the Backcasting and research team;
– Determine the methodology to be used;
– Describe the normative assumptions, requirements, and targets; and
– Define the relevant stakeholders, and how they will be involved in the process.

van der Kerkhof (2004, p 26–27) suggests that stakeholder participation in the process is essential as it increases the legitimacy of the decisions which emerge from the process resulting in increased accountability. Stakeholders therefore become co-responsible for decisions, adding an increased richness to the process due to a wider range of viewpoints, interests, information, and expertise.

Step 2: Generating One or Several Sustainable Future Visions.

It is possible to develop one or more sustainable future visions, although a single vision is generally more appropriate. There are also different methods of developing the visions, ranging from brainstorming and setting targets, to variants of morphological analysis.

Step 3: Backcasting Analysis.

This step involves developing specific questions to determine the necessary changes required to bring about the future vision, a version of which is called the WHAT-HOW -WHO questions. The 'WHAT' focuses on the technological, economic, cultural, behavioural, and societal changes required to bring about the desirable future. The 'HOW' looks at how changes can be brought about and the necessary activities and policies, regulations, communications, and education programmes. Finally, the 'WHO' looks at which actors and stakeholders are required to carry out the necessary activities to bring about the essential changes required.

Step 4: Elaboration and Defining Follow-up Activities and Agenda.

The first part of this step involves the feasibility of turning the vision into a quantified scenario and the analysis and assessment of its sustainability. The second part involves developing follow-up activities and agendas to determine the implementation pathway.

Step 5: Embedding Action Agenda and Stimulating Follow-up.

The final step involves the dissemination of results and policy recommendations, stimulating follow-up activities, and documenting the process and learning evaluations. Given that Backcasting usually focuses on solving complex social issues, the participation of representatives of several institutional stakeholders is essential, as is the linkage with decision-makers to establish a commitment to achieving the normative vision. A positive aspect of this method is its focus on discussing problems with stakeholders who have conflicting interests and reaching a common understanding of desirable futures and the steps required to achieve them. Additionally, because Backcasting focuses explicitly on policy implications and requirements, it is more closely oriented to the policy process than is the case with conventional forecasting. There are, however, several disadvantages of Backcasting. First, the process can be lengthy and requires substantial financial resources. Second, it tends to "focus on changing existing socio-technical systems while paying limited or no attention to cultural or economic changes that could support the envisioned changes" and third, it generally neglects "aspects of governance, agency and implementation" (van der Duin, 2016 p 128).

Field Anomaly Relaxation

Field Anomaly Relation (FAR), developed by Russell Rhyne in the 1970s, is a technique that maps interactions of change drivers on a systemic scale, structuring them as *sectors* and *factors*. From the interactions between these complex interconnected factors, a tree of branching scenarios can be created. The technique advocates adherence to a four-step process for projecting futures (Rhyne, 1995) as follows:

Step 1: Form an Initial View of Alternative Futures
These alternate futures could unfold within the area of interest, which can be carried out by a team of people in the form of essays describing the possible future evolution of the system in question. The purpose of the essay writing, is to generate a wide range of ideas about the sectors in the problem and to suggest the extent of their variation.

Step 2: Identify Critical Uncertainties
The next step is to identify the critical uncertainties about the socio-economic and technological developments in the future, and their range of possibilities using 'sectors' that become dimensions describing the area of interest, and 'factors' which become the alternative states within each sector. These are then expressed in a matrix to form 'whole field' (full sector range) descriptors of all possible configurations.

Step 3: Remove Anomalies
The third step requires eliminating anomalies, or factor pairs that are illogical or cannot co-exist, forming a reduced set of whole field configurations. Not all anomalies however will be clear-cut and should only be eliminated after a thorough discussion. Following a review of the anomalies eliminated, it may be necessary to reinstate some of them.

Step 4: Create a Tree with Branched Future States
The final step, which is the most subjective part of FAR, is to position the surviving whole field configurations on a 'tree' whose branches represent possible future states, with timeline transitions from one configuration to the next.

The concept behind FAR is that individuals, groups and nations, all exist within fields of interactions with other entities and events. In terms of individuals, a 'field' may include factors such as career choices, family relationships, and the financial environment, whereas for a nation a field may include factors such as the state of the economy, technological innovation, the political situation, and the stability of the region. The FAR methodology differs from conventional forecasting methods in that it deals with whole patterns rather than component variables. The objective is therefore, to describe a problem domain in terms of a complete field of several descriptors (known as sectors) and the major areas of change that could occur over 5 -10 years for an individual, or 10–30 years for a nation. Descriptors are portions of the overall field, each contributing to form a mental picture of a possible future, and the 'state' determines the level or condition of a descriptor. It is essential that the set of states of a descriptor covers the full range of behaviours of the descriptors, and that they not only describe the present situation, but are also judged to be the most appropriate to describe futures in a similar context.

Rhyne (1995) has argued that some combinations of descriptors could be seen to be anomalous in that they could involve inherent contradictions. If these anomalies are eliminated, the number of surviving pattern combinations would be reduced to a manageable number to form timeline projections of logically consistent future possibilities. Duczynski (2000) indicates that there have been several extensions to the method making it more directionally focused on the interests of practitioners, but there is only a small body of literature supporting the use of FAR, mostly relating to military and security employment.

Morphological Analysis

Morphological Analysis (MA) was developed during the Second World War by Fritz Zwicky, a Swiss astrophysicist and aerospace scientist. MA was proposed as a method for structuring and investigating the total set of relationships contained in multidimensional, non-quantifiable, problem complexes which do not lend themselves to quantification (Ritchey 2003; 2006). MA was developed essentially to facilitate group work and cooperation between different scientific disciplines and actors in different sectors and organizational levels in society. Because of the complexity of the MA process and the thousands of potential configurations mapped out in even relatively small morphological fields, MA is difficult to employ without computer support.

The iterative 5 step process defining the problem complex in terms of variables and variable conditions are:

Step 1: Identify the dimensions, parameters, or variables which best define the essential nature of the problem complex or scenario.

Step 2: Define for each variable, a range of relevant, discrete values or conditions, that the variable can express.

Step 3: Assess the internal consistency of all pairs of variable conditions, identifying all inconsistent or contradictory pairs.

Step 4: Synthesize an internally consistent outcome space.

Step 5: Iterate the process if necessary. Scrutinize the solution space and return to steps 1, 2, and 3 to adjust variables, alternatives, and consistency measures. Run steps 4 and 5 again.

Originally designed as a tool for use in the scientific community, MA has since been extended and applied by several researchers in the field of futures studies (Ritchey, 2003). As with FAR, the literature on MA in the field of futures is small, although both are included in the overview of scenario techniques by Bishop et al (2007).

Roadmapping

'Roadmapping' was developed by Motorola as a strategic foresight method in the 1970s to develop product technology and emerging technology (Romgens, 2016.) The purpose of a roadmap is to describe a desired future position, goal, or desired outcome of an organisation or industry, and the major steps required to reach it. Its flexibility and utility mean that it has, Romgens suggests, emerged as a broadly accepted foresight technique and is used extensively across industries, governments, and academic organisations to bring clarity to complex problems and alignment of purpose. Despite this, Roadmapping does not appear in the conventional literature on foresight or scenarios. This is perhaps because it is perceived more as a strategic planning technique which the Institute for Manufacturing (IfM Engage) at Cambridge University describes as integral to creating and delivering strategy and innovation in organisations and enabling strategic alignment and dialogue across functions. A detailed discussion on the history and methodology of Roadmapping can be found in Chapter 8 of the book *Foresight in Organisations. Methods and Tools* edited by Patrick van der Duin.

The Delphi Technique

The Delphi technique derived from the Oracle of Delphi (see Chapter 1), was developed in the 1950s at the Rand Corporation under a US government contract. The contract aimed to assess long-term trends in science and technology, including technology's impact on warfare and the potential outcomes of nuclear weapons in conflict. Developed by Norman Dalkey and Olaf Helmer, the technique is part of the group of 'consensus development techniques' (Avella, 2016), rather than a scenario development technique. It is a method of forecasting by gathering the opinions of experts knowledgeable about a certain topic area requiring decision-making, through a series of iterative question-naires. It has been extensively used in topics spanning a wide range of disciplines and the purpose of conducting a Delphi process is to examine a set of specific issues for goal setting, policy investigation or predicting the occurrence of future events (Hsu and Sandford, 2007). Avella describes these three versions of Delphi as 'Decision-making,' 'Policy' and 'Classical' Delphi.

The Delphi process incorporates several anonymous participants, termed 'panel-lists' selected for their expertise in a particular area. Initially, these experts are asked to identify a range of salient issues related to the topic under consideration. The ideas are then collated, summarized, anonymised, and redistributed for discussion in a second round, in which the panellists are asked to re-evaluate their previous responses. This process is iterative, allowing panellists to assess and reassess the topic based on a set of questions. This cyclical evaluation-re-evaluation process is aided by considering the anonymous, aggregated group opinion, encompassing both quantitative and qualitative data (Rowe and Wright, 1999). The method relies on the phenomenon that results from group-based discussion processes are more reliable and accurate than individual evalu-ations when the assessed topics are not a matter of fact (Rowe et al., 2005). An iterative discussion can lead to stability in the assessments or consensus among experts (Dia-mond et al., 2014; von der Gracht, 2012). Anonymity and iteration avoid the tendency of individuals to conform to majority behaviour or beliefs termed 'bandwagon effects,' which are inherent to group discussions. This allows answers to be based on individual reflections and opinions of experts, preventing the dominance of any particular individ-ual or group (von der Gracht, 2012).

Predominantly a qualitative methodology, the Delphi Technique is based on the principle that forecasts from a structured group of experts are likely to be more accu-rate than those from individuals and unstructured groups. Furthermore, it avoids the disadvantages of psychological phenomena such as 'group-think.' Commonly used in TIA, CIA, and scenario development processes, the Delphi technique is applicable in areas where there is little prior research. It is also useful in situations marked by am-biguity and where establishing cause-and-effect relationships is impossible (Yang et al., 2012). In planning a Delphi study, the main considerations are the disciplines and number of participants invited to join the process; the method and procedures of communications and feedback; and participant anonymity. The advantages of Delphi include the fact that:

- The technique is versatile and the methodology is flexible. This allows research-ers to adapt it to the research context, making it useful to tackle a wide variety of issues and situations to improve understanding of, and solve highly complex problems (Hsu and Sandford, 2007; Donohoe and Needham, 2009).
- The selection of participants can include a broad and dynamic panel of experts from a wide range of disciplines and professions. Location is not a constraint as

participants do not have to be in the same location to reach an agreement, which means they can be recruited from across the world (Dalkey and Helmer, 1963).

–   There is the potential to gather considerable quantities of data as the series of group questionnaires generate a much larger and wider set of ideas than individual participants could generate independently.

–   The iteration process allows participants to generate more insights and to clarify information presented in previous iterations, and in the process, become more problem-solving oriented (Hsu and Stanford, 2007).

–   Participants can express their opinions and critiques without restrictions or confrontations, as anonymity is maintained throughout the process. Moreover, the responses are weighed equally, so no individual can shift the opinions of the group (Donohoe and Needham, 2009; Iqbal and Pipon-Young, 2009).

–   Ideas are not dismissed, and discussions are not dominated or influenced by any individual because of their authority, personality, or professional standing. The process is democratic, allowing participants an equal opportunity to contribute (Donohoe and Needham, 2009; Iqbal and Pipon-Young, 2009); and

–   The cost of process administration and analysis is relatively low.

As with most process techniques, there are weaknesses to the Delphi method, most notably that panellists are a critical element of the process. This can be undermined if an insufficient number of panellists are selected, or if those selected lack the necessary expertise. Furthermore, the iterative nature of the process means it can be very time-consuming, and may be difficult to motivate participants to ensure their sustained involvement. This can be particularly challenging as there is no relationship-building or dialogue generation between participants. Additionally, results may be influenced by the collective bias of the participants or the survey analysis of the facilitator. There is also no evidence of reliability, since two different panels working on the same issue may arrive at a different consensus, and it is difficult to determine what exactly constitutes a sufficient consensus (Donohoe and Needham, 2009). At the same time, although a consensus may be achieved by the participants after several iterations, this does not necessarily mean that the correct opinion or judgment has been reached by the participants (Goodman, 1987).

Despite the limitations discussed above, Fink-Hafner et al. (2019) indicate that the omnipresence of the internet and internet-based research tools that support Delphi has recently seen growth in the widespread application of the method. At the same time, the Delphi method has been found to produce more accurate predictions (Parente and Anderson-Parente, 2011), making it a frequently applied method across a wide range of studies such as transportation (Piecyk and McKinnon, 2010; Spickermann et al., 2014), education, (Paul, 2014), strategic management (Loo, 2002), psychiatry (To et al., 2014), and even oncology (Xin, T, et al, 2022).

Foundations of 'The French Scenario Centre'

In Europe, the French are reputed to have been the first to systematically study the scientific and political foundations of the future using scenario techniques. As in the USA, the pioneering scenario work was almost exclusively associated with public policy and planning. While Kahn was developing scenarios for the military, in 1957 the French philosopher Gaston Berger established the Centre International de Prospective (International Centre for Foresight) in Paris. It was here that Berger developed a scenario approach to long-term planning named prospective thinking, or *La Prospective*, which emerged from the repeated failure of classical forecasting approaches (Godet, 1987). The first reported application of the *La Prospective* methodology was the study of regional futures by an interdepartmental government organization known as DATAR, the Office for Regional Planning and Development (Godet, 2001). Berger emphasized that foresight was not the same as forecasting, which was viewed as merely an extension into the future of trends observed in the past. Berger died in 1960, but the Prospectives Centre flourished; by the mid-1960s it had begun to apply the *La Prospective* methodology to a range of public issues including education, the environment, urbanisation, and regional planning.

Among those active in the Prospective group was Pierre Masse, formerly executive director of the Nationalized Electricity de France and then Commissaire General au Plan (the High Commissioner for the Plan). In preparing for the 'Fifth National Economic Plan' Masse decided to enlarge the forecasting process taking place, and introduced the use of the prospective scenario approach in the development of the plan; subsequent national economic plans have purportedly continued to use prospective scenario techniques (Gordon, 1994). Also active in Paris during the 1950s and moving in the same circles, was Bertrand de Jouvenel, who had a long-standing interest in international affairs and the future. A well-known French journalist and economist, de Jouvenel joined the Prospectives Centre in 1966 having become increasingly concerned about the long-term political and social future of France. de Jouvenel (1963) suggested that it was a particular view of the future held by small but dominant political groups within a nation, which ultimately determined how the future of that nation would unfold. This could be avoided, he argued, by encouraging futurists to act as catalysts in articulating idealistic images of what the future could be like, and which could serve as a blueprint for the nation. The underlying philosophical premise of his work was that the future is not part of a 'predetermined temporal continuity.' Instead, the future was something to be created which can be 'consciously modelled to be humanly beneficial.' Thus, the thrust of de Jouvenel's work was to use scenarios to construct positive images of the future or scientific utopias, and then specify ways in which these could be brought about to improve the lives of ordinary people (de Jouvenel, 1963).

The primary objective of the Prospectives Centre was to formulate an acceptable scenario-based methodology for developing positive images of the future, known as normative scenarios. Having developed such scenarios, the group's focus was on introducing these images into the political arena where they could serve as a guiding vision and basis for action for policymakers and the nation (van Vught, 1987). de Jouvenel passed away in 1987 yet left a lasting contribution to the futurist movement through his book *The Art of Conjecture*, published in French in 1964, and then in English in 1967.

The La Prospective School

In the mid-1970s Michel Godet, then head of the Department of Future Studies at SEMA (a firm active in the defence sector), began to develop scenarios for several French national institutions such as the electricity company EdF (Electricite de France). Firmly rooted in the *La Perspective* methodology developed by Berger, Godet began to develop his own largely mathematical and computer-based probabilistic approach to scenario development known as LIPSOR, an acronym for Laboratoire d'Investigation en Prospective, Stratégie et Organisation (Laboratory for Investigation in Prospective Strategy and Organization). The LIPSOR model is a participatory scenario planning approach, comprising five discrete modules (Stratigea and Giaoutzi, 2012; Stratigea, 2013) each serving a different purpose of the planning process, as depicted in Figure 2.2 and summarized below.

– **MICMAC** (Matrice d'Impacts Croises Multiplication Appliiquee a un Classment): this module explores key aspects of the problem area being studied, and frames questions relating to its future states to identify the internal and external driving force variables that may affect the future of the problem area. A detailed structural analysis is then undertaken to determine the influence-dependence relationships amongst a selection of both sets of variables, to ascertain the key variables that can drive the system's future state. The process provides insights into the drivers and its environment, based on causal relationships between pairs of variables and is conducted as a participatory process with local stakeholders, experts, and advisor groups.

– **MACTOR**: this module focuses on the study of the actors involved on the basis of a wide range of factors including power and dependence relationships, goals and objectives, projects in progress, preferences, motivations and past strategic behaviour, constraints, interests, potential strategic moves and personal profiles, The scope of the module is to get insights on dependence relationships among the various actors in the area of concern, providing planners with information on potential power relationships in the region, and define policies which will contribute towards conflict resolutions.

– **SMIC-PROB EXPERT**: following the above, this stage of the process adopts a participatory, qualitative approach. Several basic hypotheses are formulated by the planners based on their knowledge of the system under discussion and the results from the

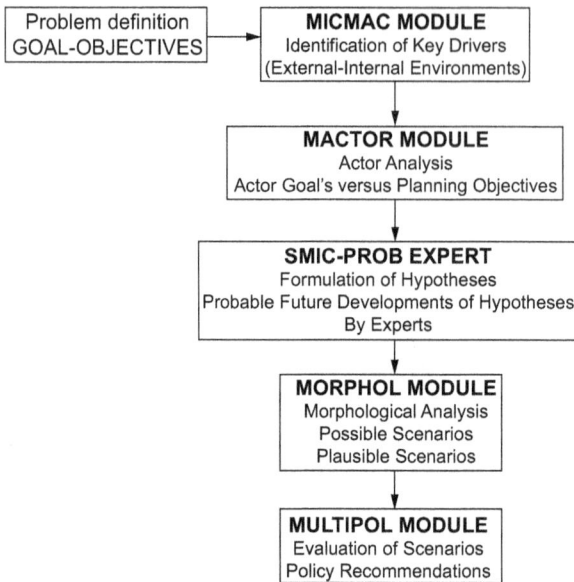

Figure 2.2: The LIPSOR Scenario Planning Model.

MICMAC and MACTOR modules. These are then given to a group of experts who, based on their professional experience, determine the single and conditional probabilities of each of the hypotheses, and are required to revise their assessments until a consensus is achieved. The objective of the module is to reduce the total number of combinations of hypotheses to a useful set of scenarios, based on a combination of their probabilities and their compatibility with the external environments, from information gathered in the previous two modules.

– **MORPHOL**: this module supports the scenario-building process by undertaking the systematic exploration of all possible future states of the area under investigation. This systematic exploration is carried out using a morphological analysis structure based on components regarded as having a high degree of uncertainty concerning their future developments. The outcome of the process, based on the integration of data from the previous modules, is that the number of plausible scenarios is reduced by eliminating those designated as low probability or which are too proximal, leaving the selection criteria for several plausible scenarios.

– **MULTIPOL**: the objective here is to evaluate scenarios developed in the MORPHOL module using multiple-criteria analysis. Two different evaluations are undertaken; the 'actions/policies' evaluation of actions in terms of policies to help policymakers determine which actions best fit each policy. This is followed by a second evaluation of the 'policies/scenario' to determine the appropriate policy specific to each scenario.

Godet et. al. (2004, p 19) suggests that the value of the LIPSOR model is that it "stands apart because of its more integrated approach and use of mixed systems, analysis tools, and procedures." This includes morphological analysis for scenario building, 'Micmac' for identifying key variables, 'Mactor' for analysis of actors' strategies and 'Smic-Prob-Expert' for determining the probability of scenarios. (Micmac, Mactor, and Smic are all acronyms for computer programs developed by Godet.)

Despite the differences in systems developed by the Futuribles Group and Godet, they have since come to be known collectively as the French school of *La Prospective*; the term, however, covers a range of concepts, and Godet (2001) suggests that as used by him, it is best translated as "strategic scenario building".

The main differentiating feature between US and French centres of scenario development is that early scenario work in the USA tended to be global in nature, while in France it was more narrowly focused on the socio-political foundations of the future of France itself (van Vught, 1987). There has since been a diffusion of scenarios into the business community, albeit scenario work in France continues to play an important role in public sector planning. While the *La Prospective* scenario approach incorporates certain features of the IL methodology, it is a more elaborate, complex, and more mechanistic rather than an openly intuitive approach to scenario development. Relying heavily on computer-based and mathematical models which have their roots in TIA and CIA, it is essentially a blending of the IL and probabilistic modified trend methodologies. Although the *La Prospective* school has been in existence for as long as the IL and probabilistic modified trends schools, it has received considerably less attention in the literature on scenario planning, which Godet asserts is a consequence of Anglo-American domination in areas related to strategy.

Following the growth of the Anglo-American and French Schools, numerous 'futures' centres and institutes have been established around the world (detailed in Appendix A). All of these centres are principally focused on tracking signals and critical trends of change around the world to help organisations and individuals make sense of the change. While the IL methodology has received the most attention in the literature, Bishop et al (2007, p 10) indicate that following a comprehensive review of the literature, they have identified "more than two dozen techniques overall" some of which are hard to classify because "they contain processes from different categories."

The Growth of Scenarios

While most scenario development and analysis has occurred in both the private sector and the military (Wilkinson and Kupers 2013; Wilkinson and Ramírez 2010), an assortment of organisations in a wide range of applications are using scenario techniques depending on needs, including:

- Crisis management, such as civil defence exercises, in which scenarios are used in the form of simulations of crises, testing the suitability of systems and equipment to respond to the situations, and increasing response preparedness.
- Scientific communities and policymakers, to understand the potential playout of drivers such as climate change, demographics, food security, fuel, and energy demands, and to communicate the increasing degree of complexity of scientific models in a readily and widely understandable format.
- Public policy makers, who use scenarios as a forum to involve multiple agencies and stakeholders in policy decisions, enabling united analysis and creating a discussion platform to assist policy implementation.
- Professional futurist institutes, of which there are many, most of which are independent research and membership organizations working to spread ideas regarding critical trends that will shape the future, and to promote future research methodologies; and
- Educational institutes, which aim to promote the research and development of future studies theories and methods and create a learning environment, so that issues are considered within an evolving futures context.

Studies of European companies by Malaska et al. (1984), Malaska (1985), and Meristo (1989) indicate that in Europe scenario planning was not widely used until after the first oil crises in 1973, following which the number of adopters of scenario planning almost doubled; there was a further surge of adoption in the period between 1976 and 1978. This led Malaska et al.(1984) to conclude that the adoption of scenario planning was largely the result of the increasing unpredictability of the corporate environment in the 1970s.

The above findings also hold in the USA. Studies by Linneman and Klein (1983) found there were few business users of scenario planning techniques before 1974, but in the two years (1974–1975) following the first oil crises, the number of adopters doubled. They then more than doubled again in the period between 1977 and 1981. Linneman and Klein estimate that in the early 1980s, almost half of all US Fortune 1000 industrial firms, US Fortune 300 non-industrial firms, and Fortune Foreign 500 industrial firms, were actively using scenario techniques in their planning process. Along with Malaska et al. (1984), they posit a correlation between the increase in disruptions and unpredictability in the contextual environment and the adoption of scenario planning.

The work of Linneman and Klein (1983) and Malaska et al (1984) also revealed that the use of scenarios in the USA was not uniform among various industry groupings, and they point to three main factors driving their adoption:
- Size of the company. By 1981, 46% of the Fortune 1000 industrials reportedly used scenarios; among the largest of the Fortune 1000, the Fortune 100, the reported usage was more than 75% of the companies surveyed. That larger companies

dominate in using scenarios is unsurprising given they have both the resources and the inclination to experiment with new planning models

-   Length of planning horizons. Most companies (72%) that used scenarios had planning horizons of 10+ years; and
-   Capital intensiveness. Most scenario users tended to be in capital-intensive industries such as aerospace, chemicals, and petroleum refining.

In Europe, the survey results of Malaska et al (1984) revealed a similar picture i.e., that the highest proportion of scenario planning users were large companies operating in capital intensive industries with long strategic planning horizons, namely, oil companies, vehicle manufacturers, electricity suppliers and transport companies. The finding that large companies predominantly use scenarios, is perhaps unsurprising given the fact that it is generally large companies which have both the resources and the inclination to experiment with new planning models such as scenarios.

This growth in scenario popularity is, however, contradicted by van Doom and von Vught (1983) who state that between 1973 and 1980 there was a decline in preference for scenarios, especially in the USA where the preference for scenarios moved from 'high' to 'medium' (Table 5, page 510). The basis of their research, however, is the analysis of only four studies, two in the US (1973 and 1980) and two in Europe (the Netherlands in 1976 and the FDR in 1978), of how individuals and organisations rated techniques of future studies. They attribute this decline to the fact that from simple beginnings in the 1960s, scenario methods quickly evolved into a complex of subtechniques which rendered them difficult to both implement and complete in a short period. To justify this assertion, they cite research findings (Balachandra, 1978; Naylor and Schauland 1976) which indicate that the perceived usefulness of a technique and ultimately its adoption, is directly proportional to the effort and the sophistication required to implement the technique.

Although there is anecdotal evidence that scenarios may have declined in popularity during the late 1980s, Martelli (2001) suggests their use comes and goes in waves, and although it has witnessed growth in the last one or two decades, it is somewhat less than expected. One reason offered for this is that scenario practitioners have so far had only limited success in finding a good balance between an excess of technicality on the one side, and a relapse into superficiality on the other. Piore (2002 p 9) contends that "futurology as a kind of faith is gone and futurists no longer have entree to the corridors of power." However, he also notes that "in some sense, the early pioneers were influential beyond their wildest dreams. The forecasting techniques, the trend analysis and market predictions spawned by futurologists are today widely used in government and private business" (p 11). A search of the Science Citation Index database reveals a dramatic surge in scenario references beginning in 1992 and continuing through to 2000. Support for this comes initially from Varum and Melo (2010, p 3) who state that following their bibliometric analysis, scenario planning has gradually "gained ground worldwide in international academic publications" and "in more recent years scenario planning has enjoyed a clear revival, apparent in the boom in published research on the matter"; and secondly from Hughes (2009), who states that recent years have seen a proliferation of policy studies using scenario techniques.

More recently, Kobes and Loy (2020) undertook an overview of the scenario literature covering the period 1980 to 2016. The objective of the undertaking was not only to identify the number of articles published in this period but also to answer the following six research questions:

– RQ 1: Does the SP literature cover a specific time trend?
– RQ 2: Has the SP literature progressed in terms of theory building versus practical application?
– RQ 3: Are there differences in meaning between the SP terms or are they used interchangeably?
– RQ 4: Is there a visible geographic pattern in the location of author research?
– RQ 5: How does the SP literature rank in terms of journal quality?
– RQ 6: Which areas of business and management research has SP gained ground?

In terms of RQ1, Kobes and Loy (2020) found that although scenario planning originated in the 1960s, there were relatively few academic papers published on the subject until the year 2000, with a steady climb thereafter through to 2015. However, the data they suggest, essentially depicts the third or maturity stage of Vernon's (1966) well-known four stage Product Life Cycle (Introduction; Growth; Maturity; Decline) and if it continues, a decline in scenario publications should be expected in the forthcoming future.

For RQ2, Kobes and Loy observed theoretical papers dominated until 2005, after which practical applications papers have led.

Data showed for RQ 3 that while the terms 'analysis' and 'planning' were the most frequently attached to the word scenario, the words were essentially regarded as synonyms and used and interpreted similarly. In answering RQ4, the authors found a growth of both international research and international research collaboration about scenarios; while North America initially dominated the field of theory development, more recently Europe has jointly contributed to theory development and practical applications. Investigating RQ5 proved challenging given scenario articles appear in such a wide range of journals. In general terms, however, the research suggests that the majority of SP papers are published in the top quartile of journals, the quality of the SP literature is of a higher average quality than other scientific methods, and publications continue to increase. As with answering RQ 5, addressing RQ 6 was difficult to answer definitively, but what is clear is that the Operations Research journal "had the most contributions in the early years and continues to publish the highest ranked papers" (p 22).

From a cursory search of the web, it would appear we are now enjoying a resurgence in the popularity of scenario publications resulting from the fact that the year

2022 has been called a '*permacrisis*' defined by the Collins English Dictionary as an "an extended period of instability and insecurity." Permacrisis is a term that "perfectly embodies the dizzying sense of lurching from one unprecedented event to another, as we wonder bleakly what new horrors might be around the corner . . . and is an ugly portmanteau that accurately encapsulates today's world as 2023 dawns" (Beddoes, 2022 p 11). Several shocks have combined to cause this situation beginning with the COVID-19 pandemic and its wide-ranging effects. This has resulted in publications and scenarios from a range of international organisations and consultancy companies such as McKinsey and Deloitte, and even academic institutions such as the International Institute for Management Development in Switzerland. Another shock is a geopolitical combination of Russia and China's challenge of "the American-led post-war western led post-world order" (Beddoes, 2022, p 11). In terms of Russia, the unprovoked invasion of Ukraine has fuelled the highest rates of inflation since the 1980s in many countries and the biggest macroeconomic challenge and loss of macroeconomic stability because of rocketing prices for fuel, food and consumer goods. This has led to double-digit inflation and the highest and fastest set of global interest rate hikes by the world's biggest central banks in the last 40 years (Beddoes, 2022). In addition to the toll of lives in Ukraine, Russia's invasion has led to the substantial displacement of Ukrainians fleeing the country. Alongside this is the war between Israel and Hamas which erupted on October 7 following an unprecedented assault on Israel citizens from the Gaza Strip by Hamas gunmen, killing more than 1,400 people and taking 241 hostages. Since then, Israel has been carrying out retaliatory strikes on Gaza, in which more than 25,000 civilians have so far been killed and several thousand forcibly displaced from their homes (https://uk.news.yahoo.com/un-chief-blasts-israel-utterly-235112573.html). Alongside these two issue, is that of Xi and China's rejection of the universal values upon which the Western order is based, and the increasing assertiveness and escalating military tensions across the Taiwan Strait as China aims to reincorporate Taiwan. At the same time the Human Rights Watch World Report 2022, reports that China has doubled down on repression, with its 'zero-tolerance' policy towards COVID-19 and harsh policies in the name of public health, a much more conservative attitude towards the gay, bisexual, and transgender (LGBT) community and women's rights, and less tolerance of criticism from private entrepreneurs.

The situations discussed above are fundamentally a challenge to Western values and the US-dominated post-war world order; Gourinchas (2022, p 42) suggests that the situation can be likened to an earthquake analogy, because "it reveals a sudden shift in underlying geopolitical tectonic plates. The danger is that these plates will drift further apart, fragmenting the global economy into distinct economic blocs with different ideologies, political systems, technology standards, cross-border payment and trade systems, and reserve currencies."

Another 'shock' is the escalating issue of asylum seekers and refugees from two sources, the first of which are individuals attempting to escape ongoing conflicts in countries such as Syria, Afghanistan, and Sudan. The second source is those affected by climate change, particularly in Africa where many rely on the environment for survival, food, shelter, energy and income-generation activities, and competition over scarce natural resources, such as water and grazing land, which lead to conflicts. Data from the United Nations High Commission for Refugee reports (2023) that at the end of 2022, there were 108.4 million forcibly displaced people in the world comprising 62.5 million internally displaced, 35.3 million refugees, 5.4 million asylum seekers, and 5.2 million requiring international protection.

While the popularity of scenarios may have moved in waves which correlate to the state of uncertainty in the business environment as discussed above, the world is currently unsettled in a permacrisis which shows no signs of abating and will undoubtedly lead to increasing existential risks over the next century as the numerous crises exist simultaneously and with a strong interrelationship between them. Given the continuous uncertainty in the business environment, it would seem that the need for scenarios will likely grow. However, the problem according to HBR (2023), is that leaders around the world are increasingly confronted with significant existential conditions that they have not previously faced, and these conditions require a larger and more sophisticated toolkit.

Discussion

The decisive factor between success and failure in scenario work according to van der Heijden (2005), is the degree to which a scenario project is 'purposeful'. The contention is that the purpose of scenario work can be categorised along two dimensions; either the work can serve specific one-off content needs as in understanding a particular issue, or it can serve as an ongoing general process aimed at longer-term strategy development and survival capability. Alternatively, the work can be undertaken either to open an organizational mind for exploration or to achieve closure on specific decisions and actions. Combining these provides a two-dimensional matrix that identifies four primary areas of purpose in scenario work illustrated in Figure 2.3.

The flexibility of the intuitive-logics methodology lends itself to a wide range of scenario purposes as it evidenced by the fact that examples of the application of the methodology to all of the above purposes can be found in the literature. While both the *La Prospective* and PMT may be theoretically applicable to a range of purposes, the objective of scenario work under these methodologies is generally to focus on a specific phenomenon and the variables which bear on the future of that phenomenon, and to determine the most likely evolutionary development of the phenomenon with a view to improving the effectiveness of policy and strategic decisions.

Both models tend to be descriptive in perspective and are limited in terms of the scope of issues to be investigated, by the need to have detailed and reliable time series data. Consequently, the objective of scenario development under these methodologies generally falls in the left-hand quadrants of the purposeful scenario work matrix –

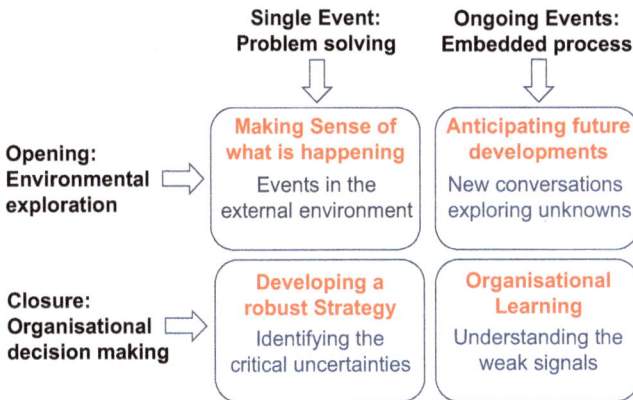

Figure 2.3: The Purpose of Scenario Work.

the work tends to be a one-off exercise associated with 'making sense' of a particular situation or with 'developing strategy.' The intuitive-logics-based scenario work meanwhile, can be either descriptive or normative, and the scope extremely broad as in the development of global scenarios, or narrowly focused on a particular issue. Common to all scenario methodologies is that the scenario horizon years typically span a period of between 3 to 20 years, but longer horizon periods are found, particularly where the focus of the scenarios is very broad.

The methodological orientation of the IL methodology is firmly an iterative, process orientation as evidenced by quotations in the literature indicating that the insights and learning arising from the process are more important than the reliability of the content of the product i.e., the scenarios. The approach taken to develop scenarios can be either inductive or deductive, with all approaches subjective and largely qualitative in nature, relying fundamentally on what Jungermann and Thuring (1987) refer to as 'disciplined intuition'. Subjectivity and intuition play a role in both *La Prospective* and PMT, but in the main, the approaches used are directed and objective, with the development of scenarios largely incorporating complex mathematical, extrapolative forecasting and computer simulation models.

Significant differences also exist between scenario methodologies in terms of the nature of scenario team participants and the role of experts in the scenario process. Under the IL methodology, a team of individuals from within the organization customarily carries out the scenario development process, which is usually designed and facilitated by an experienced, expert scenario planning practitioner. Outside experts in the form of 'remarkable people' (van der Heijden, 2005, p 308), who have some knowledge of the industry and are acute observers of the environment, may be brought into the process at junctures, to challenge and stimulate the thinking of the scenario team. While the starting point of scenario work under this methodology depends on the purpose of the scenario undertaking, it is usually related to a particular management issue or area of general concern, which in turn determines the focus in terms of the driving forces to be examined. Although the processes and tools used by scenario practitioners to achieve this vary, they commonly include desk research, individual and group brainstorming, clustering techniques, contextual environment analysis using the STEEP (Societal, Technology, Economic, Environment, Technology) framework or its derivatives, matrices, systems dynamics, stakeholder analysis and discussions with remarkable people. One further difference under the IL methodology is the learning and insights which come with the process.

The above contrasts sharply with both the *La Prospective* and PMT techniques in which external experts play a dominant role as consultants in designing and then carrying out the scenario exercise. This is because the complex and sophisticated mathematical analysis, forecasting and modelling tools utilized by *La Prospective* and PMT are not ordinarily resident in organizations, they are usually proprietary tools of consulting organizations. In the case of *La Prospective*, having identified the specific phenomenon of concern to the management of the client organization as the starting point, key individuals from within the organisation are then involved in various stages of the process. However, the process is essentially that of an external consultant-led exercise employing an arsenal of sophisticated structural analysis and cross-impact tools to identify "as exhaustive a list as possible of the variables which define the system formed by the phenomenon under study" (Godet, 2001, p 42). Under the PMT process, the starting point of the scenario work similarly revolves around management decisions and concerns, but as previously noted, is constrained by issues for which reliable historic time series data exists. The involvement of individuals from within the client organization is in most cases nominal, and the primary role of the consultant is to gather the expert judgments of external experts as input to their sophisticated, computer-based tools including Monte Carlo simulations, to arrive at modified time series forecasts.

The final output of the IL methodology is a coherent set of logically linked scenarios in discursive narrative form, supported with pictures and vivid graphics for effect, many of which are contrived. Both the *La Prospective* and PMT techniques also result in scenarios to which narratives are commonly attached; the scenarios may include numerical data in graphical form, but the data is not contrived, and visual material are seldom added for effect. The principal difference between scenarios developed under the IL methodology versus those developed under a *La Prospective* or PMT methodology, is the issue of probability. Scenarios developed under the latter two approaches are generally presented as the 'most probable' scenarios i.e., a base case plus upper and lower limit scenarios based on probabilities assigned to the scenarios. In contrast scenarios developed under IL approaches are all presented as equally probable. Consequently, while coherence, plausibility, internal consistency and logical underpinning are the common baseline criteria by which all scenarios are evaluated regardless of developmental methodology, unique to the IL model is the additional criteria of equal probability of all the scenarios within a set. Given the outcome rather than process orientation of scenario work under the *La Prospective* and PMT methods, scenarios derived under these approaches are subject to an additional evaluation criterion, namely 'verifiability in retrospect.'

The main points of commonality and departure between the three major schools of scenario are summarized in Table 2.1 below. Two final observations in this respect are that firstly, while the differences between the IL and the *La Prospective* and PMT approaches are readily apparent, the distinction between IL and *La Prospective* approaches has blurred somewhat. Fundamental differences still exist particularly in terms of methodological orientation, the nature of participants, and the role of experts in the process, but the range of tools advocated in some of the recent variants of the IL models are similar to those on which the *La Prospective* model functions. Secondly, the plethora of scenario development models noted in the introduction, and the subsequent methodological chaos stems from the fact that the differences between some of these approaches are not insignificant and categorising these approaches in terms of their differences and similarities remains an open task.

Table 2.1: Comparison of the Salient Features of the Three Schools of Scenario Techniques (Bradfield et al, 2005).

	Intuitive-Logics Models	***La Prospective* Models**	**Probabilistic Modified Trend Models**
Purpose of the scenario work:	Multiple, from a once-off activity making sense of situations and developing strategy, to an ongoing activity associated with anticipation and adaptive organisational learning.	Usually a once-off activity associated with developing more effective policy and strategic decisions and tactical plans of action.	A once-off activity to enhance extrapolative prediction and policy evaluation.
Scenario perspective:	Descriptive or normative.	Usually descriptive, can be normative.	Descriptive.
Scope of the scenario exercise:	Can be either broad or narrow scope ranging from global, regional, country, industry to an issue specific focus.	Generally a narrow scope but examination of a broad range of factors within the scope.	Narrow scope focused on the probability and impact of specific events on historic trends.
Scenario horizon year:	Varies: 3–20 years.	Varies: 3–20 years.	Varies: 3–20 years.

Table 2.1 (continued)

	Intuitive-Logics Models	*La Prospective* Models	Probabilistic Modified Trend Models
Methodological orientation:	Process orientation – inductive or deductive, essentially subjective and qualitative in approach relying on disciplined intuition.	Outcome orientation – directed and objective, quantitative and analytical approaches (with some subjectivity) relying on complex computer-based analysis and mathematical modeling.	Outcome orientation - directed and objective, quantitative and analytical approaches (with some subjectivity) using computer-based extrapolative forecasting and simulation models.
Nature of scenario team participants:	Internal – scenarios developed by a facilitated team from within the organization.	Combination of some key individuals from within the organization led by an expert external consultant.	External – scenario exercise undertaken by expert external consultants.
Role of external Experts:	Experienced scenario practitioner to design and facilitate the process; periodic use of remarkable people as catalysts of new ideas.	Dominant – expert-led process using an array of proprietary tools to undertake comprehensive analysis and expert judgments to determine scenario probabilities.	Dominant – expert-led process using proprietary tools and expert judgments to identify high impact unprecedented future events and their probability of occurrence.
Tools commonly used:	Generic – brainstorming, STEEP analysis, clustering, matrices, system dynamics and stakeholder analysis	Proprietary – structural (Micmac) and actor (Mactor) analysis, morphological analysis, Delphi, SMIC Prob-Expert, Multipol and Multicriteria evaluation.	Proprietary – Trend Impact and Cross Impact Analysis, Monte Carlo simulations.
Scenario starting point:	A particular management decision, issue or area of general concern.	A specific phenomenon of concern.	Decisions/issues for which detailed and reliable time series data exists.
Identification/ selection of key driving forces:	Intuition – brainstorming techniques, analysis of STEEP factors, research, and discussion with remarkable people.	Interviews with actors involved in the phenomenon being studied and comprehensive structural analysis using sophisticated computer tools.	Fitting curves to historical time series data to identify trends and use of expert judgment to create database of potential high impact unprecedented future events.
Establishing the scenario set:	Defining the scenario logics as organizing themes or principles (often in the form of matrices).	Matrices of sets of probable assumptions based on key variables for the future.	Monte Carlo simulations to create an envelope of uncertainty around base forecasts of key indicators.

Table 2.1 (continued)

	Intuitive-Logics Models	*La Prospective* **Models**	**Probabilistic Modified Trend Models**
Scenario Exercise Output:	Qualitative – set of equally plausible scenarios in discursive narrative form supported by graphics, some limited quantification. Implications, strategic options and early warning signals increasingly a part of scenario output.	Quantitative and qualitative – multiple scenarios of alternative futures supported by comprehensive analysis incorporating possible actions and their consequences.	Quantitative – baseline case plus upper and lower quartiles of adjusted time series forecasts. May be embellished by short storylines.
Probabilities attached to scenarios:	No, all scenarios must be equally probable.	Yes, probability of the evolution of variables under assumption sets of actors' behaviour.	Yes, conditional probability of occurrence of unprecedented and disruptive future events.
Number of Scenarios generated:	Generally 2–4.	Multiple.	Usually 3–6 dependent on the number of simulations.
Scenario evaluation criteria:	Coherence, comprehensiveness, internal consistency, novelty -underpinned by rigorous structural analysis and logics. All scenarios equally plausible.	Coherence, comprehensiveness, internal consistency – underpinned by rigorous structural and mathematical analysis; plausible and verifiable in retrospect.	Plausible and verifiable in retrospect.

Conclusions

It is clear from the literature that futurists have not yet reached a consensus as to the name or definition of their futurist activities, an appropriate universal methodology, or the balance between quantitative and qualitative methods to be used. Karlsen et al. (2010, p 62) suggest that this arises partly from the fact that the "inherent ontological and epistemological characteristics of qualitative and quantitative methods differ when it comes to capturing the complexity of issues addressed in foresight activities" albeit this has not stopped the development of scenario methods; and the choice of methodology is largely dependent on the context of the study. This being the case, a lack of consensus is understandable.

Scenario planning Bishop et al. (2007) contend, is the heart of future studies and is a key technique that distinguishes the work of professional futurists from other professions who work with the future, and they provide a comprehensive review of the current state of scenario development and an overview of techniques. While it is obvious from the literature that there are numerous scenario techniques, Khakee's (1991) contention that scenarios have given rise to so much confusion, is because there are almost as many ways of developing scenarios as there are practitioners in the field and the growth in popularity of scenarios has happened for practical reasons rather than theoretical ones. Millett (2003, p 16) contends that for many, the IL scenario method is the only scenario method for corporate planning; however, resolving the confusion over the definitions and methods of scenarios, he suggests, "is the first necessary step to bring the value of scenario thinking and development to a wider audience"

References

Andersson, J. (2018). The Future of the World: Futurology, Futurists, and the Struggle for the Post-Cold War Imagination. Oxford.

Avella J.R. (2016). Delphi Panels: Research Design, Procedures, Advantages, and Challenges. International Journal of Doctoral Studies, 11, pp 305–316.

Balachandra, R. (1978). Perceived usefulness of technological forecasting techniques. Technological Forecasting and Social Change 16, pp 155–166.

Beddoes, Z.M. (2022). Why a global recession is inevitable in 2023. The World Ahead 2023. The Economist, November 18th.

Bibri, S.E. (2020). A methodological framework for futures studies: integrating normative backcasting approaches and descriptive case study design for strategic data-driven smart sustainable city planning. Energy Inform 3, 31.

Bishop, P., Hines, A., and Collins, T. (2007). The current state of scenario development: an overview of techniques. Foresight, 9, 1 pp 5–25.

Bruce-Briggs, B. (2001). Supergenius: The Mega Worlds of Herman Kahn. North American Policy Press, New York.

Dalkey, N. and Helmer, O. (1963). An experimental application of the Delphi method to the use of experts. Management Science 9, 3, pp 458–467.

de Jouvenel, B. (1963). Introduction in: B. Jouvenel (Ed.), Futuribles: Studies in Conjecture (1), de Droz, Geneva, pp. ix–xi.

Diamond, I.R., Grant, R.C., Feldman, B.M., Pencharz, P.B., Ling, S.C., Moore. A.C., and Wales, P.W. (2014). Defining consensus: A systematic review recommends methodologic criteria for reporting of Delphi studies. Journal of Clinical Epidemiology, 67, 4, pp 401–409.

Donohoe, H.M. and Needham, R.D. (2009). Moving best practice forward: Delphi characteristics, advantages, potential problems, and solutions. International Journal of Tourism Research, 11, 5, pp 415–437.

Dreborg, K. H. (1996). Essence of Backcasting, Futures, 28, pp 813–828.

Duczynski, G.A. (2000). A practitioner's experience of using Field Anomaly Relaxation (FAR) to Craft Futures. Futures Research Quarterly 16, 3, pp 19–34.

Fink-Hafner, D., Dagen, T., Dousak, M., Novak, M. and Hafner-Fink, D. (2019). Delphi Method: Strengths and Weaknesses. Metodološki zvezki, 16, 2, pp 1–19.

Galt, M. et al, IDON Scenario Thinking: How to navigate the Uncertainties of Unknown Futures, Idon Ltd, Edradour House, Pitlochry, Scotland.

Gidley, J.M. (2017). The Future: A Very Short Introduction. Oxford University Press, Oxford.

Godet, M., Monti, R., Meunier, F. and Roubelat, F. (2004). Scenarios and Strategies: A toolbox for problem-solving. Cahiers du LIPSOR, Laboratory for Investigation in Prospective and Strategy, Paris.

Godet, M. (2001). Creating Futures: Scenario Planning as a Strategic Management Tool. Economica, London.

Godet, M. (2000). Forefront: How to be rigorous with scenario planning. Foresight 2, 1. pp 5–9.

Godet, M. (1990). Integration of scenarios and strategic management: using relevant, consistent, and likely scenarios. Futures 22, 7, pp 730–739.

Godet, M. (1987). Scenarios and Strategic Management, Butterworth, London.

Goodman, C.M. (1987). The Delhi technique: a critique. Journal of Advanced Nursing, 12, 6, pp 729–734.

Gordon, T.J. (2003). Trend Impact Analysis. Futures Research Methodology V2, the Millennium Project, American Council for the United Nations University.

Gordon, T.J. (1994). Trend Impact Analysis. AC/UNUNB Millennium Project.

Gourinchas, P.O. (2022). Shifting Geopolitical Tectonic Plates. Finance and Development, International Monetary Fund, June.

Gowing, N. and Langdon, C. (2016). Thinking the Unthinkable. A New Imperative for Leadership in the Digital Age. An interim report by Nik Gowing and Chris Langdon. Chartered Institute of Management Accountants.

Gugan, A. (2008). Successful Scenario Planning. JISC infoNet. http://www.jisc.ac.uk/publications.

Hamel, G. and Prahalad, C.K. (1994). Competing for the Future. Harvard Business Review, July-August.

Hsu, C.C. and Sandford, B.A. (2007). The Delphi technique: Making sense of consensus. Practical Assessment, Research & Evaluation, 12, 10, pp 1–8.

Hughes N. (2009). A Historical Overview of Strategic Scenario Planning, and Lessons for Undertaking Low Carbon Energy Policy, A joint working paper of the EON / EPSRC Transition Pathways Project (Working Paper 1) and the UKERC.

Huss, W.R. and Honton, E.J. (1987). Scenario planning—What style should you use? Long Range Planning, 20, 4, pp 21–29.

Iqbal, S. and Pippon-Young, L. (2009). The Delphi method. Nursing Research, 46, 2, pp 116–118.

Jungermann, H and Thuring, M. (1987). The use of mental models for generating scenarios in: G. Wright, P Ayton (Eds.), Judgmental Forecasting, Wiley, London.

Kahane, A. (2012). Transformative Scenario Planning: Working Together to Change the Future. Berrett-Koehler Publishers, San Francisco.

Karlsen, J.E., Øverland, E.F. and Karlsen, H. (2010). Sociological contributions to futures' theory building. Foresight 12, 3, pp 59–72.

Khakee, A. (1991). Scenario construction for urban planning. International Journal of Management Science, 19, 5, pp 459–469.

Kleiner, A. (2003). The man who saw the future. Thought Leaders, Spring, Issue 30 (originally published by Booz & Company).

Kleiner, A. (1996). The Age of Heretics. Nicholas Brealey Publishing, London.

Kobes, S. and Loy, T.R. (2020). Whatever happened to scenario planning? A systematic literature review. Business Energy Policy & Economics eJournal, pp 1–28.

Lindgren, M, and Bandhold, H. (2003). Scenario Planning: The Link between Future and Strategy. Palgrave MacMillan, Basingstoke.

Linneman, R. and H.E. Klein, H.E. (1983). The use of multiple scenarios by US industrial companies: a comparison study, 1977–1981. Long Range Planning 16, 6, pp 94–101.

Lorenz, C. (1990). How Shell Made its Managers Think the Unthinkable. Financial Times, 5th March.

Loo, R. (2002). The Delphi method: a powerful tool for strategic management. Policing: An International Journal of Police Strategies & Management, 25, 4, pp. 762–769.

Malaska, P. (1985). Multiple scenario approach and strategic behaviour in European companies. Strategic Management Journal, pp 339–355.

Malaska, P., Malmivirta, M., Meristo, T. and Hanson, S.O. (1984). Scenarios in Europe: Who uses them and why? Long Range Planning 17, 5, pp 45–49.

Martelli, A. (2014). Models of Scenario Planning. Facing Uncertainty and Complexity. Bocconi University Press.

Martelli, A. (2001). Scenario building and scenario planning: state of the art and prospects of evolution. Futures Research Quarterly Summer.

Mason, D.H. (1994). Scenario-based planning: decision models for the learning organisation. Planning Review March/April, pp 7–12.

Meadows,D.H., Meadows,D.L., Randers,J. and Behrens III, W.W. (1972). The Limits to Growth. A Report for The Club of Rome's Project on the Predicament of Mankind. A Potomac Associates Book.

Meristo, T. (1989). Not forecasts but multiple scenarios when coping with uncertainties in the competitive environment. European Journal of Operational Research 38, pp 350–357.

Mesarovic, M.D. and Pestel, E. (1975). Mankind at the Turning Point: The Second Report to the Club of Rome. New York: Dutton.

Millett, S. (2003). The future of scenarios: challenges and opportunities. Strategy and Leadership 31, 2, pp 16–24.

Naylor, T.H. and Schauland, H.A. (1976). A survey of users of corporate planning. Management Science, 22, 9, pp 22–27.

Orru, A.M. and Relan, D. (2013). Composing a Scenario Symphony. The Resilients website. http://libarynth. or/resilients/scenario_symphony.

Parente, R, and Anderson-Parente, J. (2011). A case study of long-term Delphi accuracy. Technological Forecasting and Social Change 78, 9, pp 1705–1711.

Paul, S. A. (2014). Assessment of critical thinking: a Delphi study. Nurse Education Today, 34, 11, pp 1357–1360.

Piecyk, M. I. and McKinnon, A.C. (2010). Forecasting the carbon footprint of road freight transport in 2020. International Journal of Production Economics. 128, 1, pp 31–42.

Piore, A. The subject of futurology has fallen on hard times. Is it time for a comeback? Newsweek 16th September (2002).

Quist, J. (2016). Backcasting in Foresight in organizations: Methods and tools, Duin, P.v.d. (Ed) Routledge, New York; London. pp 125–144.

Raubitschek, R.S. (1988). Multiple scenario analysis and business planning. Advances in Strategic Management, Vol. 5, pp 181–205.

Rhyne, R. (1995). Field anomaly relaxation: The arts of usage. Futures. 27, 6, pp. 657–674.

Ringland, G. (1998). Scenario Planning. Managing for the Future, John Wiley, Chichester.

Ritchey, T. (2006). Problem structuring using computer-aided morphological analysis. Journal of the Operational Research Society, 57, 7, pp.792–801.

Ritchey, T. (2003). "Nuclear Facilities and Sabotage: Using Morphological Analysis as a Scenario and Strategy Development Laboratory", Proceedings of the 44th Annual Meeting of the Institute of Nuclear Materials Management, Phoenix, Arizona.

Robinson, J.B. (2003). Future Subjunctive: Backcasting as Social Learning. Futures, 35, 8, pp 839–856.

Römgens, B. (2016). Roadmapping. Foresight in Organizations. Routledge, pp 145–168.

Rowe G., Wright G., McColl A. (2005). Judgment change during Delphi-like procedures: the role of majority influence, expertise, and confidence. Technological Forecasting and Social Change 72, pp 377–399.

Rowe, G. and Wright, G. (1999). The Delphi technique as a forecasting tool: issues and analysis. International Journal of Forecasting. 15, 4, pp 353–375.

Schoemaker, P.J.H. (1993). Multiple scenario development: its conceptual and behavioural foundation. Strategic Management Journal 14, pp 192–213.

Spickermann, A., Grenitz, V. and von der Gracht, H.A. (2014). Heading towards a multimodal city of the future?: Multi-stakeholder scenarios for urban mobility, Technological Forecasting and Social Change, 83,1, pp 201–221

Stratigea A., (2013). Participatory Policy making in Foresight Studies at the Regional Level – a Methodological Approach, Regional Science Inquiry Journal, Vol. V, 1, pp 145–161.

Stratigea, A. and Giaoutzi, M. (2012). Scenario Planning as a Tool in Foresight Exercises: The LIPSOR Approach. DOI: 10.1007/978-1-4614-5215-7_14, Recent Developments in Foresight Methodologies (pp.215–236), Editors: Maria Giaoutzi and Bartolomeo Sapio, Springer–Verlag.

To, W. T., Vandevelde, S., Soyez, V., De Smet, S., Boers, A., and Vanheule, S. (2014). Treatment perspectives on interned mentally ill offenders in a forensic psychiatric center (FPC): a Delphi study on experts' opinions. Psychology, crime & law, 20, 1, pp 61–77.

van der Duin, P. (2016). Foresight in Organizations: Methods and Tools. Routledge New York.

Van der Heijden, K. (2005). Scenarios: The Art of Strategic Conversation. John Wiley & Sons, Chichester.

Van der Kerkhof, M. (2004). Debating climate change: a study of stakeholder participation in an integrated assessment of long-term climate policy in the Netherlands. Amsterdam: Lemma Publishers.

van Doorn, J.W.M. and van Vught, F.A. (1983). Futures research in the Netherlands 1960–1980. Futures 15, 6, pp 504–516.

van Vught, F.A. (1987). Pitfalls of forecasting: fundamental problems for the methodology of forecasting from the philosophy of science. Futures 19, 2, pp 184–196.

Varum, C. and Melo, C. (2010). Directions in scenario planning literature – A review of the past decades. Futures, 42, 4, pp 355–369.

Vernon, R. (1966). International investment and international trade in the product cycle. Quarterly Journal of Economics, 80, pp 190–270.

von der Gracht, H. (2012). Consensus measurement in Delphi studies: Review and implications for future quality assurance. Technological Forecasting and Social Change 79, 8, pp 1525–1536.

von Reibnitz, U. (1988). Scenario Techniques. McGraw-Hill GmbH, Hamburg.

Wack, P. (1985). Scenarios: uncharted waters ahead, Harvard Business Review, 63, 5, pp 73–89.

Weimer-Jehle, W. (2006). Cross-impact balances: A system-theoretical approach to cross-impact analysis. Technological Forecasting & Social Change, 73, pp 334–361.

Wilkinson, A. and Kupers, R. (2013). Living in the Futures: How scenarios planning changed corporate strategy. Harvard Business Review, May.

Wilkinson, A. and Ramirez, R. (2010). Canaries in the Mind: Exploring How the Financial Crisis Impacts 21st Century Future-Mindfulness. Journal of Futures Studies, 14, 3, pp 45–60.

Xin, T., Ding, X., Gao, H., Li, C., Jiang, Y., and Chen, X. (2022). Using Delphi method to develop Chinese women's cervical cancer screening intention scale based on planned behavior theory. BMC Women's Health, 22, 1, pp 1–8.

Yang, X., Zeng, L., and Zhang, R. (February 2012). Cloud Delphi method. International Journal of Uncertainty, Fuzziness & Knowledge-Based Systems, 20, 1, pp 77–97.

Chapter 3
Scenario Development Process: Stage 1

Introduction

As discussed in Chapter 2, there are numerous scenario development techniques, in fact, there are almost as many ways of developing scenarios as there are practitioners in the field. The particular methodology discussed in this chapter is part of the Intuitive Logics (IL) methodology first articulated by Pierre Wack. The methodology was then developed by Peter Schwartz while first at Shell and then at Global Business Network (GBN), and subsequently refined and codified by Kees van der Heijden who oversaw scenario planning in Shell in the 1980s. van der Heijden's book, *Scenarios: The Art of Strategic Conversation* (1996 and updated in 2005), is in my opinion, the definitive work in the field.

Millett (2003, p 18) contends that the IL scenario method has many attractive features, including the fact that it:
- is non-proprietary;
- is easily taught;
- requires no particular equipment;
- can be adapted to fit any circumstances, topics, and participants, and
- it does not claim to be predictive, only proactive in stimulating people's thinking about future possible environment.

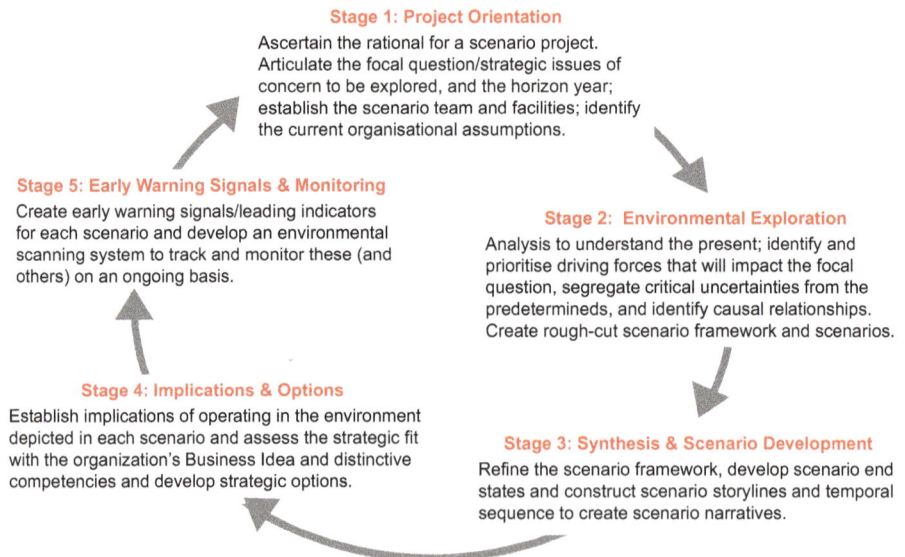

Stage 1: Project Orientation
Ascertain the rational for a scenario project. Articulate the focal question/strategic issues of concern to be explored, and the horizon year; establish the scenario team and facilities; identify the current organisational assumptions.

Stage 5: Early Warning Signals & Monitoring
Create early warning signals/leading indicators for each scenario and develop an environmental scanning system to track and monitor these (and others) on an ongoing basis.

Stage 2: Environmental Exploration
Analysis to understand the present; identify and prioritise driving forces that will impact the focal question, segregate critical uncertainties from the predetermineds, and identify causal relationships. Create rough-cut scenario framework and scenarios.

Stage 4: Implications & Options
Establish implications of operating in the environment depicted in each scenario and assess the strategic fit with the organization's Business Idea and distinctive competencies and develop strategic options.

Stage 3: Synthesis & Scenario Development
Refine the scenario framework, develop scenario end states and construct scenario storylines and temporal sequence to create scenario narratives.

Figure 3.1: The Intuitive Logics Scenario Development Framework.

https://doi.org/10.1515/9783111617442-003

Millett suggests that while there are more than two dozen techniques for developing scenarios, the IL method is the "gold standard of corporate scenario generation." Figure 3.1 below is a summarised depiction of the standard IL scenario development model.

Although the IL model is depicted as having five stages, it should be noted that there are several steps within each of the scenario development process stages themselves. This chapter will focus on the first of those stages, Project Orientation, while the subsequent stages will be discussed in detail in the chapters which follow.

Stage 1: Project Orientation

Before embarking on a scenario project, Chermack (2011) suggests it is essential there is agreement between the organisation's leaders and the scenario project leader, on five critical elements, these being.
1. Ascertaining the rationale underlying the organisation's desire to engage in a scenario initiative, and what the organisation has in mind.
2. The intended scope and time frame for the scenario project.
3. The composition of the bespoke scenario team and defined roles for each team member.
4. The general expected outcome of the scenario project.
5. Measures to assess the achievements/success of the expected outcomes.

To this list, I would add the following:
- The number of workshops, the facilities required along with the intended overall duration of the scenario project, and its cost.
- The management feedback process.

In discussing a proposed scenario intervention in an organisation, determining who should be involved in the discussion is a critical first step. It is taken for granted that the individual negotiating a scenario project with the management of the organisation is an experienced external scenario facilitator, who subsequently directs and facilitates the project from start to finish. The answer as to who in the organisation should be involved, depends to some extent, on the intended purpose of the scenario project. For example, if the organisation is facing a major strategic decision involving uncertainty and complexity, the desire is usually for a one-time problem-solving and strategy decision-making scenario project. In this case, participation in discussions regarding the project design and content, should be with the senior management team including the Chief Executive Officer (CEO). However, if the Human Resource Management (HRM) function of an organisation has proposed a scenario project to evaluate scenario planning as a tool to build adaptive organisational learning, then the senior HRM and the Training functions would normally be included in the conversation, albeit the CEO and other members of the senior management team may also wish to be involved.

Rational Underlying a Scenario Project

Ascertaining why the organisation wants to engage in a scenario initiative and what the expected benefits are, will ultimately determine whether the intended objective of a scenario project is a valid and reasonable one; if it is, this will establish the structure, content, and duration of the project process.

When approached by the senior management of an organisation regarding undertaking a scenario project, my initial questions to management are, "Why do you want to engage in a scenario project?"; "What in particular is it that you want to explore?"; and "What are the benefits you would expect to gain from undertaking it?" The answers that usually result in my agreeing to take on the scenario project, have been along the lines of:

(1) we are confused by what seems to be going on in the world, and we need to try to understand it, and what is driving the changes we are seeing;

(2) we have heard that one of our main competitors has undertaken a scenario project recently and it seems to have worked very well for them, so we would like to see if it would benefit us;

(3) we have a specific decision, project or issue we need to address and which, from our understanding, requires the same kind of analysis used in scenario exercises.

If the intended objective of undertaking a scenario project has not been thought out and clearly articulated, undertaking the project will inevitably be difficult and unlikely to result in scenarios of any value to the organisation. I have experienced several situations in which, after listening to the justification(s) offered by the senior management team to engage in a scenario project, I determined that the rationale did not align with any of the reasons above, and consequently the organisation was not ready to undertake a scenario project. An example of this is given in Box 3.1.

Box 3.1: Establishing the Rational for a Scenario Intervention

The CEO of a large Singapore-based organisation approached me because he wanted his organisation to undertake a scenario project. He was relatively new to the company and had over the months, detected growing conflicts within the organisation's management team. Although he had not been involved in a scenario project, he understood that scenario planning was an interesting and engaging process, and therefore believed that a scenario project would help bring the managers together as a team.

In preparation for a scenario project, I started interviewing the management team. During the interviews I quickly unearthed the reason for the teams' conflicts; the CEO had introduced several of what he regarded as trivial changes in the organisation's policy manual, but had not discussed any of the changes with the management team before their inclusion in the organisation's policy. This frustrated the management team as they felt that any changes, trivial or not, should have first been discussed with them before they were formally adopted and published.

It was clear a scenario project was not required; rather what I determined was needed, was a team-building program allowing the management to openly discuss their issues. I met with a professional team-building coach, who then met with the CEO and proposed a two-day executive team-building programme comprising discussion sessions interspersed with team-building activities. The CEO agreed to this, and he and the management team spent two days at a resort engaged in the programme.

After completing the team-building programme I met with several management team members. The feedback from them was that the team-building programme had been a great success. During the two days of the event, there had been many open discussions between the CEO and the management team, the overall result was that there was now a much better understanding between them, and many of the conflicts had been resolved.

The Scenario Project's Intended Scope and Time Frame

Having established the objective of the scenario workshop and that it was justifiable, the next process step is to engage with the senior management to determine:
- the focal question they want the scenarios to address i.e., the main strategic issues of concern to be explored in the scenario project;
- the scenario horizon year i.e., how far into the future the scenarios should look; and
- the time and resources the organisation is willing to invest in the scenario project.

The business environment is large and complex, and selecting the project focus/scope is often a difficult decision, as invariably senior managers from different functions in an organisation will have different concerns. For example, the project could take a broad macro-economic focus such as the economy, or a narrower focus like competition and prices in a specific industry/transactional environment. Alternatively, it could focus on a specific country or region, or perhaps concentrate on a particular societal issue. The objective of spending time discussing and agreeing on the focal question is to ensure that the scenarios subsequently developed have a strong relevance to an issue of strategic concern to management. If this is not the case, the client's expectations will not be met and the project will be deemed a failure. Research has shown that the most effective and memorable scenarios and their underlying structure, are those in which the focal question addresses issues which were alive and of concern to the organisation at the time the scenarios were developed.

Box 3.2: Example of a Broad Scenario Focal Question

I carried out a scenario project for National Petroleum Limited, a Southeast Asia national oil company commonly known as Petronas. The company had grown over the past 30 years from a small national company to a large, integrated, and profitable Fortune 500-ranked international oil and gas company, with business interests in 35 countries.

Several of the company's management team had been with the company since its beginning and were very proud of it and its achievements. However, as is not uncommon in long-established and successful companies, many of the management team had become complacent about the company's success. This led to them looking *inside* the company for improvement, rather than looking *outside* to what was happening in the world, and the potential impact this would have on the company.

In discussing the objective of the scenario project with the CEO, he stated that he was seeing some big, confusing and worrying changes going on in the world which could result in challenges negatively impacting both the industry and the company in the years ahead. However, he observed that this did not seem to bother many of the management team, who assumed that the company would simply continue to grow and prosper. While there were several issues that scenarios could address for the company, the CEO wanted to wake up the management. Specifically, he wanted to get them focused on wider, longer-term developments in the world, and how these could lead to outcomes that management had not thought about or prepared for. Consequently, it was decided that the focal question of the scenario exercise should be a wide one that explored "what will be the state of the world economies in fifteen years?"

The literature suggests that the standard suggestion regarding the scenario focal question is that it should be a very focused one designed to provide a clear idea of the nature of the specific problem to be addressed. I have, however, experienced situations where the focal question was a very broad one as shown in Box 3.2, which subsequently led to a very successful scenario project, discussed in Chapter 4.

Having established the focal question, determining the horizon year is the next important factor in scenario work. There is no one-size-fits-all rule for choosing a time horizon, as it depends on specific situations and goals. The broad factors which determine the appropriate horizon include whether the industry is fast or slow-moving, the nature of the issue(s) to be considered in the scenarios, and the state of the company and/or industry. The first specific factor to consider is the objective and context of the scenario planning i.e. what is the main objective of undertaking a scenario project, and what are the main questions or issues required to be addressed? For example, if planning for strategic decisions such as entering new markets or launching a new product, a shorter time horizon of around 5 years would normally be appropriate to focus on trends and uncertainties. If, however, the scenario exercise intends to explore a much longer-term vision, such as sustainability, one would ideally want to use a longer time horizon such as 10 to 20 years to capture the broader implications and opportunities of the scenarios.

The second factor to consider when choosing a time horizon is the benefits and challenges of using different time horizons. Each time horizon has its advantages and disadvantages, depending on the scenario's purpose and context. While shorter time horizons can help identify and respond to immediate threats and opportunities, most organisations can reliably predict what will happen in their industry over the next one to two years. However, the picture becomes dramatically less predictable the further out into the future one looks, the range of future developments expands and new threats outside of the organisation's field of activity that will impact the organisation may emerge, increasing uncertainty and complexity, as well as detaching one from current realities and actions. On the plus side, longer time horizons can help anticipate future trends, as well as stimulate innovation and learning.

Fast-moving industries such as home construction typically involve investments which are generally based on five-to-seven-year time frames. Those which are slower, such as the oil and gas sector and aviation, are more capital-intensive industries in which capital investments generally require consideration of longer periods, extending up to twenty years. But if the particular industry is in turmoil and the company is struggling to survive, it may not be able to afford the luxury of looking too far into the future. If the horizon is set too close to the present, there may be very little difference between the present and the scenario end states, in which case the scenarios will be of limited value. On the other hand, if the horizon is set too far into the future, much will likely have changed from human macro-dimensions to environmental factors, some of which will have morphed and combined in unexpected ways; consequently, making sense of the complexity and how it develops will likely be difficult. The time horizon for scenarios therefore depends largely on the industry; it must be short enough to create scenarios that are probable and useful, but far enough into the future to understand important changes which will unfold and their impact on the client's business and industry.

Horizon years can vary widely depending on the nature of the scenario subject matter. For example, a set of scenarios regarding nuclear waste may have a horizon year set at 100 years; however, the most common horizons are 10, 15 and 20 years. Cascio (2009) recommends using political cycles to consider how far into the future scenarios should explore. In the USA, this would suggest that scenarios should extend to at least 8 years to be assured of a change in the presidency and potential changes in policies.

The third factor to consider when choosing a scenario project time horizon is the availability of resources. Shorter time horizons generally require fewer resources, while longer horizons require more resources. Scenario planning is not a one-off exercise but a continuous and iterative process, consequently one has to be flexible and adaptable in terms of the time to develop a set of scenarios, which may necessitate a change in resource requirements. In my experience, as a scenario project progresses it is not uncommon to realise that the original horizon year needs to be extended and that additional workshops are required, thus increasing the costs and resources initially agreed upon.

Team Composition and Member Roles

While scenarios can be developed by an individual working alone, it is far more effective as a group activity undertaken by a small 'core' scenario project team from within the organisation, carefully recruited and led by an experienced external facilitator. The core team has three basic responsibilities, these being:
- developing an understanding of the critical uncertainties and predetermines in the business environment relevant to the scenario client;

-   constructing a set of interesting, well-structured and relevant scenarios covering
    the key alternative outcomes of the critical uncertainties; and
-   initiating a process to determine the inherent implications to the organisation, of
    operating in the environments depicted in the scenarios.

The next step in the scenario development process is to establish a bespoke core scenario project team and it is critical to get the right people in the team. This entails determining, initially, how large the team should be, what specific knowledge and skills are required of the individual team members, their availability to attend workshops, and from which departments within the organisation they should be recruited.

In the projects I have undertaken, there are usually two distinct teams. The first and major team is the core scenario team recruited from within the organisation, who are directly involved in the scenario project from start to finish, attending all workshops. The second team is usually comprised of one, two or three external ad-hoc individuals who have specific knowledge in areas relevant to the scenario topic, or are individuals with particular skills and are commonly referred to as 'Remarkable People' (RPs). This second team are not usually engaged on a full-time basis in the scenario project, but they participate in workshops at specific junctures in the scenario development process.

When it comes to the core team, as with many aspects of the IL model, there is no universal consensus regarding the ideal team size. For example, Raynaud (1976) and Mandel (1982) suggest that the core team should be between four and ten people with an outside limit of twenty. Durance and Godet (2010) however, suggest that as many people as possible should be involved in the initial phase of scenario development to mobilize the collective intelligence of the organisation, while Bezold (2010) adds that including a range of individuals from across the organisation results in a shared organisational vision and facilitates collaborative relationships working to achieve the vision. The experience of von Reibnitz (1987) is that the optimum team size is twelve people, as this allows the creation of sub-groups which can work independently on specific tasks within the scenario development process. However, there are a number of issues which need to be taken into consideration regarding team size. The first is that the larger the team, the more difficult it will usually be to arrange workshops and meeting dates that all members can attend. The second is the difficulty of getting larger groups to reach closure on discussion issues, as invariably the larger the team, the longer it takes to achieve agreement on complex and ill-defined issues. A third issue is that most teams will experience conflict at some point, and it is vital for the facilitator and team members to deal with and resolve issues as they arise. A fourth and more important concern is the active participation of all members of a team. A phenomenon in psychology commonly known as 'social loafing' refers to the occurrence where individuals exert less effort in a group task than when working alone, often due to perceived reduced accountability and shared responsibility. Discovered in 1913 by Maximilien Ringelmann, a French agricultural engineer, social loafing is more evident in tasks where the contribution of each group member is combined into a group outcome, thereby making it difficult to identify the contribution of a single person.

While too large a team will result in problems, too small a team will also lead to problems mainly in terms of workload. My suggestion therefore, based on practical experience, is that a core team of a minimum of six but no more than twelve individuals is the optimal team size. This provides the opportunity for the team to work in small sub-groups of two or three between the formal workshops, to discuss issues or undertake research.

In terms of team composition, the literature suggests that the following points are the main considerations in selecting team members:

–   The first point is that the team members selected must have the highest levels of support from the management throughout the scenario process. Millet (1988) and van der Heijden (1996) propose that the key decision-makers must be involved in the scenario process from the beginning i.e. 'Stage 1' when the objectives of the scenario initiative, the focal question and horizon year, and the scenario teams are established. They are not generally involved in the actual scenario development process but will be provided with regular updates as it unfolds; they should however, be present at the end of the project when the scenarios are presented and their implications and strategic options are considered, given that it is ultimately their responsibility to develop, implement and manage strategies. Meanwhile, de Brabandere and Iny (2010) who developed a new 'Expressway to Scenarios' methodology which they argue is considerably faster than conventional IL methods, take a more extreme view, suggesting that the scenario team should comprise *only* the senior executives of the organisation.

–   Team members should represent a broad range of functions and divisions within the organisation, including a variety of cross-level and cross-functional individuals of diverse backgrounds, familiar with a variety of intellectual disciplines, and if possible, cultures. Simpson (1992) adds that the team should include opposing views from outside the unit tasked with developing the scenarios. Mandel (1982) elaborates by proposing that team members should represent, by proxy at least, different viewpoints held by senior management and key decision-makers from various parts of the organisation. At the same time, individuals should be chosen to participate as core scenario team members for their knowledge, skills, expertise and thinking styles rather than their position in the hierarchy.

–   While diversity of thinking is critical to the success of scenario projects, equally important is that the team should include some individuals who can express dissenting views yet agree about and work towards a common objective. The key to failure suggests Ogilvy and Schwartz (2004, p 15), "is the exclusion of people who are unorthodox, challenging thinkers from inside and outside the organization"

–   Scenario teams should comprise imaginative people with open minds to avoid biases in the team which may cause knowledge to be overlooked (van der Heijden, 1996). Sviden's (1986) view is that since scenario development is more art than scientific, it is more suited to individuals with a generalist background rather than specialists in particular disciplines. Mandel (1982), however, contends that it is important to have a balance of qualitative perspectives, analytical skills, education, and professional backgrounds; thus, both specialists and generalists have a place in scenario teams. van der Heijden (1992) endorses this view, maintaining that multidisciplinary teams are required, as does von Reibnitz (1988), asserting that diversity of specialisation and qualification of the scenario team enhances the chances of developing good scenarios, generating novel ideas and strategic solutions. In addition to skills and backgrounds, Mandel (1982) claims it is essential that scenario team members understand strategy and the decisions under consideration, while at the same time being knowledgeable about the environmental forces affecting them.

– Finally, and importantly, team members should be individuals capable of working closely together as a team; it is therefore essential that team members disregard their titles and accept each other as colleagues. Raynaud (1976) argues that there should be no hierarchical connections between scenario participants, who should all be of similar age. This is not always the case, with von Reibnitz (1987) claiming that choice is governed by the openness and style of management prevailing in the organisation. At the same time, age and experience similarity can lead to a uniformity of outlook which may undermine the basic objective to consider a wide range of divergent futures.

In summarising their views on scenario team composition, Hodgkinson and Healy (2008) suggest "three design challenges in terms of selecting the scenario team and enabling the necessary forms of group information processing required to yield the necessary cognitive outcomes" (p 439). The first is to ensure there is sufficient knowledge and perspective diversity in the team to warrant effective group information processing. The second is to ensure the team comprises an appropriate blend of personality types who work well together and avoid conflicts and stress; and the third challenge is associated with adapting the facilitation process to accommodate the composition of the scenario team, increasing the likelihood of achieving the required outcomes. As indicated earlier, it is equally important that the hierarchy of managers that the team members report to in the organisation needs to be aware of and fully support, all of the team members' commitment to the scenario project.

While core project team members will periodically work alone or in sub-teams between formal workshops, all core team members must be dedicated and actively participate in all scheduled workshops and activities. However, given the state of electronic communication technology, it is acceptable that, for whatever reason, team members do not always have to be in face-to-face meetings, particularly in informal group meetings between workshops.

Although the core team of a scenario project may comprise individuals at various levels in the organisation, there are two caveats; firstly, there should be no hierarchy within the core team, all are equal players regardless of the positions they hold in the organisation, and their opinions and ideas are all equally accepted. The second is to avoid appointing the CEO or very senior managers to the team. The reason for this is that they are, because of their positions, habitually busy individuals who generally spend much time in meetings. The situation inevitably arises when they cannot attend a workshop or are called out of a workshop to attend to an urgent matter. As a consequence, they often cannot devote the time required to undertake the necessary research between the workshops, an example of which is shown in Box 3.3.

Box 3.3: Example of the wrong individual type of Scenario Team Member

In a scenario project in the Middle East several years ago, included in the seven-member scenario team was a senior vice-president (SVP) who wanted to be in the core team, and actively participated in the first workshop. The team then adjourned for two weeks to undertake the research identified in the workshop.

At the second workshop, a round-robin approach was used with each team member asked to present their research findings. When it came to the turn of the SVP to present his findings, he withdrew a typed document from his briefcase and read his research findings from the document, which was well received by the group.

At the end of the workshop, I complimented the SVP on his research presentation. He then confessed that he had not actually undertaken his allotted research; he was extremely busy and did not have the time to dedicate to research. Consequently, he assigned the research to one of the bright young individuals in his department, who undertook the research and typed the document detailing the findings.

Following a discussion, the SVP agreed to withdraw from the scenario team; while he had enjoyed being involved in the scenario development process, he had not anticipated just how much work the process involved and suggested that he be replaced by the individual who had undertaken and written up the research.

In establishing the core scenario team, it is essential to establish three key roles, a Project Leader, a Core Team Leader and a Project Scribe. As indicated earlier, the Project Leader should be an external and experienced, scenario planner and facilitator. The role of the Core Team Lead is to work closely with the project facilitator to manage the group and coordinate activities, including team attendance at workshops, managing workshop and meeting schedules, arranging venues and facilities for workshops, as well as other project administrative functions as required. Finally, the role of the Project Scribe is to collect and distribute workshop materials, record the activities of the group meetings, and capture and transcribe the outputs of each workshop including flipcharts, post-its, and whiteboard writings. While core team members must attend and participate in all of the planned formal workshops, it is often the case that some of the innovative thinking, research and breakthroughs are accomplished by sub-teams meeting and working informally between the formal workshops.

'Remarkable People'

Although not part of the core scenario team, there is a second team comprising a small number of individuals, usually one or two, who are known as 'Remarkable People.' One of Pierre Wack's most distinctive ideas regarding thinking about the future was that you needed to be associated with and talk to people outside your organisation; if you did this, you would expand your thinking in all directions. When heading scenario planning in Shell, Wack started bringing what he called 'remarkable people' (RPs) into scenario workshops, an idea he got from his mentor George Gurdieff, a Sufi mystic. Wack discovered these remarkable people on his many travels to the East, and Napier Collyns, one of the Shell scenario planning pioneers, assumed the role of finding and cultivating them for Wack.

While the word 'remarkable' conjures up pictures of famous and celebrity individuals such as Nobel laureates, sports stars, actors or best-selling authors, this was not Wack's notion of a remarkable individual. His view was that an RP was someone who had a completely different mental model or outlook from most people, and unusual insights about the world around them. They could be an academic, researcher, writer, artist or consultant – an individual who van der Heijden (1997, p 185) suggests "can produce an insightful 'aha' reaction for the client." They are known for their ability to think unconventionally and as "early detectors of a new, still emergent future possibility, an already emerging order" (Ramirez and Wilkinson, 2016, p 70) In essence, they are not actually experts but can be best described as "people who can look at the same old dots and connect them in new ways" (van der Heijden, p 222). While not all the articles on scenario development mention the use of RPs, it is increasingly widely used

Finding appropriate RPs and getting their agreement to participate in a scenario exercise is the responsibility of the project leader. However, finding RPs is not always easy and they are often selected based on experiences of conversations with individuals. I have two examples of RPs that I have come across. The first is George discussed in Box 3.4, one of several RPs I have l have used on several scenario projects.

Box 3.4: Example of a 'Remarkable Person'

George is a friend I have known for many years. He attended University in Singapore to undertake a degree in Philosophy. His family questioned his choice of degree, do you ever see advertisements for philosophers they asked? His response was that he was going to university to expand his knowledge, not to get a job. Additionally, while classes in conventional classes such as marketing or economics were very large, classes in philosophy were small which provided the opportunity to engage in discussions with the class academics.

I have brought George into several scenario initiatives and introduced him to the groups working on developing scenarios. He would look at the work detailed on flipcharts by each scenario group, and would typically ask the team members to explain how and why they saw the driving forces and their causal relationships unfolding in a particular way over time. His response to their explanations was invariably . . .

'wow that is so interesting . . . but thinking about this, what if this moved in that direction and that move there, then this happened and . . .then. . .'

George's effect on the workshop was that he brought in new and innovative ideas which essentially energised the teams to rethink the causal diagrams and restructure their scenarios and storylines. The reaction of the scenario team after George had left the workshop was always the same – 'what a man, where does he get all these ideas from?'

George is the kind of general RP who may not have specific knowledge in terms of a particular scenario project topic, but is educated, intelligent, and inquisitive, and can look at a piece of work and quickly understand it and its intentions. He then raises questions about the work and provides new ideas.

The second example in Box 3.5 is of two RPs I met in Indonesia with very specific knowledge about a particular situation in the country, which challenged widely accepted beliefs held outside Indonesia.

Box 3.5: Example of the Value Remarkable People Add

The scenario project in this case was for a South American MNC considering building an oil/gas production centre in Banda Aceh, the capital of Aceh Province and the westernmost province in Indonesia. The province has large oil/natural gas resources and is governed not as a province, but as a special territory to give it some autonomy from the central government in Jakarta.

The MNC had some concerns with the potential project around the fact that Aceh is an Islamic religiously conservative territory, and the terrorist separatist group, the 'Free Aceh' Movement (GAM) had been fighting the Indonesian authorities for independence for 29 years. Initial research by the MNC suggested that although there was a lucrative opportunity to establish a production centre in Aceh, there was also the possibility that Islamic terrorists would one day seize the centre and demand a ransom.

As part of the research for the scenario project, I met with many individuals across Indonesia and one day I received a message while in Aceh, that two individuals wanted to join me for dinner at my hotel. I met them and they asked that I not photograph them, or record our conversation. They wanted to know why I was asking questions about Aceh and GAM. Was I a member of the US or UK secret service? I explained that I was neither, but was undertaking research for a scenario project I was leading for a South American Oil/Gas MNC. They asked what I had learnt so far and I said that I had been told that several hundred Indonesian military had been killed by GAM and likewise, the military had killed a number of GAM terrorists. They laughed and then proceeded to tell me the 'facts.' GAM and the military worked together they said, and a combination of less than a hundred terrorists and soldiers had been killed. The press deliberately exaggerated the deaths resulting in international organisations sending money to help the military, who then split the money with the supposed rebels, and everyone was happy! This was a complete surprise to me, none of the research I had done or the people I had already interviewed had mentioned this.

Several years later it transpired that what I had been told was true. Following a magnitude 9.2 Indian Ocean earthquake in December 2004, Aceh coastal area was the hardest hit by the resultant tsunami with over 170,000 people killed. Following the disaster, GAM signed a peace deal with the Government in 2005 under which Aceh was granted broader autonomy, including the right to establish local political parties to represent their interests.

The value of RPs is that they understand the industry structure, language, the driving forces and how they interact, and they can bring new perspectives, new ideas and new insights. However, the type of RPs discussed in Box 3.5 are unique and difficult to find. They have knowledge underlying a situation which is essentially classified, sensitive information to be protected with access restricted to particular groups of people. Although finding these RPs is extremely difficult and time-consuming, the right RPs can dramatically change the thinking in a scenario project. When Wack was asked how he knew an RP, he purportedly said that you would know them when you meet them.

The question is, how many RPs should be brought into scenario workshops, and at what point should they be brought into the development process? Although not widely discussed in the literature, my experience is that depending on the nature of the scenario project, it is essential to bring in at least one RP into a scenario project. However, more can be used, and there are two appropriate points at which to bring them into the scenario development process:

- The first is towards the end of Stage 2 (Environmental Exploration), the precursor to developing a set of scenarios. At this point, the RP can look at what has been done in terms of identifying the driving forces, the segregation of critical uncertainties and predetermined elements, and causal relations, and provide feedback and new ideas.
- The second point is at Stage 3 (Synthesis and Scenario Development), the objective being for the RP to examine the scenario end states, storylines and temporal sequences, and provide feedback to the development team.

Depending on the feedback from the RP(s), it may be necessary to schedule one or more formal workshops.

Expected Outcome and Assessing the Success of a Scenario Project

The outcome generally expected of a scenario project is a set of three or four interesting and well-structured scenarios, but above all, scenarios which are relevant to the client. van der Heijden (2005, p 219) adds that while relevance is essential, "not much is gained if the (scenario development) process does not change the client's thinking."

Assessing scenario projects is difficult, but it is crucial, and very few articles or books on the topic discuss the assessment and evaluation of scenario interventions. Chermack (2011, p 189) states that "To establish the true contribution of scenario planning, projects must be assessed to build a suite of evidence supporting scenario planning and its utility ... The lack of effort invested to understand the outcomes of scenario projects is a serious shortcoming." The main issue is that while judging whether or not the scenarios are well written, interesting and challenging, it is difficult to judge the validity of scenarios in terms of their end states, as depending on the scenario horizon, it may take several years before factors portrayed in scenarios happen.

Swanson and Holton (1999) suggest that establishing a comprehensive assessment requires moving beyond simply establishing if the participants perceived the project as a useful and enjoyable one. They suggest that the assessment should include elements of satisfaction from both the senior management and the workshop participants, the learning that occurred in terms of what participants learnt during the process, and organisational performance (what changes to the organisation's goods or services can be made to increase their performance). For the scenario team members, this can be done either by short surveys distributed at the conclusion of the project, or by a discussion with the team. For the senior management team, this can be discussed at the project feedback session.

The metrics which I suggest are appropriate to evaluate the success of the scenario project following its completion, should include the following questions:

– Were the scenarios relevant to the organisation and the objectives which were agreed to at the start of the project?
– Were the scenarios interesting, professionally written, and supported by effective timelines and graphics?
– Were the scenarios challenging and successful in pushing out management's thinking, while remaining plausible?
– Did the scenarios provide a useful framework for strategic thinking which would help the organisation anticipate and manage risk?
– Did the scenarios produce new and original perspectives on the client's issue(s)?
– Did the early warning signals developed around the scenarios provide appropriate and timely warning signs of future developments?

Identifying 'Mental Maps' and Assumptions

Before undertaking scenario development workshops, the process of identifying 'mental maps' of the senior management team and their assumptions about the future, is required. Based on his experience in Shell, van der Heijden determined that extensive interviews with Shell's senior management were necessary to gain a thorough understanding of the current organisational assumptions as well as individual mental maps (Wilkinson and Kupers, 2014). The number of interviews undertaken depends on the organisation structure and the scope of the scenario project, but where possible, all senior management members should be interviewed. The reason for this is that interviewing some senior managers but neglecting to interview others, is likely to be of concern to those not interviewed, the inevitable question being, "Why was I not interviewed?"

Interviews would normally be conducted by the project leader following the powerful '7 Questions' technique, pioneered at the Institute of the Future (Amara and Lapinsky, 1983) and refined by Shell scenario teams. These questions serve as prompts for gathering opinions from management teams on the strategic issues that need to be addressed in contemplating the future, and can be customised as required. With the prior approval of the interviewees, interviews should be conducted under the 'Chatham House' rule, i.e., interviewers are free to use the information received, but the identity of interviewees cannot be revealed as all interview data is strictly anonymous and non-attributable, allowing for greater openness during the interviews.

The objective of the interviews is to identify the dominant organisational assumptions and individual mental maps of senior management, which the scenarios may then challenge. It is also often the case that there are quite divergent views within the management team, which are only surfaced during interviews.

There are variants of the 7 Questions regarding phrasing, but all are intended to be open-ended. A common example of the questions is as follows:

1. **Clairvoyant:** If you could speak to someone who knew the future of . . . a Clairvoyant for example, what would you like to ask, what are the critical issues for the future?
2. **Positive scenario:** What is your vision of a good, desirable but realistic future?
3. **Negative scenario:** What is your vision of a negative or unfavourable scenario?
4. **Changes required:** What internal or external operational and structural constraints do you see that will limit the company's achievements, and what changes are required?
5. **Looking back:** What would you identify as events which produced the current situation?
6. **Looking ahead:** What do you see as the roadblocks in the future, and what are the priority actions which need to be carried out?
7. **Epitaph:** When you move on from your current position, what do you hope to leave behind that people will associate with you; what do you want to be remembered for?

Not all questions are used in all interviews, but the last one, Question 7, is a well-suited question to bring interviews to a close.

Interviewing is a challenging task even for those who have experience with it, and alongside participating in a reactive mode, two activities need to be carried out simultaneously: the interviewer needs to build a trusting relationship and the critically crucial element of rapport with the interviewee, and the conversations need to be recorded. My experience is that the interviews usually take between an hour, and an hour and a half, and recording them can be done in one of three ways: by the interviewer taking handwritten notes during the interview; by the use of a second individual in the meeting who takes notes and may periodically engage in the conversation; and thirdly, the recording is done via an electronic device. While the third option is the easiest, it can be difficult as the interviewees may be wary of what might happen to the recordings, and need to be assured of complete confidentiality of the interview notes.

While good listening skills and avoiding distractions are the most crucial aspects of interviewing, some points to note include: asking one question at a time and encouraging responses with occasional nods of the head; providing a transition between the questions; showing interest in the interviewee; avoiding personal comments or engaging in debates with the interviewees; locking the conversation into a specific area, and keeping to the agreed interview timeframe. Analysis of the interviews usually reveals several important insights:

- what are the issues and uncertainties about the future of the company, its business, and the environment, that concern the organisation's key decision-makers?
- what are their hopes for the future?
- the divergent views on issues within the management team and knowledge gaps in terms of what individuals are not thinking about, but which they probably should be. An example of this is Box 3.6.

Having analysed the interview findings, the structure for interview feedback to senior management should include a summary of the significant factors and events that, according to interviewees, have evolved and led to the current situation. Specifically, this should include:

- views of the changes in contextual and transactional environments which lie ahead;
- different perspectives regarding what success in the future will be like;
- views of what should be done, when to achieve it, and the possible constraints to a successful project.

Box 3.6: Example of Senior Management Failing to See the Obvious

This occurred while I was working on a scenario project and interviewing the management team of a large port and maritime global trade enabler based in the Middle East. The standard '7 Questions' technique was used in the interviews.

In talking about their concerns for the future in the interviews, not one of the client's senior team mentioned the subject of additive manufacturing, commonly known as 3D printing. This was surprising to both myself and the scenario team given that firstly, the world's first functional 3D printed building was situated less than 5 miles from the client's offices and was well known as a unique building. Secondly, there had been numerous articles in the press regarding the major impact 3D printing would have on certain industries. Why for example, would you ship raw materials from Australia to China for manufacturing, then ship the products to the Middle East for assembly, and then transport the end products to the markets, when you could ship the raw materials directly to the end markets to be manufactured using 3D printers?

This was discussed with the scenario team and 3D printing subsequently played a significant role in successfully developing a set of well-received scenarios.

This feedback should ideally should be presented to the senior management team by the project leader at a face-to-face meeting, rather than by way of a document. Other interview findings such as knowledge gaps and what individuals are not thinking about, should *not* however be included in the feedback; these are worth discussing within the core scenario team and may have a role in the scenarios subsequently developed as discussed in Box 3.6. Surprisingly, one element of the feedback which peri-odically emerges from the interviews, is that the senior managers are often unaware of the diversity of thinking within their teams, and are taken aback by the conflicting views and different understandings of situations of the individual managers.

Workshops Number and Summary of Activities

During the five formal workshops in the IL scenario development framework shown in Figure 3.1, the team will work in groups. These workshops are usually separated by a 2–3 week break to allow team members to undertake research and for various members of the project team to meet in informal workshops. Cooperation within the groups in both formal and informal workshops is essential, and there are general meeting ground rules which need to be followed:
- Discussions as a group should use the round-robin approach so that all team members get the opportunity to express their ideas without interruption from other team members.
- There is no such thing as a bad or silly idea. The only question asked of any idea raised should be to seek clarification on some point of the idea expressed.
- Ideas expressed by any member should not be derided, or rejected without proof that the idea is wrong and that all team members accept the proof.
- Participate 100% by sharing ideas, asking questions, and contributing to discussions.
- Listen attentively to others and do not interrupt or have side conversations.

Stage 1 Workshop

The Stage 1 Workshop is usually a two-day event. The first day of the workshop is attended by both the senior management and the core scenario team, and entails:
- an introduction to the management team, the core scenario team members, and the facilitation team.
- a general discussion about and confirmation of the scenario agenda, the focal question, and the scenario horizon year. Recall that the mental maps and assumptions interviews were conducted before this first workshop to elicit this information.
- the project timetable.
- the intended project deliverables.

As a guide to the development process to be followed, those attending the workshop should be provided with a 'Scenario Workbook' which details each step of the scenario development process, along with several seminal scenario articles. This provides a background to scenario planning and some information regarding each development step process to all participants i.e. the management team and the scenario core team.

The second day of the workshop is dedicated to the core scenario team members, with an initial presentation by the facilitator of the findings from the interviews of the management team's mental maps and assumptions. This has already been given to the management team except for the findings such as knowledge gaps, and what individuals are not thinking about. The remainder of the workshop is then spent discussing these findings and the workshop concludes with establishing a research agenda validating the mental maps and assumptions, and identifying initial uncertainties as a starting point for subsequent research.

With the stage set for the scenario project, the remaining four workshops in the development process with the core scenario team are usually three-day events, of 6–8 hours per day, including presentations, exercises, and group discussions, divided by breaks. A one-day workshop is insufficient, as it takes time to pry people loose of the present and get them to start thinking of everything that could affect the focal issue in the future. Two-day workshops are acceptable, if time is limited, but in my experience a third day is more valuable as it provides an opportunity for the team to discuss findings from the first and second days, to determine what further research needs to be done.

After spending the workshop days brainstorming, the evenings are usually left open to give the team a chance to socialize and get to know each other. Experience shows that after the participants sleep on their ideas, debates, and conversations, they often awake the next day refreshed and revitalised with new insights and ideas that contribute to the scenario development. A good night's sleep is vital for exploring these new insights and ideas, with research showing that insufficient sleep can result in idea fixation, impairing our abilities to change strategies (Vartanian et al, 2014).

Workshop Facilities

There is limited discussion in the literature on the appropriate venues and facilities for scenario project workshops. However, in my experience ensuring the right physical setting and atmosphere, is as important as having the right core team members. This is supported by research (De Korte et al., 2011) which has shown that group performance during meetings is significantly influenced by the meeting room and its setup. In terms of venues, the standard requirements include:

–   a large enough room to comfortably accommodate the core scenario team, visitors, and equipment along with adequate and accessible wall space, as they will end up covered in post-it notes and flip charts.
–   the venue should be one with windows and access to plenty of natural light, rather than a venue located in a basement.
–   the venue should be self-contained, with ready access to restroom facilities.
–   a clean workplace with good ventilation, lighting and a good working temperature so it is comfortable to work in.

A hard-learned note of caution; it is best to select venues which are located away from noise and distractions, ideally offsite, i.e., not within the organisation's premises. If the venue is located at the company's premises, an individual will inevitably appear at the venue at some point in the workshop and interrupt it with an urgent request to pass a message onto one of the team participants, who then leaves the workshop. Related to this, there should be an agreement that all workshop participants must switch off their cell phones during a workshop, with calls taken during breaks if necessary.

With regards to the necessary workshop facilities, the usual workshop paraphernalia is required, namely:
- a projector and screen;
- whiteboards and whiteboard marker pens;
- flipcharts, post-it packs, notepads; and
- access to reasonable speed internet connections.

Feedback to Senior Management

As mentioned earlier, the CEO and senior management members should not be included in the core scenario team; it is, however, essential to update them periodically on developments as the project progresses. This can be done by arranging short meetings following each workshop, during which the project and core team leaders provide a brief on progress.

Scenario Project Failures

To conclude this chapter, the section which follows is a brief discussion on project failures. Although there is some general discussion in the literature on how to avoid failure in undertaking scenario projects, aside from an article by Hodgkinson and Wright (Confronting Strategic Inertia in a Top Management Team: Learning from Failure. Organisation, 2002) there is very little discussion in terms of actual failed scenario interventions. Box 3.7 is an example of a failed scenario project which was discussed with me by the management of an organisation. As indicated in the Box, the reason for the scenario failure was that firstly, there had been no discussion with the client organisation in terms of establishing the focal question to be explored, or the horizon year; and secondly, no one from the client organisation had any part at all in the scenario development process.

Box 3.7: Example of a failed Scenario Intervention

I met with the senior management of an insurance company in Scotland who were interested in undertaking a scenario project. In the discussion with the managers, it was apparent that the company was familiar with scenarios, having already undertaken a scenario project earlier in the year. When asked why they were now wanting another scenario project, the response was that they had met with members of a consultancy the previous year, who were supposedly 'experts' in the field of scenario planning. The discussions with consultants were surprisingly very short according to the management. After agreeing to fees, the consultants left and returned several months later with a report containing a set of scenarios which they presented to the company's management team. The theme of the scenarios was around the balkanization of Europe over the next 5 years. I read the scenarios and they were interesting

What was the problem with the project and the scenarios, I asked. The reply was that the whole scenario process had been a complete surprise to the company. Firstly, at the initial meeting with the consultants, there was no discussion as to what the company's concerns for the future were, what the focus of the scenarios should be, or the scenario horizon year. Secondly, the scenarios developed were done entirely by the consultants with no participation from or discussion with anyone from the company. Thirdly and more importantly was the relevance of the scenarios to the company; as a British-based company, most of the company's business was conducted within the UK, with very few dealings in Europe, and no immediate plans to expand on this.

So, albeit an interesting set of scenarios to read, they were of no relevance to the company.

Conclusions

Scenario projects are usually undertaken under a contract in which time limitations are clearly defined. While the development of a good set of scenarios delivering real insight cannot be generated from a single, one-day workshop, few clients would be comfortable with an open-ended contract. However, I have experienced instances in several scenario projects where the core scenario team concluded before the end of the contracted formal workshops, that at least one or possibly more workshops were required. This recognition, coming from the team members and/or the RPs, was usually along the lines that the scenarios:

– did not sufficiently explore causal relationships;
– contained some obvious inconsistencies;
– were insufficiently structurally different;
– lacked memorability, and were not challenging enough.

Thus, additional research, thinking and discussion on the driving forces and causal mechanisms necessitated further research workshops. Without this, the project would have failed. This would normally require approval from senior management as it results in an extension to the initial agreed project completion date and will incur additional costs.

Having established the rationale and fundamentals of a scenario planning intervention, the next chapter moves to a discussion of Stage 2, the Environmental Exploration process of scenario development.

References

Amara, R., and Lipinski, A. J. (1983). Business planning for an uncertain future. Pergamon Press.

Bezold, C. (2010). Lessons from using scenarios for strategic foresight. Technological Forecasting and Social Change, 77, 9, pp 1513–1518.

Capra, F. (1997). The Web of Life: A New Synthesis of Mind and Matter. Flamingo. HarperCollins Publishers.

Conway, M. (2012). Using Causal Layered Analysis to Explore the Relationship Between Academics and Administrators in Universities. Journal of Future Studies, 17, 2, pp 37–58.

de Brabandere, L. and Iny, A. (2010). Scenarios and creativity: Thinking in new boxes. Technological Forecasting and Social Change, 77, 9, pp 1506–1512.

de Korte, E., Kuijt, L. and van der Kleij, R. (2011). Effects of Meeting Room Interior Design on Team Performance in a Creativity Task. International Conference on Ergonomics and Health Aspects of Work with Computers EHAWC 2011: pp 59–67. Springer-Verlag Berlin Heidelberg.

Durance, P. and Godet, M. (2010). Scenario building: Uses and abuses. Technological Forecasting and Social Change, 77, 9, pp 1488–1492.

Emery, F. E., and Trist, E. L. (1965). The causal texture of organizational environments. Human Relations, 18, 1, 21–32.

Esposito,M. and Tse, T. (2017). DRIVE: The Five Megatrends that Underpin the Future Business, Social, and Economic Landscapes. Thunderbird International Business Review. https://doi.org/10.1002/tie.21889

Hodgkinson, G. P. and Healy, M. P. (2008). Cognition in Organizations, Annual Review of Psychology 59: 387–417.

Inayatullah, S. (2014). Causal Layered Analysis Defined. The Futurist; Washington.48, 1, 26.

Mandel, T.F. (1982). Scenario and Corporate Strategy: Planning in uncertain times, Menlo Park, Stanford Research Institute. Business intelligence program, Research Report 669.

Millett, S.M. (2003). The future of scenarios: challenges and opportunities. Strategy & Leadership, 31, I2, pp 16–24.

Millett, S. M. (1988). How scenarios trigger strategic thinking. Long Range Planning, 21, 5, pp 61–68.

Mintzberg, H. (2018). Strategic Thinking as "Seeing". 14th September https://mintzberg.org/blog/strategic-thinking-as-seeing.

Ogilvy, J, and Schwartz, P, (2004). Plotting Your Scenarios. Global Business Network.

Ramirez, R. and Wilkinson, A. (2016). Strategic Reframing. The Oxford Scenario Planning Approach, Oxford University Press.

Raynaud, H. (1976). Long-range forecasting within organisations. Futures, October, 8, 5, pp 420–427

Schoemaker, P.J.H. (2020). How historical analysis can enrich scenario planning. Futures and Foresight Science. 2, 3–4

Silver, N. (2015). The Signal and the Noise: Why So Many Predictions Fail–But Some Don't. Penguin, New York.

Svidén, O. (1986). Methodology: A scenario method for forecasting. Futures. 18, 5, pp 681–691.

Toffler, A. (1992). Power Shift: Knowledge, Wealth, and Power at the edge of the 21st Century. Bantam Books.

van der Heijden, K. (2005). Scenarios: The Art of Strategic Conversation. John Wiley & Sons, Chichester.

van der Heijden, K. (1996). Scenarios: The Art of Strategic Conversation. John Wiley & Sons, Chichester.

van 't Klooster, S.A. and van Asselt, M.B.A. (2006). Practising the scenario-axes technique. Futures, 38, 1, pp 15–30.

Von Reibnitz, U. (1987). Scenario Techniques. McGraw-Hill Book Co, Germany

Wilkinson, A., and Kupers, R. (2014). The Essence of Scenarios Learning from the Shell Experience. Amsterdam University Press.

Wood, G. (December 2020). The next decade could be even worse. The Atlantic

Chapter 4
Scenario Development Process Stage 2

Workshop 2: Environmental Exploration

Having spent time initially researching the mental map ideas and initial uncertainties, the scenario team returns for the second formal workshop, Stage 2 Environmental Exploration. The objective of this workshop is a first-pass scenario development task, i.e. to identify and prioritise the driving forces that impact the focal question i.e. determine which are critical uncertainties and which are predetermined, identify causal relationships, and create a rough-cut scenario framework.

Developing a good and useful set of scenarios is a lengthy and demanding process. It can be confusing and even frustrating at times because scenario work is not a precise science, it is a practitioner's art and craft and is a circular and iterative process rather than a linear one. There are essentially three environments over which the organisation has varying degrees of influence (depicted in Figure 4.1), with each discussed briefly below:

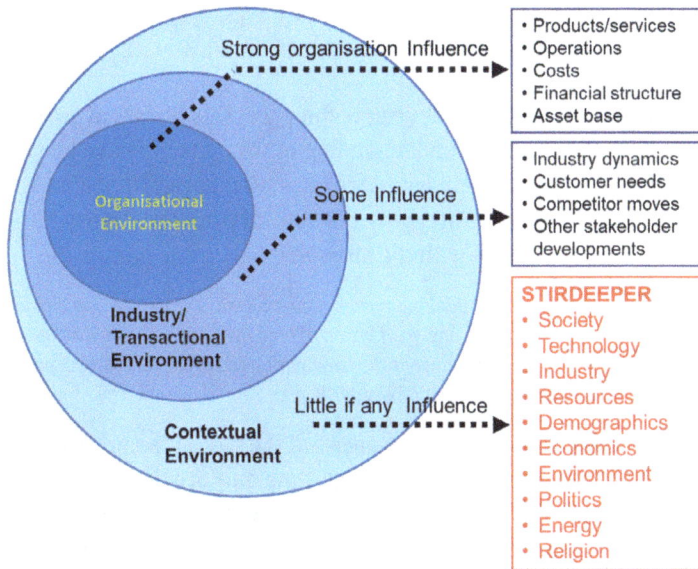

Figure 4.1: Environments and Organisational Influence.

1. The Organisational Environment: An organisation's internal environment consists of the entities, conditions, events, and factors within the organization that influence choices and activities. Factors considered part of the internal environment

https://doi.org/10.1515/9783111617442-004

include the organisation's culture, mission, leadership, products, financial structure, and asset base, all of which the organisation has a strong influence and some control over.

2. Transactional or Industry Environment: This is the part of the environment in which an organisation and its competitors operate. Depending on the organisation's size, it may be a significant player influencing some outcomes as much as being influenced by them. Customers and other stakeholders are some of the factors that occupy this environment.

3. Contextual Environment: This is the largest environment in which all organisations operate but, in most cases, have no power to influence. Thus, the organisation's major task is to develop an appropriate strategy so that it remains an effective player regardless of development in this environment.

Scenario planning is concerned essentially with the contextual environment which will shape the future and have important repercussions for organisations, but which they have little, if any, control or influence over. While the objective of scenario planning is to identify and understand the drivers in the contextual environment, the first step in exploring the contextual environment is to gain an understanding of history.

Understanding History

Before looking to the future one should first review the past. This historical review emphasizes the focal question, gaining an understanding of what factors have played out to shape the current position and their potential rates of change. Given that we are concerned about looking into the future, why does history matter? Henry Mintzberg, a Canadian academic, provides us with the answer:

> Almost everyone would agree that strategic thinking means seeing ahead. But in fact, you cannot see ahead unless you can see behind, because any good vision of how the future may evolve has to be rooted in an understanding of the past. If you want the imagination to see the future, then you'd better have the wisdom to appreciate the past (Mintzberg, 2018, p 1).

History is inescapable; it studies the past and the legacies of the past in the present. Far from being a 'dead' subject, it connects things through time and provides an understanding of the foundation of where we are today and how it will influence developments in the future. It shows us, for example, that most current trends will experience counter-vailing forces and that as the period of scenario planning lengthens, it becomes increasingly important to account for trend reversals and various pivotal moments, reflecting the disruptive events in history that have been shown to occur (Schoemaker, 2020). The role of understanding history is crucial, to first, recognise the influential forces from the past and how they have helped shape the present, which allows a better appreciation of how future changes may be different from those which have already occurred; and second, thinking accurately about the future often rests on reasonably accurate pictures of the past and the present. In reviewing history, the practice is usually to look back to the same time length as the scenarios look forward, i.e. if the scenarios look forward 10 years, then one should look back for a minimum of 10 years from the present. However, this should be extended to perhaps twenty years (or more) in the case of slow-moving industries or phenomena.

Although some regard history as boring, its value is that it provides a clear picture of how the various aspects of society have worked and developed in the past, so that we can understand how they came to work the way they do today. Only through researching history can people see and understand the reasons behind the changes that have occurred, and what elements continue regardless of continual change; however, it is not an easy task.

Environmental Change

Having established some ideas as to what has happened over the past years to arrive at the current situation, the next step is to research the contextual environment to identify a multiplicity of external wide-ranging forces, factors, trends, and events collectively known as driving forces which will determine the future. The contextual environment has received a lot of attention in the literature, one of the best-known publications being *"The Causal Texture of Organizational Environments"* by Emery and Trist (1965), describing a four-step typology (Figure 4.2):

- Step 1: A placid, randomised environment, in which things are relatively unchanging.
- Step 2: A placid, clustered environment; while still placid, factors are now clustered.
- Step 3: A disturbed, reactive environment, in which there is more than one organisation of the same kind, which is the dominant characteristic of the environment.
- Step 4: A turbulent field, in which dynamic properties arise not just from the interactions between component organisations, but also from the field itself which is in motion.

	Low Dynamism	High Dynamism
High Complexity	Placid Clustered	Turbulent
Low Complexity	Placid Randomised	Disturbed Reactive

Figure 4.2: The Turbulent field typology of Trist and Emery, 1965 (Edwards 2018).

Although these four fields have long existed, Emery and Trist suggest that the main issue in studying organisational change is that the environment in which organisations operate today is changing at accelerating rates and increasing complexity. A term now commonly used to describe the external environment is the acronym VUCA representing the terms *volatility, uncertainty, complexity and ambiguity* discussed in Chapter 1. These elements have equal and opposite forces and continue to grow. Watson and Freeman (2012) suggest that:

> *Change itself is changing . . . It appears that more things are becoming connected, which is not only acting as an accelerant to change but is also creating more systemic volatility. In short, the shocks will become more frequent and more severe. Moreover, technological change appears to be accelerating rapidly, as new attitudes and behaviours disappear with much greater velocity.* (Watson and Freeman, 2012, p 318)

As far back as 60 years ago, Max Ways, the editor of Fortune magazine, estimated that the pace of change had become fifty times as great as the average pace of previous years and he identified four categories of social change (Corniche 2004, p 11):
- Gradual change
- Revolution and major disruption
- Rapid change
- Radical change

Since the late 1960s we have been in a period of accelerated radical change and the pace will continue to accelerate. Ray Kurzweil, a well-known American computer scientist, author, inventor, and futurist, predicts that not only is the rate of technological progress increasing, but the rate at which that rate is increasing is also accelerating. Technology will have escaped human ability to control it; the result is a coming period of transition which he calls the 'Singularity,' a phase in which technology changes so fast that it's impossible to know what's on the other side Kurzweil (2010). Kurzweil has identified three principal areas of simultaneous technological advancement that he says will have the greatest impact on the world to come. The first of these is the field of biotechnology in which advances in medicine and genetic engineering will dramatically extend the human lifespan and improve the quality of life. Alongside the advances in medical science, the second area of technological advancement is nanotechnology, i.e. molecular machines building products from elemental base components by putting them together atom by atom. The third, and potentially the most transformative development, will be when we create *strong Artificial Intelligence* (AI) and computers will reproduce and exceed every aspect of human intelligence, including the attainment of conscious thought. This of course is already happening and Kurzweil describes the steps we've already taken to digitally replicate human thought, and how machine intelligence is objectively better than human intelligence. The result, Kurzweil states, is that:

The pace of change will continue and because of the explosive nature of exponential growth, the twenty-first century will be equivalent to twenty thousand years of progress at today's rate of progress; about one thousand times greater than the twentieth century (Cornish 2004, p 11).

While many agree that change is rapid and there seems to be a general consensus that it will likely accelerate, there is some doubt that it will reach the speed that Kurzweil has suggested. Theodore Modis, a scientist specialising in growth and cycles suggests we have already reached the maximum rate of growth for complexity, and that it will eventually stop accelerating and begin decelerating (Modis, 2002).

Driving Forces

A 'driving force' is loosely defined as an exogenous force, dynamic action or movement in the trends and patterns in the contextual environment that there is little control over, but which shape the future in predictable and unpredictable ways. This force underpins observable events in the world, leading to some form of change event which generates uncertainties. In addition to their connection to uncertainties, driving forces can equally be well-known visible trends, e.g. the ageing population in developed countries. Understanding the interrelatedness of driving forces provides insight into the systemic structure of the issues being explored. Lewin's Force Field Analysis is a well-established model used to analyse a situation and identify the forces that drive and resist change. Developed by Kurt Lewin in the 1940s, the idea behind Force Field Analysis is that situations are maintained by an equilibrium between forces that drive change and others that resist change; for change to happen, the driving forces must be strengthened or the resisting forces weakened.

The selection of acronyms used to categorise driving forces include DRIVE (Demographics, Resource scarcity, Inequalities, Volatility scale and complexity, and Enterprising dynamics) developed by Esposito and Tse 2017; STEEP (Society, Technology, Economics, Environment, Politics), and PESTLE (Political, Economic, Sociological, Technological, Legal, and Environmental). These typologies are somewhat restrictive and the alternative acronym proposed is STIRDEEPER. This is an expansion of existing acronyms, representing 'Society, Technology, Industry, Resources, Demographics, Economics, Environment, Politics, Energy and Religion.' However, it should be noted that whatever acronym is utilised, this only serves as the initial point of research.

The process of identifying driving forces is initially an individual brainstorming exercise using post-it notes and following the typical instructions from the Facilitator:

– Think about the driving forces that will play out in the country over the next X years; in doing so, the focus should initially be on the forces in the contextual environment likely to shape the issue areas.
– In silence (to avoid extroverts dominating) write each driving force idea on a separate post-it using a maximum of 6 words, while avoiding single words e.g. 'edu-

cation' – does this refer to the standard of education? Or its availability? Both of which may be distinct driving forces.
- Ensure each post-it represents a driving force, not its outcomes. While the wording should indicate change where relevant, it should not indicate the direction of change unless it is a predetermined element.
- When complete, place each post-it on the workshop wall space, in random order.

In researching driving forces, group members should be encouraged to consider a wide range of factors based on what they see happening in their immediate environment and the wider world around them. The more ideas generated the better, as quantity is more important than quality at this point, resulting in more ideas to work with. There are also no right or wrong answers at this stage; ideas can be adjusted or eliminated as necessary once the team discusses them and undertakes research.

Once it appears that the group has reached a point of diminishing ideas, the next phase is for the group as a whole to review each driving force listed. This is led by the Facilitator using a round-robin approach, asking the author of each post-it to explain and clarify what is meant by the driving force and then opening up discussion with the group. The process must follow the brainstorming principle of a free-thinking environment, permitting no critical, deflating comments, avoiding idea killers, or excluding ideas because of the belief that they are wrong. The idea is to suspend disbelief while questioning the individual and group's assumptions. Discussions in this phase will clarify what individuals mean by their driving force ideas, eliminating ambiguity and removing duplication. However, it is often the case that what may initially appear to be the same idea raised by another group member, is in fact quite different once it has been articulated. This process will also likely result in additional forces being identified during discussions, evidence of a free-thinking environment. The question which should be asked repeatedly is: "What have we missed, what have we not thought about?" It is a certainty that at least one or more crucial driving forces will have been missed by the group; nonetheless, these, along with new driving forces, should be picked up in the research phase.

The typical outcome of an initial brainstorming session is often a large and chaotic collection of unstructured ideas. While a set of rough-cut 'first generation' scenarios may be developed by the end of the workshop using the driving forces identified, it is often the case that, following discussion on the scenarios developed, it becomes obvious that a further one (or perhaps more) workshops are required because of issues raised during the development of the initial set of scenarios.

Clustering Driving Forces

After identifying driving forces, the next step is to cluster them into categories, with each cluster being defined as a meta-conceptualisation of causally related driving forces and uncertainties. There are no hard rules defining how clusters should be put together. Rather, the objective is to logically organize and analyse large numbers of ideas by categorising them into groups of interconnected ideas, not to reduce the number of post-its. Instructions on how to cluster the post-its include:

- Remove any duplications of idea/driving forces.
- Cluster the post-its using some form of organic taxonomy. Avoid clustering the post-its by acronyms as these are often too limiting. Broad cluster headings such as 'Society' encompass a multitude of ideas; this needs to be broken down into smaller, themed clusters, each representing a single idea, e.g. 'the role of women in society.'
- Ensure that the post-its comprising the cluster are all interrelated as each cluster must represent a single idea of interrelated concepts. The contributory driving forces are the individual 'event' driving forces that comprise each cluster.
- A particular driving force or various aspects of it may appear in more than one cluster, although this should be avoided where possible; it is also acceptable to have a cluster containing just one or two post-its.
- Assign a name to each cluster on a new post-it, with the names emerging organically from the various groupings of driving forces. The name should be short, descriptive, and themed where possible, encapsulating the essence of what the cluster represents. If it is difficult to find a name which summarizes the cluster, this usually means that the forces within the cluster are too widespread and do not form a rational grouping. Try breaking down the cluster into two or more clusters to see if this resolves the issue, and identify which clusters require further research.

The final step to ensure that the elements contained in the cluster should be part of the cluster is to determine the causal relationships between the cluster elements. This is done by drawing arrows demonstrating how the individual driving forces are linked, as causality is central to scenario building. It is important to remember that elements may exist simultaneously with strongly interwoven interrelationships between them which can lead to one of two revelations. The first is that some uncertainties are inevitable because they are already in the pipeline and will play out in ways that are well understood within specified time-frames, such as an ageing population. These are known as 'predetermined' elements, they are slow-moving but reliable and unwavering and although they will play out at some point in the future, they are unlikely to vary significantly in any scenario within the scenario timeframe. The second revelation is that some forces are fast-moving within the scenario time frame and can play out in various ways but there is no clear idea how this playout will evolve. The outcomes of these forces of change which have a big impact on the contextual environment but their outcomes are uncertain and unknown, are known as 'critical uncertainties.'

To develop multiple plausible scenarios, it is necessary to understand the relationship between cause and effect, their linkages and interactions. This exercise requires a trial-and-error approach, with several clustering attempts usually necessary before everyone agrees on each cluster. I have found that it is more effective to try out ideas quickly and reject them if necessary, rather than try to produce the ultimate answer in one go.

These process steps are very time-consuming. For larger groups, it is not unusual for the team to generate upwards of 200 driving forces. Given that the process is dealing with something with no right or wrong answer and is instead all about 'thinking,' it is a cognitively demanding process. By the end of this step, participants are invariably mentally exhausted, and a break is usually required.

Predictability/Impact Matrix

Once clustering is complete, the next step is to review the clusters and rank their headings, not the individual event post-its, on a predictability/impact matrix as shown in Figure 4.3

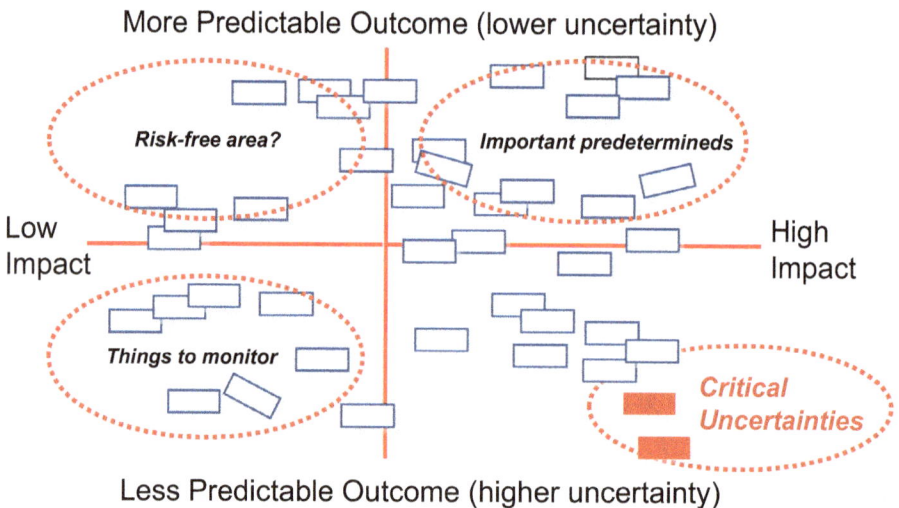

Figure 4.3: Predictability/Impact Matrix.

As with clustering, this is best done collectively as a group led by the Facilitator. This step aims to identify the critical uncertainties, i.e. those factors which are the most uncertain and have the greatest impact. *Impact* refers to the impact of the driving force on the client's areas of interest, i.e. will this driving force have a high or negligible impact? *Predictability* meanwhile relates to the cluster driving force itself: 'More Predictable Outcome' means there is a reasonable certainty that the driving force will play out and continue in ways that are well understood; 'Less Predictable Outcome' on the other hand, means there is no clear idea which of several plausible ways it might go. Some forces such as demographics are slow-moving and are therefore relatively predictable; however, other forces such as social values or technological advances are highly uncertain.

The four quadrants of the predictability/impact matrix are defined as follows:

- **More predictable outcome/Least impact:** because clusters here are relatively predictable and have the least impact, they generally represent a *risk-free area*. Forces are visible, but slow-moving incremental trends are quite predictable, and accordingly have a lower impact on business. An example of this in the financial world is U.S. Treasury securities which are considered safe-haven assets having minimal risk. With the US government unwilling to default on its debt and two-thirds of its national debt being held domestically, this reduces their vulnerability to external creditors.
- **More predictable outcome/Most impact:** Clusters in this quadrant represent factors that are completely outside the organisation's control, but which will play out in predictable ways in any story about the future, and are known as *important predetermineds*. For example, the number of high school students 10 years from now is predetermined by the number of children currently in junior school. Organisations need to take heed of these factors; addressing and planning for these predetermineds is imperative for their continued and sustained success.
- **Less predictable outcome/Least impact:** This quadrant relates to events which appear on the horizon and seem to be the 'next important thing,' but then they disappear without having made any significant impact. They should, however, be periodically *monitored* as they may come back years later once the technology or other essential impact force has developed significantly. A good example of this is driverless cars.
- **Less predictable outcome/Most impact:** Clusters in this quadrant here are those forces whose predictability is uncertain and which are also outside of the organisation's control, and thus will significantly impact the future should they play out. Here the particular focus is on those that are located in the bottom right-hand side of this quadrant, to those clusters known as *critical uncertainties*. These events are the most unpredictable driving forces clusters, and when they happen, they catch everyone off guard and have a major impact on the organisation. An example of this would be the 2007–2008 global economic crisis.

Going through the cluster forces one by one, workshop participants discuss how important each one is to the focal issue and their degree of uncertainty, and then place the cluster in one of the four scenario matrix quadrants. In terms of the critical uncertainties, it is important when placing the clusters on the matrix, that the uncertainty relates to the impact that the cluster will have on the organisation, rather than the uncertainty as to whether the cluster events materialise as envisioned. At the same time, there is no scale used on the axis to rank the clusters, it is done through a facilitated, critically discursive and usually lengthy debate within the team. Ogilvy and Schwartz (2004) suggest that rather than the team discussing and agreeing on which quadrant each force should be placed in, a quicker and more effective method is to provide every participant with several poker chips, and ask each person to assign the chips to different forces on the list – more chips for forces of greater importance and uncertainty, and fewer or no chips for forces of lesser importance and uncertainty. However, I have used this on one occasion and did not find it useful, as it generated too much discussion about the placement of the exact number of chips, rather than the placement of the cluster.

Although some debate is usually required until the group accepts the outcomes as a reasonable ranking of predictability and impact, it is important to remember that this process is not an exact science, with no ultimate truth. Thus, the ranking is intuitive, and the placing of post-its is relative to each other. When assessing the predictability and impact of the clusters, account must be taken of the time frame period as defined by the horizon year, as what may be largely predictable in 3–5 years, may be highly unpredictable when considering a 10+ year time frame. At the same time, the tendency to place all the clusters around the middle of the axis, or in one quadrant, should be avoided.

Once the two critical uncertainty clusters have been identified, they are then used as the initial framework to develop a rough-cut set of scenarios, comprising two of the dominant critical uncertainties placed across each other to create a 2x2 matrix resulting in 4 scenarios. An example is shown in Figure 4.4, taken from a scenario project I undertook in India. The 2x2 scenario matrix initially developed by Shell is a powerful and reportedly one of the most popular and widely used scenario planning templates.

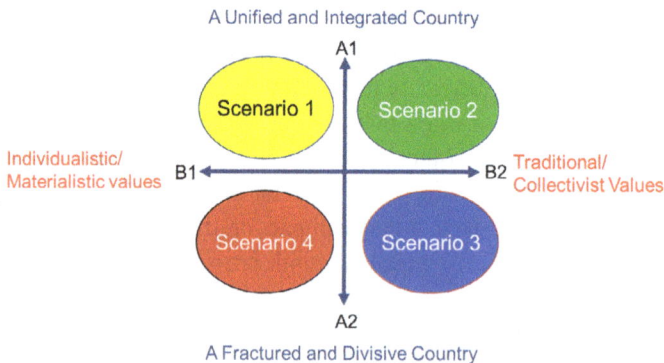

Figure 4.4: Two Critical Uncertainties Creating a Scenario Matrix.

In Figure 4.4, the A1–A2 axis represented the polar extremes of the state of the country, i.e. a unified and integrated country versus a divisive and fractured country with several states seeking independence. The B1–B2 axis represented the national value systems, i.e. India moving from a traditional and collectivist value system to one which is more individualistic and materialistic.

Before proceeding to develop the scenarios, it is crucial to test whether the two clusters used are either interdependent or are from the same driver category. If the two drivers are related to each other, they are likely to move in the same direction. For example, the state of the economy and the level of national infrastructure development are usually interdependent and conventional thinking would suggest that if the economy is poor, the level of infrastructure development would also be poor. Consequently, two of the spaces created by the intersection of these axes would not result in interesting and useful scenarios. At the same time, if the two drivers are from the same driver category, e.g. technological change and digital disruptions, they will not offer a good mix of divergence and storytelling, in which case it is necessary to select one or both new drivers. It produces a better set of scenarios if factors from different driver categories are used. It is, however, important to be careful as what at first may appear to be related or interdependent factors may, after investigation, prove not to be the case. An example of this occurred when I was involved in developing a set of scenarios for a client in the Caribbean with a focus on Cuba. Following the predictability/impact matrix ranking, the initial critical uncertainties selected were the state of the economy and the healthcare system. The scenario team's initial assumption was that these two factors were interdependent, as they could not conceive of a country with a poor economy having a good healthcare system. However, following focused research the team was surprised to discover that despite a poor economy, in virtually every area of public health and medicine, Cuba had created a high-quality primary care network and an unrivalled public health system.

One of the metrics outlined earlier for a successful scenario project was whether or not scenarios were successful in pushing out the thinking of the client's senior management team (SMT), and a good mix of matrix divergence and storytelling is essential to achieve this. Once the two drivers are agreed upon, they are then used to create a 2x2 matrix creating four distinct scenario themes at their polar extremes as exemplified in Figure 4.4.

Arriving at a consensus regarding the selection of the axes to be used is an interactive group process. Ogilvy and Schwartz (2004) claim that while the creation of this matrix is the most intuitive and intellectually challenging part of a scenario planning project, using the matrix to build scenarios provides two advantages; first, the matrix assures that the scenarios are qualitatively different in a logical, deductive, nonrandom way; and second, it guarantees that the less predictable/high-impact drivers will be in all four scenarios. van't Klooster and van Asselt (2006) meanwhile, suggest that there are three different views as to the use of the 2X2 matrix. The first is that the axes provide a backbone for scenario development. This implies that filling in the scenarios should be done within a given frame, with the workshops seen as a first opportunity to provide the building blocks for each of the four scenarios. The second view argues that the scenario axes should be perceived as akin to a building scaffold. Just as the scaffolds are removed after the building is erected, the scenario axes are simply used as a heuristic to contrast the scenarios and are removed once the scenarios have been developed. The third view is that the axes provide a foundation and rejects the idea that developing scenarios should be done within a given and fixed frame; instead, the application of the axes can vary in several ways depending on interpretations of the axes. The conclusion of van't Klooster and van Asselt is that professional futurists seem to have found ways to use the scenario axes in a more flexible and less standardised way and while they can be used to structure discussions about the future, the axes should not be considered a blueprint in scenario development.

Once the scenario matrix framework has been established and accepted by the scenario team, what follows is a four-step process:

- Step 1: Define the end state for each of the four quadrants representing a scenario, imagining what the world will look like in the horizon year in each one.
- Step 2: Revisit the clusters and allocate each to one of the scenarios in which it fits most naturally, noting that it is possible to have the same cluster in more than one scenario. The analogy is that the scenario matrix represents a 4-bedroom house and the clusters are furniture; the question then is, which furniture logically belongs in which room?
- Step 3: Develop rough-cut chronological and coherent scenario storylines. This is achieved by linking cluster events and happenings, which explain how we get from today to the end-states in each scenario. In doing so it is essential to consider those events which are already happening and are related to our current reality, as well as those which will come into effect in later years on the timeline. This is essentially a causal thinking exercise and major gaps in the story will inevitably be identified; to create a coherent and plausible storyline, groups must now create new event post-its to pull and fit everything together to address these gaps.
- Step 4: The final element is to name the four scenarios, which should be short, evocative, and thematic, encapsulating the general image of each of the end states.

At this point, what has developed are what are known as first-generation scenarios. As Wack (1985) noted, rough-cut or "first-generation scenarios are always learning scenarios; their purpose is not action but to gain understanding and insight" (p 12) into the events and the driving forces, and their interrelationships. In reviewing and discussing the first-generation scenarios, what should emerge is a detailed and wide-ranging set of questions, the main ones usually being – what have we missed? and what do we need to add or take away? In answering these questions, a research agenda is then developed with individuals or groups tasked with researching specific areas. Deep research and rigorous analysis are required, but the research is now guided by well-defined questions from the scenarios that ensure relevance and usefulness. This workshop concludes and the iterative cycle of scenario review, research-generated questions and scenario development continues.

Research

van der Heijden (2005) argues that it is preferable to use the intuitive powers of the group and let the research programme emerge, as iterating between intuition and analysis produces the quickest route to new insights. New insights, in turn, generate unique research questions leading to a revised generation of scenarios until further generations run into diminishing returns. Although this chapter introduces the scenario development process as essentially comprising two iterations, it is not uncommon that the process involves three or more, with numerous meetings between workshops, as good scenario projects are measured in months, not days or weeks (van der Heijden, 2005). Research results are invariably scattered over a wide area, initially in the form of many unrelated ideas, observations and uncertainties, and identifying the predetermined elements and the structural drivers requires considerable time and discussion.

Research questions arise mostly while trying to develop the storyline which connects the present reality with the end-states developed in the 2X2 matrix. Telling that story in detail is crucially important because in doing so you discover where there is a lack of understanding of the underlying structure of the situation. Although the main objective of the research is to understand the systemic structures that drive the contextual environment, additional objectives related to improving the quality of the final scenarios include:

- Clearing away misconceptions, the things the scenario team (who represent the views of the organisation itself) thought they knew but which were, in fact, wrong.
- Uncovering more predetermined elements, some of which may originally have been thought to be uncertainties.
- Understanding in greater detail the depth and dimensionality of uncertainties; and
- Understanding the dynamics of particular situations.

According to van der Heijden (2005), when asked to explain what scenario research was all about, Wack liked to refer to Kurt Lewin, considered one of the founders of social psychology. Lewin suggested that the traditional positivist, natural science, way of research does not work for overly complex systems such as a social system. Instead, he proposed an approach he called 'action research.' In essence, after making a significant intervention in a system, you compare the effects of this with what you were expecting. Gaps between your expectations and what really happened indicate areas where your understanding of the system is lacking. You then know where to look to improve this understanding, having generated relevant research questions about the system which need answering through focused research. However, new understanding only comes from systemic deep research involving a combination of desk research and discussions with topic specialist experts and RPs, asking questions such as:

- What is already in the pipeline?
- What seems static, but is slowly changing?
- What trends are bound to break, e.g. due to saturation?
- What seems impossible? Why is that?
- What is happening that could matter? What is the relevant system to study?
- What is the appropriate level of granularity (detail) of observation? and
- What are other ways of looking at this?

Sceptics can also play a key role in the research. For example, they can be asked why they think a scenario can or cannot happen, and then investigate why their reasons are not reflected in the scenarios. This is important because when scenarios are presented to the SMT there will inevitably be scepticism about the proposed futures, and dealing with these at an earlier stage improves the chances the scenarios are received as intended. Recall that one of the metrics for a successful scenario project was whether or not scenarios were effective in pushing out the thinking of the client's senior management team (SMT); thus, old thinking should be challenged. There are also subsidiary objectives of the research related to improving the quality of the final scenarios presented, which include:

- Increasing the depth and dimensionality of uncertainties, spelling out exactly what is meant by each one so that there are no misconceptions; and
- Identifying more probable and worked-out patterns and events, which provide the reader with a better understanding of the situation.

In terms of desk research, there are several approaches which may provide interesting insights into trends and issues. For example, Bibliometric analysis may be used to track the development of the interest in each subject. This may act as a trend indicator, albeit the success of any bibliometric analysis is strongly connected to the identification and use of key search terms. Another option is the extrapolation of historical trends or theorems which can inspire the assessment of different possible developments. As a general rule, the uptake of technologies, products, and ideas, in particular markets and societies follows an S-curve rather than developing in a linear pattern. This means that uptake or participation will be slow in the beginning, but at a certain point an almost exponential growth rate is achieved before the concept matures and growth slows and eventually stops. The challenge is to estimate the nature and location of such an S-curve. Malcolm Gladwell provides examples of how different things spread in society in his book *The Tipping Point* (2000) and compares the progress of change with that of an epidemic. Small things such as one infected individual can have a significant impact on the epidemic spreading; the tipping point is that magic moment when an idea, trend, or social behaviour crosses a threshold, tips, and spreads like wildfire. Just as a single sick person can start an epidemic of the flu, so too can a small but precisely targeted push cause a trend.

The potential use and development of technology is often an important driver of change. One way of analysing this quantitatively is to conduct a patent analysis. Because the patterns of patents help indicate the potential interest and breakthrough of technology, this approach may be an important quantitative input to scenario analysis. Although there is a range of patent analysis services and tools available, there are several pitfalls to note: (1) Companies may use patents as a strategic tool to discourage other companies from doing research in each technological field, so it is not objective. (2) There is a 'black box' effect since patents only become public after they have been filed. (3) Patent research may be time-consuming if knowledge is needed on a specific technology, as all patents require close study to understand their specifics. (4) The majority of patents never see the light of day so spending resources studying things that never amount to anything, is quite high.

Although desk research and data analysis are especially useful, participatory methods such as conversations with experts and RPs will often help provide insights and new perspectives on a subject, although identifying the right experts and RPs may present a challenge. The views of experts/RPs may be done through face-to-face discussions, telephone, online, or in focus groups, and this may be through structured, semistructured, or unstructured interviews. The objective of research with these individuals is to uncover unusual and exceptional ideas that have the power to completely change situations. Some trends are clear, such as the ageing of the population in most Western European countries. But even if they are not particularly difficult to identify, it can be extremely hard to understand exactly when and how they will begin to impact in the short-to-medium term. Other trends are exceedingly difficult to foresee, particularly unpredictable events with devastating impacts, commonly called 'wild cards.' An example of this is the September 11 attack in the US and the Indian Ocean tsunami of 2004. As Nassim Taleb explains in his book *The Black Swan* (2008), things are not always as they seem; the human tendency is to retrospectively find simplistic explanations for the occurrence and extreme impact of rare and unpredictable outlier events called Black Swans, which are a significant part of today's world. For example, the list of individuals who claimed the 2008 financial crisis was predictable *after* the event, was far higher than those heralding its arrival *before* it struck. This is an example of what is known as hindsight bias, a common bias in everyday life. Corniche (2004) suggests there are two problems in terms of research; the first is that it is exceptionally difficult to keep up with everything that is going on in our fast-changing world, and the second is that our thinking suffers greatly from antiquated beliefs about the world around us.

Iceberg Analysis

Iceberg analysis is a concept derived from 'Systems Thinking' that helps dig deeper and identify root causes. Developed by Linda Booth Sweeney and Dennis Meadows in *The Systems Thinking Playbook* (2010), it is a useful tool to gain new knowledge and understanding via what is known as the 'systems iceberg', a metaphor for the problems we are experiencing daily because what is visible is often deceiving.

The source of the analogy is that only 10% of the mass of an iceberg is visible floating above the water, while the rest is hidden from view under the water. The problem is that we generally only perceive the tip of the iceberg, while the real problem hides below the surface. It is the 90% of the iceberg which we cannot see that ocean currents act on, driving the iceberg's behaviour. Global issues can be viewed the same way and the iceberg analogy can be used to go down to four deeper levels of thinking as illustrated in Figure 4.5.

Stopping at the first level of the iceberg is merely being reactive. Getting to the second level helps to anticipate the problem, while the third level of thinking allows one to modify or design the systems. Finally, addressing the mental models themselves at the bottom levels allows one to see, understand, and transform the problem.

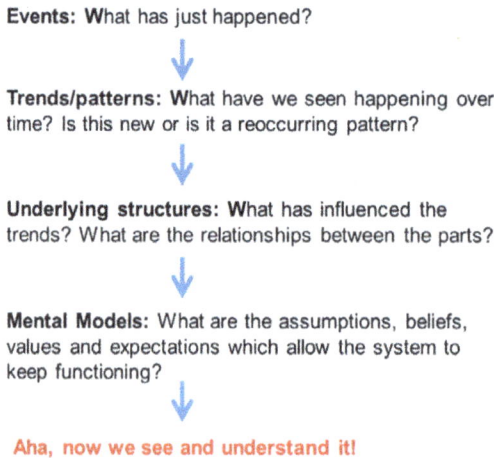

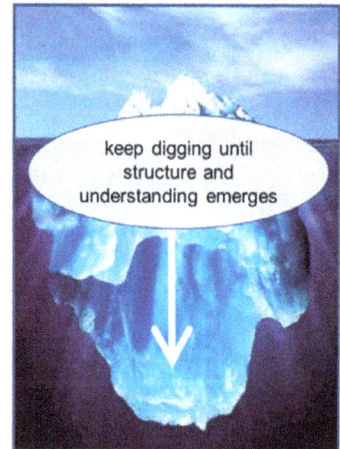

Events: What has just happened?

↓

Trends/patterns: What have we seen happening over time? Is this new or is it a reoccurring pattern?

↓

Underlying structures: What has influenced the trends? What are the relationships between the parts?

↓

Mental Models: What are the assumptions, beliefs, values and expectations which allow the system to keep functioning?

↓

Aha, now we see and understand it!

keep digging until structure and understanding emerges

Figure 4.5: Iceberg Analysis.

Events/Outcomes: usually comprise single events and are visible because they are at the surface, which is where we typically perceive the everyday world and take stock of situations. An example of an immediate, observable event level, would be if a company's stock price suddenly crashes.

Trends/Patterns: The patterns and trends level are just below the surface where some events may be new, but similar events have been taking place over time. Looking at patterns, we might for example, we might notice that 'tech' stocks often experience volatility during product launch periods.

Underlying structures: This level represents the structures and their relationships which cause the patterns and the behaviours further up the iceberg. Delving deeper, structures that influence these patterns could, for example, include the algorithms used by trading bots, the structural organization of the stock market, or the financial regulations governing trading behaviours

Mental Models/Beliefs: At the bottom of the iceberg are the assumptions, beliefs, values, and expectations which cause and allow the structures to continue functioning as they are. At this deepest level, mental models might, for example, encompass the collective belief in market rationality, the value investors place on growth versus stock value or the societal perception of the stock market as a measure of economic health.

Deep research and rigorous analysis to identify the structural drivers in a particular strategic context require a lot of time, discussion, and contemplation. Wack (1985b) argued that by rigorously exploring the business environment it is possible to identify predetermined elements, which may be:

–   Events that are inevitable in that they have already happened, although their timing and consequences may not be fully known; or
–   Events that are already in the pipeline and will emerge in time, pushing towards a particular outcome; or
–   The consequence of inertial forces within the system whose behaviour is slow to change over the long run.

Wack's view was that the purpose of scenario planning was to help managers see the inevitable forces driving change, in essence, the predetermined elements. Therefore, planning should be based on outcomes that we know will occur with certainty, rather than outcomes based on unsubstantiated assumptions.

Causal Layered Analysis

Alongside Iceberg Analysis is the technique of Causal Layered Analysis (CLA) developed by Sohail Inayatullah (2004) as a method to dig down to deeper levels of thinking. Inayatullah states that CLA, shown in Figure 4.6, is offered as a new research theory and method; "as a theory, it seeks to integrate empiricist, interpretive, critical, and action learning modes of knowing. As a method, its utility is not in predicting the future, but essentially in creating transformative spaces for the creation of alternative futures." Since its inception, CLA has been used in a variety of workshops in scenario planning and non-governmental and corporate strategy workshops.

CLA is grounded in critical futures research and is designed to identify four progressively deeper levels of causality, when an issue or strategic option is being explored in an attempt to identify the driving forces and worldviews shaping that issue. The first level is *Litany* which is the most visible and obvious. This comprises current events, issues, trends, responses, and views which are not connected, usually presented by the news media, and are often exaggerated for political purposes. The second level, *Systemic Causes*, is concerned with universal causes including social, technological, economic, environmental political, and historical factors. Interpretation here is based on quantitative data and the role of the state and other actors and interests, is often explored at this level. The third deeper level is concerned with the *Worldview* and the discourse that legitimates issues to find the deeper social and cultural processes and assumptions behind the issues. The fourth and deepest layer of analysis is at the level of *Metaphor and Myth*. Here lies the deep stories, the unconscious and often emotive dimensions of the problem, or the paradox which provides an emotional level experience to the worldview under inquiry.

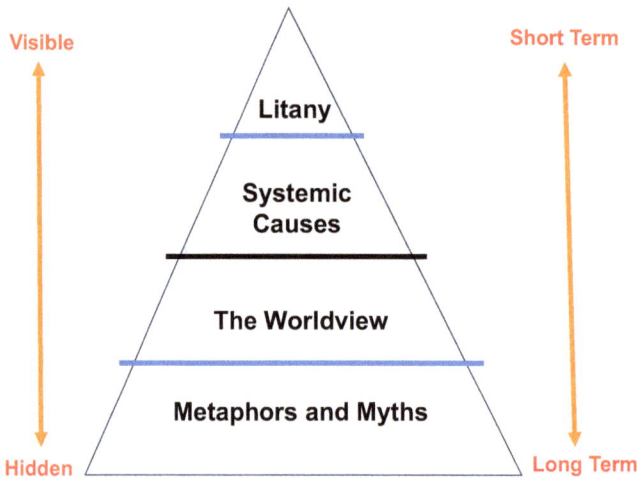

Figure 4.6: Causal Layered Analysis Inayatullah (2019).

Through this process, CLA expands the issue from the short to the long term, and from reality to the imaginative or emotive dimension, facilitating discussions on alternative realities or futures that consider different worldviews or myths held by people. The advantage of using the CLA methodology is that it moves beyond the superficiality of conventional forecasting which is "often unable to unpack worldviews, ideologies, and discourses, not to mention archetypes, myths and metaphors" (Inayatullah 2004, page 40).

In terms of scenario planning, the benefits of CLA according to Inayatullah (2004), are that it:
– Supports the development of powerful scenarios, expanding their range and richness, providing a check that scenarios are robust across diverse perspectives.
– Leads to the inclusion of diverse forms of knowledge among participants when used in a workshop setting.

– Appeals to, and can be used by, a wider range of individuals as it incorporates non-textual and poetic/artistic expression in the futures process.
– Takes recognition of, and layers of, participants' positions moving the discussion beyond the superficial and obvious, to the deeper and marginal; and
– It can help reveal alternative interpretations of an issue arising from different worldviews, discourses, myths, and metaphors.

There are also disadvantages of incorporating CLA into the scenario project, namely that it:
– Is time-consuming;
– Requires participants to be willing to share their perspectives and accept challenges to their assumptions;
– May reduce individual creativity; and
– Requires an experienced facilitator (Conway, 2012).

Slaughter (1984, p 815) argues that "CLA provides a richer account of what is being studied than the more common empiricist or predictive orientation which merely skims the surface and . . . because mastery of the different layers calls for critical and hermeneutic skills that originate in the humanities, some future practitioners may find the method challenging at first". At the same time, it has been recognised that in areas where the corporate culture is homogenous or hegemony is strong, CLA is difficult to use. It is perhaps because of these disadvantages that CLA does not appear to be widely used in scenario development in the literature.

Conclusions

This chapter has largely been about understanding and researching the future. There are several fundamental problems associated with researching the future, these being:
– Important developments occur constantly all around the world, but they may not appear significant and most people may remain unaware of them.
– 'Black Swans' events, which are beyond normal expectations in any area and are therefore extremely difficult, if not impossible, to predict.
– Recent events, especially those experienced personally, dominate thinking about the future.
– As one moves farther from the present, uncertainty increases as the quality of data declines and the number of potential causes of change grows, with the result that the accuracy with which we can explain things decline.
– A rapidly changing and increasingly interdependent world gives us so much to know about so many things, that it seems impossible to keep up.

Toffler (1992) argues that we are today living through one of those exclamation points in history where the entire structure of human knowledge is once again trembling with changes as old barriers fall. He suggests that we are not just accumulating more facts whatever they may be. Just as we are now restructuring companies and whole economies, we are reorganising the production and distribution of knowledge and the symbols we use to communicate.

While there are well-known acronyms used to categorise drivers of change, Cornish's (2004, p 9) contention is that "while we can see that technology, economy, and social institutions are all undergoing enormous change . . . it is hard to avoid noticing that the changes are intricately interconnected", a phenomenon he describes as 'the Great Transformation'. Support for this comes from Capra (1996) who suggests that the major problems of our time are systemic problems, which means they are interconnected and interdependent and cannot therefore be understood in isolation.

In terms of research to understand the Great Transformation, it is essential to determine which are the most important trends and then focus efforts on understanding them. Cornish (2004) suggests that the six most important supertrends are:

1. Technological Progress which includes improvements in many technologies such as computers, medicine, transportation, and communication to name a few.
2. Economic Progress. The accumulation of capital, consumer goods and social capital results in each new generation starting with more wealth making it easier to produce even more.
3. Improving Health leads to increasing longevity the consequences of which include more dependence on government assistance, medical and pensions, all to be funded by the younger generations.
4. Increasing Mobility. People, goods and services now move faster and in greater quantity which is the cause of globalisation, and which also causes social and cultural disruptions.
5. Environmental Decline which is a consequence of a range of factors including population growth and economic development resulting in global warming, declining freshwater supplies, overfishing of the oceans, and extinction of species of animals and plants.
6. Increasing Deculturation. This occurs when people lose key elements of their culture such as language or ingrained habits in which case accustomed ways of communicating and behaving no longer fit with the environment.

Some of the changes within these supertrends may be linear, while others may be discontinuous which is usually difficult to anticipate; tracing causal links between these trends is also difficult, but an essential part of research in developing good scenarios. While understanding ancient history can be interesting and useful, it is far more important to know and understand the more recent past as more recent circumstances are more likely to mirror the current situation and relate them to the future.

However, we can learn much from the distant past, notably that nothing is permanent, everything changes over time.

To conclude this chapter, as indicated previously, developing scenarios is a circular rather than a linear process. It is often the case that three, four or even more, iterations are required before the scenario team is satisfied with their understanding of the research.

The chapter which follows discusses in detail, Stage 3 of the scenario development process.

References

Capra, F. (1996). The Web of Life: A New Scientific Understanding of Living Systems New York: Anchor Books.

Corniche, E. (2004). Futuring. The Exploration of the Future. World Future Society, Maryland, USA.

Edwards, M. An Integral Methodology for Organisational Sustainability: Living with a crowded bottom line in chaotic times. Business Sustainability 1, 2018, p 4.

Emery, F. E. and Trist, E. L. (1965). The causal texture of organizational environments. Human Relations, 18(1), p 21–32.

Esposito, M. and Tse, T. (2017). DRIVE: The Five Megatrends that Underpin the Future Business, Social, and Economic Landscapes, Thunderbird International Business Review. Vol 60, Issue 1.

Gladwell, M. (2000). The Tipping Point: How Little Things Can Make a Big Difference. Little, Brown and Company, Boston, USA.

Inayagullah, S. (2019). Causal Layered Analysis: A Four-Level Approach to Alternative Futures Relevance and use in Foresight. Futuribles.

Inayatullah, S. (2004). The Causal Layered Analysis (CLA) Reader Theory and Case Studies of an Integrative and Transformative Methodology. Tamkang University Press.

Kurzweil, R. (2010). The Singularity Is Near. Duckworth, London.

Mintzberg, H. (2018). Strategic Thinking as "Seeing." Manage Magazine, October, Article Bank.

Modis, T. (2020). Forecasting the Growth of Complexity and Change—An Update: Korotayev, A., LePoire, D. (eds) The 21st Century Singularity and Global Futures. World-Systems Evolution and Global Futures. Springer.

Ogilvy, J. and Schwartz, P. (2004). Plotting Your Scenarios, Global Business Network, The Monitor Group.

Schoemaker, P.J. H. (2020). How historical analysis can enrich scenario planning. Futures and Foresight Science. September-December, Volume 2, Issue 3–4.

Slaughter, R, (1997). Developing and Applying Strategic Foresight, The ABN Report **5**, (10), p 7–15.

Sweeney, L.B. and Meadows, D. (2010). The Systems Thinking Playbook: Exercises to Stretch and Build Learning and Systems Thinking Capabilities. Chelsea Green Publishing Co.

Taleb, Nassim (2008). The Black Swan: The Impact of the Highly Improbable. Random House.

Toffler, A. (1991). Powershift: Knowledge, Wealth and Violence at the Edge of the 21st Century. Bantam Books

van der Heijden, C.A.M.J. (2005). Scenarios: The Art of Strategic Conversation, Chichester: John Wiley & Sons.

van 't Klooster, S.A. and van Asselt, M.B.A. (2006). Practising the Scenario-Axes Technique, Futures, Vol 38, Issue 1, p 15–30.

Wack, P. (1985b). Scenarios: Shooting the Rapids, Harvard Business Review, 63, 5, pp 3–14

Watson, R. and Freeman, O. (2012). Future Vision: scenarios for the world in 2040. Scribe Publications Pty Ltd., Sans Walk, London.

Chapter 5
Scenario Development Process Stage 3

Introduction

Following Stage 2, Stage 3 starts with a review of the research findings and what changes will be required to the scenarios. The team members invariably return from their research with new insights and ideas covering a range of subjects, necessitating a review of the rough-cut scenario framework previously developed. The process then iterates back to the scenario-building phase, the objective being to incorporate this new knowledge into a better scenario-set framework. A common occurrence is revisiting and modifying the scenario axes for one of several reasons:
- the research has indicated that one of the axes is not a critical uncertainty; it either does not have a high impact on the focal issue, or it is not as uncertain as previously thought.
- the two axes are interlinked.
- the scenarios resulting from the matrix are not particularly useful.

This review of the scenario framework may seem frustrating, particularly the review of critical uncertainties. A deeper look however shows this may be misplaced. Uncertainty is a major cause of concern for any organisation looking to stay in business and one of the benefits of SP is that through extensive research, what may initially appear to be a level 4 Uncertainty (discussed in Chapter 1), may not be so. This therefore can allow for better strategic planning.

The Scenario Framework

An example of the above is a scenario project I undertook in 2002/3 for Petronas, a Southeast Asian National Oil Company (mentioned in Chapter 3 and discussed in detail in the book *Scenario Thinking. Preparing Your Organisation for the Future in an Unpredictable World, 2nd Edition* (Cairns and Wright, 2018). Rather than scenarios focused on a particular issue or aspect of the industry, the CEO wanted a set of scenarios focused on developments in the global world as he was confused by what he saw going on in the world. As a consequence, it was determined that the first-generation scenario axes should comprise the following drivers:
- *The pace of the global economy:* the polar extremes being a vibrant, fast-paced global economic integration with a highly competitive market' at one end, and 'a dismal, slow economic integration, and fractured global market' at the other.
- *Industry structure:* one polar extreme was 'diversified and effective developments,' while the other was 'slow and consolidated development.'

https://doi.org/10.1515/9783111617442-005

These drivers were the two most uncertain but at the same time, the two with the biggest impact, which had emerged after much research and discussion in the scenario team. Happy with the scenario matrix, the team decided to run it by an RP to get their views on the matrix.

Two RPs were identified and following discussions with them, it transpired that neither considered the scenarios resulting from the matrix to be especially challenging. While the two extremes of the pace of the 'global economy integration' driver were reasonable, the first RP suggested that it had completely missed the point that the world was well on the way to a global recession. This surprised the team members; in their research, they had come across some articles suggesting that the global economy might slow down, but they had not found anything to suggest that a global recession was on the horizon. The RP suggested that there had in fact, been several internationally respected individuals who claimed that the signs were already visible that an economic collapse was likely in the near future. Examples he quoted to support this included William Poole, former president of the St. Louis Federal Reserve, who warned in 2002 that Fannie Mae and Freddie Mac did not have the cash reserves to weather a financial storm. At the same time, the Federal Reserve's strategy of maintaining low-interest rates to avoid a mild recession at the current point was risking a much deeper recession later. Meanwhile, Warren Buffett in the Berkshire 2002 Shareholder Letter stated that "Charlie and I are of one mind in how we feel about derivatives and the trading activities that go with them. We view them as time bombs, both for the parties that deal in them and the economic system." (https://www.berkshire hathaway.com/letters/2002pdf.pdf). Furthermore, the former IMF chief economist Raghu Rajan, was warning that the economy was close to a crash.

The RP suggested that the economic collapse would initially kick off in China, and then rapidly escalate and progress to the US and Europe causing a global economic crash. His reasoning for suggesting that the crash would originate in China rather than the Western world, was that he had spent much time travelling around China, and had witnessed banks drowning in bad loans, ghost towns of empty shopping malls, and abandoned real estate projects. The economy he suggested, was struggling with a massive over-investment in redundant real estate projects, mounting unmanageable debt, the growing dominance of inefficient state enterprises and chronic underconsumption. Although none of this was being reported in the regular press, he suggested that anyone who spent time in China could not miss seeing this.

The second RP meanwhile, agreed that while 'industry structure' was undoubtedly an important driver, a far more critical driver for the client's business in the future was the issue of environmental sustainability. He was surprised that given the increasing media coverage of environmental issues, none of the initial scenarios mentioned the environment. He suggested that increasing reports by the IPCC (Intergovernmental Panel on Climate Change) reiterated the fact that the world was at a crucial point in terms of global warming. This along with the publication in 1972 of the book *The Limits to Growth: A Report for the Club of Rome's Project on the Predica-*

ment of Mankind (Meadows et al) and its 30-year update, sparked an intense debate around the fact that humans were using the world's resources faster than they could be restored, and releasing wastes and pollutants faster than the Earth could absorb them. All of this was leading the world toward global environmental and economic collapse. The consequence the RP suggested, was that it was inevitable that as more governments began to see the catastrophic effects of global warming, the devastation of natural resources and pollution in their own countries, there would be a 'green awakening.' This could ultimately lead to a halt of all investments in fossil fuel exploration and extraction to mitigate the effects of climate change, along with dramatic legislation on pollutants.

Both these insights from RPs resulted in lengthy discussions in the scenario core team and the decision was eventually made to retain the one driver, the pace of the global economic integration, but with some tweaking. As the world progressed along 'The Highway to the Future' a junction would inevitably be reached, at which point the world could veer off into one of several directions:

– 'One World – their World': a scenario representing a large, fiercely competitive global market dominated by 'super-majors' controlled by the Chinese, who increasingly held the world in their hands.
– 'World of Bubbles,' a scenario in which the World Trade Organisation (WTO) would fundamentally fail as a global international organisation dealing with the rules of trade between nations, resulting in fragmentation into regional trade blocs. Meanwhile, following the Beijing Olympics, the rapidly mushrooming Chinese debt would lead to an economic collapse in China which would then quickly become a global recession. It was reasoned that the collapse in China could not happen before the Beijing Olympics as the Chinese government had successfully hosted two previous Olympics and would not allow anything to damage its reputation of the management of the Olympics.

Having adjusted the one axis, it was decided to replace the second technology advancement axis with the 'Environmental Sustainability' axis. However, rather than two polar extremes of this axis, there would be only one polar extreme named the 'Green Awakening.' The reason for one polar extreme rather than two was that the one polar extreme was to be a so-called 'TINA' (there is no alternative) scenario, i.e. following a revised Kyoto agreement, there would be no alternative, environmental sustainability and clean energy would come to dominate the world in the years ahead. The result of these changes was there were three rather than the usual four scenarios as illustrated in Figure 5.1.

The scenario diagram developed to depict the scenarios was termed the 'Highway to the future' which showed the highway unescapably leading to a more environmentally sustainable and clean world in the future. However, on the way to this future there were two branching points, either a global recession originating in China

Green Awakening

Environmental sustainability and clean energy focus dominates following revised Kyoto agreement; OPEC & OGEC de-coupling of oil and gas.

One World – Their World

One huge global market with blurred industry boundaries & 'super-majors' dominate in all areas – intensely competitive environment.

?

Highway to the future?

World of Bubbles

WTO fails and regional trade blocs (NAFTA, Mercusor, EU, ASEAN, OAFTS) consolidate. Economic collapse in China following Beijing Olympics leads to global recession.

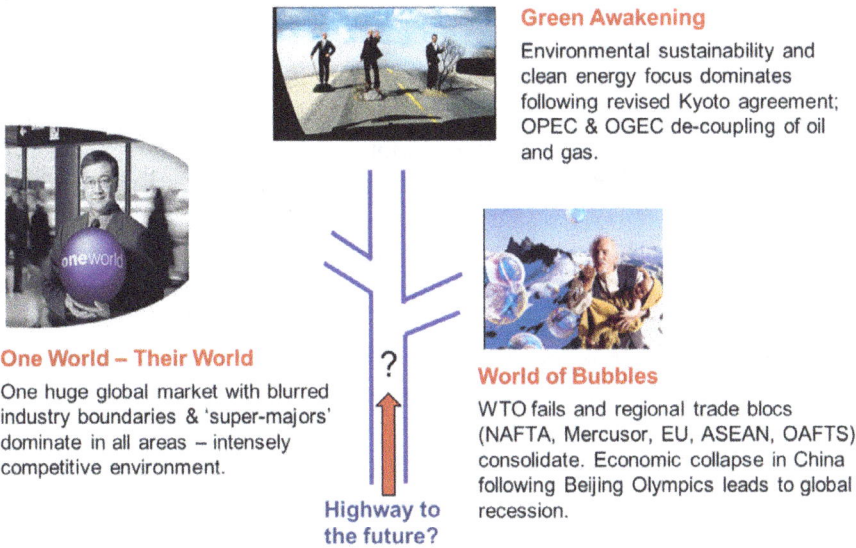

Figure 5.1: Example of a Three Scenario Framework.

(World of Bubbles), or a large global market dominated by 'super-majors' (One World -Their World) controlled by the Chinese.

Although the World of Bubbles scenario erroneously had the global recession starting in China in 2009, it had correctly foreseen a global economic downturn that ultimately devastated world financial markets, banking, and real estate industries. How did the scenario team foresee this when most of the rest of the world had not? This example is similar to the case of the Shell 'Greening of Russia' scenarios described by Schwartz, which foresaw the political and economic restructuring of Russia, but which few others had foreseen. It is ultimately the combination of deep research and conversations with RPs, which Wack (1985a) suggested eventually leads to the 'aha' moment as you start to see things few others are.

This scenario project spanning a development period of nine months was very well received by the CEO and the senior management team, and the CEO decided to establish a small scenario unit within the company which subsequently went on to undertake scenario projects for different aspects of the company's business.

The Number of Scenarios

There are no rules or empirical evidence which indicate how many scenarios should be developed, and the question of how many scenarios to generate depends to some extent on the objective of the scenario exercise. One scenario is clearly not appropriate as this is essentially a forecast which defeats the essence of scenario planning of providing a range of futures. However, the exception to this are normative scenarios, especially those of a national or public policy nature, which are a special form of scenarios, and it is usually the case that only one scenario is developed. These will be discussed later in this chapter.

Aside from normative scenarios, it is possible to develop an infinite number of scenarios and there are instances in which as many as twelve scenarios have been developed (*Twelve Scenarios for Southern California Edison*, Planning Review Case Study, Volume 20, 3, 1992). However, a large number of scenarios is cognitively difficult to handle for both the scenario development teams and the scenario client audience, thus the question of how many is not trivial. van der Heijden (2004) suggests that more than four scenarios have proven to be counterproductive and organisationally impractical. Nordfors (2007) supports this, stating that although four images of the future are better than one, the utility of scenario analysis quickly diminishes when there are more than four. Kahn and Wiener (1972). addresses this issue by stating that the objective of constructing scenarios is not to produce a range of closely spaced scenarios all with essentially the same worldview, i.e. variations around some midpoint. Rather, the purpose is to produce two or three canonical variations spanning the range of possibilities, with each scenario representing a different world rather than different outcomes in the same world.

Foster (1993) points out that although one should theoretically construct a lot of scenarios, he proposes limiting the number of scenarios to two on the basis that this is a practical number to work with. This accords with the views of Schnaars (1987) who has found two scenarios to be preferable, and Beck (1982) whose experience at Shell was that two scenarios were often the result. Mandel (1982) and Sviden (1986) suggest that the fewer the scenarios the better, as too many are likely to overwhelm the user with information and possibilities. The rationale of limiting the number of scenarios on the grounds of practical considerations is important, as the greater the number of scenarios the more likely they will blend, losing their meaningful distinctiveness and their value as decision tools. von Reibnitz (1987) agrees, observing that although numerous scenarios can be generated, there are usually only two which will optimally meet the criteria for good scenarios. Wilson (1978) however, argues that the problem of developing only two scenarios is the danger that one will be characterized as 'pessimistic' and the other as 'optimistic'. Developing three scenarios is similarly problematic as the scenarios run the risk of being labelled 'pessimistic,' 'optimistic' and the one in the 'middle' to which managers will gravitate, it being the most moderate. Several authors (Mandel, 1982; and Schwartz, 1992) echo this caveat pointing to the fact that businesses that have traditionally used three scenarios tend to focus their attention on the middle scenario, often perceived as the most likely; the remaining two are then disregarded. Surveys of corporate practice by Linneman and Klein (1983) found that, on average, users who constructed three scenarios differentiated between them based on optimistic, most likely, and pessimistic outcomes. The way to overcome this is to ensure that all scenarios developed are distinctively themed to portray all of them as being equally likely, a task easier said than done.

Wack (1985b) was adamant that the appropriate number of scenarios is 'one plus two', i.e. a surprise-free 'business-as-usual scenario', and two other scenarios portraying very different world views. The notion of a surprise-free scenario originates with Kahn and Wiener (1967) who defined it as a naive projection of the environment, which assumes a continuation of current trends and expectations. van der Heijden (1996) also advocates the use of the surprise-free scenario, as this anchors the set of scenarios in the belief systems of the decision-makers. However, while Wack's use of three scenarios was initially the standard in Shell, from 1989 onwards two scenarios have since become the norm (Wilkinson and Kupers, 2013). Although it is clear there is no consensus in the literature as to what the right number of scenarios is, my personal experience is that the appropriate number is three or four, with the actual number emerging out of the process rather than being imposed at the outset.

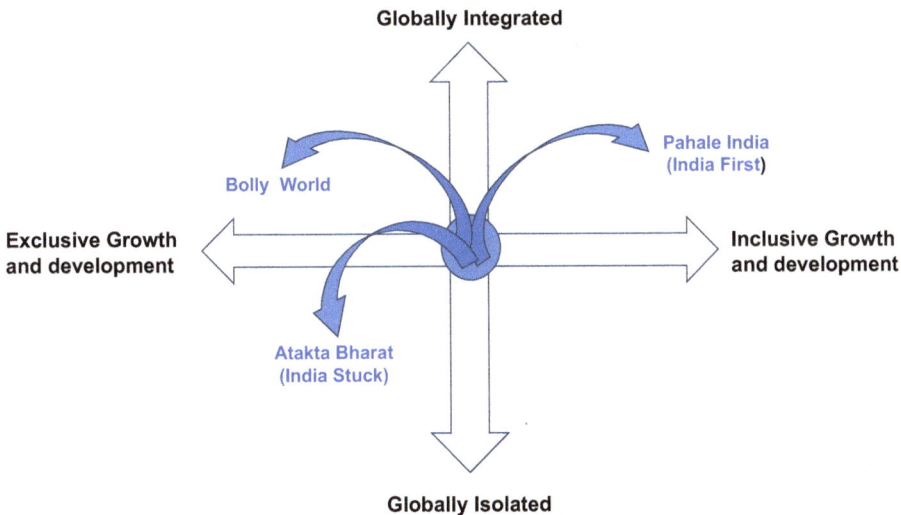

Figure 5.2: India and the World 2025.

Developing three rather than four scenarios is not unusual. The World Economic Forum (WEF), for example, use the conventional two-axis driver approach to portray scenarios, but in many cases, only three of the four are developed. An example of this is the scenarios for *India and the World 2025* published in 2005 and shown in Figure 5.2 exploring how India will take her place at the world table, and how the world will accommodate her emergence as a global player over the next 25 years. The scenarios were built on conventional two axis drivers, although only three scenarios were ultimately developed. There was no scenario for the quadrant representing 'Isolated from the World' and 'Inclusive Growth and Development,' presumably because a

scenario representing global isolation coupled with inclusive growth and development, was hardly plausible.

Scenario Diagrams

Aside from the use of images in the storylines, it is essential in scenario reports to
include a diagram or graphic of some sort to provide the reader with a visual representation of how the scenarios are linked. This then allows the reader to understand
the scenario space before reading the scenarios. This is not a problem when using a
two-by-two matrix depicting four scenarios with two critical drivers, but it is more
problematic graphically presenting the scenario space with three or more drivers.

Although not common, scenarios have been developed with more than two or
three critical uncertainties, an example of which is the UK's National Ecosystem Assessment with five critical uncertainties (environmental awareness; human well-being; governance and intervention; overseas ecological footprint; and adaptation capacity.) In
this situation, a smart graphic is required such as the use of a Venn diagram by the
Singapore Government in 1988 shown in Figure 5.3, which cleverly explains how three
drivers, Trade, Technology and Tribe, are interconnected to create three scenarios
where the drivers intersect,

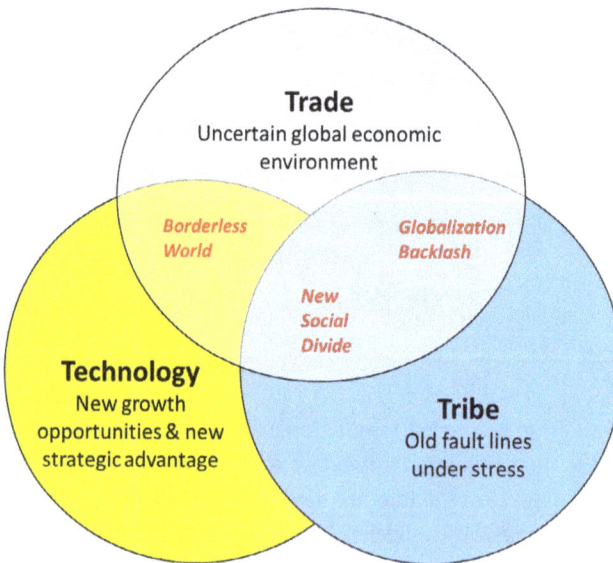

Figure 5.3: Scenario Diagram with Three Drivers.

Another example of an interesting diagram connecting three crucial uncertainties (political, economic, and social), is from the well-known South African Mont Fleur political scenarios, developed in 1991–1992 and named after the Mont Fleur centre in South Africa where the scenario workshops took place. At the beginning of the scenario process, Nelson Mandela had recently been released from prison and negotiations to end apartheid had begun; South Africa, however, was dealing with economic decline, social disintegration, and political unrest. A diverse scenario team of South Africans drawn from across the social and political spectrum of the country was provided with a remit to use the Shell scenario methodology to work together to achieve a successful transition to democracy, and what would be needed to create a better future for the country. Adam Kahane, who at the time worked for Shell, facilitated the workshops which asked the question: How will the South African transition go, and will the country succeed in taking off? Four 'transformative' scenarios shown in Figure 5.4 were developed by the scenario team, which provided a provocative road map for this transition.

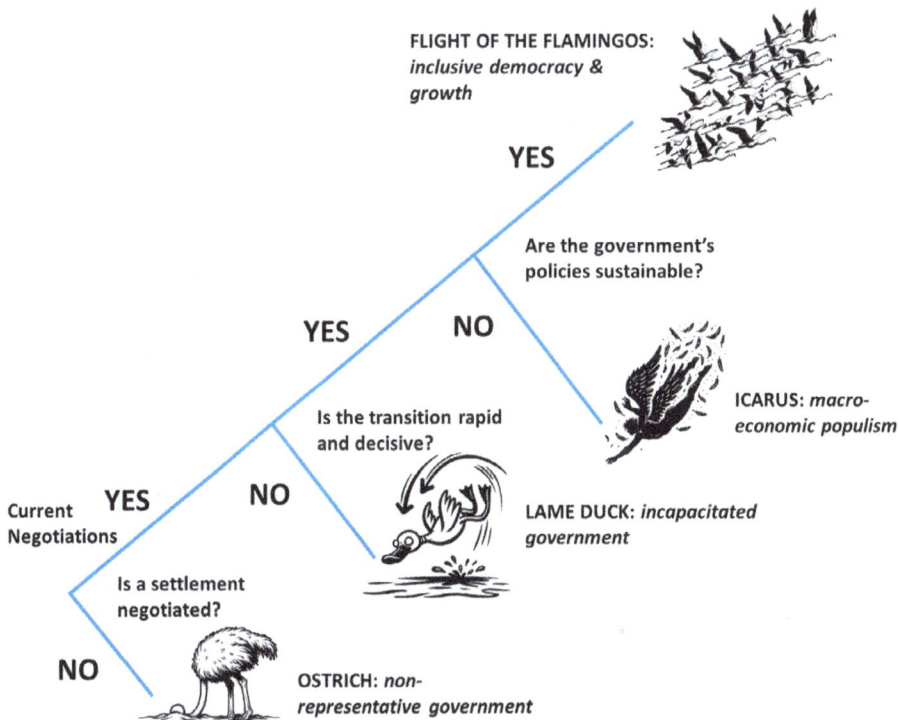

FLIGHT OF THE FLAMINGOS: *inclusive democracy & growth*

YES

Are the government's policies sustainable?

YES   **NO**

ICARUS: *macro-economic populism*

Is the transition rapid and decisive?

Current Negotiations   **YES**   **NO**

LAME DUCK: *incapacitated government*

Is a settlement negotiated?

NO

OSTRICH: *non-representative government*

Figure 5.4: The Mont Fleur Scenarios: South Reos Partners, November 2005.

The scenarios described three dark prophecies of the future to avoid, *Ostrich, Lame Duck,* and *Icarus,* and one bright vision of a future to work towards, *Flight of the Flamingos.*

- **Ostrich** represents a future in which a negotiated settlement is not achieved, and the government continues to be non-representative. The central message of this scenario was that a non-negotiated resolution to the crisis would not be sustainable.
- **Lame Duck** portrays a future in which a settlement is negotiated, but the transition to a new government is slow and indecisive. The message of this scenario was that a weak coalition government would not be able to deliver, and therefore could not last.
- **Icarus** is a future in which the transition to a new government is rapid, but the new government pursues populist, unsustainable economic policies. Thus, the scenario is a warning of the dangers of a new government taking this approach.
- **Flight of the Flamingo** is the ideal scenario in which the country takes a new and inclusive path as the government's policies are appropriate, and the transition to democracy is successful because all the key building blocks are put in place with everyone in society rising slowly and in unison.

The conundrum in this set of scenarios is that the *Flight of the Flamingos* scenario cannot take off without significant social reconstruction; however, there is the danger that attempts to deliver far more than the economy can sustain will inevitably lead to the Icarus scenario.

The scenarios were widely disseminated: published in two national newspapers, *The Weekly Mail* and *The Guardian Weekly* in July 1992; a 30-minute video was produced; and the scenario team made over 50 presentations to wide-ranging groups. All of this reportedly helped shift the economic thinking and action of the ruling African National Council to avert an economic disaster (Le Roux and Maphai, 1992). In January 2010, eighteen years after the release of the Mont Fleur scenarios, Clem Sunter (2010), an experienced corporate scenario planning practitioner, observed how well South Africa had navigated not only its transition to democracy but also in avoiding the global recession.

In addition to graphically illustrating the linkages between the scenarios, the scenario diagrams can serve other useful purposes as evident in Figure 5.5, relating to a scenario project I was involved with in 2006 on the future of Indian agriculture.

The scenarios developed on a standard two-by-two matrix focusing on two significant issues: the degree of cohesion in Indian society and the state of India's collective businesses. The vertical driver, the Social Fabric of the countryside had at one end strong, well-organised, cohesive and problem sharing rural villagers, while at the other end, the social fabric was weak, fragmented, and individualistic, resulting in the marginalization of the poor. The two polar extremes of the horizontal driver, the Economy, was government-controlled and centrally led at one end, while strongly

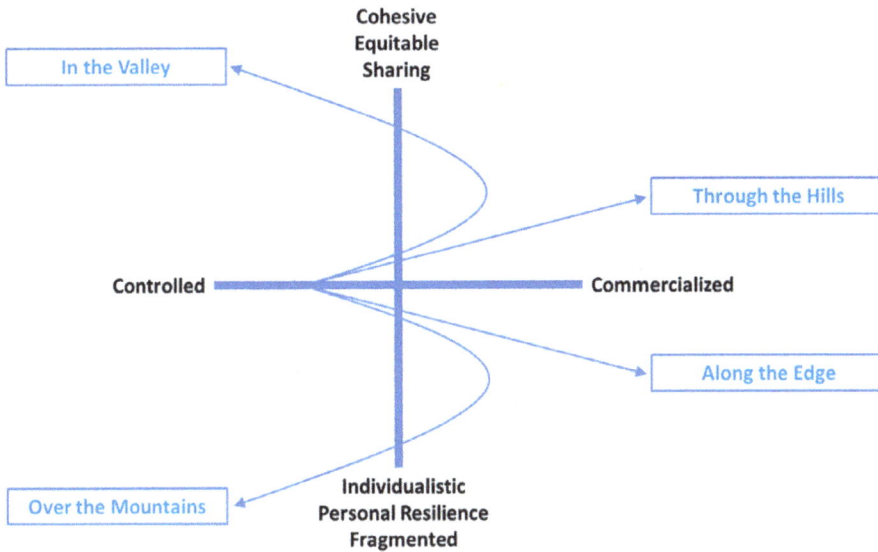

Figure 5.5: The Future of Indian Agriculture.

commercialised and market-based at the other end. Four storylines were developed. *In the Valley* was a scenario in which there is an acceptance of a significant degree of governmental control to achieve cohesion and equity in the economy. In the second, *Through the Hills*, concerns for cohesion and equity are also strong but are balanced by the desire to create incentives for productivity improvement through market forces, and a powerful base for a successful market economy was created. The third, *Along the Edge*, is a scenario in which economic development is the primary objective with significant inequity allowed to exist as a powerful incentive to increase productivity. The fourth, *Over the Mountains*, describes a society experiencing serious problems to such an extent that people call for a return to strong governmental control.

The scenario diagram developed in this case is particularly useful from several perspectives. Firstly, it reinforces the fact that all scenarios start at the same point. Secondly, the diagram shows exactly where the starting point of the scenarios is in terms of the matrix's two drivers, which in this case was midway between the Cohesive Equitable Sharing and Individualistic Personal Resilience Fragmented Social Fabric driver, and in the Controlled segment of the Economy driver, but edging towards the Commercialised segment. Thirdly, it demonstrates that not all scenarios move out in straight lines; in this case, all four scenarios start from a historically controlled economy and move towards more market liberalization. While the trend continues in two scenarios, *Through the Hills* and *Along the Edge*, in the *Over the Mountains* and *In the Valley* scenarios, the trend is reversed, and the scenarios turn around and head back to the Controlled Economy segment. Images such as this demonstrate the power of graphics regarding the information they can convey. These graphics also serve to stimulate interesting debates and raise questions such as why the turnaround, and what must have happened to have caused the change in direction, even before the stories are presented.

Scenario Plots and Narratives

There is no one right way, but rather there are many ways to develop scenario stories and timelines. It is usually an iterative process progressively building the pathway to the endpoint, with different facilitators favouring the use of one or another of the various approaches to the development of the scenarios. At the same time, there are different forms of scenarios and, depending on their use, the scenarios focus on different issues and possess different formats. Common formats of scenarios range from:
–   descriptive scenarios describing realistic situation developments.
–   complex scenarios comprising intricate webs of causally related events and processes.
–   simple scenarios limited in scope and focusing on a particular niche.
–   chain scenarios describing, in brief, the chain of events leading to the end-state.
–   snapshot scenarios depicting the end-state but only implicitly addressing how it was arrived at.

There are also global scenarios describing large-scale events and developments in countries, regions, and the world in general. They aim to achieve awareness and understanding of potential future developments, stimulating preparation for accepting and dealing with uncertainty, and they are used to inform high-level strategic thinking and planning. The alternative is focused scenarios which often take global scenarios as the starting point, and focus on specific developments within countries, regions, markets or targeted issues. Their objective is to provide decision-makers with a set of scenarios as a framework for evaluating strategic policy options. Finally, there are normative scenarios, a special form of scenarios akin to vision statements which depict a utopian scenario, an ideal future state, intending to provide a guiding vision to achieve this perfect future state.

While the interplay between critical uncertainties ultimately shapes the logic distinguishing and driving the scenarios, other significant factors identified during the research phase are used to compose or flesh out the scenario plots. When the logic of the different worlds has been determined, the scenario team must then weave the pieces together to form a narrative with a beginning, middle, and end as illustrated in Figure 5.6 below. As mentioned earlier, the starting point for each scenario in a set should be the same and although it is usually the present, it can be useful at times to have scenarios with a starting point in the recent past. For example, in developing scenarios in 2022 around the COVID-19 pandemic, the starting point of the scenario could be 2019 when the pandemic started, providing some history of its rise.

The key drivers of change are the macro-trends which form the foundation for the scenario plots. Driving forces can be roughly categorized along four lines: (1) social dynamics such as major demographic trends; (2) economics such as international trade flows; (3) politics including electoral, legislative, and regulatory possibilities; and finally (4) technology such as the impact of wireless communication advances and artificial intelligence. In addition to these, Schwartz (1991) suggests a fifth driving force, the environment. Regardless of the driving forces eventually chosen to serve as the basis for the scenario plots, these driving forces must meet two prerequisites. First, they must be important and critical to the decision(s) to be made. Second, they must be uncertain; in other words, the reactions of the driving force cannot be predetermined with any accuracy.

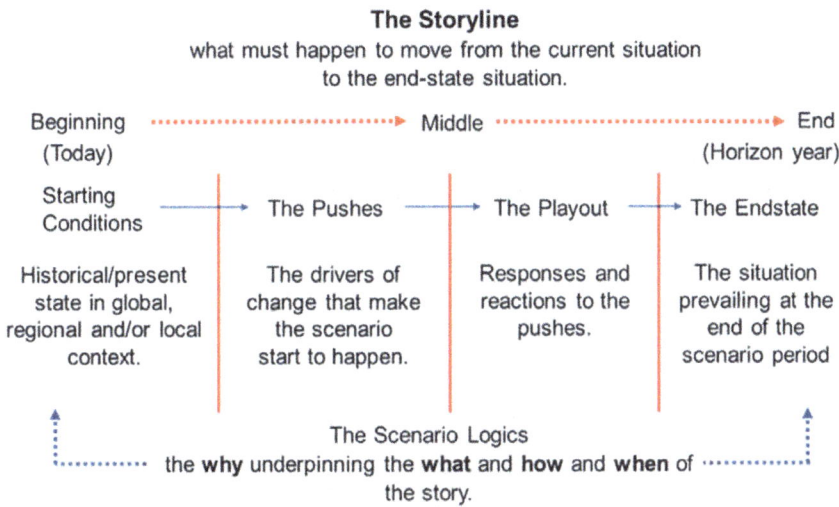

The Storyline
what must happen to move from the current situation
to the end-state situation.

Beginning (Today)	······▶ Middle ······▶	End (Horizon year)

Starting Conditions	The Pushes	The Playout	The Endstate
Historical/present state in global, regional and/or local context.	The drivers of change that make the scenario start to happen.	Responses and reactions to the pushes.	The situation prevailing at the end of the scenario period

The Scenario Logics
the **why** underpinning the **what** and **how** and **when** of
the story.

Figure 5.6: Creating the Scenario Storyline.

Although a plot and a storyline might seem to be synonymous, they are in fact two different things. Every story needs a plot, the function of which is to structure the occurrences which are driven by conflicts and resolutions that keep the narrative moving forward, and which answer the basic question: why does this event happen? The plot needs to be built around logic, meaning that when something happens there is a consequence, and it also needs to be structured correctly so that it explains the chain of events in a story, demonstrates the causal relationship between each event, and logically connects the actions and events. A storyline, on the other hand, is the timeline, the sequence of events in the narrative and the who, what, when and where of a story. Regardless of the scenario format, it is essential to explain how the world gets from the starting point to the end state proposed by each of the scenarios, and the necessary events and their sequence are required to explain how and why the story develops to the endpoint of each scenario.

Storytelling

While narratives are important to capture issues of timing and path dependency, as well as adding depth and dimensions that other ways of depicting complex data cannot capture, the question arises, why write stories? To answer this requires understanding that one of the biggest challenges for scenario practitioners is to engage management teams fully and creatively, which is difficult when trying to get top management to consider radically different business conditions that may occur in the future. One way to do this is using stories because they can communicate complex ideas simply and memorably. Additionally, stories are an effective medium for communicating knowledge, speaking to both parts of the human mind – reason and emotion – and can spark changes in resistant individuals and organizations.

Denning (2005) claims that stories are in fact the only way individuals can make sense of a rapidly changing global economy with multiple gruelling transitions happening simultaneously. Stories, he suggests, are one of the most powerful tools you can use to engage and connect with your audience. The power of stories goes far beyond simply relaying facts and data; stories give colour and depth to otherwise bland material and allow people to connect with the message in a deeper, more meaningful and memorable way.

Humans by nature are storytelling animals (Polkinghorne, 1988; Barry, 1997), and storytelling is the most powerful form of human communication. Narratives and stories have been used for thousands of years as the primary method to hand down learning and knowledge, and according to MacIntyre (1981), it is the power of stories that allows us to interpret and make sense of the world. Suzuki et al. (2018, page 9468) support the idea of the communicative power of stories because they have the ability "to illuminate fault lines, highlight oddities, and paint a picture of the past, present and future that is both compelling and easily understandable" and they are "the focus of a growing body of cognitive neuroscientific exploration." Schwartz (1992) meanwhile, suggests that stories give order and meaning to events, a crucial aspect of understanding future possibilities, and that they are fundamental to the human process of making sense of the world.

Researchers have found that storytelling is far more convincing to an audience than rational arguments, statistics, or facts. For example, in her book *Corporate Legends and Lore: The Power of Storytelling as a Management Tool* (1993), Peg Neuhauser outlines the results of a study with MBA students. This study demonstrated that learning stemming from a well-told story is recalled with greater accuracy than simply learning from facts and figures; and facts are 20 times more likely to be recalled if they are part of a story. A story makes a topic much more real to the audience because it reframes the argument in an easy-to-grasp format anyone can relate to. Consequently, when necessary to influence people, a story is always more effective than a rational, linear argument.

The difficulty in developing storylines is that while stories of the past and the present can be based on fact, "stories of the future are based on intuition, crafted as analytical structures" ('Scenarios: An Explorer' Guide' page 9). Although the stories are not intended to be entertaining works of fiction, they must make potential futures seem vivid, compelling, and believable, and this is achieved through "charismatic performers, evocative graphics, the use of memorable phrases, images, and archetypes" (Wilkinson and Kupers, 2014, p 96). When a story catches attention and engages individuals, they are more likely to absorb the message and meaning within it than if the same message was presented simply in facts and figures.

What distinguishes stories from documents, forecasts, reports, speculation, and statistics, is that stories which are emotive and entertaining, have a psychological impact that graphs, diagrams and numbers lack. Thus, they are an effective way to transmit valuable information and values from one individual or community to the next, opening people up to multiple perspectives to explain why things could happen in certain ways and give meaning to events. They are also easy to remember, with research confirming that well-designed stories are the most effective vehicle for exerting an influence (Haven, 2007). For an example of attention-grabbing storytelling, see Box 5.1. This example comes from a scenario planning project I facilitated which was undertaken over several months for a well-established Scandinavian MNC operating in a wide range of countries. The core scenario development team in the project comprised a group of seven middle-level managers in the organisation.

Box 5.1: Example of a Scenario Presentation to Senior Management
The scenario team's presentation to the senior management of the scenarios developed was organised in the amphitheatre of a hotel. The company's senior management team were seated in the front row of the theatre. On the theatre stage were three individuals from the scenario team seated at a table in a coffee shop in the city having a coffee, and reminiscing about their experiences of having lived and worked in the city many years previously.

One of the seated individuals wore a sheet arranged around himself and a large handkerchief wrapped around his head (representing a kandura and a kufiyah as he was supposedly an Arab). He began the presentation by saying: "It is so good to be back here again after 20 years, things have changed so much since I was here last, I remember when . . ." and he proceeded to tell a story of how things had evolved over the past 20 years to reach the current state. A second gentleman, dressed in casual clothes with a baseball cap and dark glasses (representing an American) said: "Ahmed, a very interesting story but you have got your facts wrong, here is what happened" and he proceeded to tell a very different story of how the present state had come about over the 20 years. The third individual, dressed in a long-sleeved white shirt and sheet wrapped around his lower half representing a traditional Indian lungi, said "Gentlemen, the problem is that you have presented an Arabic and American representation of what happened, and I am afraid you are both wrong, here is what actually happened" and he then proceeded to tell a third, very different story from the other two stories.

At the end of the presentations, the CEO said "Gentlemen, I have very much enjoyed listening to your stories. You have provided me with three very different but believable scenarios, all with some exceptional insights about the future that neither I nor my team seems to have thought about." He then directed his secretary to arrange a meeting with the management team to discuss the scenario report prepared by the scenario team.

As demonstrated in Box 5.1 the format of scenario storylines can take many different formats, from plain narratives to news reports, to film scripts, radio and TV interviews and to friends reminiscing how their lives have played out.

Box 5.2 is another example of highly effective storytelling to illustrate a set of scenarios but with a quite different outcome from that described in Box 5.1. This illustrates the point that even if well-researched, written and engagingly presented, not all scenarios are seen as easily understandable or acceptable, persuasive and compelling pictures of the future. The scenario team in this project were government department employees of various levels, who took several workshops to develop a set of scenarios.

A standard two-by-two matrix emerged from the process, the two drivers being the state of the domestic economy and regional political stability, resulting in four scenarios: *good politics/good economy*; *good economy/poor politics*; *good politics/poor economy*; and *poor politics/poor economy*. The scenario team constructed engaging storylines for three of the scenarios but had reservations regarding developing and presenting to senior government officials, a 'bad/bad' (poor politics/poor economy) scenario, as it would likely not be well received. However, the team eventually decided to go ahead with it since anyone who looked out of the window could see that this scenario was already well in motion, and the government needed to listen to the scenario as a wake-up call. Accordingly As, they went on to develop a captivating storyline which was superbly delivered by one of the team members. evident from Box 5.2, the reaction of the audience of government officials was as expected; however, the reaction of the audience of invited business leaders was very different and congratulatory.

Box 5.2: Example of Scenario Presentation rejected by Senior Management.
The scenario client in S.E. Asia was a government entity and the scenario team's presentation of four scenarios was to an audience of senior government officials and several invited senior business leaders. The scenarios were developed by the team on a two-by-two matrix, one axis being regional political stability and the second being the state of the domestic economy. The scenarios were presented as four stories, each presented by one individual. Each scenario story began with the same situation and then progressed to describe how and why life changed in four quite diverse ways. The first two scenarios (good politics/ good economy) and (good politics/poor economy) were well received with the audience smiling; the third scenario (good economy/poor politics) was met with silence from the audience.

The fourth scenario (poor politics/poor economy) story was told as a man sitting on the porch of his apartment. His wife came up to him and said "Mo, the Bank Manager has just called and said that you promised to meet him this week but have not done so." Mohammed responded, "yes dear I will meet him tomorrow, I have been busy." The wife said "okay, I am off to the mall, see you this evening" and she left. Mohammed started to think about his situation. He knew that the Bank manager wanted to see him because he was in arrears on both his mortgage and his car loan. He had just a few dollars left in his account and did not have money for living expenses, let alone make any further mortgage or loan payments. What had gone wrong?

Four years earlier Mohammed had bought the apartment and a new car. Then a year later he lost his job when the company he had been with for 10 years went into liquidation. Initially, it was not a problem as he had three brothers and they were able to help him financially while he looked for a job. Then 3 months later two of his brothers lost their jobs when their employers declared bankruptcy, and they could no longer help Mohammed who still had not found a job. He was however, not alone, the economy had collapsed plummeting the country into recession, and relationships with the neighbouring country had deteriorated with company after company closing; there were no jobs to be had.

At the conclusion of this fourth scenario presentation, one of the senior government officials stood up and said "We have invested a lot of time and money in this exercise, and you come up with ridiculous stories about the country's economy collapsing and relations with our neighbours coming apart . . ." At that point, one of the prominent invited business leaders, a CEO of a large MNC stood up and said "I do not agree with you sir, the scenario about the country's economy going into a recession and relations with our neighbours deteriorating, is not a fictitious story about the future, it is already happening. You may not want to see it, but I and many of my colleagues in business can see it already happening every day." There was clapping from the non-governmental individuals in the audience, and the presentation concluded. The government officials left the room, while the CEO and several others came to congratulate the team and asked for a copy of the scenarios.

An interesting conclusion to this scenario project was that some nine months after concluding the project, a senior government official contacted me and asked if I would come back to the country and work with the scenario team on updating the initial scenarios. In subsequent discussions with several senior government officials, it transpired that the fourth scenario (poor politics/poor economy) was not something the government officials who had arranged the scenario project expected (or wanted) to hear. However, the storyline told by a local individual was simple, well told and very believable as most of the audience knew of someone, or had heard of someone, who was experiencing a comparable situation to that facing Mohammed.

Gabriel (2000, p 18) summarises stories as highly charged narratives, "not merely recounting events, but interpreting them, enriching them, enhancing them, and infusing them with meaning". In discussing the role of scenario storytelling Wilkinson and Kupers (2014, p 96) state that the power of scenarios is that the stories "provoke rather than suppress conversation and, in turn, enable the new common ground to be forged in a process of sequential consensus building". They add that scenarios, "as unthreatening stories of the future, have enabled Shell executives to grasp futures that appear inconceivable or imperceptible and to keep their minds open to see more than they would have expected or hoped for."

One of the crucial elements required for the success of this type of political scenario project is proper timing: are public leaders ready to talk together about the future? Are they willing to talk about a potentially negative scenario? The answer as presumably other scenario planners have experienced, is that people do not generally want to believe a future story that involves significant disruption or adversarial, confrontational events. However, my experience is that those organisations who have experienced some external shock or major surprise, which is why they decided to engage in a scenario project, are usually more accepting of negative, disruptive scenarios. This should not come as much of a surprise, those who have experienced a major disruption or surprise are usually more aware of and open to considering change. However, the challenge is usually in developing this mindset before a potentially business-ending disruption occurs.

There are essentially five characteristics that make scenario conversations so powerful:
- The scenario process is logical and constructive.
- The process is open and informal, inclusive, and holistic, allowing people to openly discuss anything and encouraging people to surface and listen to multiple perspectives and to see more of the world.
- The message of the stories must be perceived as true in the minds of the listeners.
- A fundamental premise of scenario planning is that the future is not predetermined and cannot be predicted. Consequently, the choices we make can influence what happens.
- Scenarios help shift the attention away from the past and present to the future, and from looking for solutions to exploring different possibilities.

Deductive Versus Inductive Story Development

There are essentially two ways to develop scenario stories, deductively or inductively. As illustrated in Figure 5.7, in developing storylines deductively, the starting point is history and current events which are then extrapolated forward into the future through to a range of plausible end states, via a combination of forward inferences and causality.

The inductive approach on the other hand, as shown in Figure 5.8, starts with range of plausible end states and then works backwards and uses diagnostic reasoning to determine what must have happened to get to the plausible end state.

Generally, the method most used to develop scenarios is the deductive approach, sometimes referred to as a 'top down' approach. This is because it is easier to look at the top, the things that are happening around us, trying to understand and make sense of what is happening, and using forward inferences and causality to work downwards to construe how things might evolve in diverse ways as the future unfolds. An inductive approach, however, commonly referred to as 'bottom-up' is a more difficult story development process as it starts with developing plausible end states and then working backwards using backward inferences and diagnostic reasoning to get to the present state. This approach is commonly used in developing normative scenarios.

How might the forces play out to get us
from here to a range of futures?

Scenario
1

Scenario
development
starting point

History and
current events

Forward
inferences and
Causality

Scenario
2

Range of
plausible
futures

Scenario
3

Time

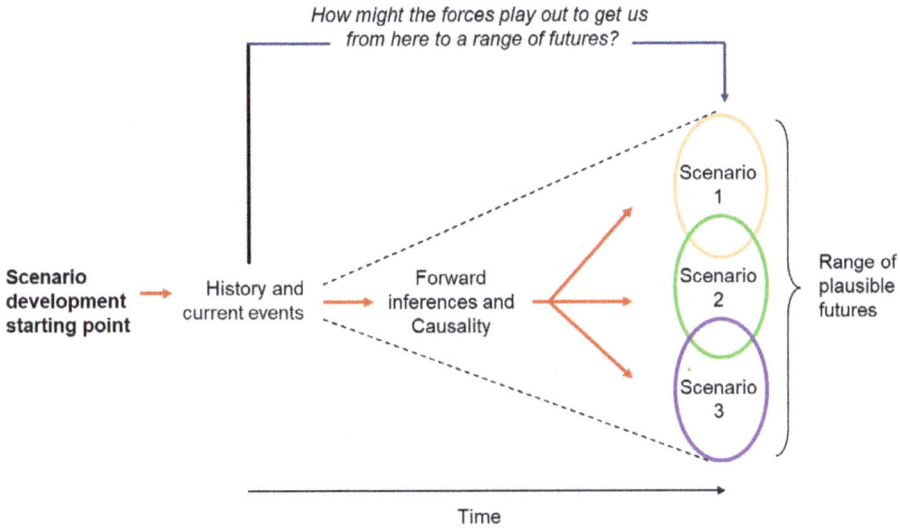

Figure 5.7: Deductive Story Development.

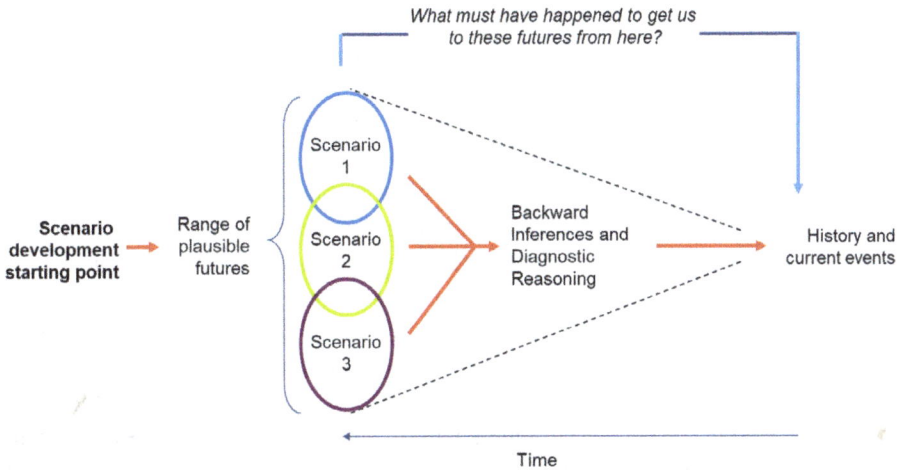

What must have happened to get us
to these futures from here?

Scenario
1

Scenario
development
starting point

Range of
plausible
futures

Scenario
2

Backward
Inferences and
Diagnostic
Reasoning

History and
current events

Scenario
3

Time

Figure 5.8: Inductive Story Development.

Jungermann (1985a, 1985b) has demonstrated that exploratory or deductive scenario developmental models that rely on forward inferences and causality result in quite different scenarios than those generated by anticipatory or inductive developmental models relying on backward inferences and diagnostic effectuality. There is empirical evidence that people make causal inferences with a greater degree of confidence than they do making diagnostic inferences, even when they are aware that the relationship between variables in the data is accidental rather than causal. Furthermore, when presented with data that have both causal and diagnostic elements, people generally accord more weight to causal data in probability judgements than to diagnostic data, even where the cause and effect provide the same information about each other.

Backward inferences or diagnostic reasoning requires 'uphill thinking' as they are at odds with the temporal order, and causal knowledge cannot be easily transferred in backward reasoning. Therefore, constructing scenarios using this approach is more difficult. However, causal thinking is also problematic given that there are no universally accepted rules for distinguishing between cause and effect. Thus, individuals distinguish cause from effect by relying on probability-based cues to causality, which include:

- the temporal order of events;
- the degree to which two events occur simultaneously;
- the number of competing variables or explanations;
- the degree to which one variable can predict another; and
- the similarity between events and prior knowledge.

These cues are related to numerous heuristics and biases. As Einhorn and Hogarth (1981) observe, one must guard against the way cues to causality quickly restrict our interpretation of the past by structuring and stabilising our perceptions of reality. In essence, the cues are apt to focus attention on the obvious and known, at the expense of creative thinking.

Regardless of the process used, developing scenario storylines is not an easy task. There is no single definition of what a good story is, and it cannot be developed according to a specific formula. However, an essential component of a good story are characters; every story should feature at least one character who will be the key to relating the audience to the story, serving as the bridge between the storyteller and the audience.

Scholars agree that stories involve a temporal sequencing of events that can be arranged chronologically or thematically, are related by time and have a mutually reinforcing logic that makes them plausible (Scholes,1981). When the storytelling is done well and convincing, some of the facts may disappear over time, but the stories remain embedded in the memory of individuals. Given the importance and difficulty in writing scenario storylines, there are instances of organisations engaging the help of professional writers; for example, Betty Sue Flowers, a professional writer and poet, served as the editor of scenarios for Shell International for several years.

In developing scenario narratives, research indicates that:

- The inclusion of events and incidents in scenarios which are causality linked plausibly, and which explain why something happens, makes it easier for decision-makers to recall available supporting evidence because it is familiar, and results in scenarios which appear more probable.
- Scenarios which are vivid and contain concrete examples, have a greater impact on the audience than scenarios relying on understanding complex causal relationships and abstract data.

- Adding more representative and salient details to a scenario, whether the details are relevant or not, will increase the scenario's representativeness and the perceived likelihood of its occurrence and acceptance; and
- Language used is important. There should be no 'this could,' or 'might' happen language, scenarios should be written as facts. Presenting a scenario as history endows it with a sense of certainty which people find difficult to ignore. The use of the past tense leads to the assumption that events described in the scenario have already taken place.

Each scenario must have a structural framework that underlies the order and way the narrative is presented to the reader. At the same time, each scenario plot or logic should be different, yet relevant to the focal question. What makes stories compelling is when the narrative challenges or changes perceptions of reality in some way, and to be effective, scenario plots must make people rethink their assumptions about the future. Thus, what happens at the scenario end state is not as important as the storyline's clarity and logic, which helps open minds to new possibilities. However, plots that are too frightening or implausible tend to be easily discounted thus weakening the value of the scenario process overall. For example, if developing a scenario in which there is increasing hostile political instability between two countries, rather than the end state being the outbreak of war, it would be better if the scene ends with signs that a war is imminent. This leaves the readers on a cliff-edge as to whether or not there will be a war, which then provides an interesting platform for discussion. Equally important is ignoring the response to change; every system has the capacity for reaction and self-correction, e.g. threats of war result in demands for peace, while high oil prices promote exploration, resulting in discoveries and the lowering of prices (Ogilvy and Schwartz, 1991).

As scenarios are being developed, the following questions should be asked:
- What is predetermined and needs to be included in the scenarios, or is obvious in each scenario, i.e. what parts of the future are already happening?
- What systemic relations are being assumed in the scenarios, and what are the principal events that need to happen?
- Are there other ways of seeing these situations?
- Are there any obvious gaps in the scenario storyline that need to be bridged?
- Do the scenario storylines make the mistake of assuming that one driver alone shapes the future?
- Is there anything that does not ring true in the storylines, any inconsistencies or logic faults? Is further research required?
- What are we not seeing, but should be, that no one else is yet seeing?

Telling that story in some detail is crucially important because in doing so you discover where there is a lack of understanding of the underlying structure of the situation. Once the storylines have been completed, they should then be considered against a range of questions which distinguish good scenarios from bad, namely, do they address the critical issues associated with the focal question, do they stretch current thinking, and are they:

- Plausible i.e. they do not explore 'Star Trek' territory?
- Balanced, allowing both negative and positive aspects to emerge?
- Challenging, engrossing, and convincing and go beyond merely stating the obvious?
- Populated with human stories, making for interesting reading?
- Linked to the present via causal loops and linkages?
- Have short but evocative names, which are themed?
- Compelling and engaging to read?
- Relevant in that they address the client's concerns and contain sufficient hooks into the client's current mental model? To be effective, the scenario must resonate in some way with what managers already know, giving them the ability to re-perceive the world.

Although what happens at the scenario horizon year is significant, more important is that the chronological and causal storyline provides a deep understanding of the underlying system leading to the end state.

A problem with scenario development is that after spending much time engaged in researching and writing the scenarios, one can become immersed in them. Consequently, it is often difficult to look at them dispassionately and see if they meet all the above. One way to ensure this is to give the scenarios to a trusted colleague who was not part of the scenario development team, to read the scenarios and provide feedback.

While storytelling involves building a visual image of the problem through words, using visual representation in different formats (such as videos, animations, newspaper headlines, images, and other evocative graphics) helps to embellish the scenario storyline. This, along with memorable phrases and charismatic presenters, is a powerful method to capture the attention of the audience and ensure the message is remembered.

In developing scenarios and storylines, Ogilvy, and Schwartz (2004, p 14) provide "Ten Tips for Successful Scenarios":

1. Stay focused: The context of the scenarios must be fixated on the focal question.
2. Keep it simple: Simple plots and a short list of characters help the manager understand and use the scenarios, there is however, a balance between plots which are too 'simple' and those that are too 'complex.'
3. Keep it interactive: The scenario plots should represent and consider insights at all levels in the organization, rather than just the powerful people in the organisation.
4. Plan to plan and allow enough time: Ensure sufficient time is allotted to cover the project from start to finish, from discussions with senior management, the interviews, research, workshops, and writing of the scenario project report.
5. Do not settle for a simple high, medium, and low set of scenarios: Each of the scenarios should represent a fundamentally different logic and different assumptions.

6. Avoid probabilities or most likely scenarios: The scenarios should represent quite different futures, all of which should be equally likely.
7. Avoid drafting too many scenarios: Four scenarios are the maximum needed, more than this is cognitively difficult for individuals to absorb and remember.
8. Invent catchy names for the scenarios: Giving scenarios evocative names which convey the changes in the environment, makes the scenario more memorable.
9. Make the decision makers own the scenarios: One of the most powerful contributions to a good scenario process is the direct involvement of key decision-makers; and
10. Budget resources for communicating the scenarios: Effectively communicating the scenarios to the senior management is a crucial element of scenario projects.

Storyline Plot Diagrams

Alongside scenario texts, a useful addition is a story timeline diagram (see Figure 5.9). This is a simple line graph of the story providing a visual representation of events, their interrelationships and their chronological sequences, helping the reader understand the story.

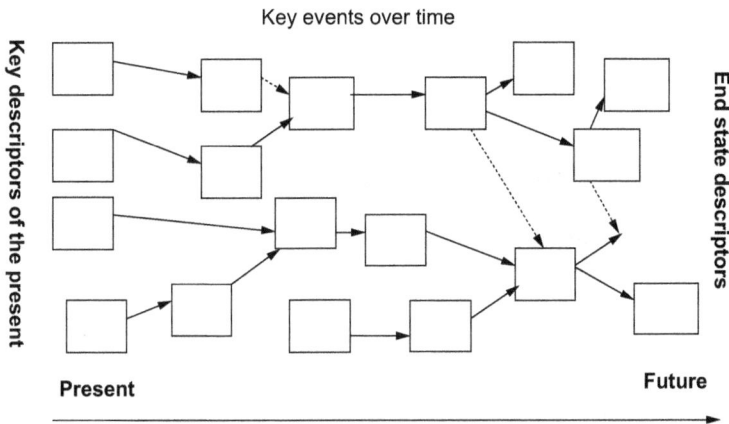

Figure 5.9: Typical Scenario Storyline Plot Graphic.

In developing the diagrams, they must portray the bare bones of a story, beginning with the story's start on the left and continuing toward the right, ending with the story's conclusion. The boxes are the variables with causal relationships depicted as an arrow between them.

The use of diagrams and graphics as aids to facilitate cognitive abilities is well covered in almost all fields ranging from physics and engineering, to design. There is truth to the adage that a picture is worth a thousand words (https://en.wikipedia.org/wiki/A_picture_is_worth_a_thousand_words). By including graphics and diagrams with the written content of the scenarios, you instantly telegraph more than the meaning of words and emphasize key points, as they will transmit an idea or meaning to the brain 90% faster than text (Source:3M). Visuals also refocus readers on the scenario text and keep them engaged in your story. It is, however, critical that the diagrams and graphics used are not so complicated that they are very difficult to follow and understand; if they are, they will be of limited value to the audience.

An example of a detailed and superbly illustrated timeline graphic of the mortgage crisis developed by Business Infographics is depicted in Figure 5.10. However aside from the fact that the diagram timeline covers a period of one hundred years, it is too complicated and not particularly easy to read or follow.

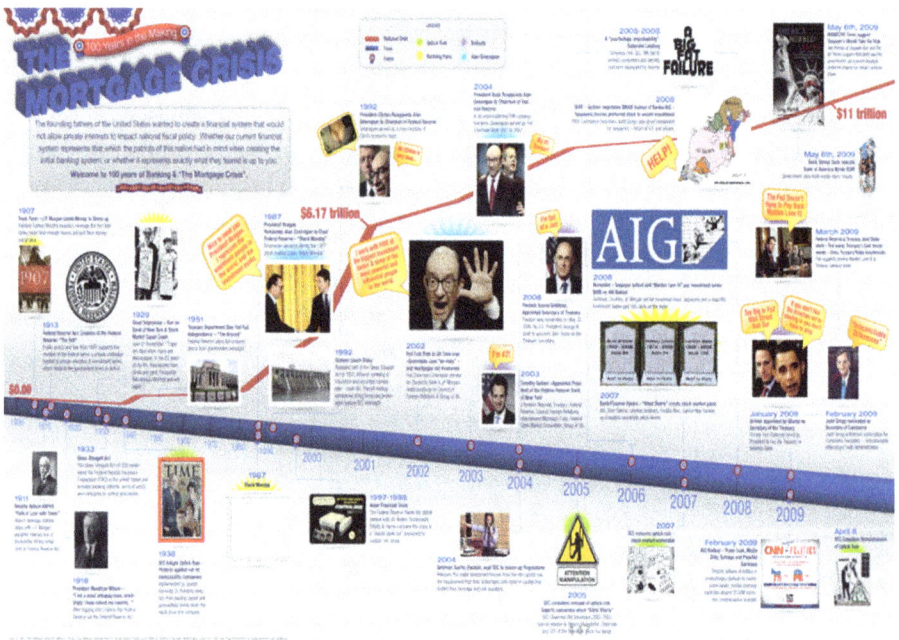

Figure 5.10: The Mortgage Crisis (Business Infographics – Pinterest).

Normative Scenarios

The scenario process discussed so far revolves around the development of descriptive or explorative scenarios. However, a different form of scenario known as 'normative scenarios' was described earlier in this chapter, which concerns a prespecified future, presenting a picture of the world achievable (or avoidable) only through certain actions. These scenarios are generally the preserve of governments and public organisations, and focus on developing desirable and preferable scenarios. These scenarios contrast with conventional explorative scenarios as they start with a prescriptive vision of the future, and then work backwards, to identify the drivers, values and conditions necessary to achieve the desired targets. Often included in developing normative scenarios is the Backcasting process (described in Chapter 2) which is particularly useful in situations where planning and actions are strongly intertwined with development planning to improve the well-being of inhabitants in particular areas (Bizikova et al., 2015).

Normative scenarios are less of an objective planning document than they are a goal statement. One of the first published examples of this was 'Wawasan 2020' or Vision 2020 developed in 1991 under the Prime Minister of Malaysia, Mahathir Mohamad, during the tabling of the Sixth Malaysia Plan. There have since been numerous country-focused normative scenario projects with 2030 as the traditional horizon year, examples of which include Abu Dhabi Economic Vision 2030, Vision 2030 Jamaica, Kenya Vision 2030, Somaliland National Vision 2030, and Vision 2030 Kingdom of Saudi Arabia.

Conclusions

Scenario thinking is not about predicting the future, producing the 'magic' answer to problems and issues, or making judgments as to what is good, bad, right, or wrong. Rather, scenario thinking facilitates creative thinking in the contexts of change, complexity, and uncertainty because of four fundamental principles:

- The long view: Scenario planning requires looking beyond immediate concerns and urgent near-term issues, and peering far enough into the future to see new possibilities, asking 'What if?'
- Outside-in thinking: Scenario planning focuses on the 'outside' world, i.e. the contextual environment. Individuals and organisations are frequently surprised by discontinuities because they typically spend most of their time thinking from the inside, about what they are most familiar with and can control. As far back as 1994, Hamel and Pralahad stated that managers spent less than 3% of their time thinking about and building a corporate perspective on the future. Managers keep looking inside the organisation where they exert more control, instead of outside, to see and understand what is happening; as a result, they invariably do not see the problem(s) until it is too late. The consequences are that in a turbulent world of radical and disruptive change, the capacity to act rather than think and imagine becomes the measure of leadership; the urgent drives out the important and firefighting becomes the mode of management, and when problems arise, the scalpel (cost cutting) becomes the answer to everything.

- Multiple perspectives: Scenario planning teams are generally composed of a diverse range of individuals, and diverse voices shed new light on strategic issues and help better understand assumptions; and
- Collaborative processes: Developing scenarios is generally a collaborative team process, albeit there are instances in which scenarios are developed by individuals.

Although there is no universally accepted definition of scenarios or scenario planning, one could summarise them briefly as being descriptions of journeys to possible futures. What do scenarios do? They challenge and stretch our current perspectives, making us aware of our assumptions and questioning our deeply held beliefs; they increase our understanding of complex structural developments and interactions, which may signal how things are evolving but can be overwhelmingly difficult to make sense of; they help relate and organise a multitude of exogenous driving forces into broad patterns and logical and coherent high-level frameworks by providing an organising schema which then allows organisations to anticipate, recognise, and address change more comprehensively; finally, they expand the range of things we pay attention to, enabling us to begin to 'see' things not previously seen because they were outside our field of view. Wack (1985a) put it very neatly:

> By presenting other ways of seeing the world, scenarios allow us to break out of a one-eyed view. They give us something very precious: the ability to reperceive reality . . . in a turbulent environment, there is more to see than we normally perceive, but highly relevant information goes unnoticed because, being locked into one way of looking, we fail to see its significance." The purpose of scenarios then is "to gather and transform information of potential strategic significance into fresh perceptions which then lead to strategic insights that were previously beyond the mind's reach . . . those that would not even have been considered.

However, Wack states that this transformation process is not trivial; it is genuinely creative. Meanwhile, Ramirez et al (2021) caution, that the fact that the practice of scenario planning has no barriers to entry, coupled with too few competent scenario planners, scenario planning interventions can often produce results which are not useful.

The chapter which follows moves on to discuss Stage 4, the Implications of operating in the environments depicted in the scenarios developed, and the strategic fit with the organisation's Business Idea. This is then followed by Stage 5, which describes the process for the development of environmental scanning systems to track and monitor early warning signals and leading indicators.

References

Barry, M. (1997). Strategy retold: toward a narrative view of strategic discourse. Academic Management Review. 22, 429–452.

Beck, P.W. (1982). Corporate planning for an uncertain future. Long Range Planning,15, 4.

Bizikova, L., Pintér, L. and Tubiello, N. (2015). Normative scenario approach: a vehicle to connect adaptation planning and development needs in developing countries. Regional Environmental Change, 15, pp 1433–1446.

Cairns, G and Wright, G. (2018). Scenario Thinking: Preparing Your Organization for the Future in an Unpredictable World. Palgrave Macmillan.

Connell, L. (2004). Making the Implausible Plausible. Merced Proceedings of the Annual Meeting of the Cognitive Science Society, 26, 26, ISSN 1069–7977.

Denning, S. (2005). The leader's guide to storytelling: Mastering the art and discipline of business narrative. Jossey-Bass, San Francisco.

Einhorn, H.J. and Hogarth, R.M. (1981). Behavioral decision theory: Processes of judgement and choice. Annual Review of Psychology, 32, pp 3–88.

Foster, M.J. (1993). Scenario planning for small businesses. Long Range Planning, 26, 1, pp 123–129

Gabriel, Y. (2000). Storytelling in Organizations: Pre-modern Narratives for Our Times. Oxford University Press.

Haven, K. (2007). Story Proof: The Science Behind the Startling Power of Story. Libraries Unlimited, Greenwood Publishing Group Ltd.

Jungermann, H. (1985a). Inferential Processes in the Construction of Scenarios. Journal of Forecasting, 4, 3, pp. 21–327.

Jungermann, H. (1985b). The Psychological Aspects of Scenarios, in V.T. Covello, J.L. Mumpower, P.J.M. Stallen and V.R.R. Uppuluri (eds.), Environmental Impact Assessment, Technology Assessment and Risk Analysis, Berlin: Springer-Verlag.

Kahn, H. and Wiener, A.J. (1972). The year 2000: A framework for speculation on the next thirty-three years. New York: Macmillan.

Khan, H. and Wiener, A.J. (1967). The Next Thirty-Three Years: A Framework for Speculation Daedalus, 96, 3, pp 705–732.

Le Roux, P. and Maphai, V. (1992). The Mont Fleur scenarios. Deeper News 7, pp 7–20.

Linneman, R. E. and Klein, H. E. (1983). The use of multiple scenarios by U.S. industrial companies: A comparison study, 1977–1981. Long Range Planning, 16, 6, pp 94–101.

Macintyre, A. (1981). After Virtue. Duckworth, London.

Mandel, T.F. (1982). Scenarios and corporate strategy: planning in uncertain times. SRI International, Business Intelligence Program.

Meadows, D., Meadows, D.L., Randers, J. and Behrens III, W.W. The Limits to Growth. (1972). Universe Books, New York.

Neuhauser, P. (1993). Corporate Legends and Lore: The Power of Storytelling as a Management Tool. McGraw-Hill. New York.

Nordfors, L. (2007). Scenarios for Success: Turning Insights into Action. Eds Sharpe, B. and van der Heijden, K.

Ogilvy, J. and Schwartz, P. (2004). Plotting Your Scenarios. Global Business Network.

Ogilvy, J. and Schwartz, P. (1991). Probabilities: Help or Hindrance in Scenario Planning? Deep News Global Business Network 2, 4.

Polkinghorne, M. (1988). Narrative Knowing and the Human Sciences. State University of New York Press, Albany, NY.

Ramirez, R., Lang, T. and Peterson, G. (2021). Seven Sure-fire Ways to do Scenario Planning Badly: A Guide to Poor Practice. Said Business School.

Schnaars, S.P. (1987). How to develop and use scenarios. Long Range Planning, 20, 1, pp 105–114.

Scholes, R. (1981). Language, narrative, and anti-narrative, in: W. Mitchell (ed.), On Narrativity, University of Chicago Press, Chicago, IL, pp 200–208.

Schwartz, P. (1991). The Art of the Long View: Planning for the Future in an Uncertain World. New York, Currency Doubleday.

Schwartz, P. (1992). Composing a plot for your scenario. Planning Review, 20, 3, pp 4–46.

Sunter, C. (2010). Learning from experience: the Mont Fleur Scenario Exercise. (https://reospartners.com/learning-from-experience-the-mont-fleur-scenario-exercise/thefuture).

Sviden, O. (1986). Methodology: A scenario method for forecasting Futures, 18, 5, pp 681–691.

Suzuki, W.A., Feliue-Mojer, M.I., Hasson, U., Yehida, R., and Zarate, J.M. (2018). Dialogues: The Science and Power of Storytelling, International Journal of Neuroscience, 38, 44, 9468–94az70.

van der Heijden, C.A.M.J. (1996). Scenarios: The Art of Strategic Conversation, Chichester: John Wiley & Sons.

Wack, P. (1985a). Scenarios: Uncharted Waters Ahead, Harvard Business Review, 63, 4, pp 73–89.

Wack, P. (1985b). Scenarios: Shooting the Rapids, Harvard Business Review, 63, 5, pp 3–14

Wilkinson, A., and Kupers, R. (2014). The Essence of Scenarios Learning from the Shell Experience. Amsterdam University Press.

Wilkinson, A. and Kupers, R. (2013). Living in the futures: how scenario planning changed corporate strategy. Harvard Business Review, pp 3–11.

Wilson I. (1978). Strategic planning for marketers. Business Horizons. 21, 6, pp 65–73.

Chapter 6
Scenario Development Process: Stage 4 & 5

Scenarios describe a particular context and how it may change over time, they do not define the implications inherent in the scenarios, which generally relate to the uncertainties portrayed in the individual scenarios. In most cases the broad implications are obvious. For example, over the past three years, several scenarios have been published around the COVID-19 pandemic. A common theme of the scenarios is that a 'new normal' factor is a more virtual-focused world with growing numbers of individuals working from home either full-time or part-time, and more individuals shopping virtually. The broad implications? As more people spend increasingly more time at home, fewer work offices and commercial buildings will be required, and strong e-commerce will increase the demand for logistics assets and infrastructure to handle home parcel delivery.

While the following sections on Stakeholder Analysis, Horizon Scanning, and Early Warning Signals are not widely considered elements of a standard scenario planning engagement, they are introduced in Kees van der Heijden's book *Scenarios: The Art of Strategic Conversation*. I have employed them in most scenario projects in which I have been involved, and they have proved to be very useful in stimulating a 'strategic conversation' in the organisation.

Stakeholder Analysis

Although time-consuming, one way of exploring implications to a greater depth is to engage in stakeholder analysis, which is a systematic process of gathering and analysing information to help determine:

- Who are the players in each scenario, what concerns them in each scenario, and how have they behaved historically in similar situations?
- Who has higher levels of power and interest in each scenario, and how would they exercise that power in each situation?
- How best to involve and communicate with each of the stakeholder groups to enlist their help and leverage their knowledge as and when required.

Stakeholders are persons, organizations, or interested parties, which can be grouped into one of the four categories based on a power/interest grid shown in Figure 6.1. The focus of analysis on the four elements of the grid is primarily on the Players and the Leaders and Context Setters. The Players are the most important stakeholders as they have a high degree of both power and influence in the business, and consequently need to be managed closely. Equally important are the Leaders and Context Setters who may have little interest in the business, but have the power to affect it, and it is

https://doi.org/10.1515/9783111617442-006

essential to keep them placated and informed of plans. While Subjects are bystanders and usually have little power to affect things, they have a great deal of interest in the business, and it is important to keep them satisfied and in regular communication to ensure that they are not experiencing problems. It is equally important to regularly monitor and pay attention to the Crowd who as bystanders, may have little power and low interest in the scenarios developed, but there are instances in history where the 'crowd' have overnight become Players. An example of this is the demonstrations which took place in central Tunisia in December 2010, catalysed by the self-immolation of Mohamed Bouazizi, a 26-year-old street vendor protesting his treatment by local officials. A protest movement dubbed the "Jasmine Revolution" (https://www.britannica.com) in the media, quickly spread through the country. The government attempted to end this using violence against the street demonstrators and offering political and economic concessions, but the protests overwhelmed the country's security forces, compelling the President, Zine al-bidine Ben Ali, to step down and flee the country on January 14, 2011.

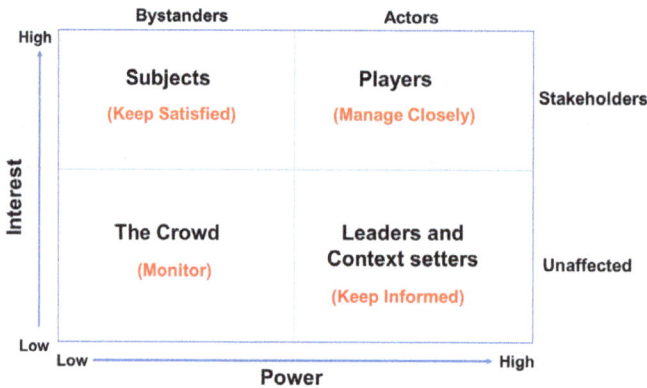

Figure 6.1: Standard Stakeholder Grid.

Once the key actors are identified, analysis can then be undertaken to assess their knowledge, interests, positions, alliances, and importance. Having analysed and understood the key actors and implications in terms of issues that matter to them and their expectations, it is then possible to uncover potential issues that could be disruptive and accordingly, determine where to spend time and resources. Following stakeholder analysis, the next step in Stage 6 is developing environmental horizon scanning systems to monitor early warning signals (EWS) and leading indicators relevant to each scenario.

Horizon Scanning

Before engaging in horizon scanning, it is essential to have developed an understanding of the environment as discussed in previous chapters, as without this understanding, developing a system to detect EWS signals would be ineffective. In studying the future, one thing is clear, there is not one certain future that we are inexorably moving to, but many possible futures comprising a combination of forces in the external environment including discontinuous change and wild cards. A primary purpose of engaging in scenario building is to raise awareness of potential developments in the world and help prepare to respond faster and more effectively to changes in their business environment. Once a set of scenarios and their implications have been developed, organisations can then engage in scanning the environment for indications of which of the dynamics raised in the scenarios, are happening and which are not. This will also help them to see when other dynamics appear, which might not have been discussed in the scenario set.

Horizon Scanning (HS) first appeared in the mid-1980s, when a Dutch study concluded that it was not satisfactory to react to technological developments only when confronted with their consequences (Jørgensen and Carlsson, 1998; Banta and Gelijns, 1998). The authors of the study called on the government to develop a permanent system for identifying new healthcare technologies, which led to the establishment of the first HS System in 1985–86 at the Dutch Health Council (Douw and Vondeling, 2006.) Since then, the concept has grown and spread to both commercial and public organisations and is used across diverse sectors to aid policy process, and research planning (Hines et al., 2019). In the UK, HS has been integrated into the government's central policymaking through the Cabinet Office (Consensus Study Report: Safeguarding the Bioeconomy, 2020) and is also reportedly used in Switzerland (Habeggar, 2009) and in Singapore, where the governments use it to consider policy challenges from healthcare to road building. In Italy, the Food and Agriculture Organisation (FAO) of the United Nations has developed an overview of HS processes, their strengths, weaknesses, and possible applications in Food Safety.

Despite its widespread use, HS is still developing as a method and there is a lack of consensus in terms of the terminology regarding tools, techniques, and processes involved. A commonly used definition is that developed by the Organisation for Economic Co-operation and Development (OECD): HS is "a technique for detecting early signs of potentially important developments through a systematic examination of potential threats and opportunities, which can be weak (or early) signals, trends, wild cards or other developments, persistent problems, risks and threats, including matters at the margins of current thinking that challenge past assumptions, with emphasis on new technology and its effects on the issue at hand. It can be a comprehensive or a limited search for information in a specific field defined by the objectives of a given task" (Attila and Matthias, 2017). Van Rij (2010a p 9) expands on this with his definition which states that HS is "the systematic examination of potential (future) problems, threats, opportunities, and likely future developments, including those at the margins of current thinking and planning." Along with the above, there are several other definitions of HS the common components of which include: a standardised and systematic methodology; criteria to ensure that the scan results are in accordance with the aim of the scan; a focus on emerging trends; and differentiation among signal types.

The approach of HS is about systematically investigating evidence about future trends and the detection of weak signals as indicators of potential change. This implies a search process, which is extended to the margins of the known environment and possibly beyond it (Loveridge, 2009). The Institute for Risk Management (IRM) states that HS is a useful tool in terms of:

– deepening the understanding of the driving forces affecting future developments of a strategy area;
– identifying gaps in understanding and building consensus amongst stakeholders regarding issues and how to address them;
– establishing difficult policy choices to develop resilient strategy, and mobilising stakeholders into action (IRM, 2018).

HS is then essentially, an instrument with two functions: firstly, an alerting function for policymakers to identify emerging issues through picking up early warning signals; and secondly, a creative function to help organisations determine if they are adequately prepared for potential opportunities and threats, and ensure that their strategies are resilient to different future environments (Amanatidou et al., 2012).

Weak signals meanwhile, are early indications concerning potential discontinuities and emerging issues. They are not yet public knowledge, only a small group of people are usually aware of their potential, and they can grow into trends, fade away, or appear as early warnings for wild cards. This includes innovative technologies which are still in their infant phase but may see a breakthrough at some point. Why should we be concerned about EWS? The answer is that when recognised and understood, EWS provide an advantage, delivering advanced insights into changes which are happening and affecting the environment.

The first step in developing an HS system is for the senior management of an organisation to establish a small core scanning team; define the terms and scope of work of the team; establish a data collection and archive infrastructure; determine how the data collected and analysed will be disseminated; and to initiate the data collection process, which typically contains the following five steps:

1. Identify potential scan sources i.e., what broad areas to investigate for emerging issues and scanning hits.
2. Design a framework for categorizing and clustering the data collected using a broad taxonomy such as STIRDEEPER (Society, Technology, Industry, Resources, Demographics, Economics, Environment, Politics, Energy and Religion) with subcategories where necessary.

3. Establish a standard by which the significance of each scan can be analysed, for example, by using cross-level and cross-layered analysis.
4. Evaluate entries by the accrual of confirming data from multiple sources, modelling issues into potential emerging issues, and prioritising the urgent time-sensitive issues.
5. The final step is to devise a method to effectively disseminate the scan findings.

Clear guidelines need to be developed that address questions such as: Who will potentially be the main users of the scans? How broad or narrow is the field of interest? Is the intention to develop broad topics or specific developments? What is the intended spatial scope of the scanning? And how far into the future should the scanning project go? Questions such as these will depend largely on the resources available and the needs of the end users. The process is not generally a linear one as HS processes inevitably involve some iteration of the cyclical actions of scanning, analysing, synthesizing, and communicating information. At the same time, expert input from a wide variety of credible sources is critical to the success of a horizon-scanning process.

There are two separate approaches to HS: continuous scanning activities, the results of which are often disseminated via regular newsletters, and ad-hoc scanning for a specific purpose or on specific occasions. Both approaches generally follow the same process of signal detection, filtration, prioritisation, assessment and dissemination. There are also two different methods to the HS process: (1) The 'Exploratory' approach which gathers data from a lengthy list of signals which are precursors for emerging issues. (2) 'Issue-centred' scanning in which the approach focuses on identifying primary signals related to parts of potential issues. In both cases signals are detected from a wide range of resources including the scientific and management literature; electronic and social media; web-based search engines; databases; inputs from industry and international institutions; expert surveys and interviews; Government bodies; universities, research institutions; think tanks; observatories and repositories; patents; conferences and public events; and conversations with individuals and expert groups. A relatively new way of collecting signals is through the blogosphere i.e. blogging and micro-blogging platforms such as Twitter, which are rapidly expanding and have the advantage of information often appearing on them before they are reported in conventional formats such as TV, radio and newspapers. Given that HS involves broad, unfocussed searches through such a wide variety of sources, it is usually beyond the capability of one individual. However, when more focused research topics of strategic interest are identified, required is at least one person with expertise in in-depth analysis. Thus, while a scanning unit may comprise one individual or a small team of people, the process should engage a broad network of individuals to handle the width of sources to be scanned and to provide specific expertise when necessary. Although the basic steps of HS are simple, the simplicity is deceptive because the goal of HS is about identifying change emerging outside an organisation's normal frames of reference, and scanners must therefore guard against bias in terms of source identification, taxonomic structure, evaluative processes, or validation criteria.

McGrath (2020) states that there are three kinds of indicators that we need to be aware of when undertaking HS:

- Lagging indicators: Most of the information we use in business is the lagging kind i.e., annual financial, sales and operational reports. Although these indicators have value in that they can be used to explain and detect internal issues, they essentially do not tell you much about the future.
- Current indicators: Current indicators are the type of indicators that tell you where you are right now and how things are, but again they do not tell you much about the future.
- Leading indicators by definition are not facts, but are the hardest indicators to get and the trickiest to consider in planning; they are pre-event or incident measurements as opposed to lagging indicators, which are measurements collected after an event or incident occurs. For example, a flat tyre is a lagging indicator because the blowout already has occurred, but an inspection that notes the poor quality of the tyre and prevents a blowout from taking place, is a leading indicator. A key competency of leading indicators is that they are measurements of events or behaviours that precede incidents, and have a predictive quality.

McGrath acknowledges that most individuals spend most of their time working with lagging indicators, whereas more time should be spent thinking about leading indicators. She indicates that there were early warnings of the current COVID-19 pandemic, but people ignored them which is why most nations were not prepared for it. To avoid this from happening, it is essential to have an early warning system based on leading indicators. McGrath suggests that things to remember with leading indicators of change are that firstly, the initial strength of a signal is very weak; secondly, as Silver (2013) states, so much noise pollutes journals, blogs, and news accounts that it is difficult to segregate out which warning signals are important; and thirdly, the strength of a signal is inversely related to the ability to change it. To get comfortable working with weak signals and indicators, McGrath proposes a form of Backcasting: one starts by identifying a time zero i.e., a point in time where the change that one is assuming to happen is visible and can identify the facts. From that point work backwards to consider what has to be true before time zero is reached.

When considering an item for potential inclusion in an environmental scanning database, the following questions should be answered:

- Is the proposed 'scan hit' objectively or subjectively new?
- Does the change represent the first mention of a new topic of change, or reinforce previous signals regarding the same topic?
- If the scan hit represents additional data on a topic, does it confirm previous scan hits, or does it contradict them?
- Is it possible to judge how quickly the change is occurring?
- How credible is the source, is it an authoritative opinion leader for that area of expertise?

The point of the process is to learn to identify a potentially significant change in time to monitor its emergence. There are two issues to be aware of. The first is to avoid collecting evidence because it supports individual preferences. The second is that the timing to disseminate information on emerging signals, especially weak signals, is crucial in terms of their acceptance as they may encounter scepticism or even be ignored. Once additional information is gathered that validates the signals and they are accepted, the signals are no longer novel and it may be too late to take remedial action. Amanatidou et al (2012) state that potential wild cards and emerging issues and their early warning signals, generally have to fight for attention in the political discourse except in situations where they are part of the present-day discourse, and do not clash with the interests of powerful stakeholders.

In searching for signals, a period of 2 to 10 years is generally the time frame considered. Anything less than 2 years would usually represent happenings which are already in late-stage development, while anything over 10 years would in most cases, be too distant and uncertain to be of any use. Having collected the signal data, the next step is organising it for efficient and useful retrieval. Traditionally, scanning databases are organised using a taxonomy that classifies each change by its point of origin; each section of the taxonomy may be further subdivided as necessary. It is then crucial to have a strategy for validating the data, especially weak signal data, and three processes can aid validation:

– Confirmation, or accruing multiple citations. Scanning is meant to be an ongoing process, monitoring emerging change as more and more cases occur. Thus, accruing evidence from a variety of sources of multiple occurrences validates the existence of a change, and indicates the direction of the emerging trend.
– Convergence, or emerging scientific consensus. Transformational weak signals will challenge current scientific paradigms. As more data is available, however, researchers will begin to discard some of the explanations the challenge provoked and come to agree on a new paradigm. A current example of this is exemplified in the history of the scientific dialogue regarding climate change.
– Parallax, or acquiring 'depth of field' on the weak signal of change by collecting views from multiple perspectives, e.g., multiple cultural viewpoints. This ensures that the original perception of the change is not merely an artefact of a cultural filter.

Lessons learnt from the use of HS include firstly, involving as many experts as possible in the process, and the IRM (IRM, 2018) process emphasizes the importance of involving a diverse group of participants with open minds. Secondly, integrating the potential for discontinuities in all topic areas to develop an appreciation for the types of discontinuities, will result in fundamental shifts (Carney, 2018). Albeit on the surface, HS appears to be a relatively simple task, designing an effective and sophisticated process of identifying, analysing to make sense of, monitoring and then disseminating the signals and insights gained, is not something which can be achieved overnight, as the example in Box 6.1 shows

---

Box 6.1: Example of Ineffective Environmental Scanning

On completion of a set of scenarios and their implications for a Malaysian multinational, the scenario team was asked to review the HS efforts of the company's environmental scanning unit. The unit which had been in operation for several years, comprised three individuals who provided 5-6 page reports every two months to all departmental managers, containing a listing of the signals identified and their industry implications.

Several senior staff were asked their opinion of the ES reports. The response from all was fundamentally the same: "I read the reports but only occasionally. I find them boring, everything they talk about in the reports is what I, and I think everyone else, already knows about – you can read about it in the newspapers. There is nothing new at all.

In reviewing several of the reports and discussing them with the ES unit, it was apparent that reports were basically a summary of events and happenings reported in the media in S.E. Asia. Rather than signals detected from the multiple resources, the unit members spent their time in the office searching print and electronic media, and then summarising their findings as reports; no effort was made to meet with any institutions or individuals.

The problem, however, was not entirely that of the team, on investigating the working of the unit two issues were uncovered. The first was that the remit of the unit was to put together periodic reports of "what was happing in the business environment;" there was no mention of the systematic examination covering a range of resources to identify potential threats, opportunities and likely developments, or of identifying early warning signals about emerging sources of change. The second issue was that none of the ES unit members had been to a HS or Foresight training course, and were not fully aware of what HS encompassed.

Early Warning Signals

Early warning signals (EWS) is a general term for dynamic patterns in system behaviour that proceed with regime shifts, and since the Indian Ocean tsunami in December 2004, there has been a surge of interest in developing early warning systems (Boettiger et al. 2013). Most complex systems including populations and markets, exhibit 'early warning' behaviours and rapid changes in the state and conditions of systems before critical transitions or disruptive changes. However, the underlying mechanisms for the changes are not always known and they are usually recognized in retrospect when it is too late to do anything.

When a system approaches a tipping point it may exhibit certain signs of instability that could potentially be used as EWS, and two main theoretical phenomena that describe this effect are 'critical slowing down' and 'flickering.' Critical slowing down is a phenomenon based on the generic mechanism that as a system gets close to a critical threshold or tipping point, the rate at which a system recovers from small perturbation becomes slow. The slowing down of one part of a system can be an indication that the system is seeking to establish a new equilibrium, and this is symptomatic of tipping points in a wide range of natural systems. Flickering meanwhile, refers to a system that switches back and forth between alternative states in response to relatively large impacts; when this happens, scientists call it 'squealing' or 'variance amplification.'

To be usable as EWS, these phenomena must be detectable well enough in advance of a major shift, and reliably distinguishable from other patterns (Boettiger et al. 2013), and there are essentially three categories of EWS:

– The first are signals designed to indicate that a known type of event, opportunity or threat may occur sometime in the future. Signals in this instance can be strong and well-known, and require only a few signals to trigger recognition and action, or they can be very subtle and weak and require several signals seen over time to trigger recognition and action. Examples would include signals designed to recognize opportunities, trends, industry changes, competitor actions, economic and financial problems, new initiatives, new partnerships, strategy changes, mergers, and takeovers.

– The second category of EWS is signals which indicate that an unknown event or one never previously seen, will occur or is imminent. These are the most difficult types of EWS, they are often anomalies and can be extremely subtle. Signals for them can be developed, but there will always be the case that it was not thought of before it happened, and is usually only clear in hindsight. An example of this is the terrorist 911 event which could have been thought of, but had never been seen before in the context of a terrorist attack.

– The third category of EWS are 'wildcards,' signals or events which when they happen, radically alter viewpoints and business reactions. They are characterised as sudden, rare, surprising and disruptive discontinuities and shocks that have a low probability of occurrence (but not a non-existent probability) and when they do occur, their impact is significant. Thus wild cards can be events that we know are possible or are expected to happen at some point based on the existing knowledge. For example, given recent pandemics such as the H1N1 Swine Flu (2009–2010), the West African Ebola epidemic (2014–2016) and the Zika Virus epidemic (2015–2021), it can be argued that the COVID pandemic should not have been a surprise.

There are two broad methods for identifying warning signals. The first is by computer software which is increasingly used to automate the process of gathering vast quantities of inputs, usually from the Internet. The process can take two forms, algorithmic-based text searches, or computer searches and scanners which take what current software suggests might be EWS, and validate this with the human mind. The issue with the first form is that it provides a high probability of accurate acquisition and recognition in only a small percentage of the signals, albeit advances in machine learning, sophisticated text analytics, and computational text mining software, are all rapidly improving accuracy. In the second case, signals that are subtle, nuanced and ambiguous, require a human mind rather than computer software to recognize them, put them into context, analyse them and pass judgment on their meaning. The suggestion in the literature is that soon, there will be a high percentage of EWS that fall into this category, despite the extraordinary advances in AI. The advantage of the manual approach is that it can access content that is not online or published, while the disadvantages are that it is labour-intensive and subject to the biases of the searchers.

The problem with EWS is that there is currently no science to detecting them, many signals are in the eye of the beholder and there will be both false positives and false negatives. At the same time, events such as the WannaCry cyber-attacks in 2017 that affected 200,000 victims across 150 nations, indicate how connected the world is, and how this affects people and locations in different and unanticipated ways. The trick is to figure out what sort of data to look for, how to make sense of it, and then to differentiate between short-term fads, sub-trends, and countertrends. It is impossible to identify all the forces at play and their interactions; it is also obvious that individuals and organisations are prone to missing, or gathering but then disregarding EWS, which often metamorphosis into major disasters. There are reasons for this; part of the problem is that our brains see what they want to see and disregard everything else because of heuristics and biases. A second, common factor for ignoring signals, is an organisational culture whereby individuals and organisations underestimate their implications in the belief that inaction will not have profound consequences. A third factor for ignoring EWS is that of political consequences. Harford (2020) suggests that what statistics we gather and share, ignore or conceal, are shaped by politics. As an example, he states that in December 2019 Taiwan had given information to the World Health Organisation (WHO) about the human-to-human transmission of COVID; however, by the middle of January, the WHO tweeted that China had found no evidence of human-to-human transmission.

Wintle et al (2020, p 29) state that although HS is evolving into a more effective tool, assessing the success of HS in identifying emerging issues is challenging. They add that "gauging the extent to which horizon-scanning outputs inform policy, future research directions and resource investments is not always straightforward, and no one has yet tested the effectiveness of this process." It is also important to note that the bulk of publications on HS and EWS come not from business, but from the ecology and ecosystems management arena. John Carney (2018), Principal Scientist within the Systems Thinking and Consulting Group of the Defence Science and Technology Laboratory (Dstl) has created the *Ten Commandments of Horizon Scanning*, based on his experiences of leading scanning activities. In summary, Carney's ten commandments are:

1. HS is not about predicting the future, it is used to change mindsets, challenge assumptions, and provide more options.
2. Do not look for 'what you know or want,' scanning is not the same as searching. HS is about asking the unasked questions or identifying the unknown unknowns.
3. Do not negate the need for a champion, a major challenge for HS analysis is in overcoming cultural resistance and a supportive stakeholder is a major help.
4. Do not forget to sustain the evidence base, a systematic and comprehensive scanning process should provide a degree of robustness which is important for credibility.

5. Do not think that there is any consistent understanding of what HS is about, there is both a lack of a mutual understanding within the HS community and a common language.
6. Do not be afraid to challenge your way of doing things, there is no magic or agreed recipe for how to do HS. Asking other teams to review your work is a wonderful way to introduce novel approaches and views.
7. Do not forget 'the team;' use a dedicated cadre of generalists, ideally recruited from very different academic backgrounds and including externals.
8. Do not negate the need for impact focus on describing the implications of the analysis, rather than the process or detailed content.
9. Do not expect to be thanked or enjoy it too much, HS is a challenging function and at times you may feel like you are on the front line of a war zone.
10. Do not give up the day job, for some, HS may become a full-time or even life-long profession, but for most, it can be a useful adjunct to a more mainstream activity.

Carney (2018) concludes by suggesting that one should be wary, while Horizon Scanning can at times seem like a cult, it should be treated not as a single bullet but as one of the many useful tools in the Futures armoury.

What follows is a general discussion on issues in understanding the contextual environment, building on the discussion in Chapter 4, beginning with the concept of complexity.

Complexity

In 2000, Stephen Hawking, in response to a question about the way that science is developing, replied: "I think the next century will be the century of complexity." Peter Ho (2017), a senior adviser to the Centre for Strategic Futures in Singapore, and previously the Head of the Civil Service in Singapore, delivered a lecture at the Institute of Policy Studies entitled *The Black Elephant Challenge for Governments.* Building on the comment from Hawking, the lecture was about complexity. He stated that it was not just cities, countries, or human systems that are complex systems, the world is complex. The issue he said, is that complexity is different from complicated.

> *Complicated systems have Newtonian characteristics in that they perform pre-determined functions that are predictable and repeatable, in which input leads to a predictable outcome. In contrast, a complex system will not behave in a repeatable and predetermined manner, it contains many autonomous parts, agents, connected and interacting in a great many ways . . . and generating their own feedback loops.*

Ho argues that to understand a complex system, it is necessary to understand the behaviour of each of these agents, how the agents interact with one another, and how they act together as a whole. The connections and interactions among the many agents in a complex system lead Ho suggests, "to outcomes that are inherently unpredictable ex-ante, and that are revealed only when they actually occur." This accords with van der Heijden's (2005) view cited in Chapter 1, that everything in life is part of a wider, non-linear, self-organising and interconnected milieu, and intractable complexity arises from the patterns of combinations and interactions between these systems, rather than from the inherent complexity of individual systems or their number.

Complexity generates 'wicked problems,' a term introduced by Rittel and Webber (1973). The characteristics of wicked problems are that they are unique; they do not have a definitive formulation; the problems lack an inherent logic that signals when they are solved; there is no way to test the solution to a wicked problem; and there is no end to the number of solutions or approaches to a wicked problem. Examples of the most disturbing wicked problems today provided by Ho include climate change, energy security, global pandemics, sustainable development, and cyberthreat all of which have complex causes and factors that are not easily determined ex-ante. To understand complexity and to deal with wicked problems, he states that we often rely on reductionism i.e., we dissect the complex world into smaller and less complex parts on the assumption that what is complex, can be reduced to simpler subsets that are easier to evaluate, and when re-aggregated, will produce results that approximate the real world. However, complexity science Ho argues, rejects reductionism for the study of how systems interact with other systems, how agents interact with other agents, and then how these lead to emergent rather than causal results. "Economics, demographics, societal issues, environment, and technology all of which interact with each other to produce the complexities of the operating environment, is a more interdisciplinary and counter-reductionist approach, and consequently, interdisciplinary collaboration is essential for solving the big challenges in all areas from science to the environment (p 3)."

There are numerous challenges associated with complexity as human cognitive limitations constrain the ability to deal with it Firstly, it is now increasingly acknowledged that the traditional belief in a mechanistic, simple cause-effect relationship often embodying implicit assumptions about linearity, is no longer valid as many relationships are non-linear and subject to ever-changing patterns of unpredictability (Nowotny et al., 2001). Secondly, adverse events, happen much more often than they are supposed to in the world of classical statistics (Kay, 2009) and as the connections between problems and solutions become less clear, there will be unintended consequences of the decisions made by policymakers.

Big Data

Martin Lindstrom (2016) suggests that "the issue right now is that the corporate world has become completely blinded by 'Big Data' . . . which is all about finding correlations, whereas 'Small Data' (SD) is all about finding the causation, the reason why".

Chatfield (2016) builds on this by suggesting that the problem with much of the big data being gathered and analysed is that the moment you start to look backwards to seek the longer view, you have far too much recent stuff and far too little of the old. Short-sightedness is built into the structure, in the form of an overwhelming tendency to overestimate short-term trends at the expense of history. The same is true of most complex phenomena in real life: stock markets, economies, success or failure of companies, war and peace, relationships, and the rise and fall of empires. Short-term analyses are not only invalid, they are unhelpful and misleading. Support for this comes from Rufus Pollock, the founder of the not-for-profit *Open Knowledge Foundation* (https://blog.okfn.org/2004/05/24/open-knowledge-foundation-launched/), who states that the hype around Big Data (BD) is misplaced, small, linked data is actually where the real value lies because it is all about finding causations.

BD represents large and complex chunks of both structured and unstructured data which conventional data processing techniques cannot manage, and the justification for BD is the assumption that more data would appear to be better than less data, albeit this is not true. The three critical components associated with BD were initially known as the 'Three Vs: 'Volume' which relates to the hundreds of complex petabytes comprising the data sets that conventional data processing software cannot handle; 'Velocity' which is the fast rate at which BD is received; and 'Variety' which refers to the many unstructured and semi-structured data types such as audio and video which require specialist additional processing to provide meaning. Two more Vs have since emerged, namely 'Value' and 'Veracity' (Laborde, 2020). The advantage of BD is that collected through a range of sources (social media platforms, mobile telephones, smart appliances, and public records) and processes such as machine learning algorithms, it can address a wide range of business activities and reveal trends which allow organisations to create tailored products and services. There are, however, disadvantages of BD, these being, firstly, the cost and difficulty in securing it as it grows exponentially; secondly, BD is generally unstructured and is costly and time-consuming to analyse. The third disadvantage is that it faces challenges in terms of privacy, security, ownership, data stewardship, and governance, as it reportedly violates the principles of privacy and can be used to manipulate customer records.

SD, meanwhile, can be defined as datasets whose data is sufficiently small that it can be accumulated in an Excel file, and whose structure is accessible, concise, and workable. The advantages of SD are that firstly, it is everywhere, and social media provides an array of SD which translates to business intelligence; secondly, it is accessible, informative, actionable, and comprehensive without using the complex set of systems and machines for carrying out analysis and interpretation; and thirdly, it is inexpensive to capture and translate. The disadvantage, however, is that it cannot provide the same breadth and depth of useful business intelligence information that BD potentially can.

In trying to understand the environment and the issues, there are several other factors to be aware of including Correlation versus Causation, Unintended (or unforeseen) Consequences, Signals versus Noise, Predictable Surprises, the Black Elephant, Fundamental Disruptive Forces, and Tipping Points and Inflection Points.

Correlation Versus Causation

One of the crucial issues in understanding the environment is correlation and causation which are deceptively similar and are often confused. They are often used interchangeably because humans are biologically inclined to recognize patterns, and the mind likes to find patterns even when they do not exist. It is often easy to find evidence of a correlation between two things when we see them happening seemingly together, but it is usually more difficult to find evidence of causation i.e., that one does cause the other. Correlation as a concept means that two things vary together and is defined as a statistical measure, expressed as a number, which describes the size and direction of a relationship between two or more variables. It is not however the same as causation. For example, Storks have been associated with the birth of babies in Europe for centuries, and the image of a stork carrying a baby in a cloth bundle dangling from its beak is ubiquitous. Numerous accounts trace the legend of storks associated with birth back to ancient Greek mythology, and more recent research has confirmed a statistically significant correlation between storks and human birth rates in several European countries. For example, George Udny Yule a statistician, and author of the book *Introduction to the Theory of Statistics* (1911), noted that in Alsace villages, the number of newborn babies correlated with the number of nesting storks. In 2004 Höfer et al. from the German Federal Institute for Risk Assessment showed in their publication *New Evidence for the Theory of the Stork*, that there was a correlation between the decrease in the stork population in the German state of Lower Saxony in the 1970s and 1980s, with a decrease in the number of baby deliveries. While research may have shown a statistically significant correlation between storks and human birth rates, there is of course no causation between the two, it is simply a case of coincidence. The human mind however subconsciously attempts to establish links between contrasting pieces of information, creating an artificial non-existent cause-and-effect relationship, examples of which can be found in business decisions, academic research, and media stories.

Causation also known as causality, means that two events appear at the same time or one after the other, and the two variables not only appear together, but the existence of one also causes the other to manifest. A positive correlation arises when one observes A increasing and B increasing as well, or if A decreases, B correspondingly decreases. A negative correlation meanwhile, is when an increase in A result in a decrease in B or vice versa. In other words, a change in one variable will typically be mirrored by a positive or negative change in the other. The strength of the linear relationship between two variables known as the correlation coefficient can range from -1 (a negative correlation) to 1 (a positive correlation). The closer the correlation coefficient is to either -1 or 1, the stronger the relationship. Meanwhile, a correlation coefficient of 0 indicates that there is no correlation between the two variables. Spurious correlations (or relationships) are instances in which two groups give an impression of a link between them, but when examined there is no logical connection. Sometimes two things can share a relationship indicating causality but without one causing the other, the possible explanations for this being the result of random chance, or where there may be a third, lurking variable that makes the relationship appear stronger (or weaker) than it is. However, confusing correlation with causation is becoming increasingly problematic as data increases and computers get more powerful. Some humorous but absurd examples of this developed by Tyler Vigen in his book *Spurious Correlations* (2015) include the following:

- US spending on science, space, and technology correlates (99.79%) with suicides by hanging, strangulation and suffocation.
- Undergraduate enrolment at U.S. universities correlates (99.6%) with injuries related to falling TVs.
- Alcohol sold in grocery stores correlates (99.3%) with the total number of bridges in the United States.
- The marriage rate in Kentucky correlates (95.2%) with people who drowned after falling out of a fishing boat.
- Per capita consumption of mozzarella cheese correlates (95.9%) with Civil Engineering doctorates awarded; and
- Divorce rates in the US state of Maine correlate (99.3%) with the per capita consumption of margarine.

There are also periodic instances of correlation being confused with causation in the press. An example of this is an article by Shari Roan in the Los Angeles Times on December 16th, 2012, with the headline "Proximity to freeways increases autism risk, study finds". The article states that children born to mothers who live close to freeways have twice the risk of autism. The study, its authors state, adds to evidence suggesting that certain environmental exposures could play a role in causing the disorder in some children, albeit this subsequently proved to be false. However, with the power of computers in today's world, one can run millions of tests and claim a discovery which is simply random noise in the data, the consequence of which is that there are numerous examples of correlations masquerading as causation.

Testing for causality is challenging, but experimental design can help. This is where a researcher can test a hypothesis whereby, they can control one variable (the independent variable) and measure its impact on another variable (the dependent variable). Most importantly, it can help them control for possible confounders to avoid potential bias in their results. The conundrum however is exactly under what conditions can experimental data be used to deduce a causal relationship between two or more variables? The standard answer to this is that causality can be inferred from a well-designed randomized controlled experiment, albeit it is often impractical or impossible to do a randomized controlled experiment.

Simpson's paradox first described by Edward Simpson in 1951, is defined in Wikipedia as a phenomenon in probability and statistics in which a trend appears in several groups of data but disappears or reverses when the groups are combined. This result is often encountered in social science and medical science statistics and is problematic when frequency data is wrongly given causal interpretations. This paradox can be resolved when confounding variables and causal relations are appropriately addressed in statistical modelling. Simpson's paradox can also arise in correlations, in which two variables appear to have a positive correlation towards one another, when in fact they have a negative correlation, the reversal having been brought about by a lurking confounder. An example of this from economics is the situation where a dataset suggests overall demand is positively correlated with a price i.e., higher prices lead to greater demand, which is contrary to expectations. In this case, analysis reveals time to be the confounding variable: plotting price and demand against time reveals the expected negative correlation over various periods, which then reverses to become positive if the influence of time is ignored by simply plotting demand against price.

Rebecca Costa (2011, p 113) suggests that the reason for what she terms 'counterfeit correlation' has become so popular is easy to understand.

> *Casually observing a relationship, any relationship between two events, is magnitudes easier than the gruelling effort required to prove one thing actually causes another to occur. The consequence is that as the world becomes more complex and more difficult to segregate the root causes of problems, the natural response to complexity is that we simply begin to lower our standard for proof . . . we simply begin accepting beliefs in lieu of knowledge.*

Unintended Consequences

he law of unintended consequences states that any purposeful action will produce some unintended consequences i.e., the actions of people and governments will inevitably have some effects that are unintended and unanticipated. Unintended consequences are at work everywhere because of the world's inherent complexity, perverse incentives, stupidity, and cognitive biases (Norton, 2021), and can be grouped into three types: *Unexpected Benefit* which is a positive unintended and unanticipated benefit that emerges from an action and is also known as luck or serendipity; *Unexpected Drawback* which is a negative unexpected consequence which emerges when a simple regulation is imposed on a complex system; and *Perverse Result* which is a perverse effect contrary to what was originally intended from a solution to a problem (Wikipedia). Some examples of negative unexpected consequences are:

- The installation of smokestacks in the 17th century to decrease pollution in local areas, led to the spread of pollution at a higher altitude, and acid rain on an international scale.
- The introduction of seat belt laws. Although the wearing of seat belts was mandated to help protect drivers and passengers, it led to an increase in pedestrian and cyclist deaths. Arguably, the reason for this is that wearing seat belts makes drivers feel more secure, so they drive more aggressively.
- Passenger-side airbags in motorcars intended as a safety feature, led to an increase in child fatalities in the mid-1990s because small children were being hit by airbags that deployed automatically during collisions. The proposed solution to this was to move the child seat to the back of the vehicle, which then led to an increase in the number of children forgotten in unattended vehicles, some of whom died under extreme temperature conditions.
- The banning of DDT in less developed countries. In the early 1970s, the US government stopped aid to any country using the insecticide DDT, arguing that the insecticide caused cancer and harmed wildlife. While many third-world countries stopped using DDT, this led to more, not fewer, deaths because the incidence of malaria increased dramatically in countries that had stopped using DDT, since the insecticide had been effective in killing the mosquitoes that carry the disease.
- The *Exxon Valdez* oil spill in 1989. Following the spill, many US coastal states enacted laws placing unlimited liability on tanker operators. As a result, big oil companies such as the Royal Dutch/Shell group, began hiring independent, unreliable tanker operators with suspect ships, to deliver oil to the USA to avoid such risk, rather than using its own tanker fleet, thereby increasing the probability of spills.
- The indiscriminate and large-scale use of antibiotics which has resulted in hardier strains of bacteria and viruses, which no longer respond to traditional antibiotics.

The first detailed analysis of the concept of unintended consequences was done in 1936 by the American sociologist Robert King Merton. In an influential article titled *The Unanticipated Consequences of Purposive Social Action*, (1936, pp 894–904), Merton identified five sources of unanticipated consequences, albeit acknowledging the problem of "ascertaining the actual purpose of a given action" (p 807). The first two, and the most pervasive, were *ignorance* and *error*. The third source was the *imperious immediacy of interest* which refers to instances in which an individual's paramount concern with the foreseen and immediate intended consequence of an action, are such that he purposefully chooses to ignore any further unintended effects. The *Basic values* was Merton's fourth source, the example being "the Protestant ethic of hard work and asceticism, paradoxically leads to its own decline through the accumulation of wealth and possessions" (p 904). The final source of unanticipated consequences was the *self-defeating prediction* which refers to situations where the public prediction of a social development proves false, precisely because the prediction changes the course of history. While there are positive unanticipated benefits which have been seen repeatedly as part of serendipity, there is also of course the well-known idiom of Murphy's Law of unanticipated consequences which states that 'What Can Go Wrong, Will Go Wrong' and there are perverse effects that result in the opposite of what was intended. Merton also listed five probable causes of unanticipated consequences, namely:

-   Ignorance, making it impossible to anticipate everything leading to incomplete analysis.
-   Errors in analysis of the problem or following habits that worked in the past, but may not apply to the current situation.
-   Immediate interests overriding long-term interests.
-   Basic values which may require or prohibit certain actions, even if the long-term result might be unfavourable.
-   Self-defeating prophecy, or the fear of consequences which drives people to find solutions before the problem occurs, and thus the non-occurrence of the problem is not anticipated.

Signals Versus Noise and the Media

In undertaking research and trying to understand what is happening in the environment, as discussed previously, is the search is for signals. The word 'signal' is a metaphor for the coherent patterns and meaningful information that is hidden in data and is typically what we want to understand. But the term has two meanings. In the general sense, it can mean the entire data recording, including the noise and other artifacts, as in the 'raw signal' before processing is applied; but it can also mean the desirable or important part of the data, the true underlying signal that you seek to measure. A fundamental problem with signals is distinguishing the true underlying signal from the noise, which means the unwanted variation or fluctuation that interferes with the signal. In short, "the noise is the sum of innumerable independent pseudorandom forces that can influence the outcome and frustrate the measurement and obscure the signal, even when there is essentially no doubt that the signal exists" (Silver, 2012, p 37). Noisy data is data rendered meaningless as it is assumed that the signal is present, but is obscured by the noise. In the age of big and ever-growing data, more data means more noise and bigger challenges in isolating the signals. The consequence in systems with noisy data Silver suggests, is a two-step process. First, people mistake the noise for a signal. Secondly, the noise pollutes journals, blogs, and news accounts with false alarms undermining our ability to understand how the system really works.

Related to the above, another key factor to be aware of is the headlines in the press and the news channels. Silver (2012 p 12) contends that "the explosive, accelerating growth of knowledge in a rapidly changing and increasingly interdependent world, gives us so much to know about so many things that it seems impossible to keep up". The human brain "can store perhaps 3 terabytes of information. And yet that is only about one-millionth of the information that IBM says is now produced in the world each day." There are an estimated 347.3 billion emails sent daily, 100 billion messages sent on WhatsApp, 5 billion daily searches online and 4.5 million YouTube videos are viewed every minute the consequence of which is too much time is wasted going through useless information (https://www.bankmycell.com).

Conjecture about the future of the macroeconomy and the social fabric of the country is a constant feature of modern journalism and the inconsequential is often elevated to a crisis in the interests of selling newspapers or airtime; moreover, the crisis will have much greater news value if it seems imminent. For example, over the years we have seen the headlines in the media regarding SARS, Avian Flu and Zika, but there has been little, if any reference to MRSA (*Methicillin-resistant Staphylococcus Aureus*) and Candia Auris which infect several million people a year, or yellow fever, diarrheal diseases, tuberculosis and malaria which in combination, annually account for more than one in eight deaths globally. The media currently fixates on the COVID-19 pandemic, yet few people are aware of the 'forgotten pandemic', a strain of flu called 'Spanish Flu', a deadly influenza pandemic caused by the H1N1 influenza A virus. Lasting from February 1918 to April 1920, it infected 500 million people in four successive waves, and reportedly killed +/- 50 million people (Wikipedia).

The press's inability to report events or trends that are not crises is not limited to public affairs and domestic news. In his book *Who Stole the News? Why We Can't Keep Up with What Happens in the World (1994),* Mort Rosenblum argues that correspondents sacrifice coverage of important but undramatic long-term trends in favour of dramatic events whose real importance may be minimal. Coups and earthquakes are he suggests, what editors want to report. Mitchell et al. (2017, p 19) states that "we live in a world of 24/7 breaking news and, sadly, every other day there seems to be a terrorist attack or break-out of violence that is worse than the one reported a week elsewhere". We are he suggests, inundated with powerful images and shocked when an atrocity happens, but as the press moves to the next big event, we quickly forget what we just saw. This of course is not new, 40 years ago Chandler and Cockle (1982, p 5) stated that "A feature of modern journalism is that the inconsequential is often elevated to a crisis in the interests of selling newspapers or airtime. Moreover, the crisis will have much greater news value if it seems imminent. We are made to live in a maelstrom of anticipation, continuously learning that we are on the brink of a new dark age." Meanwhile, Paul Weaver (1998), a former political scientist at Harvard University, contends that the news media and governments "work together in a vicious circle of mutual manipulation and self-interest. Journalists need to concoct crises to sensationalise the news, and governments need to appear to be responding to the crises; the result is that they have jointly become so entangled in a web of lies that the news media are unable to inform the public what is true, and the government is unable to govern effectively." Rolf Dobelli, author of the book *Stop Reading the News: A Manifesto for a Happier, Calmer and Wiser Life (2020)* states that news is bad for your health, it leads to fear, aggression, hinders creativity and the ability to think deeply. He goes on to say that the consumption of news is irrelevant; news has no explanatory power and the more news one digests, the less of the big picture one will understand. At the same time, news increases cognitive errors by feeding confirmation bias and inhibits thinking because it disrupts concentration, weakens comprehension and kills creativity.

Predictable Surprises

Another factor which is essential to understanding the environment, are predictable surprises defined as events and sets of events that take an individual or group by surprise, despite prior awareness of the information necessary to have anticipated the events and their consequences. In summary, everyone knew a problem existed, that it would not solve itself, and that it would get worse over time, but nothing was done. An example of this. On April 29, 1995, a small group of Greenpeace activists boarded and occupied the Brent Spar, an obsolete oil-storage platform in the North Sea that Shell's UK arm was planning to sink. The activists, however, were intent on blocking Shell's decision, arguing that the tiny amounts of low-level radioactive residue in its storage tanks would damage the environment. The Greenpeace boats were blasted with water cannons from the Shell vessel, and over the next few days, things got worse as opposition to Shell's plan increased in Europe. In Germany, several Shell petroleum stations were firebombed and vandalised and a boycott of the petroleum stations was organized. Shell finally backed down and announced on June 20th, that it would not sink the Spar. Although the attack on the Spar had come as a surprise to the company, it was clearly a predictable surprise as Shell had all the information it needed to predict what would transpire; the company's security advisers had suggested that Greenpeace had a record of occupying environmentally sensitive structures and that activists might try to block the dumping of the Spar. However, the Shell management was convinced that it had made the right decision to dump the Spar and assumed that reasonable individuals would agree with their decision.

There are numerous examples of high-profile predictable disasters following missed signals and ignored warnings, such as the Iraq War; the events of September 11, 2001; the Enron scandal; the 2008 Global Financial Crisis; Hurricane Katrina and the government response; the ageing populations and depletion of social security funds; and China and India as the new economic hubs. The most recent was the global COVID vaccine crisis despite decades of warnings from health experts who said the nation's system for vaccine supply and distribution was growing increasingly fragile. Some of the predictable surprises result in short-term losses or distractions, while others are catastrophic and cause damage that takes years to repair. Bazerman and Watkins (2008) state that all companies are vulnerable to predictable surprises and almost every organ-isational failure is followed by a post-mortem that reveals that the surprises were pre-dicted but ignored. The surprises arise from cognitive, organisational, and political failures and they indicate that the five reasons we are most likely to be surprised are:

1. We have positive illusions that lead us to conclude that a problem does not exist, or it is not severe enough to merit action.
2. We interpret events in an egocentric manner i.e., when considering the fairness of proposed solutions to a looming crisis, we assign credit and blame in self-serving ways.
3. We overly discount the future, reducing our courage to act now to prevent some disaster that we believe to be quite distant.
4. We tend to maintain the status quo refusing to accept dramatic changes will occur if we do not address a problem; rather than confronting unpalatable choices, we avoid action.
5. Most of us do not invest in preventing a problem that we have not personally ex-perienced or witnessed; and we only fix problems after we have experienced sig-nificant harm or clearly imagine ourselves, or those close to us, in peril.

The 'Black Elephant'

The Elephant in the Room is about something large and obvious that is being ignored or overlooked. The Black Swan meanwhile, is an event which seems impossible and unpredictable until it occurs at which point, we concoct an explanation that makes it appear less random, and more predictable than it was. A Black Elephant, a term coined by Peter Ho, is a cross between a black swan and the proverbial elephant in the room and is an apparently dangerous but unpredictable event that should be very predictable, and represents a problem that everyone can see, but choose to ignore rather than acknowledging and dealing with it. However, when the problem erupts, everyone acts surprised and suggests that it is a Black Swan. The example Ho gives to illustrate this is the fact that the United Kingdom Treasury and the government, ap-parently made no contingency plans for Brexit, even though the polls indicated that the referendum outcome would be a close one. The increasing news media coverage of both global warming and increasingly large-scale freshwater pollution, are com-mon examples of black elephants.

Fundamental Disruptive Forces

In their book *No Ordinary Disruption: The Four Global Forces Breaking All the Trends,* Dobbs et al (2016) suggest that there are four fundamental disruptive forces, which rank amongst the greatest changes ever witnessed affecting the global economy. The first is a combination of the shifting of the World's Economic Centre of Gravity to the east and south i.e., China and other emerging economies. The government of China began its economic reforms in 1978 under Deng Xiaoping and as a result, has the world's second-largest economy when measured by nominal GDP, and the largest when measured by Purchasing Power Parity (https://en.wikipedia.org/wiki/Economy_of_China). A forecast by Elliot (2020) states that China will become the world's largest nominal GDP economy by 2028. It currently has four of the world's top ten competitive financial centres, namely Shanghai, Hong Kong, Beijing, and Shenzhen, and three of the world's largest stock exchanges, Shanghai, Hong Kong and Shenzhen (Wikipedia). However, it should be noted that the current state of the Chinese economy suggests that China may be on the edge of a major collapse.

The 2023 population of China is estimated at 1.426 million, equivalent to 17.7% of the total world population. Meanwhile, the number of megacities (10 million +) in the world, will increase from 23 to 37 by 2025, of which 22 will be in Asia. Among the consequences of this will be altered patterns of living, family structures and social hierarchy, and the impact on the environment in terms of fuel, water, power, and sanitation demands.

The second disruptive force is the economic impact of accelerating technological innovation and Artificial Intelligence (AI) and its adoption, which combined with the data revolution, gives individuals and businesses unprecedented amounts of information, and ultimately shortens the life cycles of businesses. A figure quoted by Capgemini (Bonnet et al., 2015) is that since 2000, 52% of companies in the Fortune 500 have either gone bankrupt, been acquired, or ceased to exist largely because of digital disruption. The third force is demographics. The current global population is expected to reach 8.5 billion by 2030, and people will need 30% more water, 40% more energy and 50% more food to survive. Meanwhile, birth rates will continue to fall while life spans increase and the population of those aged 65+ will more than double from 600m to 1.1bn by 2050. The consequences of the ageing population and declining fertility rates will firstly, result in smaller workforces which will unsurprisingly increase the focus on productivity to drive growth; secondly, providing care and facilities for increasing numbers of elderly will significantly impact government finances. The fourth and final disruptive force suggested by Dobbs et al, is what the authors describe as 'accelerating flows' which represents the fact that the world is increasingly connected through a complex web of trade, capital, people and information ushering in a dynamic new phase of globalisation.

Disruption is not a passing phase, there are others such as the Harvard Business Review (10 Apr 2019) who suggest there are "7 Disruptive Forces That Leaders Should Incorporate into Growth Strategies", while MIT Sloan Management Review (March 10, 2020) suggest that there are "11 Sources of Disruption Every Company Must Monitor." Dobbs et al state that what we are seeing is no ordinary disruption, but the new facts of business life and although we may be aware of these disruptions, most executives and business leaders do not comprehend their magnitude or their knock-on effects.

The graveyard is full of companies that were once successful market leaders who subsequently failed largely because of disruptions and obsolete assumptions including:

– Statistical distribution in which the normal (bell) curve is used almost everywhere risk is quantified, and in classical statistics, the extremes generally do not matter very much to the aggregate outcome. However, Kay (2009) suggests that it has become apparent that extreme events, especially extreme adverse events, happen much more often than they are supposed to in the world of classical statistics. It is therefore essential to choose appropriate models which require an understanding of both the mathematics and the business environment.

– Nowotny (2013) states that "what produces complexity is not so much the presence of many direct cause-effect links which operate with subtlety versus precision, but rather the presence of indirect, non-linear relationships between the variables, parts, and dimensions of the whole." What makes complex systems so complex, she suggests, "is not the belief in simple cause-effect relationships often embodying implicit assumptions about linearity, but their "multiple feedback loops and their indirect cause-effect relations which play out at different speeds and on different time scales to ever-changing patterns of unpredictability."

– Drucker (1999) whose point mentioned earlier, is that executives are so internally focused and enchanted by the internal data the computer generates, that they keep looking inside the organisation instead of outside to see and understand what is happening, even though all major changes usually come from outside the company, not the inside. Support for this comes from Wack (1995a) who states that in times of rapid change strategic failure, especially in large successful companies, is often caused by the inability to see an emergent novel reality by being locked inside obsolete assumptions. Hamel and Prahalad (1994) also support this, suggesting that most managers spend less than 3% of their time thinking about and building a corporate perspective on the future. The inevitable consequence is that they do not see the problem(s) until it is too late. There is growing evidence Gowing and Langdon (2018, p 5) contend, that "what were claimed to be 'unthinkables' did often exist, but blind eyes were turned, because of a lack of will to believe the signs, or an active preference to deny, and then not to engage."

To conclude the discussion on elements to be aware of in developing an understanding of the contextual environment, the final elements are 'Tipping Points and Inflection Points' and 'Risk versus Uncertainty.'

Tipping Points and Inflection Points

Malcom Gladwell in his book *The Tipping Point: How Little Things Can Make a Big Difference, (2002)*, compares the progress of change with an epidemic and its mechanisms, and provides examples of how different things spread in society. After reaching a certain point of occurrence, the change 'tips' and is unleashed on a massive scale, which may be beneficial, or have extremely negative effects. It has become increasingly apparent that many complex systems have critical thresholds, or tipping points, at which the system shifts suddenly from one state to another. The phrase 'tipping point' was first used in sociology by Morton Grodzins who adopted the phrase from physics where it referred to the adding of a small amount of weight to a balanced object until the additional weight caused the object to topple or tip. The phrase has since been extended and applied to any process, representing the critical point in a situation beyond which a significant and often unstoppable effect or change takes place. The problem is that it is hard to foresee the critical transitions simply because the state of a system may show minor change before the tipping point, and models of complex systems are usually not accurate enough to reliably predict tipping points.

An 'Inflection Point' meanwhile is defined as "a point on a continuous plane curve at which the curve changes from being concave (concave downward) to convex (concave upward), or vice versa" (Quora.com). Similar to a tipping point, an inflection point is an event that results in a significant change in the progress of a company, industry, sector, economy, or geopolitical situation, and can be considered a turning point after which a dramatic change with either positive or negative results, is expected to result. Inflection points are more significant than the small day-to-day changes typically seen, and when an inflection point is identified, it is often a sign that the affected industry must make certain fundamental changes to continue to operate. An example of this is the introduction of the smartphone which meant that other mobile technology manufacturers had to adapt to the changing market conditions to remain in business. To qualify as an inflection point, the shift must be noticeable or decisive, attributed to a particular cause, and represent an event that changes the way we think and act. According to McGrath (2019) the reason recognizing strategic inflection points is important, is that if you get the inflection point right, it will take your business to new heights; if you get it wrong, your business can go into decline.

Risk and Uncertainty

There is a difference between risk and uncertainty. Risk is where we do not know what is going to happen next, but through repeated observations, we know what the statistical distribution looks like, and we can estimate the frequencies with which different outcomes will arise. As far as uncertainty is concerned, Courtney (2003) states that there are four levels:
- Level 1: Low uncertainty, a single and clear view of the future and dependable outcomes.
- Level 2: A limited set of possible future outcomes, one of which will occur; sufficient historical precedents can be used to estimate outcomes with reasonable certainty.

- Level 3: Outcomes are indeterminate, events are unique but bounded within a range.
- Level 4: True uncertainty, a limitless range of possible outcomes with many unknowns.

Risk analysis and management meanwhile, is a well-established profession with sophisticated methods being applied. EWS are important contributions to anticipating and managing future risks, which are often classified as:
- Hazards: The results of nature or technical failure, including human error; or
- Threats: The results of terrorist or criminal activity.

The risk from a hazard or threat is the combination of the likelihood of it occurring and the impact that it may have. The category of risk is based on a phrase from a response from Donald Rumsfeld, the former United States Secretary of Defence, at a U.S. Department of Defence (DoD) news briefing in 2002, regarding 'known knowns' from which developed four categories of information.
- Known Known: information that exists and is known.
- Known unknown: information that is understood to exist but is not in the possession of the person seeking it.
- Unknown known: information that an individual or organisation has in its possession but whose existence, relevance or value has not been realized.
- Unknown unknown: information that a person or organization is completely unaware of.

Conclusions

In a well-constructed set of scenarios, the future is likely to contain elements of each scenario in combinations, and it is therefore important to test policies against a range of scenarios to see how effective they are. This process is called 'wind-tunnelling' which can be undertaken by a policy team or through workshops with a range of stakeholders and is Goodwin and Wright (2001) contend, is an underdeveloped element of scenario planning.

While scenarios are a potentially powerful tool for developing and testing policies, they should not be seen as a mechanical approach to achieving the 'right' policy or as a tool to remove the uncertainty of the future, but a key benefit of using scenarios is that they challenge mindsets and open up consideration of a wider range of options. An equally significant role of developing scenarios is to challenge and safeguard against preconceived views of the future and associated policies. Where possible, a cross-section of stakeholders should be engaged in the policy development process as this can provide a good framework for facilitating a strategic discussion on policy options, with the stakeholders contributing to the analysis and having ownership of the outcomes. When testing policies against scenarios it is important to consider:

– Their relevance, as the factors being addressed may not be a significant issue in a particular scenario.
– Their practicality, as the policies may not be effective given the conditions in the scenario, or they may not be politically or financially deliverable; and
– Their implementation, as while a policy may be potentially successful across a range of scenarios, the way it is presented and implemented in each could be quite different.

There may be valid reasons why a policy that is contingent on a particular scenario should be implemented, and in such circumstances, the analysis can be used to consider how the policy could be adapted to make it more robust in other scenarios, and to consider the risks associated with the policy. The development of strategies or policies is a complex area and the objective of policy analysis is to explore which policies are going to maximise the opportunities and mitigate the challenges inherent in the scenarios, and which are resilient to future shocks. Hughes (2009) states that it is worth reflecting that though the work of scenarios is frequently associated with representing uncertainty, they have potentially an extremely vital role in provoking a detailed and unprejudiced review of present factors, which can sometimes result in a great deal more certainty about the future that might have been imagined. Much of this he suggests, is through ruling out impossibilities, support for which comes from Wack who noted that scenarios deny more than they affirm (Wack 1985b, p 140).

Ged Davis, the head of the Shell scenario team from 1999–2003, stated that "All successful scenarios are focused in the sense that they are derived from a fundamental consideration of their client's dilemmas and needs" (Wilkinson and Kupers, 2013). Wack meanwhile identified three essential starting points for corporate strategy: global scenarios, competitive positioning, and strategic vision. The first represents the world of possibility, the second the world of relativity, and the third the world of creativity. The challenge in effective scenario work is to go beyond the usual strategic focus on current trends and competitive positioning, to find the right scale of observation. The next challenge is to look for some degree of fit between the company's core capabilities and the variety of plausible future conditions. The success of the strategic vision thus depends on matching capabilities and context and scenarios can help that vision evolve.

Homer-Dixon (2011, p 5) sums all of this by stating that:

"The complexity and speed of today's economic, social, and ecological systems exceed the human brain's grasp, and very few of us have more than a rudimentary understanding of how these systems work . . . they are fraught with countless unknown unknowns of new threats and uncharted uncertainties . . . and the rate and scale of change is much faster than most are even prepared to concede or respond to." The result is that worries about the risk of existential risks are widespread and growing.

The chapter which follows, explores issues which have a significant impact on scenario development namely, the systematic cognitive errors in thinking and reasoning that occur when individuals activate, process, and interpret information that they are unaware of, but which affects the decisions and judgments that they make. This is an area in the scenario development process which has received little attention in the literature.

References

Amanatidou, E., Butter, M., Carabias, V., Konnola, T., Leis, M., Saritas, O., Schaper-Rinkel, P. and van Rij, V. (2012). On concepts and methods in horizon scanning: Lessons from initiating policy dialogues on emerging issues. Science and Public Policy 39, 208–221.

Attila, H. and Matthias, W.K. (2017). The Role of Foresight in Shaping the Next Production Revolution, chapter 9 in: The Next Production Revolution, Implications for Governments and Business, OECD, 303.

Banta, H.D. and Gelijns, A. (1998). An early system for the identification and assessment of future health technology. The Dutch STG Project. International Journal of Technology Assessment in Health Care, 14, 4, 607–612.

Bazeman, M. H. and Watkins, M. (2008). Predictable Surprises: The Disasters You Should Have Seen Coming and How to Prevent Them. Harvard Business School Press.

Boettiger, C., Ross, N. and Hastings, A. (2013). Early warning signals: the charted and uncharted territories. Theoretical Ecology, 6, 255–264.

Bonnet, D., Buvat, J., and Subrahmanyam, K.V.I. (2015). When Digital Disruption Strikes: How Can Incumbents Respond? Capgemini Consulting, 1–12.

Carney, J. (2018). The Ten Commandments of Horizon Scanning. Futures Capability & Resource. https://foresightprojects.blog.gov.uk/2018/03/08/the-ten-commandments-of-horizon-scanning/

Chandler, J. and Cockle, P. (1982). Techniques of Scenario Planning. McGraw-Hill Book Company, England.

Chatfield, T. (2016). There's a counter-intuitive downside to collecting vast amounts of information about economics and human behaviour: it can mean we ignore the lessons of history. BBC Future: the trouble with big data? It's called the 'recency bias'

Consensus Study Report 2020. Safeguarding the Bioeconomy. National Academies Press (US); Washington D.C.

Costa, R. D. (2011). The Watchman's Rattle: Thinking our Way out of Extinction. Virgin Books, Ebury Publishing.

Courtney, H. (2003). Decision-driven scenarios for assessing four levels of uncertainty. Strategy & Leadership, 31, 1, 14–22

Dobelli, R. (2020). Stop Reading the News: A Manifesto for a Happier, Calmer and Wiser Life. Hachette, UK.

Dobbs, R., Manyika, J. and Woetzel, J. R. (2016). No Ordinary Disruption: The Four Global Forces Breaking All the Trends. PublicAffairs.

Douw, K. and Vondeling, H. (2006). Selection of new health technologies for assessment aimed at informing decision making: A survey among horizon scanning systems. International Journal of Technology Assessment in Health Care. 22, 2, 177–183.

Drucker, P. (1999). Management Challenge for the 21st Century. Harper Collins, U.K.

Elliot, L. (2020). China to overtake US as world's biggest economy by 2028, the report predicts. The Guardian, 26 December.

Gladwell, M. (2002). The Tipping Point: How Little Things Can Make a Big Difference. Paperback. Little Brown and Company, London.

Goodwin, P and Wright, G. (2001). Enhancing Strategy Evaluation in Scenario Planning: A Role for Decision Analysis. Journal of Management Studies, 38, 1, pp 1–16.

Gowing, N. and Langdon, C.(2018). Thinking the Unthinkable. A New Imperative for Leadership in the Digital Age: An Interim Report by Nik Gowing and Chris Langdon. Chartered Institute of Management Accountants.

Habeggar, B, (2009). Horizon Scanning in Government: Concept, Country Experience, and Models for Switzerland. Political Science.

Hamel G. and Pralahad, C.K. (1994). Competing for the Future. Harvard Business Review, July- August.

Harford, T. (2020). How to Make the World Add Up. Ten Rules for Thinking Differently About Numbers. Little, Brown Book Group.

Hines, P., Yu, L.H., Guy, R.H., Brand, A., and Papaluca-Amati, M. (2019). Scanning the horizon: a systematic literature review of methodologies. BMJ Open, 1–9.

Ho, P. (2012). Coping with Complexity. Mckinsey & Company, 1–3.

Ho, P. (2017). The black elephant challenge for governments. An excerpt from a speech to the Institute of Policy Studies' S R Nathan Fellow for the Study of Singapore. The Straits Times, 7 April.

Höfer,T., Przyrembel,H. and Verleger, S. (2004). New Evidence for the Theory of the Stork. Paediatric and Perinatal Epidemiology, 18, 1, 1–92

Homer-Dixon, T. (2011). Complexity Science. Oxford Leadership Journal, 2, 1, 1–15.

Hughes, N. (2009). Transition Pathways to a Low Carbon Economy; A Historical Overview of Strategic Scenario Planning, a Joint Working Paper of the UKERC and the Eon.UK/EPSRC Transition Pathways Project.

Institute of Risk Management (2018). Horizon Scanning: A Practitioner's Guide Produced by the Innovation Special Interest Group of the Institute of Risk Management

Jørgensen, T. and Carlsson, P. (1998). Introduction: International Journal of Technology Assessment in Health Care. 14, 4, 603–606.

Kay, J. (2009). The Long and Short of it, a Guide to Finance and Investment for Normally Intelligent People who aren't in the industry. Profile books. London.

Laborde, R. (2020). The Three V's of Big Data: Volume, Velocity, and Variety. Oracle Life Sciences Blog. Data Management.

Lindstrom, M. (2016). Small Data: The Tiny Clues That Uncover Huge Trends. The St. Martin's Publishing Group

Loveridge, D. (2009). Foresight: The Art and Science of Anticipating the Future. Routledge, New York and London.

McGrath, R. (2020). Oslo Business Forum. Creating Early Warnings Scenarios. https://www.obforum.com/article/creating-early-warnings-scenarios-rita-mcgrath

McGrath, R. (2019). Seeing Around Corners: How to Spot Inflection Points in Business Before They Happen. HarperCollins.

Merton, R. K. (1936). The Unanticipated Consequences of Purposive Social Action. American Sociological Review, 1, 6, 894–904.

Mitchell, A., Gottfried, J., Shearer, E., and Lu, Kristine (2017). How Americans encounter, recall and act upon digital news. Pew Research Center.

Norton, R. (2021). Unintended Consequences. https://www.sas.upenn.edu/~haroldfs/540/handouts/french/unintconseq.html

Nowotny, H. (2013). The embarrassment of complexity. 5th global Peter Drucker Forum. November 26th.

Nowotny, H., Scott, P., Gibbons, M., (2001). Re-Thinking Science: Knowledge and the Public in an Age of Uncertainty. Polity Press, Cambridge.

Rittel, H. W. J. and Webber, M. M. (1973). Dilemmas in a General Theory of Planning. Policy Sciences, 4, 2, 155–169. Springer.

Roan, S. (2012). Proximity to freeways increases autism risk, study finds. Los Angeles Times, December 16th.

Rosenblum, M. (1994). Who Stole the News? Why We Can't Keep Up with What Happens in the World and What We Can Do About It. John Wiley & Sons.

Silver, N. (2013). The Signal and the Noise: The Art and Science of Prediction. Penguin.

van der Heijden, K. 2005. Scenarios: The Art of Strategic Conversation. Chichester, West Sussex, England; John Wiley & Sons Ltd.

Van Rij, V. (2010a). Joint horizon scanning: identifying common strategic choices and questions for knowledge. Science and Public Policy, 37, 7–18.

Vigen, T. (2015). Spurious Correlations. Hachette Books.

Wack, P. (1985a). Unchartered Waters Ahead. Harvard Business Review, September-October, 73–89.

Wack, P. (1985b). Scenarios: Shooting the Rapids. Harvard Business Review, November-December, 139–150.

Weaver, P. H. (1998). News and the Culture of Lying: How Journalism Really Works, The Free Press.

Wilkinson, A., and Kupers, R. (2013). Living in the Futures. Harvard Business Review, May.

Wintle, B., Kennicutt II., Mahlon, C, and Sutherland, W.J. (2020). Scanning horizons in research, policy and practice. Conservation Research, Policy and Practice, edited by Sutherland, W.J. and Brotherton, P. Cambridge University Press, 29–47.

Yule, G. U (1911). An introduction to the theory of statistics. C. Griffin and Company, Limited, London.

Chapter 7
How People Think

Introduction

Why in a book on scenarios, is there a chapter on how people think? The answer is in developing scenarios, the individual facilitating the development process must have a solid understanding of the cognitive factors affecting how people think and reason. Most of us are oblivious to the systematic errors in thinking that occur when processing and interpreting information, impacting our decisions and judgments. Although we like to believe that we are rational, logical people, we are influenced by cognitive biases and heuristics we have absorbed and developed throughout our lives. Due to the importance of the influence of mental models in our thinking, this chapter starts with the role of heuristics and biases, a list of which is available in Appendix G, and the following sections provide a brief review of some of the more commonly known ones.

Heuristics and Biases

Heuristics are mental shortcuts that we use to form judgments and make decisions. They help us reduce task complexity and cognitive overload in judgment and choice, allowing us to quickly reach conclusions and solutions to complex problems. Biases, on the other hand, are the systematic errors and resulting gaps between normative and heuristically determined behaviour. They can be considered like filters on how we see the world, twisting our thinking and judgement unbeknownst to us.

Herbert A. Simon, a cognitive psychologist, first introduced the concept of heuristics in the 1950s. However, it was not until the 1970s when psychologists Amos Tversky and Daniel Kahneman introduced specific heuristic models that researchers started to take a closer look at the topic. Subsequently, a large body of psychological research associated with subjective probability estimates and probability theory began to develop, and the field has expanded since (https://en.wikipedia.org/wiki/Heuristic_(psychology) with much of the reported research undertaken in the period 1960s – 1980s.

Alongside Tversky and Kahneman, pioneers in this area include Lee Beach, Ward Edwards, and Lawrence Phillips who focused principally on examining the accuracy and coherence of subjective probability judgments. Brunswick (1956) provided the rationale for this line of enquiry based on two assumptions: The first was that as future events are inherently uncertain and unpredictable, individuals would, out of necessity, learn to accurately evaluate uncertainty to cope effectively. The second assumption was that individuals would intuitively use probability theory to evaluate the unpredictability of future events, given that probability theory, in particular Bayes's theorem, was the normative model of portraying uncertainty. Consequently, research

https://doi.org/10.1515/9783111617442-007

on subjective probability focused on identifying the extent to which subjective judgments of uncertain events conformed to Bayes' theorem. However, in the early 1970s, a major line of research work by Kahneman, Tversky, Slovic and their colleagues resulted in a general set of findings which turned these assumptions on their head. The authors showed that because of apparent cognitive limitations, individuals tended to intuitively rely on a limited number of inferential judgmental rules, known as heuristics, to reduce the complex task of determining the likelihood of uncertain events. Kahneman and Tversky (1973) established that heuristic principles are valid in some situations and can even result in reasonable judgments. However, these heuristics have also been found to lead to biases, which inevitably result in errors in the intuitive judgment of probability. Subjective judgments play a significant role in scenarios; consequently, much of the research findings associated with heuristics and biases can be generalizable to scenarios. The following section examines the most widely discussed heuristics and biases in the behavioural and psychological literature, starting with representativeness, availability and anchoring and adjustment.

The Representativeness Heuristic

Tversky and Kahneman (Kahneman and Tversky, 1982a; 1973; 1972; Tversky and Kahneman, 1982b) have shown that people intuitively evaluate the probability of an event by how representative it is of their mental models. For example, when asked to judge the probability that event A occurs given that event B has already occurred, by extension, individuals assign probabilities to uncertain events according to how closely the events represent their model of the world and or their understanding of the processes; the greater the degree of representativeness, the higher the probability of occurrence assigned to the events, and the higher the confidence associated with the resultant prediction. However, Kahneman and Tversky (1973; Tversky and Kahneman, 1982a) contend that the expected accuracy of judgments based on representativeness appears to be unaffected by the quality and reliability of the information that forms the basis of the prediction. The most cited examples of this are experiments in which research subjects are given descriptions of individuals and lists of occupations, and are asked to assess the probability of which occupations they are engaged in. Subjects generally assigned occupations by assessing the degree to which the descriptions of the individuals were representative of the stereotypical image of each occupation. For example, someone described as quiet and intelligent with an eye for order and details but little interest in people or sport, is more likely to be assessed as an accountant rather than a salesperson. It appears that individuals do not consider either the reliability of the descriptions or their appropriateness, as a basis for their prediction.

Although the representativeness heuristic is generally assumed to mean the degree of similarity between a sample and a population, this is not the only interpretation. Tversky and Kahneman (1982b) claim that representativeness can also derive from other relationships such as the degree of correspondence between cause-and-effect beliefs, with a reliance on this heuristic leading to predictable errors of judgment because "it has a logic of its own which differs from the logic of probability" (Tversky and Kahneman, 1982b, p. 39).

The Availability Heuristic

Tversky and Kahneman (1973; 1982a; 1982d) demonstrated that individuals intuitively estimate the frequency of a class, or intuitively judge the probability of an event, by the ease with which they can remember or imagine instances of a similar nature. Supporting these findings, Lichtenstein et al. (1980) showed that the frequency of highly publicised events was significantly overestimated by individuals, while less publicised events were underestimated. This is commonly known as the 'availability' heuristic and is well documented in the literature; individuals have been found to apply it instinctively and attempt to justify its use, even after it has been shown to be prone to error (Maier, 1981).

In general terms, the availability heuristic suggests that: (a) instances or events which occur more frequently are more readily recalled from memory than those which occur less often; (b) instances or events which are more likely to occur are more easily imagined than those which are less likely to occur: and (c) instances of larger classes are more easily constructed in the mind than are instances of smaller classes. A cornerstone of availability is that there are essentially only two mental operations by which things are summoned to mind i.e., *recall* (retrieval from memory) and *construction* (the process of imaging), both of which are affected by several factors ultimately leading to predictable biases.

Anchoring and Adjustment

The third widely discussed heuristic identified by Tversky and Kahneman is commonly termed 'anchoring and adjustment' (Tversky and Kahneman,1982a). When making an estimate, individuals often begin with some initial value (the anchor), and then adjust the value up or down to reflect subsequent information to arrive at a final answer. The initial value is either explicit in that it exists naturally, or it is implicitly derived from how the problem is framed. Regardless of the initial anchor value or how it is obtained, once established, people tend to make insufficient adjustments to arrive at a final answer because they are influenced by the initial anchor value. Examples of this anchoring and adjustment phenomenon have been replicated extensively in the academic literature (Butler, 1986; Joyce and Biddle, 1981a/b; Slovic and Lichtenstein, 1971; Smith and Kilda, 1991). In keeping with the anchoring and adjustment heuristic, Tversky, Kahneman and others (Bar-Hillel, 1973; Cohen et al., 1972) documented the fact that when dealing with compound events, individuals tend to overestimate the probability of conjunctive events because of anchoring effects.

Although representativeness, availability and anchoring are the most frequently cited heuristics and biases in the literature, many others impact human judgment and accordingly, impact scenario development, the most common of which are discussed below.

Base Rate Fallacy

A core principle of prediction is that a base rate represents a statistical summary of the history of a particular situation. Therefore, regardless of what additional information is gathered about the situation, the base rate remains valid. However, experiments by Kahneman and Tversky and others (Johnson, 1983; Nisbett and Ross, 1980; Swieringa et al. 1976) have shown that individuals apply base rates correctly only when lacking specific details; when this information is supplied, they ignore the base rate. Thus, estimating probability by reference to representativeness means that prior probabilities are not considered. Again, this is illustrated in the individual description versus occupation experiments described earlier. Even where research subjects are given information indicating the individual is associated with a particular occupation, probabilities are estimated based on stereotypical traits rather than prior statistical evidence. This violates one of the key rules of statistical prediction and is one of the most common damaging biases (Cooke, 1991).

Sample Size Bias

Research has shown that individuals are not sensitive to sample size when relying on representativeness, and may not even be aware of the bias (Kahneman and Tversky, 1972; Borgida and Nisbett, 1977; Nisbett and Ross, 1980; Ross et al., 1977; and Schwenk, 1984). This means that samples of inadequate size are assumed to be representative of the population, and judgments based on these samples are accorded an unwarranted level of confidence. This phenomenon is described by Tversky and Kahneman (1982e, p 23) as a "belief in the law of small numbers". Studies have also shown that when presented with vivid but single samples of unknown populations, individuals tend to make unwarranted generalisations from the samples, even when made aware of the fact that the samples are highly atypical of the populations (Hamill et al., 1980; Lichtenstein et al., 1982).

Misconceptions of Random Events

There are two elements to this heuristic, the first being what may be described as the 'short-run fallacy.' This fallacy arises from the fact that individuals intuitively expect that the sequence of events generated by a random process will be representative of the essential characteristics of that process, even when the sequence is too short for this to be the case (Tversky and Kahneman, 1982a). For example, in tossing a coin, the odds are that 50% of the time 'heads' (H) will result and 50% of the time 'tails' (T) will result. Therefore, when tossing a coin six times, the sequence of H-T-H-T-H-T is generally perceived as being more likely than a sequence such as H-H-H-H-T-H which does not appear random and therefore does not accord with the '50/50' rule for a coin toss.

The second element relates to the misconception of random events known as the 'gamblers fallacy.' This is a phenomenon in which individuals intuitively, but incorrectly, believe that chance is a self-correcting process. Thus, deviations in one direction of a sequence of randomly generated, statistically independent events, are thought to automatically induce a deviation in the opposite direction to restore imbalances. The key element here is the statistical independence. This means that the occurrence of one event does not influence the probability of the occurrence of another event. For example, having witnessed several tosses of a coin all of which result in H, most people intuitively believe that the next toss of the coin is more likely to result in T to 'correct' the deviation from the expected sequence of H-T-H-T. Events which are not statistically independent are those whose occurrence is influenced by the event that took place before. For example, the probability of choosing an Ace from a deck of cards is 4 in 52 (there are four Aces from a deck of 52 cards), or 1 in 13. If an Ace is chosen, and, critically not returned to the deck, then the probability of selecting an Ace a second time is now 3 in 51, or 1 in 17. According to this heuristic, random events are not recognized as being random which results in individuals perceiving patterns or trends which do not actually exist, affecting their anticipation of the future.

The Misconception of Regression and the Conjunction Fallacy

'Regression towards the mean' describes a phenomenon whereby successive measurement or evaluation will result in random fluctuations around the mean. Thus, values initially recorded as above average will subsequently decline, whereas values initially below average will improve. For example, in the case of repeated examinations, an initial outstanding performance will usually be followed by one which is less than outstanding, whereas an initial inferior performance will generally be followed by an improved one. This is not due to some external balancing force of the universe, but rather due to the many factors that can contribute to extreme outcomes. However, Kahneman and Tversky (1973) have demonstrated empirically that individuals do not generally anticipate the phenomenon of regression, even in situations in which it is obvious it will occur. This failure is because it is counterintuitive, and when faced with the phenomenon, individuals concoct bogus causal explanations for it.

Tversky and Kahneman (1982b) argue that the greatest conflict between the logic of representativeness and that of probability, arises when individuals make probability judgments about compound events. A fundamental law of probability theory is that the probability of two or more events occurring simultaneously cannot be higher than the probability of each of the events occurring independently, a rule is known as the 'conjunction fallacy.' In experiments, Tversky and Kahneman (1982b; 1983) observed that although individuals accept the conjunction rule in its abstract form, in practice they intuitively consider the conjunction of events to be more representative and therefore more probable than the probability of the individual events comprising the conjunction, especially where the events are causally linked. The classic example of this is given by the 'Linda problem'.

Linda is a single 31-year-old, smart and outspoken individual. While a student, Linda was active in issues concerning discrimination, social justice and engaged in anti-nuclear demonstrations. People are then asked to evaluate the probability of the following statements regarding Linda:
1. Linda is a bank teller.
2. Linda is a bank teller and an active feminist.

Many people choose the second statement as being more likely, despite it containing two separate events which need to occur together i.e. Linda being a bank teller and Linda being a feminist. For the second statement to have the same probability as the first would mean that a requirement of being a bank teller is that you are active in the feminist movement. Probability theory indicates that the chance of two events occurring together in conjunction is the multiple of the two individual events occurring separately. Since both probabilities must by default be less than 1 (which is a certainty, death being the only one), then the multiple of two numbers less than 1 must be smaller than the largest of the two starting values.

The evidence demonstrates that violation of the conjunction rule is pervasive, and is based on the representativeness heuristic.

Biases Due to Retrievability of Instances

Events more easily retrieved from memory appear more numerous than events which occur with the same frequency but are more difficult to retrieve. Two interrelated biases are at work here, one associated with how individuals store information, and a second relating to how they retrieve it, with these two aspects themselves affected by several factors:
–   *Salience*: Evidence from a wide range of empirical studies has shown that vivid and concrete information is more memorable than abstract, pallid information.

Furthermore, this vivid and concrete information has a greater impact on theory development, even if it is contradictory and inferior (Abelson, 1976; Anderson, 1983b; Chapman and Chapman, 1969; Cyert and March, 1963; Hamill et al., 1980; Janis and Mann, 1977; Nisbett and Ross, 1980; Walster, 1966). An example would be someone watching a sensational news report of a plane crash, leading the individual to conclude that plane travel is more dangerous than car travel, despite statistical evidence to the contrary.

- *Recency* or *primacy*: Incidents which have occurred recently are more likely to occupy a prominent position in memory and are therefore more readily retrieved. Because they are more readily retrieved, recent incidents are given greater weight in decision-making than is warranted (Bower, 1970; Montgomery and Weinberg,1973).
- *Familiarity*: People generally prefer some things, ideas, or individuals, simply due to familiarity or repeated exposure. Familiar events or incidents can then be mistakenly judged as occurring more frequently than those which are less familiar.
- *Representativeness*: Events which are the most representative, are also those that are the most easily learned, stored, and subsequently recalled from memory. These findings are derived from research around concept formation and pattern recognition (Posner and Keele, 1968; Rosch, 1978). Individuals judge the likelihood or frequency of an event by how much the event resembles the data or group population. A common example is stereotyping, whereby an individual assumes to know someone because a few traits of that group are present in the person.

The above biases are to do with understanding data that already exists which is what scenario planning teams must do when undertaking their research. However, not everything that can happen has already occurred. Consequently, when dealing with the future, scenario teams may have to concoct plausible and imaginative situations that have not taken place before, and this process poses unique challenges.

Biases Due to Imaginability

Instances or events which are not stored in memory need to be constructed or imagined according to established rules. Interestingly, strong evidence exists that the areas in the brain that serve remembering, also play an active role in imagining future experiences or events. In situations where people must imagine, they tend to evaluate the frequency or probability of events according to how easy it is to imagine them (Schacter et al., 2012; Schacter et al., 2017; True-Love, M. et al., 2018).) This leads to bias because the most easily imagined events may not necessarily be the most frequent or most probable. The operation of imagining events is a mental simulation process which plays a key role in our judgment. Kahneman and Tversky (1982b) conducted experimental work on reconstructing the past using stories of a fatal accident resulting from extraordinary coincidences. They asked participants to imagine changes to the story and found that surviving relatives exhibited a strong preference for introducing specific types of changes that they called 'downhill changes.' Downhill changes are those in which surprising or unexpected events are removed from the story; conversely, an 'uphill change' introduces surprising or unlikely events. Thus, participants exhibited a preference for removal, rather than addition, of surprising change. The implication of this is that in imagining events, outcomes which can only be reached by invoking uphill assumptions are therefore likely to be difficult and regarded as infrequent and improbable. The bias in service of downhill thinking is dangerous because, as Kahneman and Tversky note, failure in planning is often associated with the advent of unimagined and unexpected uphill changes. Factors which affect imaginability include:

- *Effectiveness of the information search set*: Information is stored in human memory in the form of an 'associative network' in which nodes representing concepts, are connected by links representing relations between the concepts (Anderson and Bower, 1973; Collins and Loftus, 1975; Collins and Quillian, 1969; Norman and Rumelhart, 1975). Thus, the activation of one node in the network will activate other nodes in a path or search set according to the associative or causal links between nodes. Instances or events searched for and retrieved from memory are largely dependent upon what search set within the individual's knowledge base is elicited. The search set produced depends on the starting point, as the starting point, will, by activating nodes in an associative pathway, determine what information is subsequently generated. Importantly, the starting point is itself influenced by factors such as saliency. Thus, activation of different search sets results in different frequency and probability judgments being assigned to the same problem. This is because different search sets are unlikely to contain identical availability of instances or events.

- *Incomplete information*: Fischhoff et al. (1988) demonstrated that once a search set is established, individuals are insensitive to the completeness of information in the search set, even when data essential for the decision is missing. For example, in a series of experiments Fischhoff (1988) presented individuals with various decision trees for discovering why a car would not start, with some of the trees intentionally containing incomplete information. He found that when participants were assigning probabilities as to why the car would not start, only options explicitly presented to them were considered; they did not search for the missing information. Focusing the subject's attention on what information might be missing did not significantly improve their awareness of the incomplete information presented to them; individuals often overlooked elements that were missing from the tree and adding detail to the tree only slightly affected perceptions. Interestingly, splitting a branch into two separate branches seemed to increase the perceived importance of that branch. Overall, these patterns persisted among both college students and professional mechanics. This insensitivity to omissions reflects a bias where individuals do not account for all possible factors, potentially affecting decision-making and problem-solving. Moreover, the findings suggest that the way information is structured such as breaking down a problem into sub-components, can influence the perceived importance of certain aspects.

– *Illusory correlation*: A bias whereby people overestimate the frequency of co-occurrence of two outcomes or events because of seeing patterns and/or causal links between events or variables in data, despite none existing (Chapman and Chapman (1969). As an illustration of this, Chapman and Chapman cite the example of how extensively clinical psychologists develop an illusory correlation between personality tests and clinical symptoms. Another example is the use of good luck charms and winning streaks in sports.

In a series of experiments with students, Schoemaker (1995) found that most held contradictory beliefs derived from incorrectly linking unrelated events, a phenomenon he called 'incoherent beliefs.' Significantly, people do not easily relinquish these illusory correlations even in the face of contradictory evidence. Furthermore, even when a correlation exists, it is frequently misinterpreted as causation, suggesting a general difficulty in distinguishing between correlation and actual causative links.

The Experience/Framing Bias

This bias is also known as 'selective perception' and refers to how prior training and experience (i.e., our knowledge base) influence how we interpret and subsequently act on information. This is because we have a propensity to focus on those things which we already understand. This bias gives rise to two interrelated problems. First, our knowledge base, goals and values determine how we represent the problem, a process known as 'framing.' Tversky and Kahneman (1981) showed that once a situation had been framed in a certain way, it was difficult for research subjects to view the situation differently. Additionally, subjects were generally unaware of the effects of different frames in terms of how they perceived the attractiveness of the decision choices. The second problem is that because framing affects how a problem is represented, it in turn determines which elements of the decision-maker's knowledge base are activated. This is important because it is within our knowledge base that we hold perceptions as to the 'solution space' available (Newell and Simon, 1972; Simon, 1973). The result may be opposite solutions for logically identical problems. This represents a systematic violation of the elementary principles of 'consistency' and 'coherence' which underpin the notion of human rationality. Research indicates that frames are often deeply embedded in the past, formed from our prior training and experiences. Thus, in viewing problems from their frames, individuals tend to ignore and dismiss other aspects of information which may herald potentially significant changes (Dearborn and Simon, 1958; Wright and Goodwin, 2009). For example, accountants will identify with the financial aspects of information, but may dismiss technological aspects; engineers may focus on techno-logical aspects but ignore financial aspects, and so on.

Reliance on Concrete Examples

Although it is believed that individuals make decisions based on established rules and principles theorized from experience, Read (1983) demonstrated that individuals place greater reliance on concrete examples. In experiments with students relating to culture and rituals or rule-governed behaviour, Reid discovered that: firstly, where the rules or the cause-and-effect relationships underlying behaviour are complex, rather than learn and apply the rules, people are more likely to base their predictions and explain events by reference to a single, previously experienced similar instance, even where this results in behaviour which does not accord with the rules. Secondly, even where the rules governing the behaviour are simple, it appears that people still exhibit a strong tendency to predict behaviour by reference to examples of a single, previously experienced similar instance, suggesting that they rely as much on con-crete examples as they do on abstract rules. Thirdly, individuals who use the similar-ity of previous instances as the basis of their predictions, do not see themselves as guessing and are confident of their predictions. In keeping with this, Hendrickx et al. (1992) demonstrated that concrete-based scenarios had a greater effect on increased probability judgments and decreased risk-taking behaviour, than abstract scenarios.

Overconfidence and the Illusion of Control

This phenomenon describes the fact that people appear to be methodically overconfi-dent in their ability to predict because of a failure to recognise the flimsiness of the assumptions underlying their judgments (Lichtenstein et al., 1982; Russo and Schoe-maker, 2001; 1989: Schwenk, 1986; Slovic et al., 1977). Most empirical evidence in this area comes from laboratory studies in which it has been repeatedly observed that there is a discrepancy between how confident individuals are in their judgments, and the percentage of correct answers they achieve in simple metaknowledge tests. This overconfidence implies that people are generally unaware of how little they know, and how much more they need to know, to make correct judgments (Slovic et al., 1985). Research suggests that overconfidence is less prevalent in group judgments, and can be mitigated in individual judgments by regular performance feedback. How-ever, overconfidence persists despite experience, with experts no less prone to it than lay people (Russo and Schoemaker, 2001; Slovic et al., 1985).

The work of Lefcourt (1973) and others examining overconfidence has identified that when people make predictions about uncertain events, they often develop an un-founded sense of control over those events (Langer, 1975; Langer and Roth, 1975; Larwood and Whittaker, 1977). This illusion of control is a manifestation of overconfidence, where the very act of prediction itself inappropriately boosts individuals' confidence in influencing outcomes, even when no actual control or impact on the certainty of the event exists.

Single Outcome Calculation Bias

Normative decision theory supposes that individuals systematically identify and evaluate all potential actions and associated outcomes. This process involves the selection of the optimal course of action from mutually exclusive and exhaustive alternatives through the rigorous assessment of all relevant values and consequences (Elliott, 2019). However, Steinbruner (1974) postulates that people are predisposed from the outset of the decision-making process, to focus on a single outcome and a single alternative for achieving that outcome as it reduces uncertainty. This single outcome calculation bias is evidenced by Festinger's (1957) experiments demonstrating 'bolstering', a process in which individuals magnify the perceived attractiveness of desired alternatives to make them appear even more desirable than non-preferred alternatives. Not only do they attempt to magnify the attractiveness of preferred alternatives, but contrary to normative decision theory, they expend much effort identifying negative elements of non-preferred alternatives to convince themselves of the undesirability of the alternatives (Steinbruner 1974). As an example, Arino and De La Torre (1998) conducted a longitudinal case study of a failed joint venture towards developing a model of collaborative ventures. In focusing on why the venture failed, Chao (2012) argues it was due to a single outcome calculation bias that drove decision makers from one company "to make a questionable concession" (p 359).

Belief Perseverance and Confirmation Bias

As far back as the 1950s it was established that individuals have the propensity to adhere to their initial opinions and theories (Allport, 1954; Luchins, 1957). Subsequent research determined that this propensity exists even when it is made clear that the data on which they are founded is fictitious (Anderson et al., 1980; Carroll, 1978; Tversky and Kahneman, 1982d). The explanation offered for these findings is that once these beliefs have been created, they then become independent of the data on which they are founded and subsequent demonstration that the data is not true, has no effect on the beliefs.

The confirmation or prior hypotheses indicate that once formed, initial beliefs are not only difficult to dislodge because of belief perseverance, but they may also structure how subsequent evidence is interpreted (Watson, 1960; Levine, 1971; Pruitt, 1961; Kozielecki 1981). New evidence supporting initial beliefs is judged as dependable, while evidence contradicting them is dismissed as being unreliable or erroneous. Thus, individuals routinely overestimate evidence which confirms their theories and expectations, but disregard or devalue evidence which falsifies them. People have been known to maintain blatant self-contradictions by developing elaborate rationalisations to defend them (Steinbruner, 1974). Ironically, in only being receptive to supportive evidence individuals unsuspectingly receive reinforcement regarding the correctness of their theories, even though they may be wrong.

Hindsight Bias

The hindsight bias described by Fischhoff (1982; 1975a/b; Fischhoff and Beyth, 1975) identified that when asked to recall original choices on simple tests, most individuals credited themselves with more successes than they achieved. Once the individual experiences an outcome, a decision made before the outcome appears, in hindsight, to have been inevitable and easily related to cues at the time the decision was made. Hindsight bias occurs when people 'knew it all along,' that they believe they predicted an event's outcome after it happens, often revising their memories to align with what occurred (Roese and Vohs, 2012). This bias arises from a combination of cognitive factors such as selective memory and rationalization; metacognitive factors such as equating the ease of understanding an event understanding with predictability; and motivational factors such as the need for order and self-justification.

This bias leads to a narrow view of past events and overconfidence in the accuracy of one's judgment. Hogarth (1980) suggests that instead of recalling the past in terms of the uncertainties that existed at the time a decision was made, individuals reconstruct past events focusing on factors which appear to have caused the outcome, to make sense of what subsequently transpired. In retrospect, therefore, they are not surprised by what happened in the past (Hogarth and Makridakis, 1981).

Summary: Heuristics and Biases

There are several points to note concerning heuristics and biases. The first is that, although discussed separately, all are interrelated to some extent, with Schwenk (1986) showing biases interact and reinforce each other. The second point according to Evans (1982), is that biases are likely to be most prevalent when the environment is inherently complex and uncertain, i.e., when there is a multitude of factors to consider and isolating their influence is far from simple (Wright and Goodwin, 2009). The third and most important point is that the conclusions of flawed human reasoning and sub-optimal intuitive judgments and decisions are not universally accepted. There are two reasons for this: the first is that some researchers suggest the locus of some biases is not in human judgment but rather in the empirical data underpinning the biases; the second reason is that there is a long-standing debate as to whether probability theory is in fact, an appropriate standard for evaluating human reasoning. Meanwhile, the work of Tversky and Kahneman on biases has come under attack on several fronts:

- According to Beach et al. (1987), the contention that human judgment is seriously biased is not based on convincing data. They argue that of all the publications around human judgment over ten years (1972–1981), only a small percentage was based on empirical evidence and the poor performance results were cited an average of six times more often. They also question the validity of Tversky and Kahneman's research because most of the experiments conducted involved word problems. They argue that it is not clear that some of the mediocre performance results obtained were not simply the result of the research subjects' failure to understand the problems. Support for this comes from Kruglanski et al. (1984) who have shown that some judgmental biases can be overcome by using better wording of the problems, and a minor change in the wording of questions used by Tversky and Kahneman produced evidence of both good and poor judgment.
- The second contention is related to the generalisability of empirical results obtained in laboratory settings to the real world, a general critique of all experimental psychology studies (Haeiffel and Cobb, 2022). Beach et al., (1986), point out that the research of Tversky, Kahneman and others on human judgment has revolved around laboratory-type studies of word problems with undergraduate students as research subjects. They argue that word problems are not the type of activities that decision-makers get involved in, that undergraduate students usually have no expertise around word problems, that they do not have to act on the decisions they make in the experiments, and that they have no reputation to preserve. The central argument is that sample participants are not representative of organizational decision-makers, or the context of the decisions being made. Barnes (1984) however, suggests that this laboratory research is generalisable because the results were obtained across a variety of tasks, the subjects were intelligent individuals, and in an experiment with students subsequently repeated in the workplace, the results were found to be identical. Criticisms of experimental psychology laboratory studies have also highlighted the lack of diversity that influences the generalizability of findings i.e. psychology scientists and their samples are predominantly white, with upwards of 60% of authors and samples coming from the US.
- A third criticism of Tversky and Khaneman's work is that their conclusions are often too simplistic. For example, in examining several of their experiments which supposedly demonstrate the conjunction fallacy, Thuring and Jungermann (1986) argue that by using a more complex mental model framework, the results of the experiments can be interpreted quite differently in terms of a broader theoretical basis. Curley and Benson (1994) also suggest that the shortfall of research on heuristics and biases is that there is no integrating framework to it, the result being a disparate collection of heuristics and limited understanding.

– The final criticism is the contention that even if biases are common in decision-making, it is irrelevant unless it can be shown and quantified, how the outcome would improve if these biases were eliminated (Goodwin and Wright, 1991).

Having looked at specific heuristics and biases which affect human judgment and the debate as to their origin, the following section moves to a review of the literature on cognitive processes and human reasoning in terms of how knowledge is organised and processed.

Organisation and Activation of Knowledge

Although it is not yet known for certain how knowledge is stored in memory, one currently accepted theory is that knowledge is stored and organised in the brain in the form of 'cognitive schema.' Cognitive schemas are mental models of frameworks that help individuals organise and interpret information, influencing attention, perception, and memory (Dozois and Beck, 2008). These schemas are developed based on experiences and help predict and interpret the world. A core aspect of cognitive behavioural therapy (CBT) is to work on these schemas so that they may be challenged or modified (Padesky, 1994). This helps people develop more adaptive and realistic thought patterns, thereby improving emotional regulation and behaviour. Memory storage can be explained by the neural network model (Airbib, 2003) and involves distributed patterns of connections. When faced with a disparate stream of facts and events, people attempt to understand the situation by automatically applying the schema according to the similarity between it and the situation facing them. However, the problem is that while the choice of schema determines how an individual interprets the situation, it is often difficult to establish which schemata to use.

In addition to an understanding of information, schema include expectations as to what should happen in each situation, the sequence in which they should happen, what alternatives exist and what information is required. Consequently, the schema determines the relevance and significance people attach to information, as well as how they integrate this into their existing knowledge base to make sense of it. However, laboratory studies have shown that schemata limit the solution space available to individuals because they comprise deeply ingrained assumptions regarding the nature of a problem, along with a preconceived notion of the range of potential solutions to the problem (Anderson and Johnson, 1966; Newell and Simon, 1972; Simon, 1973). Once the problem set is established, the solutions are essentially predetermined, thus making it difficult to generate alternative strategies. This issue is exemplified by Pennington and Hastie (1986; 1988); in collaborating with mock juries, the authors demonstrated that albeit that all jurors heard the same evidence, each organised the information into a unique story which would then predict the verdict each juror would support.

Although schematic thought is efficient, it is also subject to distortion and error. For example, research by Bower et al. (1979) identified that when recalling situations from memory, individuals tended to fill in the elements of the situation which they had forgotten, with elements that from their schema, they would have expected to have occurred in that situation. This is achieved by a process of causal 'gap-filling' inference based on extrapolating current knowledge (Warren et al., 1979). This gap-filling does not appear consistent, depending on whether what is being recalled is an event or an object, and whether it is schema-consistent (typical) or schema-inconsistent (atypical). A further problem with schematic thought is that in thinking about the future, people attempt to construct new patterns of events which have not been seen or experienced before. In such situations, individuals cannot apply their schemata in the normal way as this requires 'productive' rather than 'reproductive' thinking. As a result, Jungermann (1985b) contends that in the process of constructing scenarios, it is likely that individuals either apply existing (and therefore inappropriate) schemata or modify the task to suit their existing schemata. In either case, it is unlikely they will generate new, unimagined facts and events which have not been previously experienced.

Script Theory

Something which appears to combine the features of representativeness and availability, and is closely allied to the concept of cognitive schema is 'script theory' (Abelson, 1981; Schank and Abelson, 1977). This theory suggests that individuals experience numerous behavioural events that occur frequently and with minor variation. In such cases, individuals develop a 'schematic conception' or a 'cognitive script' of events that are expected to occur and the order in which they are expected to occur. This script essentially guides the individual's understanding of the situation and their behaviour in it, preparing them for the next scene in the script of expected events. According to Abelson, once scripts are formed, they are a powerful influence on the individual's expectations, interpretation of immediate events and subsequent behaviour.

Causal Versus Diagnostic Reasoning and Inferences

Tversky and Kahneman (1980; 1982c) assert that individuals make sense of the world by organising and interpreting the events impacting them in terms of cause-and-effect relationships. People are predisposed to cause-and-effect reasoning because it aligns with a causal schema, where causes lead to effects in a linear, time-ordered sequence. It is a natural inclination for us to think in terms of sequential events, as it reflects our understanding of time and causality in the physical world, where past events influence future outcomes. For example, if we drop a glass, we expect it to break once it hits the ground. The transferability of causal knowledge is situation-

dependent and in more complex systems such as human behaviour or the environment, causal knowledge may not transfer so easily. Diagnostic inferences meanwhile,
require a backward inference from the consequence to the causes, which is an unnat-
ural and more complicated process. This requires individuals to mentally reverse the
temporal order in which events are assumed to have happened and is used for problem-solving and understanding how a particular outcome came to be. For example, if
you see a broken glass on the floor, you use diagnostic reasoning to figure out what
caused it to break. In essence, causal reasoning is about predicting outcomes based on
known causes, while diagnostic reasoning is about inferring causes based on known
outcomes. The police use both causal knowledge and diagnostic inference in their
work. Causal knowledge allows them to understand and anticipate the consequences
of behaviours or actions, considered critical for prevention and planning. Diagnostic
inference, on the other hand, is essential for investigations, as officers often arrive
after an event has occurred and must work backwards to piece together what happened, identifying the cause based on the available evidence. Thus, effective policing
relies on the ability to predict future events based on known patterns (causal reasoning) and to analyse past events to determine their causes (diagnostic reasoning).

Research has demonstrated that individuals make causal inferences with greater
confidence than they do making diagnostic inferences. This has been found to occur
even when they are aware that the relationship between variables in the data is accidental rather than causal. Additionally, when presented with data which has both
causal and diagnostic elements, causal data is generally accorded more weight in
probability judgments than diagnostic data. Although people can recognize that their
schemas may be incomplete and outdated, they are generally reluctant to revise their
mental models to accommodate new facts; even when revisions are made, they tend
to be marginal (Tversky and Kahneman, 1980; 1982c). Revision is essentially a difficult
diagnostic process, therefore, rather than revising their models, people are more
likely to assimilate new facts into their existing models by developing causal accounts
which satisfactorily explain the outcomes.

Several researchers (Pyszczynski and Greenberg, 1981; Weiner,1985) have established that people exhibit a high propensity to engage in causal reasoning when faced
with important, unusual, or surprising events. This is due to these events creating uncertainty, which triggers the search for a causal agent (Weiner, 1985). It has also been
shown that:

- People relate best to concrete, causally coherent narratives (Pennington and Hastie, 1988; 1986);
- Individuals judge events to be more likely if they are presented with scenarios
  containing causal information which describes how the events might occur,
  rather than just the events or outcomes alone (Hendrickx et al., 1992; 1989; Hoch,
  1985; Levi and Pryor, 1987; Tversky and Kahneman, 1983);
- Causal reasoning is more frequently engaged in, and to a greater extent when examining concrete rather than abstract data (Anderson, 1983a);

- Causal reasoning based on single, similar instances is prevalent, suggesting that causal reasoning is grounded in real-world experiences (Read, 1983).
- Causal and diagnostic processes can result in different solutions to the same problem (Becker, 1984).

The main problem with causal thinking is that research indicates the search for causality appears to be a hard-wired form of human cognition (Wright and Goodwin, 2009). Individuals tend to see patterns within random events (Ayton et al., 1989), and then invent causes which explain the patterns, even though there is no evidence to support them (Fildes and Goodwin, 2007). There are no universally accepted rules for distinguishing between cause and effect, the consequence of which is that individuals distinguish causes from effects by relying on probabilistically-based cues to causality. This includes the temporal order of events, the degree to which two events occur together, the number of competing variables or explanations, the degree to which one variable can predict another, and the similarity between events and prior knowledge. All these clues are related to heuristics and biases, with Einhorn and Hogarth (1981, p 32) observing that "one must guard against the way cues to causality restrict our interpretation of the past by structuring and stabilising our perceptions of reality". Thus, we are apt to focus attention on the obvious and known, at the expense of creative thinking. Even guarding against these cues, it is impossible to predict with any accuracy future causal chains of events, as the sequence of causal impacts is seldom a linear, cascading, domino-like process (Taleb, 2007). It is therefore only with hindsight that the chain of events underlying a significant development becomes obvious (Wright and Goodwin, 2009).

Reasoning by Analogy

Steinbruner (1974) identified that decision makers often use quite simple analogies and images to guide them in defining complex organisational problems, a process he described as 'reasoning by analogy'. The benefit of this reasoning process is that it helps to reduce perceived uncertainty and can be an effective tool in terms of developing creative solutions to problems (Huff, 1980; Neuhauser, 1993). However, the process of reasoning by analogy can also have serious adverse consequences on decision-making since using simple analogies may mislead decision-makers into taking too simplistic a view of a particular situation; secondly, decision-makers may not be aware that there are crucial differences between the analogy and the reality of the situation they face (Schwenk, 1984).

Rationality

The source of heuristics may be explained in terms of rationality concerning decision-making. Simon's notion of bounded rationality (Simon, 1956; 1955) was initially controversial as it challenged the validity of the classic 'economic man' and value-maximising human behaviour, although the concept is now widely accepted. However, the question of rationality is a complex one and there is still no universally accepted theory of bounded rationality (Simon, 2000; Gigerenzer, 2020). What is clear from numerous empirical studies (Anderson, 1983a/b; Cyert and March, 1963; Einhorn, 1974; Eisenhardt, 1989; Fischhoff et al., 1978; Fredrickson, 1984; Fredrickson and Laquinto, 1989; Fredrickson and Mitchell, 1984) is that as decision-makers, individuals have limited cognitive capabilities as evidenced by the fact that they 'satisfice' and search for information and alternatives haphazardly and opportunistically (Artinger et al., 2022; Soltwisch et al., 2022; Stevens, 2019). Although a range of alternatives may be generated, only a few will be subjected to analysis, and decisions are often arrived at by using predetermined procedures or heuristics, rather than rigorous systematic analysis. The empirical findings related to the cognitive basis of group decision-making are similar; there appears little doubt in the literature when it comes to decision-making: we simplify the process of collecting and integrating information out of necessity because of the limited cognitive processing capacity of our brain. In doing so, we do not follow procedures of rationality (Artinger et al., 2022).

Imagination and Expectation

In discussing the availability heuristics, we suggested that people tended to evaluate the frequency or probability of events according to how easy it was to imagine them. At the same time, it has been demonstrated empirically that imagining the occurrence of events using scripted scenarios will make the images of the events more available, which naturally leads to events appearing more probable. Several studies have been conducted in this area:

- Carroll (1978) established that when individuals were made to imagine a social event using elaborate scripted scenarios, they came to believe that the event would take place.
- Building on Carroll's work, Gregory et al. (1982) conducted a series of experiments in which scenario events were of a personal rather than social nature. The results were like those of Carroll (1978); subjects recorded significantly higher subjective probability estimates in terms of believing events described in the scenarios could happen to them. The findings also suggested that the process of imagining via a scripted scenario could influence behaviour.
- Anderson (1983a) performed experiments in which subjects were asked to imagine scenarios in which they or some other persons were performing/not perform-

ing a set of behaviours. The results of the experiments demonstrated that, where the research participants imagined themselves to be the scenario subject, there was a change in personal intentions towards the target behaviour on the part of the subjects, and this intention change persisted for some time. Where the research participants were not the scenario subjects, no change in personal behavioural intention was recorded. The experiments also indicated that the more frequently participants imagined themselves to be the scenario subject, the greater the personal behavioural intention change.

Groupthink and Decision Fatigue

The focus of the discussion in this chapter so far has concentrated on individual decision processes. However, in researching collective decision-making processes, Janis (1982) documented a phenomenon termed 'groupthink'. This is where individuals tend to suppress any ideas which do not accord with what they perceive to be the ideas preferred by the group, to maintain group cohesion. This leads to bias in that critical ideas are inhibited, and only those courses of action which are perceived as being preferred by the group are examined. Although anecdotal information supports the existence of this tendency to seek concurrence, there have been very few laboratory tests of Janis's theory, due in part to the difficulty of establishing a highly cohesive group in a laboratory setting, as well as mixed experimental results (Rose, 2011. There is however "very little consensus among researchers of the validity of the groupthink model" (Park, 2000, p 873), despite its widespread acceptance. Examples of calamitous group decision-making ascribed to issues of groupthink are the Bay of Pigs Invasion and the collapse of the energy giant Enron (O'Connor, 2003).

Nutt (2002) suggests five decision-making defects typify groupthink, these being when group members: (1) discuss only a limited number of options, ignoring other alternatives; (2) they fail to examine the adverse consequences of their intended actions; (3) they are quick to drop alternatives, which at first glance, appear unsatisfactory; (4) they make little attempt to solicit the advice of experts; and (5) they fail to develop contingency plans in the event that implementation of their preferred course of action is delayed. One of the benefits of scenario planning is that it can be used to mitigate groupthink in management teams by examining a variety of futures, not just those the management supports. Although the scenario team itself is not immune from the perils of groupthink, this is mitigated with expert facilitation.

Along with groupthink, there is the issue of decision fatigue, which is an individual rather than a collective issue and refers to the deteriorating quality of decisions made by an individual after a long session of decision-making. Adults make numerous decisions every day. Akin to muscle fatigue, research shows that there can be negative consequences from making these decisions, impairing our subsequent choices and behaviour control due to resource depletion, termed decision fatigue. Decision fatigue can affect even the most rational and intelligent individuals, and eventually, the brain looks for shortcuts to circumvent decision fatigue, leading to poor decision-making which applies to all decisions, not just the large or more difficult ones.

In healthcare, decision fatigue is crucial as numerous daily decisions impact patient outcomes. As an example, a study which explored decision fatigue in orthopaedic surgeons found they are 33% less likely to schedule surgeries for patients seen later in the day (Persson et al., 2019). These results suggest that decision fatigue significantly influences medical decision-making, with implications for patient care due to the prevalence of long shifts in healthcare. Baer and Schnall (2021) examined credit decisions to restructure loans at a leading bank, over a working day. They discovered the loan approval rate declined significantly as lunch approached, picking up again after, before declining again in the last two hours of work, with the higher loan rejection rates attributed to decision fatigue. Researchers have found that decision fatigue hampers the forecast accuracy of analysts leading to strategic fatigue management (Jiao, 2023). As fatigue sets in, analysts tend to make more heuristic decisions, herding with consensus forecasts or reissuing previous ones. Interestingly, the stock market implicitly acknowledges this by discounting forecasts issued during periods of high fatigue, considering the decline in decision quality over a day filled with multiple forecasts.

While the concept of decision fatigue exists in the literature, an analysis revealed a lack of consequences directly related to decision fatigue, which may result from experimental challenges (Pignatiello et al. 2020) However, the authors claim that decision analysis is a "highly relevant concept of interest" (p 132) that is worthy of further research. The recommendation to combat decision fatigue when it has been found, is to ensure that periodically, individuals are allowed to take a break and leave the work area for a short period, to recharge their mental batteries.

Punctuated Equilibrium and Coagulation

Gersick's (1991) work on group development found that groups do not evolve gradually over time, rather they alternate between periods of stasis and bursts of significant change; this model of group development was termed the punctuated equilibrium model. This appears to contrast with more linear models of group development such as Tuckman's 'forming, storming, norming and performing' (Tuckman, 1965), although Chang et al. (2003) convincingly argue that these are complementary rather than competing group models. According to the punctuated equilibrium model, a group's activity can be divided into two phases: an initial period of inertia set by the group's first meeting and a revolutionary period of change starting at the midpoint of their timeline (Chang et al., 2003). This shift is less about the work completed and more about the group's recognition of time constraints. The approach to deadlines spurs groups to revise strategies, leading to a productive second phase of inertia. There is a similar pattern discernible in most scenario planning teams, there being "periods of inertia punctuated by concentrated, revolutionary periods of quantum changes" (Gersick 1991, p 16).

A more significant phenomenon arising from punctuated equilibrium is that once the punctuated equilibrium transition is reached, groups abandon any further examination of ideas captured or exploration of new ideas; this is termed the 'coagulation' point, the instance where groups self-seal on ideas already discussed, organising and interpreting these in terms of cause-and-effect relationships. While new ideas may be surfaced by some participants, they are generally ignored or dismissed by the rest of the group after a superficial discussion. At the same time, interventions by a facilitator usually prove ineffective.

Implications for Scenarios

Having examined the research literature on cognitive limitations and processes, this section looks at the implications of the findings on scenario developmental processes, content and presentation, and the behavioural effects of scenarios.

It is a given that scenario development processes will inevitably be affected by cognitive processes. For example, Jungermann (1985a) maintains that using forward or backward inference will produce qualitatively and quantitatively different scenarios. Forward inferences are concerned with natural, cognitively easier downhill thinking and individuals will intuitively begin constructing scenarios using this approach; this means that scenarios will be developed based on causal links in sequential order. The scenarios will be plausible but not surprising, as they will be developed around familiar causal models rooted in the past and are likely to include short-run dramatic elements of high causal significance. However, they will underestimate the likelihood of events produced by slow-moving developments. On the other hand, if the more cognitively challenging backward inferences or uphill thinking process is used, there will be a focus on goals to be achieved and policies to get there, with the resulting scenarios more value than goal-oriented. Wright and Goodwin (2009) maintain that using backward logic, with a focus on organisational objectives and their plausibility, overcomes the problems inherent in forward causal thinking. This is achieved by promoting the identification of drivers which have the largest impact on the range of plausibility of the objectives. Where there are many potential causes of given future events, individuals are likely to examine only a limited number of causes ignoring the others, and the scenarios are more likely to be 'revolutionary' and 'unrealistic' which can lead to the discovery of new options.

Script theory suggests that how current events are interpreted and unfolded within a scenario is largely determined by the existing schemata of the individual developing the scenarios. This schema will contain deeply embedded assumptions as to what is and what is not feasible in terms of how the future unfolds. In instances where the individual is attempting to construct previously unexperienced patterns of events and their existing schema cannot be readily applied, they will generally force the situation to suit the existing schema. At the same time, when undertaking analysis in the scenario development process, the notion of rationality presupposes that individuals will engage in satisficing behaviour in searching for information, and are likely to use causal inferences from their cognitive schema to compensate for any memory gaps. Finally, once individuals have imagined how events might unfold in the future, it will be difficult for them to view these events from different perspectives.

In addition to the impact of cognitive processes, there are numerous heuristics and biases which potentially impact scenario development processes regarding the information that is searched for, how it is analysed, what data is accepted or rejected and how the scenario storylines are eventually constructed. For example:

- The experience bias and framing will impact what futures are explored; saliency and primacy will largely determine the starting point of the information search in the scenario development process, which in turn will determine what information is searched for as pathways of linked nodes in the neural network of the brain are activated. Once this search set is activated, individuals will likely be insensitive to missing information, sample size, prior probabilities, and the concepts of regression and illusory correlation.
- Co-occurring events will be accorded an unwarranted degree of probability as will events which are representative, well-publicised, easily imagined and which generally lead to a single outcome. Interpretation of information will be largely guided by what the individual already understands and will be constrained by the individual's belief system and cognitive anchor. The information which is supported by concrete examples, and which accords with the individual's experience and belief system, will be readily assimilated, while that which does not will be discarded.
- Because of the simulation heuristic, once individuals imagine the sequence of events encompassing a scenario, the overall scenario will appear more likely to occur than the probability of the individual events comprising the scenario.
- Finally, once individuals have developed a scenario, they will be quite confident of the predictions underlying the scenario and will be endowed with a feeling of some control over the events depicted in the scenario.

Although theoretical and empirical findings from cognitive psychology discussed in this chapter are troubling in their implications for scenario development processes, the literature, unfortunately, leaves unanswered several important questions such as:

- Do these cognitive processes, heuristics, and biases function in all cases, or are they activated or influenced by situational factors?
- Can anything be done in designing processes to offset or mitigate the effects of these cognitive processes, heuristics, and biases?

- Do some heuristics and biases offset one another as Schoemaker (1993) has suggested, and if they do, which ones and under which conditions?
- Are there other, perhaps more important impacting factors which are not discussed or have not yet been identified?

From the current state of the research literature, it is difficult to draw firm conclusions and these questions remain open. As Hodgkinson and Healey (2008) note, although scenarios can purportedly mitigate some biases, the actual process of constructing scenarios is itself susceptible to bias. Until substantially more in-depth and systematic research is undertaken, all that can be said with certainty from the current literature is that cognitive effects, heuristics, and their associated biases will impact scenario development processes; what the precise impact will be is uncertain, and how the impact might be mitigated even less so.

Scenario Content and Presentation

As with the scenario developmental processes, research on scenario content and presentation is limited and scattered. In much of the existing research, the primary focus has not been specifically on scenarios, however, the research findings are sufficiently broad enough that they may be extended to cover various aspects of scenarios. Examples of this include:

- The conjunction effect suggests that adding more representative and salient details to a scenario, whether relevant or not, increases the scenario's representativeness thereby raising the likelihood of its occurrence, and consequently its acceptance. Paradoxically increasing the level of detail in a scenario also increases the specific nature of the scenario which essentially decreases the likelihood of the scenario occurring.
- The inclusion of events in scenarios makes it easier for decision-makers to recall available supporting evidence, resulting in scenarios which appear more probable. These events however should be connected via plausible cause-and-effect relationships to explain how or why something has occurred, or to account for a recent highly publicized event.
- The more vivid the scenario, the greater the chance it will be perceived as being more probable by the scenario audience. Scenarios containing vivid, concrete examples, matching the experiences of the audience, are more likely to have an impact than scenarios relying on understanding complex causal relationships as well as abstract data. Vividly presented information is more easily recalled from memory and those scenarios which tell an engaging story are held as being more likely.

- Scenarios leading to a single outcome and which are explained in full have a higher likelihood of acceptance. It is important that the scenario story does not leave the audience with unanswered questions.
- Scenarios should be neither all good nor all bad, as these are unrealistic. The inclusion of desirable events, as well as those which threaten the scenario audience, raises the perceived probability of the scenarios occurring.
- An appealing, memorable title for a scenario strengthens its image and allows for greater memory recall therefore increasing its perceived plausibility. However, how the scenarios are labelled, whether as fact or conjecture, also affects the credibility of the scenario's credibility. At the same time, presenting a scenario in the past tense endows it with a powerful sense of certainty, as it automatically feeds the belief that the events described in the scenario have occurred, which the audience finds difficult to ignore.

Behavioural Implications of Scenarios

Several pieces of empirically based research have relevance in this area, namely:
- Anderson's experience (1983a) indicates that merely reading scenarios does not motivate organizational decision-makers sufficiently to change their plans. For this to happen, decision-makers must become actively engaged in the scenario exercise by imagining themselves playing a role in the scenarios.
- Shoemaker's (1993) laboratory experiments demonstrated that scenarios do stretch the subjective confidence range of individuals by as much as 50%; however, there is an incredulity point beyond which the ranges contract. Scenarios alter beliefs, but not necessarily in a predictable direction, and can be used to overcome availability, anchoring and overconfidence biases.
- The experiments of Langer (1975) and others (Langer and Roth, 1975; Larwood and Whittaker, 1977) demonstrated that the act of engaging in the 'prediction' of uncertain events appears to endow individuals with a misplaced sense of control over the uncertain events.
- The work of Anderson (1983b) and Gregory et al. (1982) show that decision-makers tend to anchor on scenarios which they perceive will have a greater impact on them and their organization. Work by Bolton (2003) in forecasting new products determined that individuals tend to 'anchor their judgment' on the first scenario they develop, with attempts at removing biases only succeeding in exacerbating the original bias.

Although some research exists on the behavioural effects of scenarios, it is neither extensive nor systematic. Most findings have come from psychologists testing the influence of single scenarios on decision-makers in laboratory settings, not in the way they are used in organisations. The result is a lack of knowledge about the behavioural effects of complex, long-term scenarios and the judgmental processes involved in managing them in the real world (Vlek and Otten, 1987).

Implications for Scenario Facilitators

Much of the research discussed so far is rooted in cognitive psychology and relates primarily to examining the quality of intuitive human judgement of uncertain events. However, explanations for the findings are not universally accepted in the literature. At the same time, much of the research in the area of heuristics is based on probability forecasts and scenario practitioners from the Intuitive Logics school will be quick to point out that scenarios have nothing at all to do with either probabilities or forecasts. How can we reconcile these apparent contradictions and make them useful for scenario facilitators? The cognitive sciences tell us that we are bounded in our rationality. We interpret and make sense of what we see going on around us through unique and interacting ontological and epistemological lenses. These lenses comprise our mental models but we are generally unaware, or at best vaguely aware of their existence. As Pierre Wack has noted,

> . . . in times of rapid change and increased complexity, the mental model becomes a dangerously mixed bag; enormously rich detail and deep understanding can coexist with dubious assumptions, selective inattention to alternative ways of interpreting evidence and projections that are a mere pretence. It is here that the scenario approach can make the difference (Wack, 1985a, 1985b).

The key then is to effectively leverage the science by exposing the flaws in mental models of people and to engage them in new ways of thinking. To achieve this, it is essential to understand how people think, how knowledge is stored and organized in their brains, and how they subsequently search for and interpret information.

Conclusions

Several observations can be drawn from the review of the academic literature on heuristics and biases, organization and activation of knowledge, and reasoning on the scenario development process. The first is that there is a paucity of systematic research regarding the cognitive and behavioural implications of scenario development. Jungermann (1985a; 1985b) argues there is a need to focus on the process of scenario construction, with more experimental work and case studies required, to understand how cognitive factors affect it. At the same time, there is a requirement for the development and testing of techniques that may mitigate or counteract cognitive biases.

The second observation is that most of the reported research stems from cognitive psychology, focusing on individual cognitive styles of decision-making and behaviour. While little research relates specifically to scenarios, their findings appear largely applicable. Scenario-specific research that has been conducted relates predominantly to individuals in artificial or laboratory settings, rather than the real-world organisational context for which scenarios were intended.

The third observation is that Goodwin and Wright (1991) suggest that the work of Tversky and Kahneman gained popularity because their studies are easily understood by non-technical readers. However, their interpretations of the data appear ad hoc and a more comprehensive conceptual, empirically grounded model is yet to be developed. Although the psychological research discussed above may be troubling in its potential implications concerning scenario development processes, the research is either unknown or appears to be ignored by scenario practitioners. Nevertheless, the lack of empirical validation does not appear to have hampered the popularity and growth of scenarios.

Empirical evidence from the cognitive sciences suggests that scenario developmental processes will be affected by a range of cognitive processes. In addition to the impact of cognitive processes, a range of heuristics and biases will impact scenario developmental processes in varying degrees, specifically regarding what information is searched for and analysed, and what data are accepted or rejected. Factors such as experience bias, framing, saliency, and primacy will determine the starting point of the information search, which in turn determines what information is searched for, as pathways of linked nodes in the neural network of the brain are activated. Once the search set is activated, individuals will likely be insensitive to missing information, and events that are representative, well-publicized, easily imagined and generally lead to a single outcome will dominate the thinking. Interpretation of information will be guided by issues that individuals already understand and will be constrained by belief systems and cognitive anchors. Information that accords with experiences and belief systems will be readily assimilated; that which does not will be discarded. Once the individuals have developed a scenario, they will be quite confident of the inherent predictions underlying the scenario.

Experience scenario practitioners may be intuitively aware of much of the above. Practitioners in general however appear generally unaware of, or at best only vaguely aware of, these phenomena and their ramifications on the scenario developmental process. That few of the articles on scenarios in the anecdotal, experienced-based literature make references to these phenomena is evidence of this. Additionally, in advocating particular methodologies, only a small number of articles report supporting empirical evidence. The communication of scenarios must be tailored to the audience. This includes scenarios each having a distinctive and ideally theme catchy title, high literary quality, appropriate imagery, and memorable events in the timeline, all of which make superb reading. The objective is not only to communicate the facts about the scenario but also emotions so that the audience can 'live' the scenarios. Again, however, there is little discussion of this in the literature.

A significant omission in the literature on scenario planning is the fact that there is an absence of discussion on 'failed' scenario interventions. Undoubtedly the cause of failure in some cases could be traced back to the discussions in this chapter on the effects of heuristics and biases, causal and diagnostics thinking, and how knowledge is structured and used. Many however do not appear aware of these influences based on the lack of discussion or mention in the literature, and I trust that this chapter will provide those interested in scenarios, with useful information to increase their understanding of the scenario development process.

The chapter which follows is the concluding chapter in this book and focuses on the criticisms and issues in scenario planning.

References

Abelson, R.P. (1981). The Psychological Status of the Script Concept, American Psychologist, 36, 715–729.

Abelson, R.P. (1976). Script Processing in Attitude Formation and Decision Making, in J.S. Carroll and J.W. Payne (eds.), Cognition and Social Behaviour, Hillsdale, NJ: Erlbaum.

Allport, G.W. (1954). The Nature of Prejudice, Reading, Mass.: Addison-Wesley.

Anderson, C.A. (1983a). Abstract and Concrete Data in the Perseverance of Social Theories: When Weak Data Leads to Unshakeable Beliefs, Journal of Experimental Social Psychology, 19, 93–108.

Anderson, C.A. (1983b). Imagination and Expectation: The Effects of Imagining Behavioral Scripts on Personal Intentions. Journal of Personality and Social Psychology, 45, (2), 293–305.

Anderson, C.A., Lepper, M.R. and Ross, L. (1980). Perseverance of Social Theories: The Role of Explanation in the Persistence of Discredited Information, Journal of Personality and Social Psychology, 39, 1037–1049.

Anderson, J.R. and Bower, G.H. (1973). Human Associative Memory, Washington: Winston.

Anderson, B.F. and Johnson, W. (1966). Two kinds of Set in Problem Solving, Psychological Reports, 19, 851–858.

Airbib, M.A. (2003). (Ed). The Handbook of brain theory and neural networks. MIT Press.

Arino, A. and de la Torre, A. A. (1998). Learning from Failure: Towards an Evolutionary Model of Collaborative Ventures. Organization Science, 9, (3), 306–326

Artinger, F.M., Gigerenzer, G., and Jacobs, P. (2022). Satisficing: Integration Two Traditions, Journal of Economic Literature. 60 (2) 598–635.

Ayton, P., Hunt, A.J. and Wright, G. (1989). Psychological conceptions of randomness, Journal of Behavioural Decision Making, 2, 221–238.

Baer, T. and Schnall, S. (2021). Quantifying the cost of decision fatigue: suboptimal risk decisions in finance. Royal Society Open Science. 8: 201059.

Bar-Hillel, M. (1973). On the Subjective Probability of Compound Events, Organisational Behavior and Human Performance, 9, 396–406.

Barnes, V.E. (1984). The Quality of Human Judgement: An Alternative Perspective, unpublished PhD dissertation, University of Washington, Seattle.

Beach, L.R., Christensen-Szalanski, J.J. and Barnes V. (1987). Assessing Human Judgement: Has it Been Done, Can it be Done, Should it be Done? in G. Wright and P. Ayton, (Eds.), Subjective Probability. John Wiley & Sons, Chichester.

Beach, L.R., Barnes, V.E. and Christensen-Szalanski, J.J. (1986). Beyond Heuristics and Biases: A Contingency Model of Judgmental Forecasts, Journal of Forecasting, 5, 143–157.

Bolton, L.E, (2003). Stickier Priors: The Effects of Nonanalytic Versus Analytic Thinking in New Product Forecasting, Journal of Marketing Research, 40, 1, 65–79.

Borgida, E. and Nisbett, R.E. (1977). The Differential Impact of Abstract versus Concrete Information on Decisions, Journal of Applied Psychology, 7, 258–271.

Bower, G.H., Black, J. and Turner, T. (1979). Scripts in Text Comprehension and Memory, Cognitive Psychology, 11, 177–220.

Bower, J.L. (1970). Managing the Resource Allocation Process, Division of Research, Harvard University.

Brunswick, E. (1956). Perception and the Representative Design of Experiments, Berkley, CA: University of California Presssimpon.

Butler, S. (1986). Anchoring in The Judgmental Evaluation of Audit Samples, The Accounting Review, 61, 101–111.

Cardenas, A., Crozier, W. and Strange, D. (2021). Right place, wrong time: the limitations of mental reinstatement of context on alibi-elicitation. Psychology, Crime and Law. 27, 3, 201–230.

Carroll, J.S. (1978). The Effects of Imagining an Event on Expectations for the Event: An Interpretation in Terms of the Availability Heuristics, Journal of Experimental Social Psychology, 14, 88–96.

Chang, A., Bordia, P. and Duck, J. (2003). Punctuated Equilibrium and Linear Progression: Toward a New Understanding of Group Development, The Academy of Management Journal, 46, 1, 106–117.

Chao, Y. (2012). Decision-making biases in the alliance life cycle: implications for alliance failure, Management Decisions, 49, 3, 350–364.

Chapman, P.F. and Chapman, J.P. (1969). Illusory Correlation as an Obstacle to the Use of Valid Diagnostic Signs, Journal of Abnormal Psychology, 74, 193–204.

Cohen, J., Chesnick, E.I. and Haran, D.A. (1972). Confirmation of the Inertial Effect in Sequential Choice and Design, British Journal of Psychology, 63, 1, 41–46.

Collins, A.M. and Loftus, E.F. (1975). A Spreading-activation Theory of Semantic Memory, Psychology Review, 82, 407–428.

Collins, A.M. and Quillian, M.R. (1969). Retrieval Time from Semantic Memory, Journal of Verbal Learning and Verbal Behaviour, 8, 241–248.

Cooke, R.M. (1991). Experts in Uncertainty: Opinion and Subjective Probability in Science, New York: Oxford University Press.

Curley, S.P. and Benson, P.G. (1994). Applying a Cognitive Perspective to Probability Construction, in G. Wright and P. Ayton (eds.), Subjective Probability, Chichester: John Wiley & Sons.

Cyert, M. and Marsh, J.G. (1963). A Behavioral Theory of the Firm, Eaglewood Cliffs, NJ: Prentice-Hall.

Dearborn, D.C. and Simon, H.A. (1958). Selective Perception: A Note on the Departmental Identification of Executives, Sociometry, 21, 140–144.

Dozois, D.J. and Beck, A.T. (2008). Cognitive schemas, beliefs and assumptions. Risk Factors in Depression, 119–143.

Einhorn, H.J. and Hogarth, R.M. (1981). Behavioral Decision Theory: Processes of Judgement and Choice, Annual Review of Psychology, 32, 53–88.

Einhorn, H.J. (1974). Expert Judgement: Some Necessary Conditions and an Example, Journal of Applied Psychology, 59, 652–571.

Eisenhardt. K.M. (1989). Making Fast Strategic Decisions in High-velocity Environments, Academy of Management Journal, 32, 543–576.

Elliott. E. (2019). Normative Decision Theory. Analysis, 79, 4, 755–772.

Evans, J. St. B.T. (1982). Psychological Pitfalls in Forecasting, Futures, 14, 4, 258–265.

Fildes, R. and Goodwin, P. (2007). Good and bad judgment forecasting: Lessons from four companies, Foresight, 8, 5–10.

Fischhoff, B. (1988). Judgmental Aspects of Forecasting: Needs and Possible Trends, International Journal of Forecasting, 4, 3, 331–339.

Fischhoff, B. (1982). For Those Condemned to Study the Past: Heuristics and Biases in Hindsight, in D. Kahneman, P. Slovic, and A. Tversky, (eds.), Judgement Under Uncertainty: Heuristics and Biases, Cambridge: Cambridge University Press.

Fischoff, B., Slovic, P. and Lichtenstein, S. (1978). Fault Trees: Sensitivity of Estimated Failure Probabilities to Problem Representation, Journal of Experimental Psychology: Human Perception and Performance, 4, 330–334.

Fischoff, B., Slovic, P. and Lichtenstein, S. (1977). Knowing with Certainty: The Appropriateness of Extreme Confidence, Journal of Experimental Psychology: Human Perception and Performance, 3, 552–564.

Fischhoff, B. (1975). Hindsight #1 Foresight: The Effects of Outcome Knowledge on Judgement Under Uncertainty, Journal of Experimental Psychology: Human Perception and Performance, 1, 288–200.

Fischhoff, B. and Beyth, R. (1975). I Knew It Would Happen – Remembered Probabilities of Once-future Things, Organisational Behaviour and Performance, 13, 1–16.

Fischoff, B. (1975a). Hindsight and Foresight: The Effects of Outcome Knowledge on Judgement Under Uncertainty, Journal of Experimental Psychology: Human Perceptions and Performance, 1, 288–299.

Fischoff, B. (1975b). Hindsight: Thinking Backward? Psychology Today, 8, 70–76.

Fredrickson, J.W. and Laquinto, A.L. (1989). Inertia and Creeping Rationality in Strategic Decision Processes, Academy of Management Journal, 32, 516–542.

Fredrickson, J.W. (1984). The Comprehensiveness of Strategic Decision Processes: Extension, Observation, Future Directions, Academy of Management Journal, 28, 821–843.

Fredrickson, J.W. and Mitchell, T.R. (1984). Strategic Decision Processes: Comprehensiveness and Performance in an Industry with an Unstable Environment, Administrative Science Quarterly, 27, 399–423.

Gersick, C.J.G. (1991). Revolutionary Change Theories: A Multilevel Exploration of the Punctuated Equilibrium Paradigm. The Academy of Management Review, 16, 1, pp. 10–36.

Gigerenzer, G. (2020). What is bounded rationality? Routledge Handbook of Bounded Rationality. Routledge.

Goodwin, P. and Wright, G. (1991). Decision Analysis for Management Judgement, Chichester: John Wiley & Sons.

Gregory, W.L., Cialdini, R.B. and Carpenter, K.M. (1982). Self-relevant Scenarios as Mediators of Likelihood Estimates and Compliance: Does Imagining it Make it So? Journal of Personality and Social Psychology, 43, 1, 89–99.

Haeiffel, G.J. and Cobb, W.R. (2022). Tests of generalizability can diversify psychology and improve theories. National Review of Psychology, 1, 186–187.

Hamill, R., Wilson, T.D. and Nisbett, R.E. (1980). Insensitivity to Sample Bias: Generalizing from Atypical Cases, Journal of Personality and Social Psychology, 39, 4, 578–589.

Hendrickx, L., Vlek, C. and Caljie, H. (1992). Effects of Frequency and Scenario Information on the Evaluation of Large-scale Risks, Organisational Behaviour and Human Decision Processes, 52, 256–275.

Hendrickx, L., Vlek, C. and Oppenwal, H. (1989). Relative Importance of Scenario Information and Frequency Information in the Judgement of Risk, Acta Psychologica, 72, 41–63.

Hoch, S.J. (1985). Counterfactual Reasoning and Accuracy in Predicting Personal Events, Journal of Experimental Psychology: Learning, Memory, and Cognition, 11, 719–731.

Hodgkinson, G.P. and Healey, M. P. (2008). Toward a (Pragmatic) Science of Strategic Intervention: Design Propositions for Scenario Planning, Organization Studies, 29, 435–457.

Hogarth, R.M. and Makridakis, S. (1981). Forecasting and Planning: An Evaluation, Management Science, February, 115–138.

Hogarth, R. (1980). Judgement and Choice: The Psychology of Decisions, New York: John Wiley & Sons.

Huff, A.S. (1980). Evocative Metaphors, Human Systems Management, 1, 1–10.

Janis, I.R. (1982). Groupthink, 2nd Edn. Boston: Houghton Mifflin.

Janis, I.R. and Mann, L. (1977). Decision Making: A Psychological Analysis of Conflict, Choice and Commitment, London: Collier McMillan.

Jiao, Y. (2023). Managing decision fatigue: Evidence from analysts' earnings forecasts. Journal of Accounting and Economics. https://doi.org/10.1016/.jacceco.2023.101615.

Johnson, W.B. (1983). Representativeness in Judgmental Predictions of Corporate Bankruptcy, The Accounting Review, 63, 78–79.

Joyce, E.J. and Biddle, G.C. (1981a). Anchoring and Adjustment in Probabilistic Inferences in Auditing, Journal of Accounting Research, 19, 1, 120–145.

Joyce E.J. and Biddle, G.C. (1981b). Are Auditor's Judgements Sufficiently Regressive? Journal of Accounting Research, 19, 1, 323–349.

Jungermann, H. (1985a). Inferential Processes in the Construction of Scenarios, Journal of Forecasting, 4, 3, 21–327.

Jungermann, H. (1985b). The Psychological Aspects of Scenarios, in V.T. Covello, J.L. Mumpower, P.J.M. Stallen and V.R.R. Uppuluri (Eds.), Environmental Impact Assessment, Technology Assessment and Risk Analysis, Berlin: Springer-Verlag.

Kahneman, D. and Tversky, A. (1982). The Psychology of Preferences, Scientific American, 39, 136–142.

Kahneman, D. and Tversky, A. (1982a). On the Psychology of Prediction, in D. Kahanerman, P. Slovic and A. Tversky (Eds.), Judgement Under Uncertainty: Heuristics and Biases, Cambridge: Cambridge University Press.

Kahneman, D. and Tversky, A. (1982b). The Simulation Heuristic, in D. Kahanerman, P. Slovic and A. Tversky (eds.), Judgement Under Uncertainty: Heuristics and Biases, Cambridge: Cambridge University Press.

Kahneman, D. and Tversky, A. (1979). Intuitive Predictions: Biases and Corrective Procedures, TIMS Studies in Management Science, 12, 313–327.

Kahneman, D. and Tversky, A. (1973). On the Psychology of Prediction, Psychological Review, 80, 237–251.

Kahneman, D. and Tversky, A. (1972). Subjective Probability: A Judgement of Representativeness, Cognitive Psychology, 3, 450–454.

Kozielecki, J. (1981). Psychological decision theory, Boston: D. Reidel.

Kruglanski, A.W., Friedland, N. and Farkash, E. (1984), Lay Persons' Sensitivity to Statistical Information: The Case of High Perceived Applicability, Journal of Personality and Social Psychology, 46, 503–518.

Langer, E.J. (1975). The Illusion of Control, Journal of Personality and Social Psychology, 32, 311–328.

Langer, E.J. and Roth, J. (1975). The Effect of Sequence of Outcomes in a Chance Task on the Illusion of Control, Journal of Personality and Social Psychology, 32, 951–955.

Larwood, L. and Whittaker, W. (1977). Managerial Myopia: Self-Serving Biases in Organizational Planning, Journal of Applied Psychology, 62, 2, 194–198.

Lefcourt, H.M. (1973). The Function of The Illusions of Control and Freedom, American Psychologist, 28, 417–425.

Levi, A.S. and Pryor, J.B. (1987). Use of the Availability Heuristic in Probability Estimates of Future Events: The Effects of Imagining Outcomes versus Imagining Reasons, Organisational Behaviour and Human Decision Processes, 40, 219–234.

Levine, M. (1971). Hypothesis Theory and Non-learning Despite Ideal S-R Reinforcement Contingencies, Psychological Review, 78, 130–140.

Lichtenstein, S., Fischhoff, B. and Phillips, L.D. (1982). Calibration of Probabilities: The State of the Art to 1980, in D. Kahanerman, P. Slovic and A. Tversky (Eds.), Judgement Under Uncertainty: Heuristics and Biases, Cambridge: Cambridge University Press.

Lichtenstein, S., Slovic, P., Fischhoff, B., Layman, M. and Combs, B. (1980). Judged Frequency of Lethal Events, Journal of Experimental Psychology: Human Learning and Memory, 4, 551–578.

Luchins, A.S. (1957). Essential Attempts to Minimise the Impact of First Impressions, in I.C. Hovland, (Ed.), The Order of Presentations in Persuasion New Haven, Conn: Yale University Press.

Maier, N.R.F. (1981). Reasoning in Humans: The Solution of a Problem and Its Appearance in Consciousness, Journal of Comparative Psychology, 12, 181–194.

Mintzberg, H. (2018). Strategic Thinking as "Seeing." Manage Magazine, October 18.

Montgomery, D.B. and Weinberg, C.B. (1973). Modeling Marketing Phenomena: A Managerial Perspective, Journal of Contemporary Business, Autumn, 17–43.

Neuhauser, P. (1993). Corporate Legends and Legends: The Power of Storytelling as a Management Tool, New York: McGraw-Hill.

Newell, A. and Simon, H.A. (1972). Human Problem Solving, Englewood Cliffs, NJ: Prentice-Hall.

Nisbett, R.E. and Ross, L.D. (1980). Human inferences: Strategies and Shortcomings of Social Judgement, Englewood Cliffs, NJ: Prentice-Hall.

Norman, D.A. and Rumelhart, D.E. (1975). Explorations in Cognition, San Francisco: Freeman Press.

Nutt, P.C. (2002). Why Decisions Fail, New York: Berrett-Koehler.

O'Connor, M. A. (2003). The Enron board: the perils of groupthink. University of Cincinnati Law Review. 71, 4. 1233–1320

Padesky, C.A. (1994). Scherma change processes in cognitive theory. Clinical Psychology and Psychotherapy. 1, 5, 267–278.

Park, W. (2000). A comprehensive empirical investigation of the relationships among variables of the groupthink model. Journal of Organisational Behavior, 21, 873–887.

Pennington, N. and Hastie, R. (1988). Explanation-based Decision Making: The effects of Memory Structure on Judgement, Journal of Experimental Psychology: Learning, Memory, and Cognition, 14, 521–533.

Pennington, N. and Hastie, R. (1986). Evidence Evaluation in Complex Decision Making, Journal of Personality and Social Psychology, 51, 242–258.

Persson, E., Barrafrem, K., Meunier, A., and Tinghog. G. (2019). The effects of decision fatigue on surgeons' clinical decisions. Health Economics, 28, 1194–1203.

Pignatiello, G. A., Martin, R. I., and Hickman, R.L. (2020). Decision fatigue: A conceptual analysis. Journal of Health Psychology, 25, 1, 123–135.

Posner, M.I. and Keele, S.W. (1968). On the Generation of Abstract Ideas, Journal of Experimental Psychology, 77, 353–363.

Pruitt, D.G. (1961). Informational Requirements in Decision Making, American Journal of Psychology, 74, 433–439.

Pyszczynski, T. and Greenberg, J. (1981). Role of disconfirmed expectancies in the instigation of attributional processing, Journal of Personality and Social Psychology, 40, 31–38.

Read, S.J. (1983). Once is Enough: Causal Reasoning from a Single Instance, Journal of Personality and Social Psychology, 45, 2, 323–334.

Roese, N.J. and Vohs, K.D. (2012). Hindsight Bias. Perspectives on Psychological Science, 7, 5, 411–426.

Rosch, E. (1978). Principles of Categorization, in E. Rosch and B.B. Floyd, (Eds.), Cognition and Categorization, Hillsdale, NJ: Erlbaum.

Rose, J.D. (2011). Diverse perspectives on the groupthink theory-a literary review. Emerging Leadership Journeys, 4, 1, 37–57.

Ross, L.D., Arnabile, T.M. and Steinmetz, J.L. (1977). Social Roles, Social Control and Biases in Social-Perception Processes, Journal of Personality and Social Psychology, 35, 485–494.

Russo, J.E., and Shoemaker, P.J.H, (2001). Winning Decisions: Getting it Right the First Time, New York: Doubleday.

Russo, J.E. and Schoemaker, P.J.H. (1989). Decision Traps: The Ten Barriers to Brilliant Decision Making and How to Overcome Them, New York: Doubleday Currency.

Schank R.C. and Abelson, R.P. (1977). Scripts, Plans, Goals and Understanding, Hillsdale, NJ: Erlbaum.

Schacter, D.L., Addis, D.R., Haasabis, D., Martin. V.C., Spreng, R.N. and Szpunar, K.K. (2012). The Future of Memory: Remembering, Imagining, and the Brain Neuron, 76, (4), 10.1016/i.neuron.11.001.

Schacter, D.L., Benoit, R.G., and Szpunar K.K. (2017). Episodic Future Thinking: Mechanisms and Functions, Current Opinion in Behavioural Sciences, 17, 41–50.

Schoemaker, P.J.H. (1993). Multiple Scenario Development: Its Conceptual and Behavioural Foundation, Strategic Management Journal, 14, 192–213.

Schwenk, C.R. (1986). Information, Cognitive Biases and Commitment to a Course of Action, Academy of Management Review, 11, 298–310.

Schwenk, C.R. (1984). Cognitive Simplification Processes in Strategic Decision-making, Strategic Management Journal, 5, 111–128.

Simon, H.A. (2000). Bounded Rationality in Social Science: Today and Tomorrow, Mind & Society, 1, 25–39.

Simon, H. A. (1991). Bounded Rationality and Organisational Learning, Organization Science, 2, 1, 125–134.

Simon, H.A. (1973). The Structure of Ill-structured Problems, Artificial Intelligence, 4, 181–201.

Simon, H.A. (1956). Rational Choice and The Structure of the Environment, Psychological Review, 63, 129–138.

Simon, H.A. (1955). A Behavioral Model of Rational Choice, Quarterly Journal of Economics, 69, 99–118.

Slovic, P., Fischhoff, B. and Lichtenstein, S. (1985). Rating the Risks: The Structure of Expert and Lay Perceptions in V.T. Covello, J.L. Mumpower, P.J.M. Stallen and V.R.R. Uppuluri (Eds.), Environmental Impact Assessment, Technology Assessment, and Risk Analysis, Berlin: Springer Verlag.

Slovic, P., Fischhoff, B. and Lichtenstein, S. (1977). Behavioral Decision Theory, Annual Review of Psychology, 28, 1–39.

Slovic, P. and Lichtenstein, S. (1971). Comparison of Bayesian and Regression Approaches to The Study of Information Processing in Judgement, Organisational Behavior and Human Performance, 6, 649–744.

Smith, J.F. and Kilda, T. (1991). Heuristics and Biases: Expertise and Task Realism in Auditing, Psychological Bulletin, 109, 472–485.

Soltwisch, B; Ma, D., and Syed, I. (2022). When 'Good Enough' is Not Enough: The Role of Maximizing or Satisficing Decision Decision-Making Styles, Innovation Behavior, and Entrepreneurial Alertness in the Pursuit of New Business Opportunities. Journal of Small Business Strategy. 32, 4, 63–81.

Steinbruner, J. D. (1974). The Cybernetics Theory of Decisions, Princeton, NJ: Princeton University Press.

Stevens, D. (2019). Satisficing in Political Decision-Making. Oxford Research Encyclopaedia of Politics.

Swieringa, R., Gibbons, M., Larson, L. and Sweeney, J.L. (1976). Experiments in The Heuristics of Information Processing, Journal of Accounting Research, 4 (Supp), 159–187.

Taleb, Nassim Nicholas (2007). Black Swan: The Impact of the Improbable. Penguin Books.

Thuring, M. and Jungermann. H. (1986). Constructing and Running Mental Models for Inferences About the Future, in B. Brehmer, H. Jungermann, P. Lourens and G. Sevon, (Eds.), New Directions in Research on Decision Making, North Holland: Elsevier Science Publishers BV.

True-Love, M., Erickson, B.A., Anderson, J., Kossoyan, M. and Kunions, J. (2018). A Growth-Curve Analysis of the Effects of Future-Thought Priming on Insight and Analytical Problem-Solving. Frontiers in Psychology, 9.

Tuckman, B.W. (1965). Developmental sequence in small groups. Psychological Bulletin 63 (6), 384–399.

Tversky, A. and Kahneman, D. (1983). Extensional Versus Intuitive Reasoning: The Conjunctive Fallacy in Probability Judgement, Psychological Review, 90, 4, 293–315.

Tversky, A. and Kahneman, D. (1982a). Judgements Under Uncertainty: Heuristics and Biases, in D. Kahneman, P. Slovic and A. Tversky (Eds.), Judgement Under Uncertainty: Heuristics and Biases, Cambridge: Cambridge University Press.

Tversky, A. and Kahneman, D. (1982b). Judgements of and by Representativeness, in D. Kahanerman, P. Slovic and A. Tversky (Eds.), Judgement Under Uncertainty: Heuristics and Biases, Cambridge: Cambridge University Press.

Tversky, A. and Kahneman, D. (1982c). Causal Schemas in Judgements Under Uncertainty, in D. Kahneman, P. Slovic and A. Tversky (Eds.), Judgement Under Uncertainty: Heuristics and Biases, Cambridge: Cambridge University Press.

Tversky, A. and Kahneman, D. (1982d). Availability: A Heuristic for Judging Frequency and Probability, in D. Kahneman, P. Slovic and A. Tversky (Eds.), Judgement Under Uncertainty: Heuristics and Biases, Cambridge: Cambridge University Press.

Tversky, A. and Kahneman, D. (1982e). Belief in The Law of Small Numbers, in D. Kahneman, P. Slovic and A. Tversky (Eds.), Judgement Under Uncertainty: Heuristics and Biases, Cambridge: Cambridge University Press.

Tversky, A. and Kahneman, D. (1981). The Framing of Decisions and the Psychology of Choice, Science, 211, 453–458.

Tversky, A. and Kahneman, D. (1980). Causal Schemas in Judgements Under Uncertainty, in M. Fishbuein (ed.), Progress is Social Psychology, Hillsdale: Earlbaum.

Tversky, A. and Kahneman, D. (1971). Beliefs in The Law of Small Numbers, Psychological Bulletin, 76, 105–110.

Vlek, C. and Otten, W. (1987). Judgmental Handling of Energy Scenarios: A Psychological Analysis and Experiment, in G. Wright and P. Ayton (Eds.), Judgmental Forecasting, Chichester: John Wiley & Sons.

Wack, P. (1985a). Unchartered Waters Ahead. Harvard Business Review, September-October, 73–89.

Wack, P. (1985b). Scenarios: Shooting the Rapids. Harvard Business Review, November-December, 139–150.

Walster, E. (1966). Assignment of Responsibility for an Accident, Journal of Personality and Social Psychology, 3, 73–70.

Warren, W.H., Nicholas, D.W. and Trebasso, T. (1979). Event Chains and Inferences in Understanding Narratives, in R.O. Freedle (ed.), New Directions in Discourse Processing. Norwood, NJ: Ablex.

Watson, P.C. (1960). On the Failure to Eliminate Hypothesis in a Conceptual Task, Quarterly Journal of Experimental Psychology, 12, 129–140.

Weiner, B. (1985). Spontaneous' Causal Thinking, Psychological Bulletin, 97, 74–84.

Wright, G. and Goodwin, P. (2009). Decision making and planning under low levels of predictability: Enhancing the scenario method, International Journal of Forecasting, 25, 813–825.

Chapter 8
Issues in Scenario Planning

Introduction

Chapter 7, the final chapter in the book, discusses some of the important issues in futures and scenario planning methods. At the end of the book are 7 appendices which should prove useful to those who want to learn more about scenario planning, these being:
– Foresight and Futurist Organisations
– Futures Journals, Magazines, and Networks
– Foresight Glossary
– Useful Guides and Tools
– Select Readings
– Scenario Examples
– Common Heuristics and Cognitive Biases

Scenario Typologies

Over the years, several SP typologies have been published: Ducot and Lubben (1980); Duncan and Wack (1994); Godet and Roubelat, 1996; and Heugens and van Oosterhout, 2001). However, the problem with these typologies according to van Notten (2005), is that they do not capture the full range of diverse up-to-date scenario development processes. While the typologies may reflect the state of play at the time they are published, as the field develops, they become outdated. The result is that the existing classifications are not "detailed enough nor broad enough to do justice to the variety of today's scenario development approaches" (van Notten, 2005, p 23).

In response to criticisms and to bring some clarity, Bishop et al (2007) offer some basic vocabulary definitions for commonly used terms, and classify individual techniques into eight general categories, albeit there are several variations for each of the eight types with specific techniques for each category. They provide tables which compare the process, products and advantages and disadvantages of each technique, and at the same time, they point to three articles in the literature which provide typologies of scenario types.
– The first is from van Notten et. al. (2003). Their taxonomy focuses on the attributes of the scenarios, and they propose three categories of scenarios based on major overarching themes, namely: the project goal – exploration versus decision support; the process – intuitive versus formal; and the scenario content – complex versus simple.

https://doi.org/10.1515/9783111617442-008

- The second is from Bradfield (et al. 2005). They provide a higher-level framework of scenarios by tracing the evolution and development of three different scenario schools, two of which originated in the UK/USA and the third in France.
- The third typology is from Borjeson et al. (2006), who propose a typology of scenarios based on the diverse types of futures, namely: probable or predictive scenarios which answer the question of what will happen; possible or exploratory scenarios which answer the question what can happen; and preferable futures or normative scenarios which address how can a specific target be reached?

More recently Hughes (2009) has developed a detailed scenario family tree depicting key practitioners and institutions involved in scenario building, and the important methodological tools which they developed or have been associated with. Although the tree does not provide any additional typological clarity, it demonstrates 'lineages of influence' with several branches corresponding to scenario development schools, and it emphasizes the range of approaches.

Classification of Futures Methods

The issue that receives the most attention in journals is the categorisation of scenario planning (SP) and future studies; Poli (2018) contends that the classification of futures methods is one of the SP field's weakest points, and most classifications score poorly on two criteria. The first criterion is that SP must prove that it contributes knowledge and viewpoints which are different from those distinctive of other established fields. The second criterion is the futurist's toolbox contains methods such as Delphi and brainstorming which are not unique to SP, but are widely used in other fields such as economics. To become an autonomous field of research and application, Poli states that the futurist's toolbox should be distinguished from those used by other system practitioners. The classification issue therefore, is Poli suggests, finding methods that distinguish future studies from other social sciences, or distinguish them according to the different ways in which they use the future, and organizing those methods according to a futures literacy typology.

Masini (1993, p 23) suggests that 'scientificity' is the most debated of the characteristics of Future Studies and according to many scholars, is not to be considered a quality of Future Studies. While futurists such as Malaska, (1995) regard Future Studies as a science, pioneers in the field such as de Jouvenel (2004) contend that by its very nature, the field cannot be a science. Meanwhile, futurists such as Schwartz and van der Heijden contend that scenario work integrates facts and data based on rational and objective analysis, and as such, SP is an art form and must be recognised and valued as such. Amara (1981) however, sees it as both art and science.

Wendell Bell (2003, p 189) examines both sides of the argument and suggests that future studies are a "transdisciplinary, action and social science" on the basis that it is:

- 'Transdisciplinary' because it encompasses numerous disciplines in reaching and justifying its findings and assertions.
- 'Action science' because it aims to inform human action designed to shape the future.
- 'Social science' because decision-making and action are social processes and act within social contexts.

Bell continues that art and science share many similar characteristics, and as with science, art has its "technical and rigorous, mechanical, codified, standardized, and objective aspects." The fact that the future is nonevidential is not an issue as "evidential and existing phenomena that bear on the future can be studied with the standard methods of science." To conclude, Bell (2017, p 168) suggests that it "is silly to quibble over terms and individuals should assign the field any name they want and get on with the job." However, the debate as to whether future studies are art or science has not been resolved and continues.

A second issue is the long-standing argument that foresight lacks a coherent and rational *theory*-based model (Mermet et al, 2009; Chermack, 2004), and this has contributed to fragmenting the global community of futurists, many of whom go off in different philosophical and professional directions. Loveridge (2009, p 155) states that while attempts by individuals such as Chermack have been made to create a theory of SP, "There is not and, I will assert, there cannot be a theoretical basis to scenario planning any more than there can be a theoretical basis to a playwright's art". Piirainen and Gonzalez (2015, p 191) meanwhile, suggest that while the issue of theory is problematic, they ask the questions: "What does a theory of foresight even mean?" and "What is there to achieve with more theory?" In terms of the second question, they argue that theory development is essentially an important mark of progress and legitimacy, it would make the field of foresight more progressive and better understood, and it would "improve the quality and impact of foresight as well as legitimacy of the field" (p 193). In exploring the gap between the theory and practice of foresight, Hideg (2007, p 36) suggests that two different types of practical foresight activities have developed, one termed *praxis foresight* (PF), which has no theoretical basis, and the other termed *foresight of critical futures studies* (FCFS) which is an application of a theory of future studies. However, a brief search of the scenario and foresight literature has not revealed any publications supporting this suggestion.

Spaniol and Rowland (2017, p 33) suggest that "there is probably no greater point of consensus in future studies than the reality that there is no scholarly consensus concerning the application of theory to support scenario methodology". Derbyshire (2017 p 78) however, states that although the contention held by many scenario scholars that scenario planning is theoretically underdeveloped and requires more solid theoretical foundations, "theoretical frameworks that could potentially fulfil this role have already, from time to time, been identified, only to remain undeveloped and, eventually forgotten." The example Derbyshire gives is the similarity, recognised by

Shell in the 1980s, between G.L.S. Shackle's theory of 'potential surprise' (PST) and scenario planning which has gone overlooked by SP scholars. Derbyshire suggests this is a significant oversight as PST and SP share many similarities including the use of plausibility, the focus on extreme outcomes, and the same ontology i.e. the construction of futures through the imaginations of individuals. At the same time, scenario planning underpinned by PST can provide the means to overcome the current divide between constructivist and deductivist approaches in scenario planning practice. Derbyshire concludes that ignoring PST as an underpinning theoretical framework on the foundations of which SP can be further developed as an academic discipline lending support to its use as a practical tool, is "a considerable oversight."

Scenario Definitions

Like any field, the futures field has its esoteric language. There is an ongoing discussion in the literature regarding the definition of foresight and scenarios, and futurists have not yet reached a consensus on either the name or definition of their activity, the result being the names commonly used include *foresight, futurism, futurology, future thinking*, and *scenario planning*, while those in France and francophone African countries prefer the name *prospective analysis* or *prospective studies*. The word scenario is originally derived from the Latin *scaena* meaning scene, and was originally used in the context of films and theatres. The earliest and most comprehensive definitions in the literature was that put forward by Kahn and Wiener (1967, p 32) who defined scenarios as:

> *Hypothetical sequences of events constructed for the purpose of focusing attention on causal processes and decision points. They answer two kinds of questions: (1) precisely how might some hypothetical situation come about, step-by-step; and (2) what alternatives exist, for each actor, at each step, for preventing, diverting, or facilitating the process?*

Hideg (2006, p 81) states that Richard Slaughter (1995) was the first to define foresight in the future studies literature, in which he defined it as

> *. . . a universal human capacity which allows people to think ahead, consider, model, create and respond to future eventualities . . . founded on the rich and inclusive environment of the human brain-mind system which, crudely put, has sufficiently complex neural wiring to support an extended mode of perception, whose main functions are proactive and facilitating.*

Since then, numerous, diverse definitions of foresight and scenarios have appeared in the literature, many of which are somewhat similar, and there are several overlapping camps of opinion as to the name or definition of activities. For example, Chermack et al (2001), state that Porter (1985) defines scenarios as "an internally consistent view of what the future may turn out to be", while Schwartz (1991) suggests that "SP is a tool for ordering one's perceptions about alternative future environments in which one's decisions might be played out right." In line with this Schoemaker proposes that SP "is a disciplined method for imaging possible futures in which organizational decisions may be played out." Ringland (1998) meanwhile, states that SP is "that part of strategic planning which relates to the tools and technologies for managing the uncertainties of the future", while van Notten (2005) suggests that "scenarios are consistent and coherent descriptions of hypothetical futures which reflect different perspectives on past, present, and future developments, which can serve as a basis action," which he suggests, covers many of the characteristics proposed by other definitions. Godet's (2001, p 3) definition is probably the simplest, "A scenario is simply a means to represent a future reality to shed light on current action in view of possible and desirable futures." To get clarity on the issue of definitions, Chermack et al. (2001, p 8) conducted a review of the available definitions and outcome variables of SP using a keyword search which identified 18 definitions. While some definitions did not explicitly state the outcomes of SP, many featured "embedded outcome variables, which may support the notion that some definitions are unclear about their primary intentions." Chermack et al suggest that this is evidence that SP professionals are just beginning to consider the importance of defining what they do, and explicitly stating what they intend to achieve by doing it.

The reason that there is no single best definition of the term scenario is that it means different things to different people and consequentially, is defined and applied in widely divergent ways (Millet 1988). For example, in the context of game theory, the term scenario refers to the operating environment within which the simulation is played out (Brown 1968); in financial analysis, scenarios are regarded as a form of judgmental forecasting as evidenced by the fact the multiple forecasts generated by changing assumptions regarding the future values of key variables, are routinely referred to as scenarios. Bishop et al (2007, p 6) suggest that because future studies are a relatively new field, it is "blessed with an abundance of creative and entrepreneurial practitioners" who develop different techniques to suit their client's needs, the result of which is that "after a period of time the growth becomes chaotic." However, although there are numerous definitions, Millet (2003) states that there are terms in the literature relating to the goal, role and form of scenarios that refer to remarkably similar concepts, the result of which there is semantic and technical overlap. Although there are numerous definitions of scenarios, there is one point on which there is unanimous agreement: scenarios are not predictions (van der Heijden et al, 2002).

Aside from the different meanings ascribed to scenarios, many of the definitions indicate a different conceptualization of the term, an example of which is the chronological nature of scenarios. Several writers (DuMoulin and Eyre, 1979; Georgoff and Murdick, 1986; Gershuny 1976; Goldfarb and Huss, 1988; MacNulty 1977; Mandel 1982; Porter 1985) appear to emphasize in their definitions, the depiction of the situation being examined at a given point in the future i.e., the focus of the scenarios is on the end-state. Meanwhile, definitions provided by Kahn and Weiner (1967) and others (Becker and van Houten, 1984; Brauers and Weber, 1988; Godet 1987; Millett and Randles, 1986; Millet, 1988; Raubitschek 1988) accentuate understanding of the evolution of the chains of events and their causal processes that lead to the end-states. Jungermann and Thuring (1987) describe these two different conceptual approaches as 'snapshot' and 'chain' scenarios, while Godet (1987) refers to them as 'situational' and 'developmental' scenarios and Schnaars (1987) describes them as 'cross-sectional' and 'longitudinal'.

Writers such as Huss (1988) indicate that the focus of scenarios should be on future business environments whereas writers such as Becker and van Houten (1984) take a more social perspective and circumscribe scenarios in terms of the state of society. Other writers (Bunn and Salo, 1993; Jungermann, 1985a; Kahn and Wiener, 1967; and van der Heijden, 1996) incorporate the concept of decision-making in their definitions which few others appear to, although this can be implied in their definitions, or is discussed in terms of the objectives of scenarios. Similarly, aside from Mobasheri et al. (1989), Ringland (1998), and van der Heijden (1996), none of the other writers specifically reference scenarios to business strategy in their definitions, albeit this may be implied by the readers of the work, or is addressed elsewhere in their discussions.

Despite the many definitions in the literature, Jungermann,1985a, Jungermann and Thuring, 1987, contend that the term scenario is not a very precisely defined concept. This is endorsed by Durance and Godet (2010) and Godet and Roubelat (1996), who suggest that the term scenario is increasingly misused and abused, and Simpson (1992) who states that the term elicits an array of imprecise, ambiguously defined concepts. The result concludes Mason (1994), is that the term scenario has become as ill-defined as the term strategy, while Vlek and Otten (1987) question whether it is possible to define the scenario concept with precision. Accepting that the term scenario lacks a precise, universally accepted definition, Jungermann (1985a) declares that there are five attributes common to most of the definitions and interpretations of the term scenario, these being that a scenario:

– Is hypothetical in nature in that it describes some probable future state, but it is selective in that it represents only one possible state;
– Describes a process representing a sequence of specific events over a period;
– Is bounded in that it consists of a limited number of states, events, actions, and consequences which are conditionally or causally related;
– Is assessable in that the scenario elements can be judged in terms of their importance, desirability and or probability; and
– It includes the depiction of an initial state which usually, but not necessarily lies in the present, and of a final state at a fixed time horizon in the future.

It is Jungermann (1985a) argues, that these five common features in effect, constitute the term scenario and differentiate it from other terms.

Scenario Development Methods

The first comprehensive model for the development of scenarios to be published in a journal was that provided by Zentner in 1975. Since then, numerous models have been published, and the literature is replete with methodological descriptions of ideal models for generating scenarios, ranging from simple to elaborate and highly structured techniques, quantitative versus qualitative, and exploratory versus normative. Most of the models and techniques discussed in the literature are highly prescriptive, each identifying several discrete steps, varying from 5 to 12 or more, depending on the scenario approach used, and the features of scenarios that are highlighted or ignored. Although there are notable differences between the models, in broad terms they appear to adhere to a similar structure consisting of a series of distinct phases completed sequentially. However, in most cases, specifics of the construction process are generally vague, and some 20 years ago Jungermann (1985a) reported that "most techniques discussed in the literature are only loosely defined procedures with little theoretical justification or empirical validation and none are immutable" (p28). Eight years on, Bunn and Salo (1993) maintained that notwithstanding the considerable changes that the scenario approach had undergone since its rise, protocols for scenario development were still essentially improvised and not justifiable. Despite the outpouring of books and journal publications about scenarios over the years, the situation remains essentially unchanged. Whilst numerous guidelines concerning scenario construction process are provided in the literature (Schoemaker, 1995); van der Heijden (1996); Wright and Goodwin (1999); Dominiak, (2006); Montibeller and Franco (2010), there is no consensus in the literature on the appropriate methodology, or the balance between quantitative and qualitative methods to be used. This Karlsen et al. (2010) contend, arises partly from the fact that the inherent ontological and epistemological presumptions in foresight studies differ when it comes to capturing the complexity of issues. Secondly, the choice of methodology is largely dependent on the context of the study. Consequently, a lack of consensus is understandable.

Schnaars (1987) states that most of what is known about SP techniques comes from three sources. The first are articles by scenario practitioners and consultants describing how SP projects are undertaken and offering experienced-based advice on conducting scenario projects. The second source is articles from the future research literature which offer numerous models for constructing scenarios, many of which are impractical and have not been thoroughly tested. The third source is a growing body of research based on empirical studies of related topics, which offer evidence as to the value of scenarios as a long-range planning tool. In reviewing publications from the three sources, the first observation is that numerous approaches and techniques go by the name scenarios, but there is no consensus as to what framework the scenarios belong to as there are several overlapping camps of opinion. Testimony to this is the fact that the terms *planning, thinking, forecasting, development, analysis, learning, adaptive, alternative, predictive, exploratory,* and *normative* are commonly attached to the word scenario.

There are, however, terms in the literature relating to the goal, role and form of scenarios that refer to similar concepts, the consequence of which Millett (2003) suggests, is that there is semantic and technical overlap. The second observation is that there is a plethora of scenario development models, the result of which is that the existing methodological chaos is unlikely to disappear in the foreseeable future (Martelli, 2001). Support for this comes from Masini and Vasquez (2000, p 50) who suggest that the flexibility in scenario development models has its pitfalls:

> Scenario development has become a Swiss pocketknife of multiple uses or a magic wand, and the development of scenarios is no more than a cosmetic exercise that adds superficial legitimacy to policy-making exercises; the resulting scenarios are hollow diamonds, attractive to look at but lacking in content.

The third observation is that there appears to be virtually no area in scenarios on which there is widespread consensus; the literature reveals many different and conflicting definitions, characteristics, principles, and methodological ideas. Mason (1994) states that the term scenario has become as ill-defined as the term strategy, while Simpson (1992) suggests that the term elicits a plethora of vague and loosely defined concepts. Ramirez and Wilkinson (2014) state that the fact that SP practices have continued to evolve over the years has resulted in an assortment of and within methods, leading ultimately to misunderstandings and methodological confusion. The futurist's toolkit is now crowded with foresight/scenario systems from the French School, the Intuitive Logics methodology and its variants, the Delphi technique, Causal Layered Analysis and recent approaches like the Integral Futures, Systemic Foresight Methodology and RIMA (Reflexive, Interventionist, Multi-agent scenario practices). Writers such as Hodkinson and Sparrow (2002) criticise SP planning as a practitioner tool but with little theoretical underpinning, while others (Hamel, 2000; Hyde, 1999; Mintzberg, 1994; Porter, 1985) suggest that it is an imperfect tool which offers mere speculation on the nature of the future dealing with opinions rather than facts, and which then raises the question of how should managers be expected to respond to matters of speculation as opposed to fact? Aside from the confusion caused by the different scenario typologies, definitions and methods, is the uncertainty about when and how to apply scenarios in the business environment.

Godet and Roubelat (1996) add that the term scenario is increasingly 'misused and abused' while Millet (2003 p 17), asserts that "perhaps no other method of futuring has caused as much confusion as scenarios because of the variations in definitions of them, and the methods of generating them. Virtually every manager may say that he or she understands and uses scenarios, but few really do." The consequence of all of this suggests Khakee (1991), is that there are few techniques in future studies which have given rise to so much confusion as scenarios. Crawford (2019, p 1) however, refutes the contention that the numerous typologies and ever-emerging methods and schools of scenario planning have given rise to chaos and confusion. She suggests firstly, that the many differences have in fact, been responsible for expanding the field of SP; secondly, she states that she sees the field "as a collective of experiences and knowledge that play upon a theme, where emerging realities slowly reveal a structure to the system" and proposes the name 'Comprehensive Scenario Intervention Typology' which incorporates all dimensions of existing typologies.

Marcus (2009, p 63) meanwhile states that the important critiques of SP revolve around the fact that firstly, scenarios "emphasize preparation for external events rather than actions that participants in organisations can take to shape these events". The very reason for engaging in scenarios work is not to submit to the inevitably of the possible futures depicted in the scenarios, but to influence them. Secondly, it is usually the "organisational elites, top-level or central organisational thinkers and their consultants" who develop the scenarios, fix them at a point in time, and "arrive at a premature consensus about how the future will evolve" which stifles dissent (p 10). Marcus (p 23) goes on to suggest that scenarios should be "more central to the decision-making process and all members of the organisation should be involved in thinking and acting about the future" (rather than just the organisational elites), . . . and "the scenarios should "rest on a culture of pluralism and dissent". Schmidt-Scheele (2020, p 216) builds on Marcus's points, stating that because researchers and developers actively involved in the development of scenarios are preoccupied, only those directly involved in the process are considered. She suggests that users who are targeted by the scenarios but are not directly involved in their development process, are unexplored territory, and "investigating their expectations, beliefs and cognitive assessment style is worthwhile for any successful scenario activity." The alternative to the comments by Marcus and Schmidt-Scheele, albeit a somewhat impractical suggestion, would be to give every individual in the organisation the opportunity to examine the future and allow the scenarios to be subjected to criticism and revision from people across the organisation.

A second comment by Schmidt-Scheele (2020 p 216) is that while the objective of scenarios is usually associated with learning and exposure to new and challenging assumptions, "when talking about effectiveness, scenario studies and research and analysis are rather vague regarding the ultimate purpose of scenario activity." Additionally, scenario objectives such as stretching mental models beyond current beliefs are difficult, because "challenging scenarios are usually disregarded and only have a chance of being accepted if the scenario source and method are considered highly credible." At the same time, Schmidt-Scheele states that the field of SP is full of contradictions and paradoxes, namely:

- What is the main purpose of the scenario planning activity?
- Should the scenarios emphasize probable futures or plausible futures, or both?
- Although rich, complex scenario sets are useful to explore and create preparedness for the future, they do not provide the simplicity and security that managers like best.
- Scenario planning designed for innovation purposes, is necessarily different from processes aiming to evaluate existing concepts and strategies.

- In the short term, trend-based scenarios are enough since most changes have already happened, but in the long term, uncertainties and discontinuities are more critical. When the focus is on the action, a short-term view is appropriate but long-term perspectives are needed to provide a relevant contextual framing for the short-term decisions.
- Scenarios can be developed through either a present-to-future perspective or through a retrospective approach using back-casting, and may be used with a specific decision in mind, but may also be a more open-ended explorative process.
- How much should line managers and other decision-makers be involved in the process?

Despite the many criticisms in the literature regarding classifications, definitions, processes, and apparent contradictions and paradoxes, there is extensive testimony to the value of SP in the literature. Their strength is that they do not describe just one future, but several realisable futures which are placed side by side for consideration. SP is also an appropriate way to recognise discontinuities or disruptive events and include them in long-range planning, the result of which organisations are then better prepared to handle new situations and promote proactive leadership initiatives (Mietzner and Reger, 2005).

Probability and Plausibility

The question often asked by management when presented with a set of scenarios is: 'Which is the most likely of these scenarios, which one should we prepare for?" The issue of probabilities and scenarios is well discussed in the literature and Millett (2009) states that a persistent controversy among practitioners is whether probabilities should ever be assigned to scenarios. There are according to Ramirez and Selin (2014, p 61), two incompatible cultures on how to engage uncertain future contexts" i.e. plausibility and probability, and the IL methodologies which are the most widely used, consider probability to be irrelevant because "it considers scenarios to be used in situations where probability cannot operate and forecasting is impossible" and accordingly, favour the criteria of plausibility. Meanwhile, methodologies used by Battelle and Godet (2000) which use more complex, quantitative methods placing factors in cross-impact tables and using expert judgement, software and algorithms, are more tied to attributing probability to the scenarios arising from the analysis.

On the basis that managers should consider all scenarios as equally likely representing possible rather than likely futures and should prepare for each scenario, Millet (2009) suggests that scenarios should not be assigned any probabilities. The arguments against assigning probabilities to scenarios include the fact that:

- It creates an expectation of predictability. The crucial characteristic of scenarios is their focus on possibility, rather than probability, trading precision for in-

creased awareness of the future by presenting the expanse of possibilities grounded in plausibility.
- There are usually multidimensional developments in a scenario, each having only an infinitesimal probability of occurring, making calculating the overall probability of a scenario a complex problem. De Finetti (1975) claims that no matter how much information we have, there is no scientific method to assign probability to an event; if a probability is assigned it is no more than just an opinion of an individual.
- Estimating probabilities for aspects or events we do not know, or even do not know we do not know, such as 'wild cards,' is exceptionally difficult if not impossible. "Probability looks objective and scientific, it crunches a large volume of numbers, but it is quite fuzzy and subjective and mathematical probability only concerns repetitive situations" (Gaspars-Wieloch, 2019 p 114).
- Probabilities are invariably subjective, based on the experience and knowledge of the individuals who assigned them. Gaspars-Wieloch makes the point that "there are numerous, even contradictory, probability definitions . . . unfortunately, a unanimous and universal interpretation does not exist . . . the majority of probability definitions were called into question by a lot of writers." (2019, p 114).

While scenarios deal with uncertainty, there are according to the literature, three sources of uncertainty – incomplete domain knowledge, noisy and conflicting data, and incomplete information, and four basic levels of uncertainty (Courtney, Kirkland and Viquerie, 1997; Larbi, Konieczny et al. 2011; Gaspars-Wieloch, 2019;). The first level is uncertainty but with known probabilities; the second level is uncertainty with partially known probabilities; the third level is uncertainty with unknown probabilities, and the fourth level is total ignorance. All four levels will often be a factor in scenarios, but the important ones in terms of attaching probabilities to, are levels three and four.

As pioneers of scenario planning, both Wack and Khan were very much against assigning probabilities to scenarios. They considered the objective of scenarios was to break away from the traditional reliance on quantitative forecasting of the most likely future often representing a linear projection of the past to the future, but rather to stimulate senior management thinking about the future by providing a range of equally possible outcomes. The use of probabilities implies precision and predictive accuracy which distracts from the storytelling qualities of scenarios, and while probability forecasts may capture trends, they cannot capture the discontinuities of change.

One last point against the use of probabilities is that it compromises team building as experience has shown that while teams can achieve consensus on plausible scenarios, they can rarely agree on probabilities of occurrence (Schwartz, 1991; Fahey and Randall, 1998; Ralston and Wilson, 2006.) Shell does not assign probabilities to their scenarios for several reasons. Firstly, the scenarios are deliberately intended to be equally plausible to avoid any one of them being dismissed; secondly, by definition, any given scenario has only a small probability of being right because so many varia-tions are possible; and thirdly, the reason to be wary of any quantification is that there is a strong tendency for people to focus on what appears to be the most likely scenario. This defeats the whole purpose of the process, which is to make strategic choices that are fairly robust under all scenarios.

Although all scenarios should be treated equally, they are not, as individuals typi-cally gravitate to the scenario which they find most interesting, or which aligns with their beliefs. There are, as a result, arguments for using probabilities with scenarios, but the probabilities should be Bayesian in that they explicitly include assumptions, imagination, and expert judgment, and that they go beyond trend projections. Millett (2009, p 66) contends that "Probabilities compel scenario teams to examine scenarios that they might otherwise dismiss as unattractive, while Bayesian probabilities en-courage people to explain their judgments, thereby exposing hidden assumptions, biases, and expectations that too often go unarticulated in the generation of purely intuitive scenarios." While there is not a complete consensus on the use of probabili-ties in scenarios, Millett (2009) suggests that it is appropriate to attach probabilities to scenarios where: (1) There is sufficient time and resources to calculate and attach probabilities to the scenarios; (2) The scenario team is familiar and comfortable with the concept of Bayesian probabilities; and (3) In scientific and technical organisations where the corporate culture and management cognitive style favour the use of proba-bilities over qualitative reasoning. Thus, if attaching probabilities to scenarios fits the corporate culture and stimulates creative thinking, then it is appropriate to use them.

Despite the many variations of scenarios, scenario planning guidelines and meth-odological reviews generally name plausibility as a key criterion for the development and usage of scenarios (Urueña, 2019; Schmidt-Scheele, 2020). However, there is con-tinued controversy over the ties (or lack of) between the probability and plausibility of scenarios. Probability refers to concepts of chance and likeliness and a probable future is a future that is more likely than some other future. Plausibility on the other hand refers to the structure of the argument, where truth-value is based on the con-vincingness and the credibility of the discourse describing the future, and its ability to convince the reader or audience.

Plausibility has been implicated as playing a critical role in many cognitive phenom-ena from comprehension to problem-solving. "Every day in many different situations, we judge plausibility . . . and in the cognitive science and psychology literature, plausi-bility judgement is useful in a diverse range of cognitive tasks" (Connell, 2004, p 244). While plausibility rather than probability has emerged as a central quality criterion of scenarios that allows exploring the future with credibility, Kahn and Wiener (1967) state that any scenario may contain paranoid ideas, but this must be judged based on the plausibility of the scenario. This is often a difficult judgment in a world of many sur-prises. Although the literature on scenario methodologies demonstrates an overwhelm-ing dominance of plausibility as an 'effectiveness criterion' for scenario work (Amer et al 2013; Ramírez and Selin, 2014), paradoxically it has not resulted in significant detailed investigations of the concept. Scenario plausibility has simply been contrasted with possibility, probability, and desirability (Selin and Guimarães Pereira 2013). Wiek et al. (2013) ask what exactly is plausibility vis-à-vis probability, consistency, and desirability, and how can plausibility be constructed and evaluated in scenarios. Swinney (2020) suggests that plausibility is a moving if not fuzzy target, and one can never know with complete certainty if participants will accept it, which leads to concerns. Plausible for whom? Plausible in what context? Indeed, plausibility is not just about connecting the dots (casually or logically) but also about believability and perceptual acuity; in other words, what is plausible for one individual might seem entirely implausible to another. Weik et al. (2013) suggest that firstly, the literature remains ambivalent and opaque as to exactly what plausibility entails; secondly, it is even less clear how to construct plausible scenarios; and finally, how can the plausibility of scenarios be evaluated.

Connell and Keane (2006; 2003b) developed the 'Knowledge-Fitting Theory of Plausibility' which posits that a plausible scenario fits well with our knowledge of the world and has good 'concept-coherence'. Thus, when people make plausibility judgements about a scenario, they are relating the scenario to their prior experiences and assessing in some way if it fits with what they have experienced. Scenarios in which the events are linked by causal inferences are considered more plausible than events that were linked by temporal inferences, because causal inferences fit more closely with prior experiences. The temporal sequence can, however, increase the plausibility of a scenario. Following a series of experiments Connell and Keane (2006) found that people judge plausibility with a certain 'cognitive laziness' i.e., when presented with a scenario, if a possible connection between events is not immediately apparent, then people do not take the trouble to connect the events and dismiss the scenario as implausible. It is only when situations demand that people overcome their cognitive laziness that they attempt to reason out the connections between events.

Weik et al. (2013) provide six indicators to evaluate the plausibility of scenarios or their elements. A scenario is thus considered plausible if it:
1. Can theoretically occur evidenced by early warnings, soft signals or theoretical insight.
2. Has occurred in the past under different framing conditions.
3. Is already happening somewhere in the world under different framing conditions.
4. Is currently occurring elsewhere in the world in a location with similar framing conditions.
5. Occurred in the past at the same location under similar framing conditions.
6. The scenario or elements of it currently exist at the same location.

Individual scenario elements are evaluated against these six indicators which require information on the elements comprising the scenarios including their origin and information on their historical and current cases.

Alongside and related to the above, are several heuristics identified by Tversky and Kahneman (1973) that impact plausibility and the likelihood of events. When faced with the challenging task of judging probability or frequency, people employ a limited number of heuristics such as representativeness, which reduce these judgments to simpler ones. Under this heuristic, an event is judged probable to the extent that it represents the essential features of its parent population or generating process. Tversky and Kahneman also established that although these heuristic principles are valid in some situations and can result in reasonable judgments, they lead to biases which inevitably result in systematic errors in the intuitive judgment of probability. Connell and Keane (2006, p 95) provide perhaps the best examination of how, as a practical matter, human beings implicitly define plausibility when it comes to scenarios:

- Aligning well with existing knowledge.
- Supported by various pieces of prior information to strengthen necessary conclusions.
- Avoiding any extended or complicated justifications.
- Minimising the use of numerous hypothetical assumptions where possible.

Writing in the 1940s, the English economist George Shackle proposed what he called 'Potential Surprise Theory' as an alternative to the use of subjective probability when thinking about potential future outcomes. Shackle's objection to the use of subjective probability was what he termed the problem of additivity in situations of uncertainty, where the full range of possible outcomes was unknown. In complex adaptive systems, new outcomes can emerge unexpectedly so one can never know in advance the full set of possible outcomes that such systems can produce. This uncertainty makes it impossible for the probabilities associated with the identified possibilities to logically sum to 100%. Instead of quantitative probabilities, Shackle suggested that we focus on the degree of implausibility associated with possible future outcomes, measured by the degree of surprise one would feel if a given outcome occurred. The extent of disbelief (potential surprise) in a set of hypotheses does not need to sum to 100%, nor does the degree of disbelief in individual hypotheses need to be adjusted if additional hypotheses are added to a set.

To summarise the discussion, Weik et al (2013) argue that scenario plausibility and probability are correlated. If a scenario is deemed highly probable, then it is equally highly plausible; nevertheless, a less probable scenario can still be plausible. However, Schmidt-Scheele (2021) claims that there are no conceptual or empirical findings on how the plausibility of scenarios is perceived and assessed by users who have not been involved in the development process. Ramírez and Selin (2014) note that if the scenarios are not used exclusively by those who produced them, or are to be shared, different dynamics around plausibility and probability erupt given that different users, cultures and scenario formats may trigger different plausibility assessments. To conclude, Selin (2011, p 241) argues that "rather than dealing with plausibility as a fixed quality criterion, it can function as a worthwhile sparring partner that brings up interesting [. . .] questions around evidence, trust, science and culture and decision-making."

Conflicting Terms in Scenario Development

The SP literature uses several terms (key factors, driving forces) to describe the business environment, but does not define them. Precise definitions of these terms are necessary as the scenario development process refers to different terms in different steps, and instead of precise definitions, authors use various terms to illustrate the same aspects of the scenario creation process. For instance, van der Heijden uses the term environmental factors to describe contextual variables related to environmental aspects driving business factors, or circumstances in the environment that could have a major impact on a business, but are essentially outside the control of the business. This parallels Schwartz's description of driving forces as the environmental variables, which neither individuals nor companies have control over. Furthermore, Schwartz uses the terms 'driving forces' and 'driving trends' interchangeably, while also using the term 'trend' to refer to predetermined elements of the environment, which are distinct from other types of driving forces. The semantic confusion has been reported by Bishop, et al. (2007) in their extensive review of the SP literature, noting that the literature reveals many different and at times conflicting definitions, and pointing out that even the most basic vocabulary is used every which way in this field.

At the same time while the IL scenario development process lists what steps to follow, it does not describe specifically how each step in the process should be undertaken and by who. This raised three questions in executing each process step in SP projects:

- Who should execute each step, and what data sources should be used?
- What methods should be used for gathering the necessary information?
- What is the rationale for making the above choices?

The Scenario Matrix

The 2x2 dimensional scenario matrix is a well-established scenario development tool widely used by practitioners; van Asselt et al (2010) and Ringland (2002) state that it is generally referred to as a standard by both practitioners and scholars in non-probabilistic scenario development. Proof substantiating this comes from a review of 35 sets of scenarios in 2009 by Compendium, Natural England Commissioned Report NECR031, in which over 24 (68%) of the scenarios were noted as being developed using the 2x2 method. Although the matrix is often mistaken for the Shell method, no 2x2 matrixes have been identified in the SP literature documenting Shell scenarios. However, the axis method was widely used by the Global Business Network, a former scenario consulting firm headquartered in San Francisco and established by Peter Schwartz and several other ex-Shell employees.

As discussed previously, developing the matrix method appears to be a relatively simple process; two contextual factor clusters developed in the clustering process and considered to be causally independent of each other, are placed across each other to create a 2x2 matrix as the structure for four scenarios. The selection of the two cluster factors from the list of driving force clusters developed, is based on those two factors regarded as having both the potentially highest uncertainty and the greatest impact over the scenario-building time horizon, and are known as the critical uncertainties. Ramirez and Wilkinson (2014) state that the success of the matrix may be explained by:

- How easy it is to implement and generate highly contrasted scenarios in a short period using the matrix, as it is simple to use and memorable.
- The 2x2 matrix is an easy-to-communicate structure that allows the four scenarios built to be differentiated from each other with little, if any, overlap among them.
- The matrix models a complex situation in a way that enables consideration of alternative perspectives and new solutions, and the polarised outcome of each key driving force encourages consideration of more extreme future outcomes.

Schwartz notes that choosing the clusters to create scenario axes is among the most important steps in the scenario creation process; he states that it is a difficult task and is the most intellectually challenging and intuitively analytical exercise that takes place during an SP project. While the use of the 2x2 matrix has several advantages, the disadvantages of the matrix approach are:

- Assuming independence between variables in a scenario set rather than exploring more interesting challenges implied by their co-evolution, may be considered too simplistic.
- Using two driving forces to shape a whole set of possibilities may limit the appreciation and understanding of complex systems and does not explicitly consider the interactions between many variables.
- In creating four distinctive scenarios, what needs to be considered is the time and resources needed to use the scenarios in a scenario-to-strategy process.
- It is sometimes the case that the highest-ranked uncertainties do not offer a good mix of divergence and storytelling.
- The four scenarios developed may not always considered to be equally plausible, in which case one quadrant is dismissed, as is often the case in the scenarios developed by the World Economic Forum.

The literature does not provide a systematic method for performing the task of selecting the scenario framework. The choice of the scenario logic seems to be a highly subjective decision and studies have revealed that even experienced futurists struggled to choose a scenario axis, even after several rounds of discussion. It is also the case as previously discussed, that one of the axes initially selected, may subsequently be rejected for one of two reasons. Firstly, if the drivers of change which have scored the highest on importance/uncertainty are related to each other or are interdependent. Secondly, when the two highest-scoring drivers of change are from the same driver category, e.g., 'the rate of climate change' and resource depletion' which are both

components of the environmental driver. It generally leads to broader and more enriching scenarios to choose factors from different driver categories.

Scenario Project Facilitation

Facilitation is defined by ICA:UK as "a set of skills to be used in working with a group,
enabling, and supporting them to achieve their objectives in a way that involves and
respects all contributions, builds ownership and releases the potential of the group
and its members. It helps differentiate between process and content." Inherent in facilitation are the principles of equality, inclusion, participation, and affirmation which in
group terms, means recognising the value of each person's contribution and encouraging the active participation of each group member in the SP development process. At
the same time, facilitators need to approach the scenario project as a programme of
action learning, which requires both an understanding of various scenario techniques
and a skill in managing group processes. Some of the tools and processes used are relatively straightforward to manage, while others require the facilitator to think through the
process and identify any adjustments that might need to be made. Facilitating scenario
development processes is not an easy task and some of the basic requirements are:

- Investment in time: Facilitators need to be prepared to invest significant time and
  resources in facilitating an SP process, which includes preparing the team participants in terms of the process, and agreeing with expectations at the outset. It
  should be remembered that SP is an iterative rather than a linear process, and
  the final set of scenarios developed are customarily the result of multiple, time-
  consuming iterations.
- Confidentiality: To participate fully, group members must be confident that things
  can be discussed freely within the group without inappropriate reporting outside
  the group. At the start of the process, it should be agreed by the group as to what
  level of detail can be reported to those outside of the group.
- Group process: Facilitation requires giving attention to how the group operates.
  This includes; listening to what people are saying and tuning in to what they are
  not saying; being aware of verbal and non-verbal means of communication; attempting to resolve conflict or any other difficulty that might arise in the group;
  respecting each individual; and preventing other group members from undermining the respect that should be accorded to every member of the group. To ensure maximum participation, the facilitator must encourage the development of
  trust and safety with every member of the group stimulated to participate and
  share ideas. In doing so, the facilitator must remain neutral and not take a particular position in the discussions.
- The importance of a positive experience: Facilitators must recognise that everyone is entitled to a positive experience in the group. This means the facilitator
  meets realistic individual needs and is aware of and challenges any unrealistic

expectations of the group. Consultation with group members on direction, pace, content, and method with an openness to change, is vital and includes recognising and managing the existential anxieties of the participants.

– Help team members understand the mental models and assumptions of the senior management, which are influential in determining the strategies of the organisation.

SP practice has reportedly endured well, supposedly because it is operationally easy relative to other techniques. Conceptually it is not a hard idea to grasp and is an easy fit for the human brain as storytelling is what people normally do. It would appear therefore that the scenario development process is relatively straightforward; constructing scenarios is simply a matter of progressing through a series of well-defined, sequential steps. While this may be true for experienced practitioners, anyone who has carefully observed the development process in detail will quickly realize that it is not that simple, there is substantially more going on in the process than is generally ascribed to in the literature. As Napier Collyns suggests, it's really closer to magic than technique. However, if scenario techniques do have the ability to stretch managers' mental models and engage them in strategic conversation, then an understanding of how people think is essential for anyone designing and facilitating a scenario process. By taking a hypothetical example of an individual constructing a scenario and then tracing the cognitive activity required, Jungermann (1985a) describes what constitutes a generic, four-stage scenario generation process model:

– Activation of problem knowledge within the world knowledge of the individual.
– Constitution of the mental model in terms of the activated problem knowledge.
– Stimulation of the mental model to draw inferences; and
– Selection of the inferences which appear appropriate for scenario construction.

As discussed in the previous chapter, four areas encompassing the above are likely to impact this generic development process in terms of how people think. The first are the cognitive processes related to how knowledge is organized and activated in the human mind; the second is the area of cognitive simplification processes individuals use to deal with uncertainty and complexity as they cope with the flood of data; the third area is to be aware how people's judgments and decisions deviate from normative standards because of the effects of heuristics and biases, and the fourth area concerns inductive versus deductive thinking.

The facilitator should also be aware of 'decision fatigue' discussed in the previous chapter which refers to the deteriorating quality of decisions made by individuals after a long session of decision-making and can affect even the most rational and intelligent individuals.

Implications for Scenario Facilitators

Most of the research discussed above is rooted in the discipline of cognitive psychol-ogy and relates primarily to examining the quality of intuitive human judgement of uncertain events. It was conducted more than 20 years ago, and explanations for its findings are not unanimous in the literature. At the same time, much of the research, particularly around heuristics, is based on probability forecasts. However, as scenario practitioners from the IL school will be quick to point out, scenarios have nothing at all to do with either probabilities or forecasts. What then is the relevance of the pre-ceding discussion, and how does it relate to scenario facilitators? The cognitive scien-ces tell us that humans are bounded in their rationality; they interpret and make sense of what they see going on around them through unique and interacting ontolog-ical and epistemological lenses that comprise their mental models. As Pierre Wack (Wack, 1985a, 1985b) has noted,

> In times of rapid change and increased complexity, the mental model becomes a dangerously mixed bag; enormously rich detail and deep understanding can coexist with dubious assumptions, selective inattention to alternative ways of interpreting evidence, and projections that are a mere pretence. It is here that the scenario approach can make a difference.

The contention then is that to exercise this leverage by exposing the flaws in the men-tal models of individuals and engage them in new ways of thinking, it is essential to understand how they think, how knowledge is stored and organized in their brains, how they subsequently search for and then interpret information, and so on. The above can be illustrated by some examples from a research project undertaken some years ago, with postgraduate students at the Centre for Scenario Planning within the University of Strathclyde Business School. I covertly recorded and analysed the behav-iour of syndicate groups of students undertaking a scenario development process de-signed and facilitated by Kees van der Heijden. In terms of exploring the drivers of change in the contextual environment and developing the scenarios, the observations included the following:

– The initial search set triggered in the groups determined which variables the group subsequently explored in depth, and the trigger related to topical happen-ings highly publicized in the media. Thus, events such as AIDS and Bird Flu, the war in Afghanistan and the Middle East tensions, the situation in North Korea, the question of the sustainability of the US economy, and stem cell research, were the initial issues raised in all groups as the likely dominant drivers of change. Nu-merous other issues were raised but accorded relatively minor attention. Even when provided with evidence that, for example, pneumonia, diarrhoeal diseases, and malaria were responsible for more childhood deaths in developing countries than AIDS/HIV, the groups dismissed this and continued to focus their discussions on AIDS/HIV.

- In exploring these recent events, each of the groups tended to have a clear view of how they would unfold within the scenario period. Although the groups supposedly engaged in 'freewheel' thinking in terms of possible combinations and alternative future developments, they invariably returned to contemplate combinations and alternatives that were either already well-known or easily imagined. In reviewing these it was apparent that developments envisaged by all groups represented variations around a common, already articulated midpoint. Extreme developments were raised but lay dormant and were eventually discarded as being unrealistic and implausible. For example, in discussing global economics, the headline news at the time was that the US economy showed signs of slowing while the Chinese economy was overheating. In contemplating this, the combinations and outcomes discussed in the syndicates ranged from the US and Chinese economies continuing to grow, to the US economy slowing, while the Chinese economy managed a soft landing. A collapse of the economies precipitating a global depression was raised, but summarily rejected by all syndicates as an implausible development.
- Once the groups had determined what constituted the most plausible future developments, they were generally insensitive to missing information, sample size and the concept of regression and correlation, among other things. Activities at this point centred largely on identifying supporting events and data that could be causally linked plausibly, to explain why a particular event would or would not occur.

Having established the critical uncertainties and an initial scenario matrix, several of the groups were tasked with using a deductive approach to develop the scenarios defined by the matrix. As discussed earlier, a deductive approach is likely to result in more revolutionary scenarios, potentially leading to the discovery of new options that would not ordinarily surface under a causal process. As a starting point in the deductive process, groups were told to imagine themselves sitting at a Starbucks coffee shop in a particular location in the scenario horizon year within each of the scenario end-states defined in the matrix, and asked to look around them and visualize what the world looked like – what people were doing, reading, talking about, and so on. Having imagined the state of the world in the horizon year, the next step was to work backwards to determine what must have happened in the intervening years for the end-state situation to have arisen. In observing the groups throughout this process stage, it was apparent that none found this an easy process, problems in developing diagnostic reasoning were encountered, and the groups invariably abandoned the task and resorted to an inductive approach. At the same time, the punctuated equilibrium phenomenon was evident in all groups as they progressed through the stages of scenario development. However, unlike the model described by Gersick (1991), the transition point was not in all cases, the midpoint in the time allotted for the various exercises; it varied within each group. More significant, however, was the observation that once the punctuated equilibrium transition point was launched, the groups abandoned any further exploratory discussions, self-sealing on ideas already discussed. At this point, interventions by the facilitator proved ineffective. While group members appeared to pay attention to the facilitator, on his departure from the room they dismissed his comments and continued to develop their existing ideas with an escalating commitment, invoking elaborate causal reasoning to justify the ideas, and massaging data to fit the existing schema and dispel any doubts raised by the facilitator. Some revisions were made based on the facilitator's comments, but these were minimal in scope.

The events and student actions witnessed in the scenario project in the Business School were not unique; I have since led numerous scenario consulting projects in a wide range of countries and my observations of the consulting groups were very similar to those which I witnessed with students at the Business School.

Process and Content Pitfalls

Schoemaker (2015) provides a list of twenty common pitfalls in the SP process, divided into ten processes and ten content pitfalls, which in summary are:

Process Pitfalls

1. Failure to gain top management support: It is essential to secure the political support and active involvement of senior executives from the start of a scenario project, by making them stakeholders in the scenario process, as they will determine any significant changes to the organisation's strategy.
2. Lack of diverse inputs: Given that scenarios address the contextual environment rather than the organisation, inputs from a range of outside experts (customers, suppliers, regulators, analysts, academics and 'remarkable people') should be invited into the process as this diversity will expand the knowledge and view of possible developments in the future.
3. Poor balance of line and staff people in the scenario team: Scenario teams should include both staff and line managers and not just those at a senior level, as the line managers are usually the ones tasked with delivering the strategy.
4. Unrealistic goals and expectations: The objective of scenario planning is not to produce plans contributing to the bottom line within a short time, but to help managers understand how the future may develop, the impact this will have on their plans and the fact that there are key uncertainties that cannot be predicted.
5. Confusion about roles: It is imperative at the start of a scenario project to clarify the process and the roles in the process of the core scenario team, the supporting

individuals, and the senior management team. The core team should be tasked with setting milestones and ensuring activities remain on track.

6. Failure to develop a clear road map: It is essential at the start of a scenario project to have a clear plan detailing the process, dates, milestones, and deliverables, along with the responsibilities of the individuals involved in the project.

7. Developing too many scenarios: Two to a maximum of four scenarios which are distinctly different, is the norm. More than four scenarios are too difficult to comprehend

8. Insufficient time to learn from the scenarios: Scenarios are designed to be a learning activity; therefore, a slow and detailed development process is more beneficial.

9. Failing to link into the planning process: Scenario planning should not be an isolated activity unconnected to other organisational decision-making processes, but linked to existing organisational processes such as budgeting and planning.

10. Not tracking the scenarios via signposts: The scenarios should be tracked via specific signposts or early warning signals.

Content Pitfalls

1. Inappropriate time frame and scope: It is essential not to focus only on the short-term and current issues, but to consider emerging drivers and new developments.

2. Too limited a range of outcomes: Although firms may have experienced deregulation, globalization and new technologies which have created havoc, this does not mean that there will not be more unexpected discontinuities in the future.

3. Too much focus on trends: Focusing too much on current trends leads to a reliance on the past, rather than focusing on the unknowns which will determine the future.

4. Lack of diversity of viewpoints: As a test of the diversity of the scenario themes, do they reflect the opinions of a wide range of innovative thinkers from both inside and outside of the industry?

5. Scenario internal consistency: The logic of the scenarios must be internally consistent to ensure credible stories.

6. Insufficient focus on drivers: The emphasis in organisations is on elements such as profit, and margins, but scenarios need to focus on and explore symptoms of the deeper forces and the underlying drivers.

7. Not breaking out of the paradigm: A scenario which confirms conventional wisdom is less useful than a scenario that challenges fundamental beliefs.

8. Failing to tell a dynamic story: A scenario should be an engaging story which takes the reader from the present and explains how the future unfolds through to the end-state.

9. Failure to connect with managerial concerns: The scenarios must be relevant to the key decision makers, confronting their concerns in terms of the issues they face.
10. Failure to stimulate new strategic options: The ultimate payoff of scenario planning occurs when the organisation embarks on successful new strategic issues, albeit the scenario process can fail to create acceptable strategic options.

Roxburgh (2009) adds some general principles to the above, namely:
- Rather than relying on an excessively narrow set of outcomes in the scenario set, one should ensure that the scenarios cover a broad range of outcomes including extremes.
- If the scenarios do not have catchy, memorable names, they will not enter the organization's lexicon. Avoid long, descriptive titles, the names of well-known film titles, books and historical events are recommended.
- Learn from being wrong and do not discard a set of scenarios too quickly just because short-term reality appears to refute them.
- Understand when not enough is known to sketch out a scenario, and additional research is required.
- Always listen to contrary voices as this is a good corrective to groupthink.

Roxburgh (p 8) concludes that while developing scenarios is not rocket science:

> Scenarios are harder than they look – harder to conceptualize, harder to build, and uncomfortably rich in shortcomings. A good one takes time to build, and so a whole set takes a correspondingly larger investment of time and energy. Scenarios will not provide all the answers, but they help executives ask better questions and prepare for the unexpected. And that makes them a very valuable tool indeed.

Challenges

The surprising thing about SP is that although it has been around for 50-plus years during which time a multitude of techniques and methodologies have developed, there has been relatively little academic research in the area which has been slow to interrogate and theorize about the effectiveness of SP methods. This is a puzzle, as it has become a widely adopted strategic planning approach for understanding environmental complexity and uncertainty, by challenging managerial assumptions and improving long-term strategic thinking about a complex future. Scholarly research into the operational process of formulating scenarios remains scarce, with most of the accounts relating mainly to successful interventions. Though its subjective and heuristic nature might explain this paucity of academic concern, there is a need for a more systematic body of research to better understand the effectiveness of different scenario interventions.

Despite multiple clarification attempts, methodological confusion remains rampant and extends to the epistemological disagreements of what is subsumed to what. A scenarios approach can only be credible and useful if it complies with four prerequisites: relevance, coherence, likelihood, and transparency. Consequently, one must ask the right questions. The last prerequisite needed to ensure the credibility and usefulness of the scenario method implies that a clear concept can always be stated clearly, which should be the case for any problem, for the methods used to solve it, for the reasoning behind it, and for the results and the conclusions regarding the scenarios envisaged (Godet, 2003). Too often, either the simple reading of the scenarios proves laborious, and the reader must invest considerable effort in ascertaining the prerequisite conditions (relevance, consistency), or the literary quality is so low that the reader finds it indigestible and sets it aside. Scenarios with catchy titles, or which are presented in an emotion-ridden, pleasurable or doomsday style can be convincing and often make for superb reading.

Millet (2003) suggests that three major challenges must be addressed for the future of the scenario method:

–   Resolve the confusion over the definitions and methods of scenarios;
–   Clarify and enlarge the appropriate application of scenarios; and
–   Reduce the resources required to perform scenario planning.

However, Spaniol and Rowland (2017, p 36) state that despite the many claims in the literature that the academic community of futures and foresight science suffers from significant confusion over the many definitions of scenarios, their analysis of the published literature indicates that different definitions "do not appear to confuse neither the practitioner nor scholars in their communications."

Conclusions

Linneman and Klein (1985) note that few companies heed the advice offered in the scenario literature; they do not generally follow the guidelines regarding team composition, and only a small number employ consultants, experienced external facilitators, and experts to assist in the scenario development process.

In closing the discussion on the scenario development process, it is evident that aside from a limited set of tools, the task is essentially a creative one and the process has been described as "a practitioner's art" and it is, therefore, more a craft than a science (van der Heijden 1996, p 133). All the procedures described in the literature rely heavily on subjective judgments which is a necessary ingredient in SP as there is no hard data about the future. Decisions regarding the future must be highly subjective and, unlike conventional scientific research, futures research problems are "usually ill-defined, imprecisely structured and probability relationships are largely unknown" (Athey 1987, p 170). Accordingly, the "modelling of developmental processes combining both uncertain factors and conditional decisions whose combined probable effects have to be assessed" is the most controversial part of scenario construction (Vlek and Otten 1987, p 273). Consequently, the basic methodological assumptions are seldom agreed upon in scenario exercises (Athey, 1987).

In the very long term where very little is predictable, scenario planning is not a useful activity. It is in the intermediate and relatively near future where uncertainty and predictability are both significant, that scenario-based planning makes its contribution. This is also the area of strategy and consequently, strategic management, and scenario-based planning are closely linked. Scenarios can help in dealing with uncertainty in three specific ways: Firstly, they help the organisation to understand the environment better. Secondly, scenarios put structural uncertainty on the agenda, driving home to the organisation what sort of things are waiting to happen, which helps managers avoid taking undue chances. Thirdly, scenarios help the organisation to become more adaptable by expanding their mental models of the environment and enhancing their perceptual capabilities to recognise unexpected events and take proactive action. Athey (1987) states that, unlike conventional research in the physical and behavioural sciences, 'futures' research is not considered an academic undertaking and poses considerable methodological problems for the researcher. In the words of Simmonds (1988, p 380), "A typical futures problem is almost exactly the inverse or opposite of normal science." Simmonds goes on to explain that, unlike classical scientific research, "futures research problems are usually ill-defined, imprecisely (if at all) structured, probability relationships are largely unknown, and basic methodological assumptions are seldom agreed upon." Similarly, Amara has observed that due to the extreme uncertainty with which the future must be studied, only the most basic tools of scientific research can be applied.

The result of these methodological constraints has been the development of an interesting paradox for futures researchers. On the one hand, increasingly sophisticated and technically complex forecasting methods have been developed to make futures research more accurate and scientifically respectable, but on the other hand, futures research is characterized by its reliance on unscientific methods such as intuition, and imagination. This paradox can be represented by what Loye (1998) describes as the contrast between left-brain forecasting (reliance on logical analytical and mathematical research methods) and right-brain foreseeing (reliance on intuitive, prescriptive, and imaginative methods). Consequently, futures research requires one to have a genuine interest in the unknowable future and challenging assumptions about it, while simultaneously being capable of understanding and using complex analytical methods and still being willing to tolerate considerable reliance on intuitive judgment in conducting the research. This requires flexibility and ambiguity tolerance demands on researchers, which many individuals are unable to accept.

As there are no criteria for being a futurist, the field has grown to encompass participants from a wide range of social and behavioural sciences, humanities, and business. This is a necessity given that studying how and why the future may develop in different ways is essentially a multidisciplinary examination of change in all aspects of life and their interacting dynamics creating the changes. It is likely that as the field of futures research progresses, confusion reliance on multi-disciplinarity systematic approaches in both research methods and thinking will become more important, given that firstly scenario projects invariably result in three to four scenarios each depicting a different scenario rather than a single scenario depicting one 'right' answer. Secondly, although scenario development processes incorporate rigorous analysis, the scenarios are often based on intuition and are usually qualitative, which does not always fit well with traditional numbers-oriented business minds.

To conclude this discussion, Peter Schwartz who has a degree in aeronautical engineering once said "Scenario planning isn't rocket science. Believe me. I used to be a rocket scientist." However, neither is it quite as straightforward and effortless as it is often made out to be in the literature, testimony to which are the following comments:

- Developing scenarios is a challenging task requiring substantial investment in resources, competence, professionalism, and a wide range of knowledge (Shell 'Guides to Planning' Series No 5, 1986).
- Scenario planning is a potentially enormous undertaking, and it can take months to create, and the apparent simplicity (of the scenario planning process) belies, however, the considerable skills required by its practitioners (Grinyer, 2000).
- MacKay and McKiernan (2018, p 57) state that although the scenario can have a powerful influence on the creative aspects of human behaviour, "embedding scenario thinking in well-established organisations is not easy."
- Following an intense, detailed five-year study of the activities that futurists perform, van Asselt et al, (2010) observe that "foresight presents an extraordinary challenge in intellectual and methodological terms, methodological accounts are usually a (very) brief description of some main steps or are confined to a simple scheme. As a result, a linear and stepwise process is suggested: choices, considerations, discussions, struggles, compromises, unproductive steps, flaws, practical adjustments, experiments, difficulties, challenges, and local solutions are concealed . . . foresight practice is messier and more complex than is suggested in futurists' accounts."

This concludes the book text, and I trust that it provides a useful guide to those wanting to know more about scenario planning. As indicated at the start of this chapter, at the end of the book is a series of appendices which should prove useful to those who wish to earn more about the subject of scenario planning.

References

Amara, A. (1981). The futures field: searching for definitions and boundaries. The Futurist, 15, 1, pp 25–29.
Amer, M., Tugrul, D., and Jetter, A.J. (2013). Futures. A review of scenario planning, 46, p 23–40.
Athey, T.R. (1987). The Dynamics of Volunteer Participation in Futures Research. Futures, 19, 2, pp 168–183.
Becker, P. (2002). Corporate Foresight in Europe. Foresight Brief No. 082 The European Foresight Monitoring Network
Becker, H.A. and Van Houten, D.J. (1984). Energie in Scenarios. Beleid en Maatschappij, 3, p 55–65.
Bell, W. (2017). Volume 2: Values, Objectivity, and the Good Society. Human Science for a New Era. Routledge, New York.
Bell, W. (2003). Volume 1: Foundations of Futures Studies: History, Purposes, and Knowledge. Human Science for a New Era. Routledge, New York.
Bishop, P., Hines, A. and Collins, T. (2007). The current state of scenario development: an overview of techniques. Foresight 9, 1, p 5–25.
Borjestson, L., Hojer, M., Dreborg, K. H., Ekval, T. and Finnveden, T. (2006). Scenario types and techniques: Towards a user's guide. Futures. 38, p 723–739.
Bradfield, R., Wright, G., Burt, G., Cairns, G. and van der Heijden, K. (2005). The origins and evolution of scenario techniques in long range business planning. Futures, p 795–812.
Brauers, J. and Weber, M. (1988). A New Method of Scenario Analysis for Strategic Planners. Journal of Forecasting, 7, 1, p 21–47.
Brown, S. (1968). Scenarios in Systems Analysis. Systems Analysis and Policy Planning: Applications in Defense. E. S. Quade and W. I. Boucher (eds.), American Elsevier Publishing Company, New York, p 298–310.
Bunn, D. W. and Salo, A. A. (1993). Forecasting with scenarios. European Journal of Operational Research, 68, 3, p 291–303.
Burmeister, K., Neef, A., Beyers, B. (2004). Corporate Foresight. Unternehmen gestalten Zukunft, Murmann Publishers, Hamburg.
Chermack, T. J. (2004). A Theoretical Model of Scenario Planning. Human Resource Development Review. 3, 4. p 301–325.
Chermack, T.J., Lynham, S.A. and Ruona W.F.A. (2001). A Review of Scenario Planning Literature. Futures Research Quarterly 17, p 7–31.
Connell, L. and Keane, M.T. (2006). A Model of Plausibility. Cognitive Science A Multidisciplinary Journal 30, 1, p 95–120
Connell, L. (2004). A cognitive theory and model of plausibility. Ph.D. thesis, Department of Computer Science, University College Dublin, Ireland.
Connell, L, and Keane, M.T. (2003b). PAM: A Cognitive Model of Plausibility, Department of Computer Science, University College Dublin, Belfield, Dublin 4, Ireland
Courtney, H., Kirkland, J. and Viguerie, P. (1997). Strategy Under Uncertainty. Harvard Business Review, Decision Making and Problem Solving, November-December.
Crawford, M.M. (2019). A Comprehensive Scenario Intervention Typology. Technological Forecasting and Social Change. Volume 149, December.
Daheim, C. and Uerz, G. (2008). Corporate foresight in Europe; from trend-based logics to open foresight. Technology Analysis and Strategic Management, 20, 3.
de Finetti, B. (1975). Theory of Probability: A Critical Introductory Treatment. John Wiley & Sons, London. New York.
De Jouvenel, B. (2004). Invitation à la prospective. Futuribles, 87.
Derbyshire, J. (2016). Potential surprise theory as a theoretical foundation for scenario planning. Technological Forecasting and Social Change. Volume 124, p 77–87.

Dominiak, C. (2006). Multicriteria decision aid under uncertainty. Multiple criteria decision making, 5, p 63–81.

Ducot, C. and Lubben, H.J. (1980). A typology for scenarios. Futures, 12, 1, pp 15–57.

DuMoulin, H. and Eyre, J. (1979). Energy scenarios a learning process. Energy Economics.1, 2, p 76–86.

Duncan, N. E and Wack, P. (1994). Scenarios Designed to Improve Decision Making. Planning Review, 22, 4. pp 18–46.

Durance, P. and Godet, P. (2010). Scenario building: Uses and abuses. Technological Forecasting and Social Change, 77, 9, p 1488–1492.

Fahey, L. and Randall, R.M. (Eds.) (2001). Learning from the future: Competitive foresight scenarios. New York: John Wiley & Sons.

Gaspars-Wieloch (2019). Project Net Present Value estimation under uncertainty. Central European Journal of Operations Research, 27, 1, 9, p 179–197

Georgoff, D.M. and Murdick, R.G. (1986). Manager's guide to forecasting, Harvard Business Review, 64, p 110–120.

Gershuny, J. (1976). The choice of scenarios. Futures, 8, 6, pp 496–508.

Gersick, C.J.G. (1991). Revolutionary Change Theories: A Multilevel Exploration of the Punctuated Equilibrium Paradigm. The Academy of Management Review, 16, 1, p 10–36.

Godet, M. (2003). Scenarios and Strategic Management, London: Butterworths.

Godet, M (2001). Creating Futures: Scenario Planning as a Strategic Management Tool. Brookings Institution Press, Business & Economics.

Godet, M. (2000). The Art of Scenarios and Strategic Planning. Technological Forecasting and Social Change 65, 1. p 3–22.

Godet, M. and Roubelat, F. (1996). Creating the future: The use and misuse of scenarios. Long Range Planning, 29, 2, p 164–171.

Godet, M. (1987). Scenarios and Strategic Management. Butterworths, London.

Goldfarb, D.L. and Huss, W.R, (1988). Building scenarios for an electric utility. Long Range Planning. 21, 2, p 78–85.

Grinyer, P. H. (2000). A cognitive approach to group strategic decision-taking: A discussion of evolved practice in light of received research results. Journal of the Operational Research Society, 62, 5.

Hamel, G. (2000). Leading the Revolution. Boston, MA: Harvard Business School Press.

Heugens,P.P.M.A.R and van Oosterhout, J. (2001). To boldly go where no man has gone before: integrating cognitive and physical features in scenario studies. Futures. 33,10, p 861–872.

Hideg, E. (2006). Emergence in the Foresight, Interdisciplinary Description of Complex Systems 4, 2, p 80–88.

Hideg, E. (2007). Theory and Practice in the Field of Foresight. Foresight 9, 6, p 36–46.

Hodgkinson, G.P. and Sparrow, P. (2002). The Competent Organization: A Psychological Analysis of The Strategic Management Process. Open University Press.

Hughes, N. (2009). A Historical Overview of Strategic Scenario Planning: A Joint Working Paper of the UKERC and the EON.UK/EPSRC Transition Pathways Project.

Huss, W.R. (1988). A Move toward Scenario Analysis. International Journal of Forecasting, 4, p 377–388.

Hyde, A.C. (1999). Scenario planning: strategic thinking goes back to the future. The Public Manager: The New Bureaucrat, 28, 62.

Jungermann, H. (1985a). Inferential Processes in the Construction of Scenarios. Journal of Forecasting, 4, (3), p 21–327.

Jungermann, H. and Thuring, M. (1987). The Use of Mental Models for Generating Scenarios, in G. Wright and P. Ayton, (eds.), Judgmental Forecasting, London: John Wiley & Sons.

Kahn, H. and Wiener, A.J. (1967). The Year 2000, A Framework for Speculation. MacMillan New York

Karlsen, J.E., Øverland, E. F. and Karlsen, H. (2010). Sociological contributions to futures' theory building. Foresight, 12, 3 p 59–72.

Konieczny, S., Marquis, P. and Schwind, N. (2011). Belief base rationalization for propositional merging. In IJCAI'11, 951–956.

Linneman, R.E. and Klein, H.E. (1985). Using scenarios in strategic decision making. Business Horizons, 28, 1, pp 64–74.

Larbi, R., S. Konieczny, S., and Marquis, P. (2010). Characterization of Optimality Criteria for Decision Making under Complete Ignorance. The Principles of Knowledge Representation and Reasoning: Proceedings of The Twelfth International Conference Published in Book 1, (Kr2010).

Loye, D. (1998). The Knowable Future: A Psychology of Forecasting and Prophecy, Excel Press, Lincoln, Nebraska.

Loveridge, D. (2009). Foresight. The Art and Science of Anticipating the Future. Routledge, New York.

MacKay, R.B. and McKiernan, P. (2018). Scenario Thinking. A Historical Evolution of Strategic Foresight, University Printing House, Cambridge.

MacNulty, C.A.R. (1977). Scenario development for corporate planning. Futures, 9, 2, p 128–138.

Malaska, P. (1985). Multiple Scenario Approach and Strategic behaviour in European Companies. Strategic Management Journal, 6, pp 339–355.

Mandel, T.F. Scenarios and Corporate Strategy: Planning in Uncertain Times (1982). SRI International, Business Intelligence Program.

Marcus, A. (2009). Strategic Foresight: A new look at Scenarios. Palgrave MacMillan.

Martelli, A. (2001). Scenario Building and Scenario Planning: State of the Art and Prospects of Evolution. Futures Research Quarterly.

Masini, E.B. and Vasquez, J.M. (2000). Scenarios as seen from a Human and Social Perspective. Technological Forecasting and Social Change, 5, p 49–66.

Masini, E. (1993). Why Future Studies? London, Grey Seal Books.

Mason, D.H. (1994). Scenario-based Planning: Decision Models for the Learning Organisation, Planning Review, March/April, p 7–12.

Mermet, L., Fuller, T. and van der Helm, R. (2009). Re-examining and Renewing Theoretical underpinnings of the Futures Field: A pressing and Long-Term Challenge. Futures, 41, 2, p 67–70

Mietzner, D, and Reger, G. (2005). Advantages and disadvantages of scenario approaches for strategic foresight. International Journal of Technology Intelligence and Planning, I, p 220–239.

Miller, R. (2006). Futures Studies, Scenarios, and the Possibility-space Approach, in Think Scenarios, Rethink Education, OECD Publishing, https://doi.org/10.1787/9789264023642-7-en.

Millett, S.M. (2003). The future of scenarios: Challenges and opportunities. Strategy and Leadership, 31, 2, p 16–24.

Millett, S.M. (1988). How Scenarios Trigger Strategic Thinking, Long Range Planning, 21, 5, p 61–68.

Millett, S.M. and Randles, F. (1986). Scenarios for Strategic Business Planning: A Case History for Aerospace and Defence Companies. Interfaces, 16, 6, p 64–72.

Mintzberg, H. (1994). The Rise and Fall of Strategic Planning. Prentice Hall, New York.

Mobasheri, F., Orren, L.H. and Sioshansi, F.P. (1989). Scenario Planning at Southern California Edison. Interfaces, 19, 5, p 31–44.

Montibeller, G. and Franco, A. (2010). Multi-Criteria Decision Analysis for Strategic Decision Making, In C. Zopounidis and P. Pardalos (eds) Handbook of Multicriteria Analysis. Applied Optimization, vol 103. Springer, Berlin, Heidelberg.

Piirainen, K. and Gonzalez, R.A. (2015). Theory of and within foresight – What does a theory of foresight even mean? Technological Forecasting and Social Change. 96, p 91–201.

Poli, R. (2018). A note on the classification of future-related methods. European Journal of Futures Research, 6, 15.

Porter, M. E. (1985). Competitive Advantage: Creating and Sustaining Superior Performance. Simon & Schuster UK.

Ralston. B. and Wilson, 1. (2006). The scenario-planning handbook: a practitioner's guide to developing and using scenarios to direct strategy in today's uncertain times. Thomson/South-Western

Ramirez, R. and Selin, C. (2014). Plausibility and Probability in Scenario Planning. Foresight, 16, 1, p 54–57.

Ramirez, R. and Wilkinson, A. (2014). Re-thinking the 2X2 scenario method: grid or frames? Technological Forecasting and Social Change.

Raubitschek, R. (1988). Multiple Scenario Analysis and Business Planning, in R. Lamb and P. Shrivastava (eds.), Advances in Strategic Management, Volume 5, London: JAI Press Inc.

Ringland, G. (1998). Scenario Planning: Managing for the Future. Chichester: John Wiley & Sons.

Ringland, G. (2002). Scenarios in Public Policy. Chichester, John Wiley and Sons.

Roxburgh, C. (2009). The use and abuse of scenarios. McKinsey Quarterly. November, p 1–10.

Schoemaker, P.J.H. (2015). Twenty common pitfalls in scenario planning. https://www.researchgate.net/publication/285797815.

Schoemaker, P.J.H. (1995). Scenario Planning: A Tool for Strategic Thinking. Sloan Management Review, Winter, p 25–40.

Schnaars, S. P. (1987). How to develop and use scenarios. Long Range Planning. 20, 1, p 105–114.

Schmidt-Scheele, R. (2020). The Plausibility of Future Scenarios Conceptualising an Unexplored Criterion in Scenario Planning, Science Studies. Columbia University Press.

Schwartz, P. (1991). The Art of the Long View. Doubleday. New York.

Selin, C. and Guimarães Pereira, A. (2013). Pursuing plausibility, International Journal of Foresight and Innovation Policy, 9 (2/3/4) p 93–109.

Selin, C. 2011 Negotiating Plausibility: Intervening in the Future of Nanotechnology. Science and Engineering Ethics, 17,4, p 723–737.

Simmonds, W.H.C. (1988). Futures research: New starting points. Technological Forecasting and Social Change, 33, 4, p 377–387.

Simpson, D.G. (1992). Key Lessons for Adopting Scenario Planning in Diversified Companies. Planning Review, 20, 3, p 10–17.

Slaughter, R. (1995). The Foresight Principle; Cultural Recovery in the 21st Century. Bloomsbury Academic, UK.

Spaniol, M.J. and Rowland, N.J. (2017). The scenario planning paradox. Futures, Volume 95, p 33–43.

Tversky, A. and Kahneman, D. (1983). Extensional Versus Intuitive Reasoning: The Conjunction Fallacy in Probability Judgment. Psychological Review, 90, 4.

Urueña, S. (2019). Understanding "plausibility": A relational approach to the anticipatory heuristics of future scenarios. Futures, Volume 111, p 15–25

van Asselt, M.B.A; van't Klooster; van Notten, P. W. F. and Smits, L.S. (2010). Foresight in Action. Developing Policy-Oriented Scenarios. Earthscan, London.

van der Heijden, K., Bradfield, R., Burt, G., Cairns, G. and Wright, G. (2002). The Sixth Sense: Accelerating Organisational Learning with Scenarios. Chichester: John Wiley & Sons.

van der Heijden, K. (1996). Scenarios: the art of strategic conversation. John Wiley & Sons, New York.

van Notten, P. W. F. (2005). Writing on the Wall: Scenario Development in Times of Discontinuity. Dissertation.com, Florida.

van Notten, P.W.F., Rotmans, J., van Asselt, M.B.A. and Rothman, D.S. (2003). An updated scenario typology. Futures, 35, 5, p 423–443.

Vlek, C. H. and Otten, W. (1987). Judgmental handling of energy scenarios: a psychological analysis and experiment, in G. Wright, and P. Ayton (eds), Judgmental Forecasting, Chichester/New York: Wiley.

Wack, P. (1985a). Scenarios: Uncharted Waters Ahead. Harvard Business Review, 63, 4, pp 73–89.

Wack, P. (1985b). Scenarios: Shooting the Rapids. Harvard Business Review, 63, 5, pp 3–14.

Wiek, A., Withycombe Keeler, L., Schweizer, V. and Lang, D.J. (2013). Plausibility indications in future scenarios, Int. J. Foresight and Innovation Policy, Vol. 9, Nos. 2/3/4, p 133–147.

Wright, G. and Goodwin, P. (1999). Future-focussed thinking: combining scenario planning with decision analysis. Journal of Multi-criteria Decision Analysis, 8, p 311–321.

Zentner, R.D. (1975). Scenarios in Forecasting. Chemical and Engineering News, October 6, p 22–34.

Appendix A: Foresight and Futurist Organisations

Association of Professional Futurists (APF).
Founded in 2002, APF is a global community of futurists, dedicated to promoting professional excellence, demonstrating the value of and advancing the practice of professional foresight.
Washington DC. USA.
Website: https://www.apf.org/general/
For general inquiry: contact@apf.org

Australian Foresight Institute (AFI).
The AFI was founded by Richard Slaughter in 1998 at Swinburne University, Melbourne, Australia, which offered the first-ever post-graduate course unit on Integral Futures (IF).
Swinburne University of Technology, P.O. Box 218, Hawthorn, Vic. 3122, Australia.
Telephone: 03 92 14 5981.

Centre for Strategic Futures (CSF).
Established in 2009, the CSF was established as a 'futures think tank' within the Singapore Strategic Policy Office to strengthen links between foresight work and strategy formulation.
The Treasury, 100 High Street, #03–01, Singapore 179434.
Email: pmo_csf@pmo.gov.sg

Copenhagen Institute for Future Studies.
Founded in 1969, the Copenhagen Institute for Futures Studies is a not-for-profit futures think tank, and a global leader in the use of futurist methods to solve strategic challenges.
BLOXHUB, Bryghuspladsen 8, Entrance C 3 floor DK 1473, Copenhagen. Denmark.
Telephone: +45 33117176
Email: cifs@cifs.dk

Dubai Future Foundation (DFF).
Dubai's future is at the heart of the Foundation's remit which was born out of a key belief that leading in the present is not sufficient; it is the future that we must imagine, design and execute.
5th Floor, Emirates Towers, Dubai, UAE.
Telephone: +971 4 516 6567
Email: info@dubaifuture.gov.ae

Finland Futures Research Centre (FFRC).
Finland Futures Research Centre founded in 1992 and situated at the University of Turku, is the only academic futures research organization in Finland and the biggest in the Nordic countries.

https://doi.org/10.1515/9783111617442-009

F1-20014 Turun Ylioplisto, Finland.
Telephone: +358 29 450 5000
Email: communications@utu.fi

Foresight Institute.
Founded in 1987, the Institute is a research organisation and non-profit that supports the beneficial development of high-impact technologies for the long-term benefit of life.
101A Clay Street, Box 185, San Francisco, CA. 94111. USA.
Email: foresight@foresight.org

Futures Group.
Future thinking is focused on leading change in careers, advice, skills, and training, supporting people and businesses to be the best they can, unlocking the potential in people of all ages.
Futures Group, 57 Maid Marian Way, Nottingham. England. NG1 6GE.
Email: communications@the-futures-group.com

Futures Platform.
Futures Platform was founded by a group of professional futurists, and is a standard source for future trends, scenarios, and long-term change.
Bulevardi 21, Entrance Albertinkatu 25, FI-00180 Helsinki, Finland.
Telephone: 358 10 325 7070
Email: info@futuresplatform.com

Futuribles International.
A French centre for foresight thinking and studies, founded in 1960 and which has played a leading role in the development of foresight studies in France and through-out the world.
47 rue de Babylone. FR-75007 Paris. France.
Telephone: +33 (0)1 53 63 37 70.
Email: diffusion@futuribles.com

Global Futures and Foresight (GFF).
Founded in 2006, Global Futures & Foresight helps clients to adapt to the fast-changing world with the use of diverse futures methods, reducing their risk of being blindsided by change.
Contact: CEO david.smith@thegff.com
Telephone: +44 (0) 7932 408901

Hawaii Research Centre for Futures Studies.
The centre was established by the Hawaii State Legislature in 1971 and is located within the Department of Political Science, College of Social Sciences, University of Hawai'i at Mānoa.
2424 Maile Way, Saunders Hall - Room 617, Honolulu, Hawaii 96822. USA.

Telephone: (808) 561-6077
Email: jairusg@hawaii.edu

Institute for the Future (IFTF).
The Institute for the Future was established in 1968 as a spin-off from the RAND Corporation and is the world's oldest continuously running futures research and educational organisation.
201 Hamilton Avenue, Palo Alto, CA. 94301. USA.
Telephone: 650-854-6322
Email: info@iftf.org

Institute for Futures Research (IFR).
Established in 1974 IFR is a research institution of the University of Stellenbosch Business School, South Africa, specialising in futurology for knowledge and strategic management.
Telephone: +27 (0)21 918 4144
Email: futures@ifr.sun.ac.za.

Institute for Global Futures (IGF).
Founded in 1990, the Institute for Global Futures is a San Francisco-based think tank that offers business strategy and forecasts about leading-edge innovations and trends.
2084 Union St, San Francisco, 94123 California, United States
Telephone: 1 415 563 0720
E-mail: jcanton@globalfuturist.com

International Futures Forum (IFF).
IFF is a registered charity founded in 2001 in Scotland, with the mission to support the development of competencies required to flourish in today's complex operating environment.
The Boathouse, Silversands, Hawkcraig Road, Aberdour, Fife. Scotland. KY3 0TZ.
Telephone: +44 (0)1383 324002
Email: editorial@internationalfuturesforum.com

Frederick S. Pardee Centre for International Futures.
The centre builds and uses data and tools to analyse the complex world and the long-term dynamics of change in human, social, and natural systems to plan for the global future.
Joseph Korbel School of International Studies, University of Denver, Anna and John J. Sie International Relations Complex, 2201 S. Gaylord St. Denver, CO 80208.
Telephone: 303 871 2324
Email: korbeladm@du.edu

Police Futurists International (PFI).
PFI grew out of an FBI Academy course and was established in 1991 and has grown to include academics, researchers, practitioners and a range of technology and security experts.
Fort Worth, Texas, USA.
https://www.policefuturists.org

Scenario Planning Institute (SPI).
The purpose of the Scenario Planning Institute is to create new knowledge about scenario planning and advance scenario planning practices through research and projects.
Colorado State University, 223 Education Building, Fort Collins, Colorado. 80532-1588.
Telephone: (970) 491 1157
Email: scenario@colostate.edu

School of International Futures (SOIF).
SOIF founded in 2012, SOIF operates globally with decision makers and use futures and foresight tools to help them get to innovative and imaginative solutions for the wider good.
Onega House, 112 Main Road, Sidcup, Kent. England. DA14 6NE.
Telephone: +44 (0) 300 302 0486.
Email: info@soif.org.uk

Shaping Tomorrow.
Shaping Tomorrow established in 2002, is an online horizon scanning and foresight service that provides organisations with scenario planning tools and strategic intelligence.
Office: +44 (0) 1273 832221
info@shapingtomorrow.com

The Bavarian Foresight Institute.
The Bavarian Foresight Institute focuses on technology-oriented research and economic and social interdependencies in the areas of artificial intelligence, sustainability and mobility.
Technische Hochschule Ingolstadt, Esplanade 10, 85049, Ingolstadt, Germany.
Telephone: 49 8419348-0
Email: info@thi.de

The Centre for Future Studies.
CFS was founded in 1996 as a strategic futures consultancy enabling organisations to anticipate and manage change in their external environment.
Innovation Centre, Kent University. England. CT2 7FG
Telephone: +44 (0)800 881 5279
Email: insights@futurestudies.co.uk

The Club of Rome.
The Club of Rome is a platform of thought leaders who identify solutions to complex global issues and promote initiatives to enable humanity to emerge from planetary emergencies.
Club of Rome Secretariat, Lagerhausstrasse 9, 8400 Winterthur, Canton Zurich. Switzerland.
https://www.worldfuture.org/

The Future Laboratory.
The Future Laboratory and LS:N Global has joined a group of industry-leading agencies in the lifestyle sectors, allowing the Future Laboratory to inspire and future proof organisations.
6 Orsman Road, London. England. N1 5RA.
Telephone: 020 7791 2020
Email: hello@thefuturelaboratory.com Website: www.thefuturelaboratory.com

The Millennium Project.
A global think tank established in 1996 as part of the UN University, that became independent in 2009, with the objective of improving humanity's prospects for building a better future.
4421 Garrison Street, N.W. Washington, D.C. 20016-4055. USA.
Telephone: +1 (202) 686-5179
Website: https://www.millennium-project.org/about-us/

World Future Society (WFS).
Founded in 1966, the World Future Society is the largest and longest-running community of future thinkers in the world with WFS members establishing the foundations of future thinking.
https://www.worldfuture.org/

World Futures Studies Federation (WFSF).
Founded in1973, WFSF is a UNESCO/UN partner and global NGO bringing together academics, researchers, practitioners and futures-focused institutions in 60 countries.
Website: www.wfsf.org
LinkedIn: https://www.linkedin.com/company/world-futures-studies-federation/

World Network of Religious Futurists.
Founded in 1980 as the Joint Strategy Network of World Council of Churches, it adopted the current name in 1989 and is a society advancing research into the future of religion.
Website: http://www.wnrf.org

Select National Futurist Associations

- **Centre for Philippine Futuristics Studies and Management Inc. (APF)**
  https://futuristicsph.webs.com/
- **Dutch Futures Society (DFS)**
  https://dutchfuturesociety.nl
- **Finnish Society for Futures Studies**
  https://www.tutuseura.fi/
- **Italian Institute for the Future (IIF)**
  https://www.instituteforthefuture.it
- **Kansallinen ennakointiverkosto (KEV) (Finnish National Foresight Network)**
  https://foresight.fi/info-in-english/
- **Prospective 2100** (France)
  https://2100.org/asso/
- **The Futures Foundation** (Australia)
  https://futuresfoundation.org.au/

Appendix B: Futures Journals, Magazines and Networks

Journals

European Journal of Futures Research.
This SpringerOpen journal publishes articles about European traditions and perspectives in futures research and theoretical and methodological underpinnings of futures studies.
https://eujournalfuturesresearch.springeropen.com/

Foresight: The Journal of Futures Studies, Strategic Thinking and Policy.
An Emerald *journal* founded in 1999, focusing on themes and issues shaping the future, using quantitative and qualitative methods, tools, techniques and case studies.
https://www.emeraldgrouppublishing.com/journal/fs

Foresight and STI Governance.
A journal offering new theoretical insights and practical knowledge related to strategic planning, science, technology, and innovation (STI) policy, foresight and futures studies.
https://pr.hse.ru/en/

Futures: The Journal of Policy, Planning and Futures Studies.
An Elsevier journal founded in 1968, for the study of futures, anticipation, and foresight which aims *to promote divergent and pluralistic visions and ideas about the future.*
https://www.journals.elsevier.com/futures\

Futures & Foresight Science.
A new Wiley journal focused on methods that aid anticipation of the future and documents the status of a particular method's application and use, and its future potential.
https://onlinelibrary.wiley.com/journal/25735152

Futuribles.
A French language journal which carries out foresight activities to aid the construction of desirable futures and provides indications of environmental megatrends/weak signals.
https://www.futuribles.com/fr/

Innovation: Organization & Management Journal.
A relatively new journal which seeks to publish outstanding research on innovation within and across organizations.
https://www.researchgate.net/project/Innovation-Organization-Management-IOM-Journal

https://doi.org/10.1515/9783111617442-010

International Journal of Forecasting.
The official journal of the International Institute of Forecasters (IIF) published by Elsevier, covers all aspects of **forecasting to** bridge the gap between theory and practice.
https://www.journals.elsevier.com/international-journal-of-forecasting

International Journal of Foresight and Innovation Policy.
An Elsevier journal founded in 2004, which deals with the methodology and practice of **technological forecasting** and future studies as planning tools.
https://www.inderscience.com/jhome.php?jcode=ijfip

Journal of Future Studies: Epistemology, Methods, and Alternative Futures.
Founded in 1996, the journal published by the Graduate Institute of Futures Studies at Tamkang University, Taiwan, publishes the main research frameworks of futures studies.
https://jfsdigital.org/

Journal of Tourism Futures.
An Emerald journal that publishes research in the fields of tourism and tourism futures, and is published in association with NHL Stenden Hogeschool.
https://www.emeraldgrouppublishing.com/journal/jtf

Long Range Planning: International Journal of Strategic Management.
LRP is an Elsevier journal for the field of strategic management and has been publishing original research since 1968 involving empirical research and theoretical articles.
https://www.journals.elsevier.com/long-range-planning

On the Horizon: The International Journal of Learning Futures.
The journal focuses on the increasingly complex intersection of forces that are impinging on education and learning, and to which all committed to human potential must respond.
https://www.emeraldgrouppublishing.com/journal/oth/horizon-call-papers

Policy Futures in Education.
A futures-oriented publication founded in 2003, committed to promoting debate in education among academics, policy analysts, governments and world policy agencies.
https://journals.sagepub.com/home/pfe

Prospective et Stratégie.
Founded in 2010, published in French, the journal publishes methodological, theoretical, and case-based papers exploring strategic issues for private and public organisations.
https://www.cairn.info/revue-prospective-et-strategie.htm

Technological Forecasting and Social Change: An International Journal.
An Elsevier journal founded in 1970 for those wishing to deal with the methodology and practice of **technological forecasting** and future studies as planning tools.
https://www.journals.elsevier.com/technological-forecasting-and-social-change

The International Journal of Forecasting.
Founded in 1985, the journal covers all aspects of forecasting and is open to many points of view with the intention to make forecasting useful to decision and policy makers.
https://www.sciencedirect.com/journal/international-journal-of-forecasting

The Journal of Forecasting.
The journal founded in 1982, publishes papers dealing with all aspects of forecasting from theoretical, practical, computational and methodological, in diverse applications.
https://onlinelibrary.wiley.com/journal/1099131x

World Futures: The Journal of New Paradigm Research.
A Taylor & Francis journal focused on the exploration, articulation, and application of human potentialities, and the implications for building a sustainable and humanistic future.
https://www.tandfonline.com/toc/gwof20/current

World Futures Review: A Journal of Strategic Foresight.
The journal is about futures studies as an academic/applied discipline covering the roots of futures studies, basic concepts, theories, methods and how it has changed over time.
https://journals.sagepub.com/aims-scope/WFR

Magazines

BBC Science Focus Magazine.
Each annual issue is packed with news, discoveries, ideas and innovations to keep one up-to-speed with the complexities of the fast-moving world around us.
https://www.sciencefocus.com/

COMPASS.
Compass is a quarterly magazine edited and designed by a volunteer team of APF members to share the diverse voices of professional futurists from around the world.
https://www.apf.org/compass

RAND Review.
RAND is a research organization that develops solutions to public policy challenges, while *Review* is the flagship magazine covering the big issues with an eye for important details.
https://www.rand.org/pubs/periodicals/rand-review.html

Scenario Magazine

A quarterly print magazine from the Copenhagen Institute for Future Studies which keeps you up-to-date with the world of tomorrow.
https://cifs.dk/publications/

The Classical Futurist.
Founded in September 2021, The Classical Futurist seeks to formulate visions of the future inspired by classical antiquity, with one new essay per month.
https://classicalfuturist.substack.com/

The Club of Amsterdam Journal.
A free online magazine published every two weeks by an independent, international, future-oriented think tank involved in channelling **preferred futures.**
https://clubofamsterdam.com/about-us/

The Economist.
The Economist is a British weekly newspaper available in both print and digital format, and which focuses on current affairs, international business, politics, technology, and culture.
https://www.economist.com

The Futurist.
The Futurist publishes inspiring articles about a wide range of topics that fuel curiosity so that one always stays a step ahead of the rest.
https://www.getthefuturist.com/news

The Future Laboratory.
The Future Laboratory is a futures consultancy with a blend of trend forecasting, consumer insight, foresight, brand strategy and innovation to future-proof organisations.
https://www.thefuturelaboratory.com/

The Manoa Journal of Fried and Half-Fried Ideas.
An occasional paper series about the future published by the Hawai'i Research Centre for Future Studies.
https://www.academia.edu/8609383/Manoa_Journal_of_Fried_and_Half_Baked_Ideas_about_the_future_

The Medical Futurist.
The Medical Futurist works to build a community of healthcare organisations, governments and medical professionals to drive healthcare innovations world-wide.
https://medicalfuturist.com/our-vision

Think Magazine.
Produced by the University of Malta, the magazine tells the stories of students, alumni, researchers, and professors, sharing their work and discoveries with a general audience.
https://thinkmagazine.mt/

WIRED.
Wired is a magazine, published in print and online editions, that focuses on how emerging technologies affect culture, the economy, and politics, changing every aspect of our lives.
https://www.wired.co.uk

Networks

Davinci Institute.
The mission of the institute is to understand the future of humanity and the myriad of technologies causing it to change.
https://davinciinstitute.com/

European Foresight Platform (EFP).
EFP is a network building program supported by the EC to build a network of communities & individuals to share knowledge about foresight and other methods of future studies.
http://foresight-platform.eu/

EU-wide Foresight Network.
One objective of the European Commission, initiated in 2021, is to develop foresight to integrate foresight into policymaking to create future policies equipped for change.
https://vnk.fi/en/foresight/eu-wide-foresight-network

Foresight Europe Network (FEN).
FEN is a network of individuals active in futures/foresight research, education, and practice, to foster connections between members to enable opportunities for cooperation.
https://www.millennium-project.org/about-us/nodes/foresight-europe-network/

Future Exploration Network.

The Future Exploration Network helps leading organizations globally to explore the potential of the future, and take the actions that will create success.
Http://www.futureexploration.net

Futures4Europe.

Futures4europe platform collects and distributes foresight activities about Europe, hosted by the Foresight on Demand consortium (FOD) supported by the European Commission.
https://www.futures4europe.eu/

Global Foresight Network (GFN).

GFN is a network of thinkers, designers and researchers focusing on strategic foresight to create future sensitive, adaptive and resilient organisational and city architectures.
https://globalforesight.net/

The Futures Foundation.

The Foundation promotes interest in, and understanding of, the future and provides tools and perspectives to assist individuals and businesses in preparing a more ideal *tomorrow*.
http://www.futuresfoundation.org.au

The Next Generation Foresight Practitioners (NGFP).

NGFP is a global network of next-generation future-alert changemakers and leaders from over 90 countries across 6 continents, using futures/foresight to drive positive change.
https://nextgenforesight.org/our-network/

The Public Sector Foresight Network (PSFN).

The PSFN's aim is to spread awareness of foresight activities taking place at all levels of governments, to support government foresight practitioners and to share best practices.
https://www.publicsectorforesight.org/

The South Asia Foresight Network (SAFN).

SAFN functions under the Millennium Project in Washington, DC. and comprises of individuals/institutions active and interested in Futures Research in South Asian countries.
https://southasiaforesight.org/aboutus/

Appendix C: Foresight Glossary

(Reference: Foresight: A Glossary. Centre for Strategic Futures and Civil Service College, Singapore)

Back-Casting A facilitation method which works backwards from a future scenario to the present day; back-casting involves fleshing out the steps needed to arrive at the scenario.

Black Swan A rare, large-impact, hard-to-predict and discontinuous event beyond the realm of normal expectations. Taking reference from how people believed that all swans were white up to the discovery of black swans in Australia, "Black Swans" illustrate the fragility of human knowledge and the weakness of a purely empirical approach to preparing for the future.

Causal Layered Analysis (CLA) A sense-making tool designed to help uncover the underlying issues beneath observable events and trends. Commonly described as a process of uncovering the story beneath the tip of the iceberg, CLA begins with identifying an obvious and superficial phenomenon (litany), analysing the cause of the phenomenon (systemic perspective), and then unravelling the deeper ideological assumptions (worldview). These assumptions help uncover the unconscious emotive aspects of the issue (myth/metaphor).

Cognitive Bias Psychological tendencies that result in systematic errors in the way humans receive, process, retain or recall information, or make inferences, judgements, and predictions. Many cognitive biases result from the heuristics or mental shortcuts that human beings unconsciously use to process information; while heuristics are useful in making simple daily decisions, in more complex situations, they can lead to an overestimation or underestimation of actual odds.

Cognitive Dissonance The psychological discomfort a person feels at the discrepancy between his existing beliefs and new information or views he is confronted with that contradict those beliefs. Since it is difficult to hold two opposing ideas in one's mind simultaneously, individuals tend to reduce their cognitive dissonance by denying or devaluing the new information or views they are confronted with, or by rationalising their own views.

Complexity A phenomenon involving multiple components in a dense network of interactions or relationships, where cause-effect relationships are not clear, stable, or predictably repeatable. Complex systems are often self-organising; they exhibit new patterns and behaviours that cannot be predicted or by examining the component parts of the system, but can only be discerned and understood after the fact and usually cannot be replicated. Complex systems are also characterised by non-linearity, i.e., where changes are random and/or discontinuous, and do not follow a gradual and orderly pattern. As a result, cause-effect relations between components are difficult to establish in a complex system.

Crisis Management The process by which an organisation deals with a major event that threatens to harm the organisation, its stakeholders, or the general public.

Crowd-Sourcing The process of canvassing for views and ideas across a broad spectrum of people, drawing upon the idea of cognitive diversity, where a group contains a variety of ways of thinking. This can help to overcome the cognitive biases and blind spots of an individual or team.

Cross-Cutting Issues Issues that, in the context of government, do not fall neatly within the purview of a single agency.

https://doi.org/10.1515/9783111617442-011

Cynefin Framework A sense-making and decision-making tool to help decision-makers analyse and evaluate issues, determine their significance, and take appropriate follow-up action. The framework classifies issues into four types: simple, complicated, complex, and chaotic, with each type requiring distinct responses.

Delphi Method A method of crowd-sourcing inputs that involves two or more rounds of consultations with a group of experts. After each round, a facilitator circulates an anonymised summary of the group's responses to the previous round's questions. The members of the group then respond to the new set of information, revising their previous answers, if necessary. The underlying philosophy here is that, over time, the group will converge towards the "correct" answer, or at least arrive at a working consensus on the issues discussed.

Design Thinking An approach to problem-solving that takes the end-user's experience as the starting point in developing the solution. Instead of focusing only on the purely rational parameters of a given situation, design thinking recognises that there is bound to be some messiness and unpredictability in the way situations develop and the way people respond to those situations.

Drivers/Driving Forces Significant trends, observable in the present, which are expected to continue to affect the future. There is a distinction between driving forces that are "predetermined" and those that are "critical uncertainties." "Predetermined" driving forces are likely to remain stable and predictable e.g., because demographics take a long time to shift, China's ageing population is likely to be a predetermined element across multiple development trajectories. "Critical uncertainties" are driving forces for which a range of plausible future trajectories exists e.g., as China gradually opens its doors to trade with other countries, its own growth trajectory will increasingly be subject to the uncertainty and volatility of the international economy.

Early Warning System A system such as Horizon Scanning is established to track indicators identified as warning signs that possible future trends or events are imminent. A good early warning system should be easily tracked on a regular basis and give sufficient advance warning so that there is the opportunity to act at the appropriate time.

Emerging Strategic Issues (ESIs) Issues that could pose institutional surprises and are plausible. They have implications that have not yet been fully accounted for, and there is sufficient evidence that they may occur in future. They can arise for several reasons; they can develop as the result of an acceleration of existing phenomena; arise as second or third-order effects of existing phenomena; or arise as combinations of two or more existing phenomena.

Environmental Scanning The systematic process of picking up weak signals and trends to identify and monitor driving forces, potential discontinuities, and emerging issues from regular scanning of diverse information sources. Often referred to as "horizon scanning."

Forecasting A process for making justified statements on future events, based on quantitative analysis and modelling which can be combined with sensitivity analysis to establish a range of trajectories, and are entirely extrapolative in nature.

Futures A concept that indicates the presence of alternatives that might happen, and the need to consider them.

Game Theory Game theory is a study of strategic decision-making, i.e., situations where two or more players (or agents) must make decisions, and the way things turn out for each player may depend on the other player or players' choices. Game theory examines the strategies that a group of decision-makers will converge on as they try to maximise their own payoffs and may be used to analyse the behaviours of agents and the stability of the outcomes in agent-based modelling.

Management by Discovery A management style that emphasises the importance of continual reframing and adaptation. It builds on the traditional approach of Management by Objectives, which assumes that a project's objectives can be clearly defined in advance and will remain fixed throughout the project.

Morphological Analysis A method for exploring practical solutions to a multi-dimensional problem. In the context of foresight work, morphological analysis can be used as a tool to generate alternative scenarios or strategies. It is most suited for multi-dimensional problems with many variables, where systems maps, and simulations do not function well.

Narrative Inquiry A sense-making process that helps analysts identify key patterns, weak signals, and key perspectives. These may surface from the narratives provided by participants through activities such as interviews.

Prototyping The process of creating models (for objects) or early sketches of a policy which can help to evaluate ideas and spot potential problems so that subsequent prototypes come closer to addressing the issues at hand.

Retrospective coherence The idea that a current situation always makes sense in hindsight. However, being able to explain the current state of affairs does not mean we are operating in a knowable world. In a complex system, even if we were to start again and make the same decisions, we cannot be sure that we will end up in the same situation.

Risk This can be distinguished in several ways and is defined as the effect of uncertainty on objectives i.e., we do not know what is going to happen next but through repeated observations, we know what the statistical distribution looks like and can estimate frequencies with which different outcomes will arise.

Sandbox Sandbox is a working-level meeting with members of other foresight and strategic planning agencies, which helps to build networks and trust within the foresight community.

Scenario Planning A process that generates a group of plausible stories about the future, which can then be used to aid long-term planning. The traditional scenario planning methodology, pioneered by Royal Dutch Shell, emphasises that scenarios are not intended to present definitive predictions about the future, but to help articulate the risks and opportunities present in a range of plausible futures, and serve as a discussion tool to stimulate debate about strategies to shape the future.

Sense-making The process of clarifying and articulating an organisation's understanding of complex situations to build situational awareness and shared understanding within the organisation. It supports decision-making by establishing an understanding of the interconnections between various elements and actors within a complex system.

Signposts Indicators that mark milestones or "waypoints" between a given future and the present day. They can take the form of discrete events or thresholds, but they can also be much more loosely defined, such as trends or patterns. In the context of foresight work, signposts help to gauge the extent to which a particular scenario has materialised and can help to update decision-maker's thinking as new information becomes available.

STEEP Analysis A framework for a holistic scan of the external environment for factors, from various domains, which need to be taken into consideration in its decision-making. STEEP stands for: Social, Technological, Economic, Ecological/Environmental, and Political factors. Similar frameworks include STEEPLED (adding Legal, Ethics and Demographic factors) and STEER (Socio-cultural, Technological, Economic, Ecological and Regulatory factors).

Strategic Planning The process of determining and articulating what goals should be achieved in the medium to long term, where the nature of the operating environment is subject to change, as well as how to reach these goals. Strategic planning contrasts with operations planning, which seeks to maximise an organisation's efficiency within near-term constraints, without considering how things might change in the longer term.

Stress-Testing A method of identifying weaknesses or flaws in existing policies to help decision-makers assess and evaluate the robustness of their policies by identifying potential breaking points and instances of failure along policy trajectories.

SWOT Analysis A tool typically deployed in planning or facilitated discussions that helps to surface the internal Strengths and Weaknesses of an organisation and the Opportunities and Threats it faces, and which are external to the organisation.

Systems Thinking An analytical approach that considers the full range of interactions between different elements in a system. This is different from traditional analyses, which tend to focus on particular elements or a limited range of interactions in isolation of the system as a whole.

Unknown Unknowns Issues which have not yet been surfaced to the organisation and are blind spots. The phrase was used by the US Secretary of Defence Donald Rumsfeld in a press briefing in 2002 to explain that, despite intelligence agencies' best efforts, it was often not possible to get a complete picture of a situation, and that it was important to acknowledge that there would always be gaps in knowledge and unrecognised blind spots.

Wicked Problem A problem which has no simple solution because the precise nature of the problem cannot be readily defined. Wicked problems are commonly found within complex environments, where constantly evolving interdependencies make it difficult to define problems precisely. An example of a wicked problem is climate change as there is no single or definitive solution.

Wild Cards Low probability, high impact opportunities and threats that would be disruptive should they occur, but for which there may not be any evidence today that they will eventually happen, e.g., an asteroid from space striking a large population centre on Earth.

Wind-Tunnelling A means of assessing the robustness of strategies in multiple scenarios, as part of the scenarios-to-strategies effort. Wind-tunnelling is a term borrowed from aerodynamic research and refers to a tool used to study the effects of air moving past airframes to find the weak points. Likewise, the robustness of a strategy is assessed by placing it in each scenario to see which of the strategies holds up best in all the scenarios

Appendix D: Some Useful Guides and Tools

Foresight/Scenarios

- **BSC Designer: Scenarios in Strategic Planning: Full Guide with Examples.**
  https://bscdesigner.com/scenario-planning.htm
- **ETF Frame: Skills for the Future – Foresight.**
  https://www.etf.europa.eu/sites/default/files/m/7836A795A2AD6DB8C1257
  D90003E99BC_Foresight%20guide.pdf
- **European Commission Strategic Foresight.**
  https://commission.europa.eu/strategy-and-policy/strategic-planning/strategic-fore
  sight_en#what-is-strategic-foresight-
- **Futures Platform. 2x2 Scenario Planning Matrix: A Step-by-Step Guide.**
  https://www.futuresplatform.com/blog/2x2-scenario-planning-matrix-guideline
- **GEWENT PSB: Futures Toolkit.**
  https://www.newport.gov.uk/documents/One-Newport/Gwent-Futures-Toolkit.pdf
- **JISC: Scenario Planning Guide.**
  https://www.jisc.ac.uk/guides/scenario-planning
- **A Guide to Scenario Planning for Voluntary Organisations.**
  https://www.bayes.city.ac.uk/__data/assets/pdf_file/0010/37297/picture_this.pdf.
- **Replicon: Scenario Planning: A Detailed Guide.**
  https://www.replicon.com/blog/scenario-planning/
- **RHNTC: Scenario Planning Tool.**
  https://rhntc.org/sites/default/files/resources/fpntc_scenario_planning_2020-09-
  28.pdf
- **Shell International: Scenarios – An Explorer's Guide.**
  http://opanalytics.ca/aus/pdf/shell-scenarios-explorersguide.pdf
- **UK Government Office for Science: The Futures Toolkit.**
  https://assets.publishing.service.gov.uk/government/uploads/system/uploads/at
  tachment_data/file/674209/futures-toolkit-edition-1.pdf
- **UNDP Global Centre for Public Service Excellence: Foresight Manual.**
  https://www.undp.org/sites/g/files/zskgke326/files/publications/UNDP_ForesightMa
  nual_2018.pdf

https://doi.org/10.1515/9783111617442-012

Horizon Scanning

- **How to Do Horizon Scanning: A Step-by-Step Guide.**
  https://www.futuresplatform.com/blog/how-to-horizon-scanning-guideline
- **Horizon Scanning Toolkit.**
  https://www.sepa.org.uk/media/367059/lsw-b4-horizon-scanning-toolkit-v10.pdf
- **IRM Horizon Scanning: A Practitioner Guide.**
  https://www.theirm.org/media/7423/horizon-scanning_final2-1.pdf

Appendix E: Select Readings

Scenarios and Foresight Books

- Bell, W. (2003). Foundations of Futures Studies, Volume 1. History, Purposes, and Knowledge (Human Science for a New Era).
- Bell, W. (2005). Foundations of Futures Studies, Volume 2. Values, Objectivity, and the Good Society (Human Science for a New Era).
- Cairns, G. and Wright, G. (2018). Scenario Thinking, 2nd Edition.
- Chermack, T.J. (2011). Scenario Planning in Organisations. How to Create, Use and Assess Scenarios.
- Cornish, E. (2004). Futuring. The Exploration of the Future.
- Costanzo. L.A. and MacKay, R.B. (2009). (Eds). Handbook of Research on Strategy and Foresight.
- Courtney, H. (2001). 20/20 Foresight: Crafting Strategy in an Uncertain World.
- Fahey, L. and Randall, R.M. (1997). Learning from the Future. Competitive Foresight Scenarios.
- Fowles, J. (1978). (Ed). Handbook of Futures Research.
- Giaoutzi, M. and Sapio, B.S. (2013). (Eds). Recent Developments in Foresight Methodologies.
- Gidley, J. (2017). The Future. A Very Short Introduction.
- Godet, M., Durance, P. and Gerber, A. (2006). Strategic Foresight. Problems & Methods.
- Gordon, T.G. and Todorova, M. (2017). Future Studies and Counterfactual Analysis.
- Helmer, O. (1983). Looking Forward. A Guide to Futures Research.
- Hines, A. and Bishop, P. (2013). (Eds). Thinking about the Future. Guideline for Strategic Foresight.
- Kahane, A. (2013). Transformative Scenario Planning. Working Together to Change the Future.
- Lindgren, M. and Bandhold, H. (2009). Scenario Planning. The link between Future and Strategy.
- Loverage, D. Foresight. (2009). The Art and Science of Anticipating the Future.
- Lustig, P. (2017). Strategic Foresight. Learning from the Future.
- MacKay, R.B. and McKiernan, P. (2018). Scenario Thinking. A Historical Evolution of Strategic Foresight.
- Marcus, A. (2009). Strategic Foresight. A New Look at Scenarios.
- Ramirez, R. and Wilkinson, A. (2016). Strategic Reframing. The Oxford Scenario Planning Approach.
- Ringland. G. (2002). Scenarios for Business (and Scenarios for the Public Sector).
- Sanderson, A. and Dingley, R. (2000). (Eds). Histories of the Future Studies in Fact, Fantasy, and Science Fiction.

https://doi.org/10.1515/9783111617442-013

- Schwartz, P. (1992). The Art of the Long View. Planning for the Future in an Uncertain World.
- Slaughter, R. (1996). (Ed). New Thinking for a New Millennium. The Knowledge Base of Futures Studies.
- Sunter, C. and Illbury, C. (2011). The Mind of a Fox: Scenario Planning in Action.
- van Asselt, M., van 't Klooster, S.A., van Notten, P.W.F. and Smits, L.A. (2015). Foresight in Action: Developing Policy-Oriented Scenarios.
- van der Heijden, K., Bradfield, R., Burt, G., Cairns, G. and Wright, G. (2002). The Sixth Sense. Accelerating Organisational Learning with Scenarios.
- van der Heijden, K. (2005). Scenarios. The Art of Strategic Conversation. 2nd Edition.
- Wilkinson, A. and Kupers, R. (2014). The Essence of Scenarios. Learning from the Shell Experience.
- Zakarov, D. (2021). Future-Fluent: How Organizations Use Foresight to Thrive in Turbulent Times.

Futures Related - Interesting Reads

- Costa, R. (2011). The Watchman's Rattle: Thinking our Way out of Extinction.
- Dewey, E.R. and Dalkin, E. F. (1987). Cycles. The Science of Prediction.
- Dobelli, R. (2013). The Art of Thinking Clearly.
- Gordon, A. (2008). Future Savvy: Identifying Trends to Make Better Decisions, Manage Uncertainty, and Profit from Change.
- Ilbury, C. and Sunter, C. (2015). The Fox Trilogy. Imagining the unimaginable and dealing with it.
- Inayatullah, S. and Wildman, P. (Eds). Future Studies: Methods, Emerging Issues and Civilisational Issues.
- Kleiner, A. (2008). The Age of Heretics: Heroes, Outlaws, and the Forerunners of Corporate Change.
- Meadows, D., Meadows, D.L. and Randers, J. (1992). Beyond The Limits. Confronting Global Collapse - Envisioning a Sustainable Future.
- Schwab, K. (2017). The Fourth Industrial Revolution.
- Sherden, W.A. (2011). Best Laid Plans: The Tyranny of Unintended Consequences.
- Sunter, C. (2015). Flagwatching. How a Fox Decodes the Future.
- Toffler, A. (1970). Future Shock.
- Vigen, T. (2015). Spurious Correlations.
- Web, A. (2016). The Signals are Talking. Why today's Fringe is Tomorrow's Mainstream.

Forecasting, Prediction and Statistical Analysis

– Armstrong, J.S. (2001). Principles of Forecasting: A Handbook for Researchers and Practitioners.
– de Smith, M.J. (2018). Statistical Analysis Handbook. A Comprehensive Handbook of Statistical Concepts, Techniques and Software Tools.
– Dewey, E.R. and Dakin, E.F. (2011). Cycles: The Science of Prediction.
– Gibson, W. (2003). Pattern Recognition.
– Levitin, D. (2016). A field Guide to Lies (and Statistics).
– Sherden, W. (1999). The Fortune Sellers: The Big Business of Buying and Selling Predictions.
– Silver, N. (2012). The Signal and the Noise. The Art and Science of Prediction.
– Tetlock, P. and Gardner, D. (2016). Superforecasting: The Art and Science of Prediction.
– Westfahl, G., Wong, K.Y. and Chan, A, K-S. (2011). Science Fiction and the Prediction of the Future.

Trends

– Global Strategic Trends out to 2045. Ministry of Defence 2014.
– Global Megatrends. European Environment Agency 2017.
– Global Trends: Challenges and Opportunities. UNDP 2017.

Heuristics, Biases, and Judgement

– Bazerman, M.H. and Moore, D.A. (2012). Judgment in Managerial Decision Making, 8th Edition.
– Kahneman, D., Slovic, P. and Tversky, A. (1972). Judgment under uncertainty: Heuristics and biases.
– Kahneman, D., Sibony, O. and Sunstein, C.R. (2022). NOISE: A Flaw in Human Judgement.

Global Foresight Reports

A small list of high-quality annual to semi-annual reports that professionals concerned with global and organizational foresight should be aware of.

- **Economic Freedom of the World,** Cato Institute (Annual).
- **Global Risks Report,** World Economic Forum (Annual).
- **Global Trends Report,** National Intelligence Council (Every Five Years).
- **State of the Future,** The Millennium Project (Biennial).
- **State of the World,** Worldwatch Institute (Annual).
- **The World in 20XX.** The Economist (Annual).

Appendix F: Examples of a Range of Published Scenarios

ARUP: 2050 Scenarios: Four Plausible Futures.
Arup's Foresight teams, explore four plausible, divergent future scenarios based on the intersection between the planet's health and societal conditions, and ranging from the collapse of society and natural systems to living in sustainable harmony.
https://www.arup.com/perspectives/publications/research/section/2050-scenarios-four-plausible-futures

BEIS/ARUP: The Future Offshore Wind Scenarios (FOWS).
The Future Wind Scenarios (FOWS) project was commissioned by BEIS, The Crown Estate and Crown Estate Scotland, with the analysis undertaken by Arup. Its objective is to understand the spatial implications of the deployment potential needed to meet net zero.
https://www.marinedataexchange.co.uk/

Deloitte: Four Futures of the War in Ukraine.
Deloitte developed four scenarios about the future that describe different ways the Russia-Ukraine war could evolve throughout 2022 and how businesses will be impacted.
https://www2.deloitte.com/us/en/pages/consulting/articles/russia-and-ukraine-war-economy-business-scenarios.html

Deloitte: Scenarios for Transportation in a Post-Coronavirus World.
Deloitte offers four possible scenarios for the future of mobility following the pandemic which shut millions of people in their homes and disrupted the transportation domain.
https://www2.deloitte.com/us/en/insights/economy/covid-19/future-of-mobility-after-covid-19-transportation-scenarios.html

DHL: The World in 2050 – A Scenario Study.
In a new study entitled "Delivering Tomorrow: Logistics in 2050," Deutsche Post DHL Group presents five sweeping, radical, prospects for the world in 2050 as well as the impact they would have on the logistics industry.
https://www.dhl.com/global-en/home/insights-and-innovation/thought-leadership/case-studies/logistics-2050.html

FocusWire: Four Scenarios for the Future of Travel.
The organisation developed four potential scenarios for the future of the travel sector and the wider geopolitical environment, plotted along two axes.
https://www.phocuswire.com/scenario-planning-travel-future-Amadeus#

https://doi.org/10.1515/9783111617442-014

Millennium Project Technology 2050: Scenarios and Action.
Report on an international study that produced three detailed scenarios from 30 national workshops conducted in 29 countries.
https://www.millennium-project.org/projects/workshops-on-future-of-worktechnology-2050-scenarios/

Office of Science and Technology: Intelligent Infrastructure Futures: The Scenarios – Towards 2055.
These scenarios explore how science and technology can be applied to the design and implementation of safe transport, telecommunications, water and energy infrastructure.
https://www.foodsecurity.ac.uk/document/category/reports/

The Future of Education: Four OECD Scenarios for Schooling.
Four OECD Scenarios for Schooling is a tool to support long-term strategic thinking in education inspired by the ground-breaking 2001 OECD Schooling for Tomorrow scenarios.
https://www.oecd-ilibrary.org/education/back-to-the-future-s-of-education_178ef527-en

Shell: Energy Scenarios to 2050.
To help think about the future of energy, Shell developed two scenarios which describe alternative ways it may develop.
https://rjohnwilliams.files.wordpress.com/2016/02/shell-energy-scenarios2050.pdf

Shell: New Lens Scenarios.
Shell's 'New Lens' scenarios explore two possible ways the 21st century could unfold, with dramatically different implications for society and the world's energy system.
https://www.biee.org/new-lens-scenarios-from-shell/

TempAG: Future Trade Scenarios and the impact on Agricultural Economies.
The scenarios explore how economic, social, environmental and political drivers may impact future trade, and how this shapes agricultural economies and their research agendas.
https://www.foodsecurity.ac.uk/document/category/reports/

WEF: Scenarios for the Russian Federation.
The report presents three different scenarios aimed at challenging conventional wisdom and existing assumptions about Russia's economic future.
https://www.weforum.org/reports/scenarios-russian-federation/

WEF: The Kingdom of Saudi Arabia and the World: Scenarios to 2025.
Will the KSA leaders be able to implement the necessary economic/political reforms to maintain internal order and stability, in light of a complex and uncertain regional situation?
https://www3.weforum.org/docs/WEF_Scenario_SoudiaArabiaWorld2025_Report_2010.pdf

WEF: Scenarios for Mongolia.
Scenarios in this report suggest possible future contexts for Mongolia by 2040. While it is a long way off mining projects, other opportunities for diversification have long lead times
https://www3.weforum.org/docs/WEF_ScenariosSeries_Mongolia_Report_2014.pdf

WEF: Shaping the Future of Construction. Future Scenarios and Implications for the Industry.
The Infrastructure and Urban Development (IU) industry is important in shaping a desirable future for our planet.
https://www3.weforum.org/docs/Future_Scenarios_Implications_Industry_report_2018.pdf

WEF: Four Futures for Economic Globalization & Their Implications.
These scenarios outline how the nature of globalization may shift as economic powers choose between fragmentation or isolation, in both physical and virtual integration.
https://www.weforum.org/whitepapers/four-futures-for-economic-globalization-scenarios-and-their-implications/e-prommaryedataexchange.co.uk/details/3558/2022-beis-the-crown-estate-crown

Appendix G: Common Heuristics and Cognitive Biases

A list of the most common heuristics and biases which affect human behaviour and decision-making.

- Action Bias: Why we prefer doing something rather than doing nothing.
- Affect Heuristic: Why we rely on our current emotions when making quick decisions.
- Ambiguity Effect: Why we prefer options that are known to us.
- Anchoring Bias: Why we rely heavily on the first piece of information that we receive.
- Attentional Bias: Why we focus more on some things than others.
- Availability Heuristic: Why we think that things that have happened recently are more likely to happen again.
- Base Rate Fallacy: Why we rely on specific information over statistics.
- Bounded Rationality: Why we are satisfied by "good enough."
- Category Size Bias: Why we think we are more likely to win at the big casino versus the small one.
- Choice Overload: Why we have a harder time choosing when we have more options.
- Cognitive Dissonance: Why is it so hard to change someone's beliefs.
- Commitment Bias: Why people support their past ideas, even when presented with evidence that they are wrong.
- Confirmation Bias: Why we favour our existing beliefs.
- Dunning-Kruger Effect: Why we cannot perceive our own abilities.
- Decision Fatigue: Why we make worse decisions at the end of the day.
- Diclinism Bias: Why view the present or future in an excessively negative light and romanticize the past in a positive light.
- Exposure Effect: Why we prefer things with which we are familiar.
- Framing Effect: Why our decisions depend on how options are presented to us.
- Functional Fixedness: Why we have trouble "thinking outside the box."
- Fundamental Attribution Error: Why we underestimate the influence of the situation on people's behaviour.
- Gambler's Fallacy: Why we think a random event is more or less likely to occur if it happened several times in the past.
- Google Effect: Why we forget information that we just looked up.
- Halo Effect: Why positive impressions produced in one area, positively influence our opinions in another area.
- Hard-easy Effect: Why our confidence is disproportionate to the difficulty of a task.
- Heuristics: Why we take mental shortcuts.

https://doi.org/10.1515/9783111617442-015

- Hindsight Bias: Why we see unpredictable events as predictable after they occur.
- Hyperbolic Discounting: Why we value immediate rewards more than long-term rewards.
- IKEA effect: Why we place disproportionately high value on things we helped to create.
- Illusion of Control: Why we believe we have more control over the world than we do.
- Illusion of Validity: Why we are overconfident in our predictions.
- Illusory Correlation: Why we think things are related when they are clearly not.
- Illusory Truth Effect: Why we believe misinformation more easily when it is repeated many times.
- Negativity Bias: Why the news is always so depressing.
- Nostalgia Effect: Why our sentimental feeling or the past influence our present actions.
- Optimism Bias: Why we overestimate the probability of success.
- Ostrich Effect: Why we prefer to ignore negative information.
- Peak-end Rule: How our memories differ from our experiences.
- Pessimism Bias: Why we think that we are destined to fail.
- Planning Fallacy: Why we underestimate how long it will take to complete a task.
- Priming Effect: Why some ideas prompt other ideas later, without our conscious awareness of this.
- Projection bias: Why we think current preferences will remain the same in the future.
- Representativeness Heuristic: Why we use similarity to gauge statistical probability.
- Rosy Retrospection: Why we think that the good old days were so good.
- Salience Bias: Why outstanding and prominent features receive more attention than justified, and influence how we interpret the past and how we imagine the future.
- Self-serving Bias: Why we attribute success to ourselves, but failures to external factors for our own mistakes.
- Status Quo Bias: Why we tend to leave things as they are.
- Sunk Cost Fallacy: Why we continue with an investment when current costs outweigh the benefits, and it would be rational to give the investment up.
- Telescoping Effect: Why some things seem like they just happened yesterday.
- The Illusion of Explanatory Depth: Why we think that we understand the world far more than we do.
- Zero Risk Bias: Why we seek certainty in risky situations.

List of Figures

https://doi.org/10.1515/9783111617442-016

List of Boxes

https://doi.org/10.1515/9783111617442-017

Index

Amanatidou, E. 143
Amara, A. 200, 223
Anderson, C. A. 183, 189
Andersson, J. 34
Armstrong, J. S. 10–11, 15, 251
artificial intelligence (AI) 92, 121, 158
The Art of Conjecture (de Jouvenel) 51
ARUP: 2050 Scenarios 253
Athey, T. R. 223

back-casting technique 42–45, 133, 142, 208, 243
Baer, T. 185
Bandhold, H. 249
Bazerman, M. H. 156–157, 251
Beach, L. R. 178
Beck, P. W. 114
Becker, H. A. 204
Bell, W. 8, 200–201
Bennet, N. 3, 4
Big Data (BD) 148–150
Bishop, P. 8, 39, 47, 63, 123, 199, 203, 249
The Black Swan (Taleb) 103
Black Swan events 103, 107, 157, 243
Borjeson, L. 200
Bower, G. H. 180
Bradfield, R. 200, 250
BrainReserve (consultancy firm) 27–28
Brunswick, E. 166
Bunn, D. W. 205
Burt, G. 250
Butterfly Effect 12

Cairns, G. 110, 249, 250
Capra, F. 108
Carney, J. 146, 147
Carroll, J. S. 18
Causal Layered Analysis (CLA) 105–107, 206, 243
The Causal Texture of Organizational Environments
    (Emery and Trist) 91
cause-and-effect relationships 4, 48, 148, 150, 175,
    180, 186, 188
Cerf, C. 18
Chan, A. K. -S. 251
Chandler, J. 155
Chang, A. 185
Chao, Y. 176
Chatfield, T. 148

Chermack, T. J. 69, 80, 201–203, 249
Chief Executive Officer (CEO) 28, 69–72, 77, 110,
    124, 125
Chung, H. 19
Cockle, P. 155
cognitive bias 16, 20, 152, 190, 199, 243, 257–258
cognitive dissonance 243, 257
cognitive schemas 179–180
complexity/complex systems 1, 3, 4, 6, 22, 24, 41,
    92, 147–148, 243
– and cognitive overload 166
– scientific models 54
– uncertainty and 69, 216
Connell, L. 211, 212
contextual environment 24, 54, 60, 90, 93, 133, 157
– complexity 147–148
– correlation *vs.* causation 150–152
– disruptive forces 157–159
– risk and uncertainty 160–161
– signals *vs.* noise and media 154–156
– tipping and inflection points 159–160
– unintended consequences 28, 152–154
Cornish, E. 16–17, 103, 108, 249
Corporate Legends and Lore: The Power of Storytelling
    as a Management Tool (Neuhauser) 122
correlation 54, 148, 174
Cosmic Bazaar (forecasting tournament) 20–21
Costa, R. D. 152, 250
Costanzo. L. A. 249
Courtney, H. 6, 160, 249
COVID-19 pandemic 3, 57, 120, 137, 142, 155
Crawford, M. M. 206
crisis management 54, 243
Cross-Impact Analysis (CIA) 17, 41–42, 48, 53
crowd-sourcing 15–16, 243
Cynefin framework 244

Dalkin, E. F. 250, 251
de Brabandere, L. 75
decision-making processes 16, 35, 48, 172, 176, 184,
    185, 207, 220
Defence Science and Technology Laboratory
    (Dstl) 146–147
de Jouvenel, B. 50, 51, 200
Deloitte company 253
Delphi technique 47–49, 206, 244
Denning, S. 122

https://doi.org/10.1515/9783111617442-018

www.ingramcontent.com/pod-product-compliance
Lightning Source LLC
Chambersburg PA
CBHW081057220326
41598CB00038B/7131